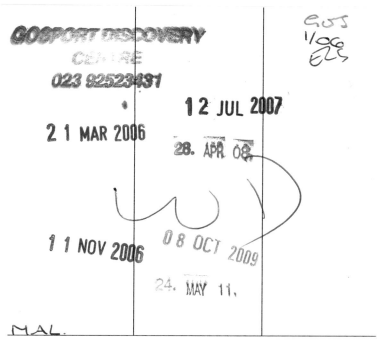

Hampshire
County Council

Please return/renew this item
by the last date shown.
Books may also be renewed by
phone or the Internet.

**Hampshire County Council
Library & Information Service**

http://libcat.hants.gov.uk

Duran Duran

NOTORIOUS

Duran Duran
NOTORIOUS

Steve Malins

André Deutsch

First published in Great Britain in 2005 by

André Deutsch
an imprint of the
Carlton Publishing Group
20 Mortimer Street
London W1T 3JW

The publishers would like to thank the following sources for their kind
permission to reproduce the pictures in this book:

Plate Section One: Page 1: (top) Paul Edmonds/Retna Pictures; (bottom)
Paul Edmonds/Retna Pictures; Page 2: (top) Paul Edmonds/Retna Pictures;
(bottom) Virginia Turbett/Redferns; Pages 3-7: Denis O'Regan; Page 8: (top)
Denis O'Regan; (bottom) Andre Csillag/Rex Features.

Plate Section Two: Page 1: (top) Andy Earl/Retna Pictures; (bottom) Fin
Costello/Redferns; Pages 2-3: Denis O'Regan; Page 4: (top) Denis O'Regan;
(bottom) Sipa Press/Rex Features; Page 5: (top) Stills Press Agency/Rex Features;
(bottom) Mick Hutson/Redferns; Pages 6-8: Denis O'Regan.

A catalogue record for this book is available from the British Library

ISBN 0-233-00137-9

Typeset by E-Type, Liverpool
Printed and bound in Great Britain by Mackays

CONTENTS

For Isobel

Given the excitement and pace of Duran Duran's story, which accelerates from early 1970s Birmingham glam-rock to a triumphant comeback in the 21st Century with barely a pause for breath, it is astonishing that this is the first in-depth biography on the band. They are paradoxically one of the most underrated pop bands of all time, yet also one of the most written about – a reflection of and comment on the celebrity rock'n'roll lifestyle that we've become so obsessed with. It is, after all, a modern fairytale where Simon Le Bon chooses his future wife from a model agency portfolio, John Taylor lives out his James Bond fantasies by dating an *Octopussy* girl and driving a classic Aston Martin, and Nick Rhodes meets his cult heroes, including Andy Warhol and Federico Fellini ('He didn't disappoint').

There are sky-scraping highs, in particular the band's 1984 debut show at New York's Madison Square Garden, plus the artistic and commercial zeniths of the lilting 'Save A Prayer' (a number-two hit in the UK and sixteen in America) and 'Ordinary World' a decade later. I also describe the flipside, such as the dark, rainy mornings on the M1 as the band drove up to London in a Citroen estate to record their debut album or drummer Roger Taylor suffering heart palpitations every time the phone rang in the months leading up to his decision to quit. At the start of the new century, John Taylor's solo career was crash-diving: one night in Florida he ended up playing in front of twenty people; Andy Taylor hadn't recorded an album in years and Roger Taylor found himself experimenting with dance music just as everyone else was trading in their turntables for real instruments. At almost the same moment, Duran were dropped by the Disney-owned Hollywood Records, witheringly described by Nick Rhodes recently in an interview with *Rolling Stone*: 'Never was there a place that felt less like a record company: seven giant dwarves hold up the building. You're listening to these people and finally I had to say, "How funny that your corporate logo is a large pair of ears, yet none of you in here happens to have any."'

Although a pop band (Le Bon: 'We're not afraid of being sold a bit, we're not afraid of being prostitutes'), the character of Duran Duran's music is rooted in bizarre, extreme twists. Their songs are fuelled by a love of films, fashion, electronics, glam, hedonism, punk, funk and art that is light years away from the modern definition of 'pop' as a stage-school, characterless pursuit. Duran Duran's inspiration ranges from Simon Le Bon being stuck out in a desert in Israel in 1978 listening to Patti Smith's *Horses* album over and over to the arrival of eccentric Brooklyn guitarist Warren Cuccurullo, a man who used to perform so regularly in drag with his mentor Frank Zappa that he was nicknamed 'Sophia Warren'.

Now in 2005, their beautiful wives from the 1980s have maintained their looks and raised families or, in the case of John Taylor's ex-fiancée Renee Simonsen, left him to take a diploma in psychology, and the band themselves have kept all of their hair. In fact, always aware of their image, the first thing Duran Duran did when they met up again in 2001 to discuss the reunion was to take a Polaroid of themselves together. Le Bon: 'We stand for the fans' youth and if you start to look a little ropey, they're going to start feeling ropey themselves.' In Nick Rhodes, they also possess one of the most cartoonishly uncompromising figures in pop music, a man who – unlike Kiss – has never taken off his makeup. This recently prompted the 'Anti-Christ superstar' Marilyn Manson to comment approvingly, 'Duran Duran confused a lot of boys into thinking they were gay', although the forty-three-year-old's teenage daughter Tatjana feels very differently and shrivels in embarrassment at the sight of her father's kohl. 'When my daughter sees me putting on eyeliner, she'll say, "Oh Dad",' laughed Rhodes in 2004. So speaks the middle-aged man whose face was recently 'immortalized' by a line of T-shirts sold in Topman with the caption 'still a fashion legend'.

It is Duran Duran's durability that is so fascinating, proving that 'disposable' pop often lasts longer than music that is self-consciously designed to be 'timeless'. Recently they've been name-checked as an influence by The Killers, Dandy Warhols,

Gwen Stefani, The Bravery, Scissor Sisters and The Faint, although in truth even during their darkest moments in the 1990s they had fans that included Smashing Pumpkins, Snoop Doggy Dogg, Hole, Puff Daddy, and who knows what was going through Kurt Cobain's mind in 1993 when Nirvana played a version of 'Rio' at a concert in Brazil. While many artists have struggled to convert re-discovered interest into a fully-fledged, revitalised career, Duran Duran are now operating at a level that's as high as their 1980s peak, at least in terms of their live shows. Back in 1997, Nick Rhodes declared 'history will be very kind to us' but surely even he didn't expect their reinvention to include sold-out arenas and awards from MTV, *Q* Magazine and the Brits. They played to 250,000 people on their 2004 UK tour and in spring 2005 they grossed between $700,000 and $800,000 a night during their forty-venue tour in North America.

I hope this book captures some of the bullet-train speed of Duran Duran's moment-to-moment existence and gives some insights into the characters themselves. I've conducted over fifty interviews in the last few months, as well as setting out to uncover every feature written about the band in the last twenty-five years. Although I'm sure I didn't achieve that, I did have access to some prime sources, especially *Smash Hits* and *Sounds* in the UK. I owe a debt to all the other writers and journalists who have interviewed Duran Duran, in addition to various books and articles on related subjects.

Most of all thanks to Duran Duran, who are becoming an iconic act in a way that few would have dreamed possible twenty-five years ago. Their tale is all the more engaging because it begins in Hollywood, Birmingham, not California – and it's refreshing that even the band's über-fop Rhodes sometimes shows the Brummie within. His arty veneer dropped when he told one journalist about a 'proper disgusting' porn video he used to own as a fourteen-year-old. 'Apparently now it's in Wolverhampton,' he said dreamily. Meanwhile, LA resident John Taylor recently confessed that he often finds himself reminiscing about 'the beautiful countryside around Redditch'.

Steve Malins, London

CHAPTER ONE

John Taylor: *'We wouldn't buy records by ugly groups.'*

Andy Warhol: *'Business art is the step that comes after Art. I started as a commercial artist, and I want to finish as a business artist. After I did the thing called "art" or whatever it's called, I went into business art. I wanted to be an Art Businessman or a Business Artist. Being good in business is the most fascinating kind of art.'*

John Taylor: *'I think we know more about music than people who write about it – we were filling in the NME crossword when we were eleven.'*

Nick Rhodes: *'I saw the Pistols a few times and I've never witnessed a band with energy like that – ever.'*

John Taylor: *'When we were starting, Nick and I actually envisaged what stage we should be at each year, worldwide. It wasn't just sitting and dreaming, it was Hammersmith in '82, Wembley by '83, Madison Square Garden by '84 ...'*

Nigel John Taylor was born on 20 June 1960 at Sorrento Hospital, Birmingham and grew up in Hollywood, south Birmingham. Seven miles from the city centre, in the 1970s it was an area surrounded by beautiful countryside and a rural, slow-paced atmosphere that was culturally light-years away from Birmingham's high-rise flats, Bull Ring shopping-mall nightmare and the ring-road horror of the infamous 'Spaghetti Junction'. Taylor lived on a 1960s housing estate built for baby boomers, many of whom worked at the local car plants such as British Leyland and Lucas. According to his childhood friend, David Twist, 'Every house had a young family in it. Hollywood was a nice area just outside the Birmingham boundary but it was by no means posh. John's dad Jack worked at Lucas cars and his mum, my "Auntie" Jean, was a dinner lady. My mum and Jean were in the next beds in the maternity wards having John and me, so everyone knew each other very well.' Known as Nigel by everyone until his late teens, from a young age this only child was 'strangely drawn' towards his grandmother's 'out-of-tune piano' and if he wasn't imitating a concert pianist on the breakfast table, he was doing an impression of a drummer in the back seat of the family car. The Beatles also formed a significant part of his early memories. Taylor was fascinated by the flickering, black-and-white images of the 'Fab Four' on television, 'arriving at airports, giving concerts, everywhere they went pandemonium, screaming girls throwing themselves at them, it sure looked fun. I don't know if I ever set out to mirror that experience but what appealed to me was the brotherhood of the Beatles. They were never alone, always together, like a gang of princes.'

From the age of five until he was eleven, Taylor went to a Catholic school, Our Lady of the Wayside, and attended mass every Sunday. His form mistress at the school observed early signs of a creative talent in his 1968 school report: 'I have found Nigel an interesting boy to teach. He is keen to learn and is always a lively contributor to the oral lessons. His work shows imagination and originality. Unfortunately, he does not always express his ideas very clearly in his written work.' It would take a few years but eventually Catholicism became an early source of disillusionment for the sensitive, intense Taylor as he gradually lost his handed-down faith. Although his parents provided a safe, normal and stable environment for their son to grow up in, there were secrets in the house too. Jack Taylor was a veteran of the Second World War and had been held as a prisoner of war in Africa where many of his friends had died but, 'my mum never wanted it talked about, so I grew up confused and afraid of what really might have gone down with Dad'.

After turning nine in June 1969, Taylor experienced 'the first stirrings of adolescence' when he was left alone one morning with 'three wonderful things': his 'gorgeous' eight-year-old cousin Andrea, a portable record player and a copy of Desmond Dekker's 'The Israelites'. However, this remained a tantalizing glimpse of another world for Jack and Jean's quiet son and for the next three years the short-sighted, bespectacled 'Nigel' (he started wearing glasses from the age of five) invested 'long hours in Catholicism', along with boyish obsessions typical of the early 1970s: Lego, model cars, planes, tanks and metal soldiers. He took all this very seriously, not only mixing talcum powder in his paints to create a realistic 'smooth cloth effect' on his toy figures, but also hanging out with the super-nerds of that period, 'war-gamers'. Taylor's partner in these games was David Twist, with the pair staging epic battles in the former's bedroom, using biscuit tins for drums and arranging their soldiers into long, neat lines. 'John and I knew each other when we were absolutely tiny but we really became big friends a lot later, when we were about ten or eleven,' remembers Twist. 'It sounds a bit nerdy now, but times were very different then – we bonded over making and painting military models – you know, little lead toy soldiers which we'd paint up and play war games with.'

By 1973 Taylor was taking the school bus every day to Redditch Grammar, ignoring the 'beautiful countryside' around him as he hit adolescence. In spite of his enthusiastic attempts to put his hand on a girl's knee, John Taylor wasn't an early or natural lothario: 'I didn't have any brothers or sisters, so I had very little experience with girls. I didn't know how to communicate with them.' The gangly thirteen-year-old also started to take an interest in the glam rock of Roxy Music, David Bowie, T. Rex and Lou Reed: 'It all began to get under my skin ... certain songs: "Starman", "Virginia Plain", "Walk on the Wild Side" and "Ride a White Swan", had been like beacons to me, beckoning me out from isolation and the collecting of Napoleonic toy soldiers, with promises of something more interesting and sexual.' *NME* scribe Charles Shaar Murray sums up the importance of this new musical movement: 'Glam was the first real pop thing that happened in the 1970s and it brought a great cast with it of geniuses and madmen, poseurs and philosophers, winners and losers, clowns and warriors, stars and fools ... giving the impetus for kids to dye their hair fantasy colours like blue, green, scarlet and purple; to wear clothes based on Flash Gordon comics and 1930s movies; to be exactly what they wanted to be and screw reality.' Science fiction and fantasy were an essential part of the gaudy fabric of glam, spearheaded by the boogie riffage and painted teardrop of Marc Bolan's T. Rex; David Bowie's androgynous, emaciated extraterrestrial alter ego Ziggy Stardust and the more musically innovative art-rock band Roxy Music. There were also the bandwagon-hopping, brickies-in-make up bands at this time: the faintly ludicrous Sweet, Birmingham's more lovably anthemic Slade, and Gary Glitter (the camp, extroverted Paul Raven, who had also considered calling himself Terry Tinsel or Horace Hydrogen), but it was the scene's artier moments that really inspired Taylor. After cleaning cars on Sunday morning with his mate Colin, he earned enough money to start buying his own records, starting with David Bowie's *Aladdin Sane* and the street punk wit of *Transformer* by Lou Reed. It was around this time that David Twist introduced Taylor to a younger kid from his school, an album-buying, pop culture prodigy named Nick Bates. Although two years his junior, according to Taylor, 'Nick already had stacks of albums and took delivery of every music weekly, every week. He had a girlfriend too, but let's not talk about that.' 'Nick and I were kind of friendly rivals,' says Twist. 'I went around to his place all the time and as a child he was indulged, shall we say. He had everything he wanted. In fact Nick's mum owned a toy shop up in the precinct at the Maypole, so called because there's a giant pub called the Maypole there. I don't mean this in a nasty way at all, but his dad Roger [who worked as an engineer and restored houses] horrified Nick sometimes. He was the anti-Nick in some ways, a very blokey bloke. He'd do things like eat mad stuff for a bet. But Nick was always a very different type of character. Nick was a big music fan, although very faddish. He'd be into everything for three weeks and then he'd move on. The only one who was pretty consistent in his taste was David Bowie and we all liked Roxy Music. I was crazy about the Velvet Underground but Nick thought they were appalling at first. He said they sounded like Gerry and the Pacemakers, although he later changed his mind and they became his favourite band. To be fair, he was younger than me, but he did like his music to be a bit more polished at that stage. I remember he even favoured Genesis for a while.'

Born Nicholas James Bates on 8 June 1962 in his grandmother's home in Moseley, Nick Rhodes was also an only child and lived just down the road from both Twist and Taylor.

According to his mother, Sylvia, 'Nick was a lovely little child. When he was good, he was very good but when he was bad he was awful. As a young boy he was very much a chatterbox, very lively and extremely inquisitive. He always wanted to know what was going on around him. He asked questions constantly and wanted to know absolutely everything.' Like most young lads of the time, Rhodes loved Gerry Anderson's sci-fi 'supermarionation' TV shows such as *Thunderbirds* and *Captain Scarlet and the Mysterons*, sometimes dressing up as the 'indestructible' Scarlet complete with Spectrum cap and 'working visor'. Given his evident appreciation of cultured, stylishly attired, leggy females, one suspects he was fond of Spectrum's 'Angels', five beautiful pilots in white leather jumpsuits called Destiny, Symphony, Harmony, Rhapsody and Melody. He's also described Marina from *Stingray* as his 'first crush'.

The ten-year-old Bates was still at Silvermead Junior School when his life changed as a result of buying David Bowie's *The Rise and Fall of Ziggy Stardust and the Spiders from Mars*. He was mesmerized by Bowie's otherworldly transmission from a trashy, apocalyptic future of leper messiahs and rock'n'roll suicides: 'Pop music got to be more and more of an important thing for me, it became almost an obsession. My life began to be engulfed by music. I was in junior school in Hollywood, Birmingham, and all the groovy kids were into Bowie, Roxy and T-Rex.' This fashionable, self-assured youngster already had a keen eye for contemporary culture, observing that the 'horrible kids' at his school were easily identified by their 'parkas' and their love of 'noisy prog-rock and heavy metal'. He was still only ten years old when he 'calmly announced' to his parents that he was going to be a 'pop star'. By the time Rhodes had started at Woodrush High School in 1974, he'd also confided in his art teacher, Mr Hart: 'Nicholas knew what he wanted to do at an early age and was one of the few schoolkids who've said to me, "I want to be a pop star" – and actually achieved his ambition.'

Rhodes and Taylor bonded as they enthusiastically traded photos of their favourite artists, both fascinated by the images of their heroes as much as their music. At a time when Bowie was experimenting with Kabuki-influenced outfits and Reed was making a stark, sinister visual impact in shades and black leather, this was hardly surprising. Roxy Music also made a deep impression on the pair. Mixing rock'n'roll with avant-garde guitars and electronics, they looked like a sci-fi vision of the 1950s delivered with an art school twist. Rhodes was particularly impressed by the band's performances on BBC's *Top of the Pops* and *The Old Grey Whistle Test*: 'They just looked so different on television. I loved Phil Manzanera's sunglasses – straight out of a bug horror movie.'

Taylor and Rhodes also started to go to concerts together, beginning with Mick Ronson at Birmingham Town Hall in April 1974 (Rhodes had already attended a Gary Glitter concert two years earlier). It was the former Bowie sidekick's first full UK tour in support of his debut album, *Slaughter on 10th Avenue*, and expectations for the much-hyped guitar hero ran high. Taylor remembers: 'The Bowie machine appeared so huge and unstoppable (he had six albums in the UK Top Fifty that year) it seemed a no brainer that Mick Ronson would become equally huge as a front man and star in his own right. It was a school night – the first time I'd been allowed into town at night on my own. Birmingham's Town Hall was mock Grecian but upon first entering, the grandeur was replaced by the new to me odour of pot and hash, doing battle with the milder forms of hippie-stink, beer and incense. The show itself made me so nervy I don't remember much about it. To be honest, no one else who saw that tour would talk of it as being particularly memorable.'

Despite Bowie's management spending a fortune on breaking him, Ronson failed to make it as a solo star and released only one further album in his lifetime, the underrated *Play Don't Worry*.

Roxy Music's gig at the Birmingham Odeon a few months later was the one the two friends had really been waiting for and they turned up at the venue several hours before the tickets went on sale to make sure that they were going to get in. According to John Taylor, 'On this tour Roxy Music were promoting their fourth album *Country Life*, opening with what would remain one of my favourite songs of theirs, "Prairie Rose". Bryan Ferry wore a white and black Spanish cowboy outfit which would be much maligned by the *NME* the next Thursday, but I thought it looked pretty good. The band was brilliant that night and I am almost too embarrassed to admit hanging around the Holiday Inn the next day. Our waiting was rewarded by a friendly chat with Eddie Jobson, Roxy Music's violinist, who looked barely out of his teens himself, and a rare sighting of Bob Monkhouse, television celebrity host of *The Golden Shot* and already a major media pain. Whether we asked him for his autograph or not that afternoon must remain, I feel, a secret.'

The impact of Roxy Music on the pair was life-changing. Although they loved the music, it was singer Bryan Ferry's witty use of fashion, art and Hollywood kitsch in his lyrics, image and via the band's striking artwork that ultimately made the deepest impression. Fashion designer Anthony Price met up with Ferry in 1971 and describes how they 'had this idea to fuse music and fashion, which was outrageous at the time but it worked. Until then fashion saw music as sweaty and disgusting, so here was the first person to change all that.' Taylor and Rhodes immediately connected with Ferry's vision. 'I've been obsessed with clothes and fashion ever since I was ten,' said the latter in 1983. 'When I was very young I used to read books about Dior and Chanel, all those fantastic early couturiers who really shaped style and fashion. I became interested in everything stylistically. I still am. It's detail – I'm absolutely obsessed with detail.' In fact, one of Rhodes's proudest moments as a kid was when he won a local competition after decorating the shop window of Bates's Toy Corner.

As well as fashion, the 1960s Pop Art movement was a big influence on Ferry's ideas, including Richard Hamilton's small collage in 1956, *What is It About Today's Homes That Makes Them So Different, So Appealing?*. Hamilton, who tutored Ferry as an art student, wrote a manifesto to go with the collage, some of which sounds strikingly like a description of Duran Duran's vision: 'Pop Art is: Popular (designed for mass audience), Transient (short-term solution) ... Low Cost, Mass Produced, Young (aimed at youth), Witty, Sexy, Gimmicky, Glamorous, Big Business.' Roxy Music also revelled in the notion that they were 'inspired amateurs' who totally rejected the rock'n'roll clichés. 'Other bands wanted to wreck hotel rooms, Roxy Music wanted to redecorate them,' deadpanned Ferry, setting the tone for Bates's chin-stroking, witty reinvention as the platinum-haired Nick Rhodes. Bryan Ferry also talked eloquently in interviews about artists such as Dali, Duchamp and Warhol. In 1972 Ferry told the *Melody Maker*, 'Warhol's idea is to make art with as little effort as possible – he's an ideas man, really. And if you have faith in an idea, it's really easy to make it happen.' All this stuff must've been absolutely intoxicating for Taylor and Rhodes, offering a glamorous, arty world that could be reached if you had a good idea and were focused enough. It didn't even matter if you were from Birmingham. After all, Newcastle-born Ferry had, by his own admission, created a new form of himself, a stylized, articulate and slightly absurd expression of his own teenage fantasies.

Taking encouragement from a clairvoyant who visited his parents' shop and told them their son was destined for great things, the bright, uncompromising Rhodes started to pick and choose his interests at school. 'It really stifled me. I really didn't feel that I needed to know what sodium bicarbonate and sulphuric acid make. Society continually tries to make people conform rather than to develop their individuality. It begins when you are very young and you have to try to fulfil your parents' expectations. After that you are forever pushed into becoming a part of various institutions: school, church, college and so on. Institutions like that cater only for the majority. They're inflexible and cause an awful lot of pain and damage.' The young dreamer was more interested in writing 'stuff' down in a journal, mixing fact with fiction as he combined a flair for stories with a keen, almost voyeuristic fascination with observing people.

By the mid-1970s his physical appearance was inspired by his hero, David Bowie: long brown hair, quite bushy, a bit like the cut Bowie had on the cover of his *Space Oddity* album. As for his fellow Bowie-freak, Taylor was nicknamed 'Tigger' by his schoolmates because he was often spotted wearing a distinctly un-rock'n'roll pullover with red and black hoops all over it. And he was still wearing spectacles. 'He was only nerdy in the way that people with glasses are thought of as nerdy,' insists Twist. 'If central casting wants to depict a nerd they stick a pair of glasses on someone called Nigel. If you take the glasses off and change their name to John, they become the world's most beautiful man!' Although Rhodes and Taylor had been trading records and talking about their favourite artists for years, it was the latter who first started making music. According to Twist, 'When John and I were about twelve years old, our families would get together at Christmas and we would try to play some music together. I had an acoustic guitar, which neither of us could play. We'd feed it through the speakers in my bedroom and make the most horrible noise.'

Not long after these basic experiments, punk hit Birmingham with a more nihilistic brand of DIY attitude and Rhodes, Twist and Taylor often went to the same gigs together at the city's two main punk venues, Rebecca's and Barbarella's. They saw the Sex Pistols several times and the Clash became a particular favourite of John Taylor, who idolized the cool, iconic rebel, Joe Strummer. They were also crazy about the New York Dolls, so when their guitarist Johnny Thunders came to play at Birmingham University they had to be there. 'I'm sure that Nigel was happy to change his name to John Taylor because it meant he had the same initials as Johnny Thunders,' laughs Twist. 'We were also huge fans of the Only Ones; Nick in particular really liked them. He started looking a bit like Peter Perrett – kind of bouffant hair, eyeliner and leopard-skin jacket.' Although Rhodes hadn't picked up a musical instrument in 'anger', he flirted with some of the punk fashions: 'I didn't go in for safety pins or other such torment but in 1976 I adopted drainpipe trousers. That caused a huge fuss. My appearance was even announced in assembly – I'd managed to pin my tie and make it straight instead of wide, and it was announced that just because I had decided to change my school uniform it didn't mean that everybody else had to.'

The energy and raw, apparent amateurishness of punk inspired Twist and Taylor to form their first band, Shock Treatment, inspired by the Ramones song 'Gimme Gimme Shock Treatment'. 'When punk came along we thought we'd been doing that sort of stuff already – making horrible noises and being non-musicians,' asserts David Twist with a dry smile. 'So we formed our own band. I used to whine pitifully like Johnny Rotten, a diabolical impression, and Taylor just made a terrible noise by running his fingers up and down the strings. Even though all we could do was make a racket, we booked ourselves a couple of gigs, the first one being at a punk club called Rebecca's where we'd seen Adam and the Ants, Siouxsie and the Banshees and the Heartbreakers. When we turned up we realized that actually a lot of the other punk bands had learned how to play. My mate Gaz, who now works at record shop called Swordfish, held the bass and stood with his back to the audience so that they couldn't see he wasn't actually playing. John made a huge distorting racket and I howled over the top. I seem to remember the reaction was stunned silence. You see the local promoters also believed what they read in the music papers: so as long as you were sixteen-year-olds with spiky hair, you were all right, they'd book you. Anyway, we listened to the other punk bands and the headliner that night was a band called TV Eye. They came on after us and we thought, "Jesus Christ, they're fantastic." They were far more sussed, the same age as us, but a lot more worldly-wise. They were from the Moseley area of Birmingham, which was a bit more bohemian.' Taylor financed his growing passion for playing music by working in a large supermarket in Birmingham. 'It was a Saturday job, and most of the time I could get away with working the checkouts (only ducking into the back room when some other local punks came in for cigarettes), or stocking the shelves – but oh, the butchery department was the short straw, freezing to death and smelling of dead meat for days afterwards.'

The next band Taylor and Twist formed was Dada, an electronic-inflected, post-punk outfit, named after the early-twentieth-century art movement which satirized society through absurd humour and shock tactics. The pair's new ideas reflected a change in the UK's music scene. After the initial energy of the Sex Pistols, the Clash and the Ramones, punk had rapidly stagnated into a movement dominated by blank-eyed, gobbing, safety-pinned droids. It had lost its sense of individualism and become a mindless, artless pantomime epitomized by Sham 69, Stiff Little Fingers, UK Subs and numerous, anonymous garage bands. This was the antithesis to the experimental tastes of the original punks, many of whom were old Bowie and Roxy Music fans. The Bromley contingent of Siouxsie Sioux, Steve Severin, Billy Idol, Berlin and Catwoman were the most infamous mutation of punk and glam alter egos but they were not untypical. When the *NME*'s Charles Shaar Murray reviewed the Sex Pistols' era-defining Screen on the Green gig in Islington, London, in 1976, he observed: 'All kinds of folks in bizarre costumes – the kind of clothes you used to find at Bowie gigs "before 'e went all funny-like" – are milling around the foyer playing the wild mutation and dancing around to a barrage of Ferry and Bowie records.' By late 1977 the cutting edge was redefined by *Sounds* magazine and in particular the writer Jon Savage as 'New Musick'. Savage described the new sound as 'nuclear night dreams' conjured up by the likes of Wire, Siouxsie and the Banshees, the Slits, Throbbing Gristle, Cabaret Voltaire and Subway Sect. They were swiftly followed by

Joy Division, Magazine and the Cure, in creating a minimalist, artily DIY sensibility by punking up the more avant-garde elements of Bowie, Roxy Music, Velvet Underground, Iggy Pop, Kraftwerk, Can and Neu!. Twist and Taylor's Dada was a simple, reactive take on New Musick, sounding 'strangely like the industrial music of Cabaret Voltaire', according to Twist. 'I think we arrived at a certain style through ineptitude. I was desperately naïve on the drums, our keyboard player Marcus had a pre-Wasp synthesizer, virtually a child's Casio keyboard, and John Taylor performed his same one-finger-on-the-guitar technique but masked it through his guitar pedals, putting lots of effects on it.' Dada's set also included a cover of Brian Eno's off-beat, proto-electronic pop song, 'The True Wheel', taken from his 1974 album, *Taking Tiger Mountain (By Strategy)*. The short-lived outfit played five or six gigs, including one at the local punk pub the Crown on the Hill, which was advertised, naturally with Dada-esque, photocopied posters. They'd been inspired to experiment with graphics by a school trip to an art exhibition in London and the band also took their Dada ideas on stage, where they used an ironing board as a rather bizarre keyboard stand. They soon broke up and David Twist joined the group who had headlined Rebeccas at that first Shock Treatment appearance: TV Eye. 'I think John would have jumped at the chance to join with me but they didn't need a bass player,' claims Twist.

For the moment the two friends continued to hang out together and in autumn 1978 they started attending an art foundation course at Birmingham Polytechnic on Fazely Street. The course was designed as an experimental workshop where students were encouraged to try out ideas and be as creative as they liked. Set in an old Victorian building underneath a flyover, the college didn't have many facilities, but it was proof that the pioneering, socialist 'golden age' of art schools in the 1970s was still alive. As Twist and Taylor walked towards the college for their first day, they were spotted whistling the theme tune to the *Banana Splits* by a skinny young punk in heavy makeup called Stephen Duffy. 'Back then Stephen was a very over-the-top, camp character,' recalls Twist. 'He was a lot more extrovert than he is now. I remember on some college trip, Stephen forward-rolling up and down the coach screaming that we were all going to die, as a laugh. I couldn't imagine him doing something like that now! He also used to wear this fantastic, box-shouldered elderly women's crimplene clothing. He was as thin as a rake and these things used to just hang off him and he looked great.' Duffy had created his own theoretical Richard Hell-influenced band called the Urbanoids, followed by a single gig in a punk band with a bunch of lads who, according to Twist, 'were as hard as nails. They got him in just because he'd learned how to play the bass.' Inspired by the do-it-yourself simplicity of punk, Duffy had bought a bass guitar, but was so embarrassed by his lack of skill that he didn't play it in the shop. It was only when he got it home that he realized it was fretless. On that first grey September morning in 1978, Duffy was too nervous to talk to a local punk celebrity from TV Eye and instead struck up a conversation with the less intimidating, bespectacled Taylor. He soon realized that Taylor was the guitarist he'd seen playing in Dada earlier that year. Duffy also discovered that Taylor's other claim to fame was that he'd bought New York Dolls' Johnny Thunders a drink with his bus fare home at the punk hang-out, Rebecca's. Plus, all three art student punks and the sixteen-year-old Nick Rhodes were regulars at the city's biggest club, the 2,000-capacity Barbarella's, which had embraced many of the new punk acts. 'It was so glamorous walking down that red corridor at Barbarella's and hearing the music of the club,' romanticized Duffy in 2002. 'It was like a Kubrick movie. It was so red inside, panning down the corridor ... And then walking in there would be girls wearing just a skirt and nothing else.' He wrote in his memoir, *Memory and Desire*, 'You could see the Clash, Buzzcocks, Subway Sect and (by far the best of all) the Slits, steal a pint of lager and still have change out of a pound.' Meanwhile Ultravox! had become a particular favourite of Nick Rhodes. Fronted by an ex-art school student John Foxx, Ultravox! lashed together acid-tongued vignettes about sex, machines and the seedier aspects of city life with punky guitars and pioneering electronics. Their self-titled debut album, released back in 1976, was Brian Eno's first production job and initially confused people at the height of punk. 'Electronic stuff was considered something that you couldn't touch,' says John Foxx from a studio in London. 'It was too close to Pink Floyd, forbidden by Johnny Lydon, declared un-good.' Although an articulate, thoughtful character off-stage, when he was fronting Ultravox! Foxx became transformed into a twitchy, electric presence clothed in black shirt and jeans, dog collar and plastic mac. 'I had these ideas about ruined, half electronic people,' he explains, 'and it was sort of like cyber hippies – ripped and torn, people who've come unplugged.' Rhodes adds, 'They were the link between punk and what came next. I guess Duran Duran wouldn't have existed had we not seen those bands at that time. Everyone should own the first three Ultravox! albums in their collection.' Rhodes also developed a taste for pretty synthesizer ballads from listening to the early Ultravox! songs, 'My Sex', 'Hiroshima Mon Amour' and 'Just for a Moment'. '"My Sex" was the first electro-ballad,' says Foxx, who quit the band in 1979. 'When we finished that, I knew it was a direction that no one else was anywhere near at that point.'

Now that Twist was signed up to TV Eye it was a natural move for Taylor, Rhodes and Duffy to form their own band. Rhodes recalls: 'We had vivid ideas of what we wanted to look and sound like, but we looked at the instruments and said, "Do we have to learn to play those things?"' He initially tried his hand at guitar. 'When I was fifteen, I spent about a year learning a few chords, struggling with my fingers and rehearsing every day. Seeing as John was about six months ahead of me, I decided to let him play it. I figured that there must be something more interesting to do than play guitar anyway and keyboards seemed the obvious answer because they give you so much scope.' Although he was on social security at the time, Rhodes saved up for a Wasp synthesizer by doing odd jobs for his parents. Famous for its distinctive yellow and black markings, this simple, monophonic synth created a buzzy artificial sound that was primitive but oddly effective. Years later the fully formed electronic convert declared: 'I love playing with keyboards. They're fascinating to me. I'm a real sucker for any gadget that does something or makes a noise. I love toy shops. I go around playing with all the little guns and robots. I still haven't really grown up in that respect. So, any time I have a chance to sit down in front of any sort of keyboard, including the piano, I do it.'

Rhodes's switch to electronics was in tune with another style shift in the British music scene. Two years on from Ultravox!'s debut, synthesizers had become voguishly cool and, just as importantly, affordable for the first time. In 1978, Sheffield's The Human League pioneered a very English style of electro-pop with their *Electronically Yours* EP, featuring the classic 'Being Boiled'. The Normal's icily paranoid 'Warm Leatherette' was another early benchmark and of course, by that time David Bowie had hooked up with Eno (the pair had talked while the ex-Roxy Music man was working on the Utravox! album) to produce the classic *Low* LP, released in early 1977. In fact, Brian Eno, the 'inspired amateur' and operator of 'synthesizer and tapes' on Roxy Music's first two albums, became a renewed source of inspiration for Rhodes, along with Daniel Miller from the Normal, who enthused about 'the possibilities of the synthesizer as an instrument for the person who isn't a musician'. By the autumn of 1978, the sixteen-year-old was not only 'quite certain synthesizers are the future of rock'n'roll', he'd also started to dye his hair – initially blond and then purple and orange – and experimented with mascara, panstick and lip-gloss. His reinvention was later completed when he changed his name to Nick Rhodes for 'aesthetic' reasons, although he was briefly chris- tened as a synthesizer player called Dior in one of the band's early photocopied posters. The same year, he reiterated his childhood announcement that he was going to be a pop star. His father remembers that, 'after school one day he told us he wasn't going back after his "O" levels [he passed eight in the end]. We decided to give him two years – until he was eighteen – to see if he could make it. We said we would help him financially.' Nick Rhodes says: 'When John and I formed the band we were very ambitious, very optimistic and very naïve. And out of that came this total belief that the thing was going to work, because it couldn't possibly fail. What on earth else were we going to do?' This confidence was handy when the local job centre stopped his dole money because he refused to be a petrol pump attendant at a garage 300 yards from his front door. He claimed he was allergic to the fumes. Oddly enough, Rhodes has remained a non-driver to this day, despite his parents giving him a car when he was seventeen: 'I took the driving test and was very irritated when I failed. I drove in this really quiet area of Birmingham and I think I only saw one guy on a bicycle the whole time. Then they failed me for not paying enough attention to oncoming traffic! So I decided I had to make enough money to be driven around for the rest of my life.'

Stephen Duffy describes the trio's early experiments as a cross between the Normal and the first Echo and the Bunnymen single, 'Pictures on My Wall', while according to Taylor it was a 'hotchpotch of influence – early Human League one minute, Lou Reed or Syd

Barrett the next'. The first song they wrote together was a track called 'Lost Decade', which highlighted Duffy's natural melodic ability, backed up by the sound of Rhodes's Wasp and Taylor's primitive riffs. Rhodes remembers: 'Stephen had all the words and tunes for some of the pieces, but when we all played together it became something else. Once I turned a rhythm unit on and John started making this noise with his guitar, we'd have something new and special, whatever it was.' 'It's true, Stephen was a lot more musical than any of us and came from a slightly bohemian, more arty background,' explains Twist, who remembers that his friend's family actually had a piano in their front room. 'Even then he was writing songs that were streets ahead of what any of the rest of us could do. His songs were brilliant.' Duffy has remained self-effacing about his own abilities: 'It's quite astounding now, but I thought you could take great chunks of *The Great Gatsby* by F. Scott Fitzgerald and sing it. The lyrics to one of our early songs, "Aztec Moon" were influenced by Jack Kerouac's *Mexico City Blues* and "Hawks Do Not Share" was inspired by Hemingway. All I'd done at that stage was listen to records and read books. I had no idea about writing from my own experience.'

Enthused by their early efforts, the trio used to meet up in Rackham's department store cafeteria where they fantasized about sounding like 'the Velvet Underground produced by Giorgio Moroder'. According to Duffy, 'We were so hungry to consume everything that was out there. Nick and John were so much more knowledgeable about music than I was, they seemed to know everything. I had to try and catch up with them. John could sit and complete the *NME* crossword and Nick had more records than anyone else I knew. The first time I ever went to Nick's house we listened to *Autobahn* by Kraftwerk, we watched the Elvis 1968 Special and played Elvis Costello's *Armed Forces* because it was the day it came out. It was exciting because we started the band at a point before music started repeating itself. Immediately after, what happened then was mod and ska, that's when repetition started and since then most music has been more or less derivative. But with things like Kraftwerk and Bowie's *Low* and "*Heroes*" you just thought it was going to go more and more futuristic.'

They had enough songs to plan their first gig, but they still needed a name. After toying with various options including RAF and Jazz, the young hopefuls settled on Duran Duran following a conversation between Rhodes and Taylor in the Hole in the Wall, a pub located in the city centre. It was the day after the ultra-camp, 1960s sci-fi movie *Barbarella* had aired on British television. The film stars Jane Fonda as a voluptuous space agent, Barbarella, on a mission to locate an evil renegade scientist called Durand Durand (played by Milo O'Shea). Later that day, Taylor asked Duffy if he'd seen the film. Of course he had, although he said it had nothing to do with Fonda's zero gravity striptease as she morphs into an inter-planetary sex kitten or the pop culture trivia of Anita Pallenberg as a bizarre dominatrix. He claimed that, like many other Birmingham music fans, he'd been curious about the source of the name of their favourite punk hangout. Duffy writes in his memoir, *Memory and Desire*: 'Taylor and I stood in the stairwell outside the college kitchen, Victorian and untouched since the war. He said that we should call ourselves Duran Duran. It was an exciting moment. To hear the space-age name in such a dark old place, to hear the future christened in the past. For some time it was by far the best thing about the band.'

Armed with a growing collection of songs, such as the Warholian 'Big Store', 'So Cold in El Dorado' and 'Hold Me Pose Me' (inspired by some writing on the side of a doll's box in the toy shop where they rehearsed), Duran Duran played their debut gig in the lecture theatre of Birmingham Polytechnic on 5 April 1979. To set the correct off-beat, avant-garde mood, Taylor covered all their speakers and amplifiers with white plastic, nearly glueing his fingers together in the process. They played to about ten people including Andy Wickett (the singer in TV Eye), various members of local band the Prefects, Mike Caddick and Gaz from a record shop in Hurst Street (they would later open Swordfish Records) and a girl who was waiting for her prints to dry. 'Duran Duran were a real art student band,' says Duffy in 2005. 'We spent hours at the college photocopying Warhol books, ripping bits of fashion magazines and so on. Duran Duran's roots were post-punk, a dark, provincial, red-brick type of thing. We felt close to what was happening in Liverpool and Manchester with bands like Echo and the Bunnymen and Teardrop Explodes. One of the reasons why we liked Warhol so much was that he was this working-class guy from Pittsburgh who drew shoes and then completely redefined art, invented a whole new school of thought.'

For their next gig they accommodated catering student Simon Colley on clarinet and bass, freeing Duffy to play the pallid, foppish front man without distraction. Behind him Taylor scratched out fuzzy, rudimentary guitar riffs and Rhodes operated pulsing electronics and the childlike drum machine. The show took place at a puppet theatre in Cannon's Art Centre. 'We figured that maybe we could fill the puppet theatre, although the puppets still got the larger dressing room,' quips Duffy in his memoir. It was his nineteenth birthday and his mother drove the band's gear to the gig in her Mini. Duran Duran added back projection for this gig although even with a set that was only half an hour long they didn't have enough slides to fill the time without mind-numbing repetition. Duffy says, 'It was therefore only slightly surprising to turn during "Signals in Smoke" and see John's geography field trip flashing up behind me.' They were still a long way from fulfilling Nick Rhodes's awakening ambitions to develop Duran Duran into a kind of 'multi-media company', but it was a start. The band's third concert took place in Birmingham University's Grand Hall where they supported Here and Now, a band with hippy connections to abstract stoners Gong. Calling himself Dufait to complete his Parisian art fop image, the singer chain-smoked Gitanes and wore a second-hand 'pink and black hexagonal blouse ... Nick wondered if I wasn't overdoing the makeup and before I could reassure him that in six months all men would look like this, it was too late as the p.a. droned: "Ladies and gentlemen, all the way from Birmingham, Duran Duran." Of course, I was wrong, in six months only Nick would wear as much makeup.'

Compared to the first three shows, Duran Duran must have felt they'd arrived as they lined up supporting local heroes, Fashion, at Barbarella's on 1 June 1979. 'I think Duran were very in awe of Fashion,' opines Mike Caddick from Swordfish Records. 'They sounded a bit like the Police and a lot of people thought Fashion were the ones who'd break through, not Duran.' 'Mulligan from the band Fashion probably had an influence on Nick,' agrees David Twist. 'He was a genuine art school character and represented everything that Nick wanted to be at the time. He had bleached blond hair, a black suit, skinny tie and went to the local art college.' Duffy comments, 'I remember Mulligan talking about the aesthetics of the cassette. He was an important figure in the art school scene at that time. In fact, various members of Fashion worked with me on my first version of "Kiss Me" [Duffy's only UK Top Ten solo hit] which I also wrote in 1979.' As for the gig itself, Nick Rhodes recalled in 2002: 'I have a very vivid memory of walking on stage at Barbarella's in Birmingham. We were supporting a group called Fashion who were pretty popular then. It was a Friday night, still Birmingham punk times, and we walked on stage wearing our outfits that certainly weren't punk style, in fact I think we were all wearing women's clothing. My home-made synthesizer stand was constructed from an old Meccano set and I had banks of reel-to-reel tape recorders all set, hoping that everything would work. The punk crowd usually liked pogoing and spitting and were occasionally prone to throwing bottles but for some reason we had decided to begin our set with a slow instrumental – "Toy Room to Tokyo". I started the song by pressing the waltz button on my antiquated drum machine and I looked out and thought, "I'm not sure that people are going to like this." At the end of the song was polite applause as I waited for the bottles to start flying. Stephen stepped up to the microphone and in his most fey voice eloquently announced, "This next song was influenced by F. Scott Fitzgerald." I thought, "They're going to kill us" and we launched into another one of our pretentious classics. By the end of it they were loving it.' In their moment of triumph, no one suspected that Stephen Duffy and Simon Colley were about to walk out on the band. 'I don't know why I left Duran Duran. I have no idea,' Duffy says now. 'I wanted to be Bob Dylan and I suppose I had to do everything I've done. I certainly don't think it did them any harm!' At nineteen years old, the skinny Beat poet enthusiast was finished with synthesizer music, especially when he sensed that his latest Fitzgerald-influenced song, 'All the Sad Young Men', wasn't liked by the other band members. So, Duffy and Colley joined Obviously Five Believers (also known as Hawks Don't Share, Subterranean Hawks and the Hawks) along with David Twist and Dave Cusworth from TV Eye, and he was replaced in Duran Duran by the latter band's singer, Andy Wickett. 'We lifted Stephen,' says Twist, 'and I don't think John ever forgave me. By then the guy who joined Duran, Andy Wickett, had drifted away from us. He was always a bit of a Syd Barrett-type figure, quite an intense character.' Stephen Duffy and Nick Rhodes reunited twenty years later to record much of the set they'd performed as Duran Duran at Barbarella's. Calling themselves The Devils, they re-created songs stowed away on a long-forgotten cassette hidden in Duffy's writing desk. Mike Caddick confirms that, 'The Devils' album is pretty much what they sounded like, although they were a bit shakier then. But the songs themselves haven't changed that much.' For Duran Duran the summer of 1979 marked the end of the band's art school era as Duffy articulates in *Memory and Desire*. Recalling the last time he went out to a gig with Rhodes and Taylor, he writes: 'The symbolism is vivid. Roxy Music at the Birmingham Odeon on the night Margaret Thatcher was elected prime minister. The socialist utopia that had financed the art schools and filled them with Lennons, Keith Richards, Kinks, Hockneys, Brian Ferry and Enos was over. We were due for a season in hell.'

Andy Taylor: *'Bowie and Roxy were the stylists. Gary Numan and Kraftwerk were the inventors. But AC/DC was the band I liked!'*

Simon Le Bon: *'It was glamorous but not when you saw the alleyway to that converted warehouse, which is what the Rum Runner was, for the first time. The people were glamorous, that was the thing.'*

Roger Taylor: *'I was a very shy kid. When I was little, if I saw someone I knew walking down the road I would cross over.'*

John Taylor: *'None of us would underestimate the role our managers, Paul and Michael Berrow, played in the band's success.'*

Simon Le Bon: *'I remember sitting in a Birmingham club with John and thinking, "This guy's got great cheekbones. If only he could take off his glasses and learn to eat with his mouth shut."'*

Simon Le Bon: *'The others did things like clean, cook, glue mirror tiles on the wall and bus tables – Nick DJ'd.'*

In spring 1979 Stephen Duffy took his songs with him, leaving Duran Duran with only musical sections and ideas. However, they did now have the willowy, intense, off-the-wall Andy Wickett. As the former front man of local heroes TV Eye, he was considered by most local music fans to be a more promising talent than the remaining lads in Duran Duran. Wickett had an experimental, creative approach to both everyday life and his music, which flickered between invention and self-destruction, although the worst of the latter would surface in years to come. He also had a very distinctive voice, described by Twist as 'great, quite high and when he let fly it would sound almost like Patti Smith'.

On the surface Wickett's commitment to Duran Duran gave them new momentum, but he was a very different character to the other band members. The skinny singer was more street-wise, living in a squat at the centre of an ugly, industrial wasteland, while Rhodes and Taylor were still at home with their parents. Wickett recalls with a dry smile, 'Nick always had plenty of stuff. I remember going around with him and his dad to a music shop in town and Nick went in to buy this Roland synthesizer. He brought it out to the car and then went, "Dad, Dad, I just can't have it without the side-bits." He was well looked after and he was always a very confident, secure person.' Although Duran Duran's second front man also experimented with makeup, there was a disparity in approach. 'Nick's always styled himself as a bit of a dandy, an Andy Warhol-type character. In TV Eye we'd worn makeup, I'd had dyed black hair, a bit Gothy. But in Duran Duran we had scarves and stuff; it was quite foppish. It was a little more glitzy and cheesy.'

Gradually this would grow into a widening division between the unorthodox, wayward spirit of Wickett and the ambitious but unworldly Rhodes and Taylor. For the moment Duffy's sudden departure had given them a scare, but they had no intention of abandoning their dreams of pop stardom. If anything it hardened their desire, especially as the music scene was changing in line with their own tastes. Duffy remembers a conversation with Nick Rhodes shortly before the fey, Fitzgerald-loving singer flounced out of Duran Duran: 'Nick wanted to be successful and famous, whatever it took. He said that once and I didn't think I'd heard him right. I didn't think you said that kind of thing.'

While Duran's adoption of electronics and drum machine, a clarinettist and Max Factor 28 was not an especially commercial move in 1978, within a few months Gary Numan's Tubeway Army had completely reshaped the pop landscape. Numan made a virtue of being an 'outsider', sensationalizing the strange through his number-one single, 'Are "Friends" Electric?'. The track was built around a voice that was a whisper away from crying; a compulsive, motorik beat, starkly atmospheric synthesizers that seemed as if they'd been teleported in from another dimension and lyrics about machines, sex and alienation. In May 1979 the quietly spoken man-in-black struck a chord with young fans who felt that their own insecurities and dreams were expressed by his combination of introspection and theatricality. He also pioneered the idea that electronic music was 'pop', rather than an avant-garde and esoteric pursuit. This was in stark contrast to David Bowie, who had actively retreated from the spotlight to experiment with synthesizers on 1977's *Low* album, while the genre's leaders Kraftwerk hid their personalities behind faceless, robotic imagery. Still only twenty-one-years-old at the time of his breakthrough success (within eighteen months he'd scored three number-one albums) Numan's machine-made sound was a new fusion of glam's showmanship and punk's DIY ethic. He told *Sounds* writer Jon Savage, 'I was excited by the thing [punk] as a whole, that all of a sudden there was something that was completely new – new fashion, new music. Hopefully when it got started, something really great would come out of it, but it sort of got destroyed by its own ideas. The anti-hero thing could never happen because this country has always had the heroes, it always will do – I think it's a very English thing to make heroes.' As a result he became the first fully fledged pop star in years, as *Melody Maker*'s Karl Dallas noted when observing Numan on stage: 'Hearing the massed sub-teen girls behind me squeal with delight brought back memories of an attitude to the artist-as-demigod which I thought had died with Beatlemania. I doubt if there was a dry pair of knickers in the house.'

For Rhodes and Taylor it must have felt that their instincts were right, as they too pursued an individualistic, ambitious, synthesizer-led direction. While there was something slightly retro about drawing inspiration from the glam rock heroes of your recent past, in this case it was exactly what everybody wanted. This left Stephen Duffy and his Subterranean Hawks feeling increasingly isolated. Twist comments, 'We've been painted as these philistines for referencing back to things like the Rolling Stones and Dylan, but the odd thing is that it felt to us more retro to be inspired by the recent past – you know, things like Bowie and Roxy. We felt we were digging a bit deeper for ideas.' Rivalry between the two bands intensified when they started rehearsing in the same Cheapside house where all the members of TV Eye had lived, including Wickett and Twist. 'It had a veranda at the back and was great because it was the only house in an area full of factories, so you could make as much noise as you liked,' recalls Twist. 'What a slum!' declared Taylor in 2003. 'We rehearsed upstairs and the Hawks were downstairs.' Duran Duran also tried out their new songs in Bates's Toy Corner, 'surrounded by boxes of toys, which was a little surreal', laughs Wickett.

According to Rhodes, Duran Duran endured a 'hellish' period in 1979, but it was vital to their development. Rhodes continued to experiment with synthesizers and Taylor started to explore disco music, strengthening Duran Duran's anti-purist ethic. In June 1979 Chic scored their fifth Top Five hit in the UK with 'Good Times'. The intuitive Taylor was paying attention, as Daryl Easlea reveals in his fascinating biograpy, *Everybody Dance: Chic and the Politics of Dance*: 'I was in a pub in 1979 and the Sex Pistols and Chic came on back to back on the jukebox. I remember saying, "I love both of these records, why can't we fuse the two?" instead of them being so removed from each other. There was tremendous power and energy in both their records; power was almost exclusively synonymous with out-of-tune guitar players and fast drummers. Chic had tremendous energy and power but with refinement and sophistica- tion. It was around the time I started playing bass. To that point I'd had no interest in the instrument – bass players were the quiet ones. I'd always been attracted to guitarists; they were like the sex symbols of the band. Bernard Edwards from Chic became the new model for me.'

Chic's streamlined, sculptured funk sound makes them the Kraftwerk of their genre, creating movement and beauty where others simply fashioned 4/4 beats and chanted. However, disco was generally regarded as 'uncool' and their rivals the Hawks weren't impressed by Duran Duran's new direction. John Taylor recalls, 'They considered themselves authentic holders of the "real rock" flame, in the Rolling Stone tradition. One night, in a scene worthy of Stephen King, we arrived to find the words "disco sucks" daubed on our door in gruesome red paint.' Taylor's enthusiasm for bass guitar played in a funkier, crossover style required a real drummer rather than a crude rhythm box. They were already aware of Roger Taylor after seeing him perform with his punk outfit the Scent Organs at Barbarella's but fate gave them a helping hand when Andy Wickett bumped into the drummer at a party. They decided

to recruit this darkly handsome, fellow Roxy Music fan after audi-
tioning him in the Cheapside squat. 'I sat in for the audition and the
music was exactly the sort of thing I was into at the time – sort of a
cross between funk and rock,' recalled Roger Taylor years later. He
was also struck by the band's 'positive' attitude: 'The music wasn't
really that important at first because Nick was just learning to play.
John had just picked up the bass and was playing around with it, so
it was a bit of a racket at first but even in those days we used to talk
about playing New York's Madison Square Garden.' The introspective percussionist with the quietly intense James Dean looks
immediately warmed to the outgoing, generous-spirited John
Taylor: 'He was very bubbly, very enthusiastic. John had all these
mad ideas shooting out of his head every ten minutes. He was very
friendly – I couldn't believe how friendly he was the first time I met
him. I think everybody thinks that when they meet him. He relates
to people easily.' Roger Taylor found Rhodes harder to figure out at
first. 'Nick was very … almost shy, I suppose. The first time I met
him he was standing in a corner with his head down and he had this
big mop of hair. I walked in the room and said "Hi" and he said …
"Hi" … and put his head back down again. So I thought he was
quite stand-offish.' Rhodes soon let his guard down, finding Roger
to be 'a very calm, reassuring kind of spirit to have around. He
never argued. He always tried to keep the peace and agree with the
majority on most occasions.' What Rhodes didn't realize was that
Duran had just recruited their second Taylor. 'For months I just
knew him as Roger,' laughs the man with the permanently spectral
complexion.

Born Roger Andrew Taylor at Heathville Hospital, Castle
Bromwich on 26 April 1960, the shy-mannered drummer has one
older brother, Steve, whom his mother Jean describes as 'very
outgoing, while Roger was always more reserved'. When Roger
was a kid, Jean did a nine-to-five job as an accounts clerk and his
father Hughie worked in a car factory, later running his own business. A big animal lover, the shy Brummie grew up with lots of
pets, especially the family dog, Kelly. He also developed a passion
for sailing, spending hours at the local sailing club with his dad.
His school life was 'uneventful … I tried to keep as low a profile
as possible. I didn't really like school – I was very quiet. I was the
one who sat at the back and never really said much of anything. I

never used to have birthday parties because I was terrified of the idea of someone coming around because of me and the idea that I'd have to be on show all day.' When he was fourteen, he sold a small boat he owned in order to buy a drum kit for £60. 'I was always interested in drums, ever since I can remember. I used to bang on things with knitting needles, pots and pans. I drove my mum crazy.' He learned by playing along to records by Yes, Genesis and Jethro Tull, and didn't bother having any lessons. Aged fifteen, the unobtrusive schoolkid joined a band called Crucified Toad, practising at home every night for half an hour until his parents came home. 'It was a guitarist, a bass player, me and an electric violinist. We were really bad.' Crucified Toad used to do covers of Cream and the Rolling Stones, plus a couple of Steeleye Span songs, simply because they too had an electric violinist. After that he joined the Scent Organs, although as far as he was concerned, 'it was nothing more than a silly band with schoolfriends. Punk was coming about at that time, so we got involved in that a bit. We played a couple of clubs but it was nothing much. It was actually new wave-oriented, not like the Dead Kennedys or anything like that.' When Roger Taylor left school with five 'O' levels, his parents encouraged him to work at the Land Rover factory for a couple of weeks and he also spent one day at the local post office, sorting mail. According to his mother, 'We couldn't see any future in being a drummer, so we tried to put him off. I think most parents would have done the same in our position. But he was quiet and determined and once he sets his mind on something that's it. He won't move. He used to say to me, "This is all I want to do." '

Although still very raw, Duran Duran's new line-up cut their first demo tapes at Bob Lamb's studio in Birmingham, with John Taylor playing bass and guitar. A laid-back, jeans-clad figure, Lamb had recorded UB40's first album in his living room studio and was a very important influence on all the hipper local talent at the time. He'd been the drummer in 1970s rockers the Steve Gibbons Band, but had set up his Moseley-based studio in the wake of punk. 'I liked Duran Duran with Andy because it was very off-the-wall and different. They had this disco format with a slightly wacky front man. And some great songs.' Duran Duran cut four tracks in that session, 'Dreaming of Your Cars',

'Reincarnation', 'Working the Steel' and an embryonic version of 'Girls on Film'. Wickett takes up the story of the last track: 'It came about because I was working on the nightshift at the time at Cadbury's Bournville factory and I used to write songs there. I remember getting this one riff and sang it all around, got some lyrics and put it down on tape.' Initially the chorus went, 'Girls in film, they look better, girls in film always smile.' 'John suggested we change it to "Girls on Film",' says Wickett, sticking blankly to the facts. 'Then we rehearsed it. Often songs would come about because John would take something and build on it. Sometimes we'd steal a whole arrangement and adapt it. I remember taking chord structures from Roxy Music songs and then we'd build a song on top of it. John did most of the music and arrangements at the start, because he was playing bass parts and guitar, but there was also a lot of collaboration between everyone. They were always very methodical about their influences and knew exactly what they wanted in there. Anyway, I said to Nick, "Try this riff on the string machine" and that was "Girls on Film". The sound was a bit more alternative than what it eventually became, I guess.'

After Duran Duran had recorded the demos, Rhodes's father Roger whisked the two original members down to London in his car, where they met up with A&R men at various record companies. They were turned down by everyone, although perhaps putting a brave face on the situation, Nick Rhodes phoned Andy Wickett at Cadbury's to tell him that some people had mentioned they quite liked 'Girls on Film'. The reality, as Rhodes himself acknowledged, was that they were probably being let down gently and no one was taking any serious interest in the band.

In late 1979 Duran Duran's line-up was briefly augmented by the arrival of Alan Curtis, a talented guitar player from London, described by Mike Caddick as 'having spiky, reddish hair, quite a nervous chap but a great guitarist – a bit like Tom Verlaine'. Duran Duran played 'once or twice' with Wickett, Curtis, Taylor, Taylor and Rhodes, performing a set that included an early version of 'Rio' called 'See Me, Repeat Me'. However, it all finished in farce one night at Birmingham University. Rhodes remembers, 'It so happened that the rugby club first, second and third teams and the reserves and the basketball team all turned up. And they didn't want to listen to Duran Duran, they wanted to sing "Knees up Mother Brown". Paper plates, tomato ketchup and sausages started flying towards us and then it graduated to ashtrays and glasses.' 'My girlfriend was managing the band at the time,' says Wickett. 'She'd booked us in at Birmingham University but what she hadn't realized was that it was a rugby club night. I was off my head on mushrooms at the time and I remember loads of plates coming over towards us, like the movie *Mars Attacks* or something. These guys were coming for us and the next minute Roger got up and hit someone with his cymbal.' Although people came up afterwards and said that it wasn't anything personal, they just wanted to have a 'good time', it would prove to be Wickett's last appearance in Duran Duran. 'There were a couple of reasons why I left the band,' he explains. 'Me and my girlfriend split up and she went out with Nick for a couple of weeks, then came back with me, so there was an atmosphere. Also, I had a skinhead haircut and they didn't like that. I wasn't into being too smooth, and they were going in that direction even at that stage. I was into rougher stuff.' Mike Caddick at Swordfish also remembers thinking that 'when Andy cut all his hair it didn't fit at all. He was dressed all in black, a skinhead in Doc Martens. He would never have gone along with that whole pop thing.' According to the sleepy-voiced Rhodes, 'Andy's personality was very different from the rest of us. Some of his lyrics weren't exactly evoking what we wanted to put forward. I think the last straw came when Andy, who used to always drink a pint of beer on stage, spilled it into a keyboard. And then he turned up at the next rehearsal with that skinhead haircut.' As for going out with Wickett's girlfriend, Rhodes recalls with a nasal laugh, 'It was a very different time back then. Both John and I had little flings with the girlfriends of the other band members.'

'If Andy had stayed their singer I think they would have exploded into a million pieces,' says Twist, hinting at Wickett's self-destructive nature. 'But when he left they lost their credibility. They would have been perceived very differently if he had remained. It must have hurt them at the time. They'd lost two of their best people in terms of talent: Stephen Duffy and now Andy Wickett. Perhaps that made them more determined and cut-throat than anyone else.' Twist is alluding to the deal Duran Duran made with Andy Wickett a couple of years later over ownership of the track 'Girls on Film'. No one disputes the fact that Wickett came up with the original chorus idea – the 'Girls on Film' part – so Duran Duran were encouraged to clarify the situation legally or it might lead to problems later. On 7 July 1981 Wickett signed his part of the song away for a one-off payment of £600. The contract reads, 'I hereby confirm that I have no interest as a writer in any of the musical works and compositions by the musicians now presently professionally known together as Duran Duran.'

According to Wickett, 'I really needed an organ at the time because I was trying to get that Hammond sound. I phoned my solicitor and asked what I should do and he said, "Sign it as it's proof that you actually have a claim on the song and then we can take them to court." So I signed it, took the money. But later I realised I wasn't going to be able to fight EMI and that they were just going to blow me out of court. I'd been hearing the song on the radio, thinking I would have part of that and then I had nothing.' Legally, Duran Duran have done nothing wrong, but it's not hard to imagine how Wickett must have felt.

In the immediate short term, the indefatigable Duran Duran replaced him with Jeff Thomas from the Scent Organs and they continued to record demos and play live, including a second support slot for Fashion. According to John Taylor, their new front man had a 'demeanour not unlike Bono' and a very esoteric writing style reflected in bizarre song titles such as 'Enigmatic Swimmer'. In his hands 'See Me, Repeat Me' became 'Ami à Go Go'. Bob Lamb remembers Thomas as 'really looking the part' but 'not having a great voice'. This was the band's line-up when twenty-five years ago, in 1980, Rhodes and John Taylor walked into local Birmingham nightclub the Rum Runner with a demo tape. They were looking to play at the venue, apparently unaware that the owners had put the word out that they were interested in managing a local band. The club was run by two brothers, Paul and Michael Berrow, who had taken it on after their father decided to sell it. Located at 273 Broad Street in central Birmingham, it used to be home to a casino but the Berrow family had switched their gambling business over to

Birmingham's Grand Hotel, leaving an increasingly rundown building that was used as a storeroom as much as anything and opening as a club only three nights a week. However, when Paul and Michael took over, they injected some New York-inspired glitz and entrepreneurial daring into the place. Many of their ambitious plans were dreamed up during their visits to New York's disco Valhalla, Studio 54, which was opened by Steve Rubell and his lawyer Ian Schrager on 26 April 1977 with an invite reading, 'Attire – spectacular'. Manhattan's nocturnal palace featured a massive dance floor, a state-of-the-art lighting rig and humungous sound system, plus a depiction of a man-in-the-moon that included an animated cocaine spoon. Bill Brewster and Frank Broughton commented in their book, *Last Night a DJ Saved My Life*, that Studio 54 was 'the last throw of the 1970s dice. Blowjobs in the balcony; adultery in the ante-rooms; buggery in the bathroom'. Pop stars and artists gilded Studio 54 with their own glamour, including Debbie Harry, Grace Jones, Mick Jagger and Andy Warhol.

The Berrow brothers set out to create a club in Birmingham which possessed some of Studio 54's opulence and sense of style. The ultra-ambitious Paul Berrow explains. 'I'd not run a club before but I'd been washer-upper, glass-collector, bar-manager, reception manager. It was more to do with, "How do we market this place out of this financial hole?" This was around early 1979 and the first thing we did was we shot off to New York and got a sense of what was happening over there and then we refocused the club immediately along those lines. We put in a huge sound system – there wasn't anything else like it in the UK at the time. We filled the club with lots of lights and plants, created a big dance floor and painted stuff matt-black to brush it all out. We added loads of green glass and then we started to mirror all the walls, slowly but surely working our way around as and when we could afford it. And it was cool, it was a good vibe. We turned it from loss to profit within three weeks. When we first took the club over it was largely the New York dance scene we focused on. It was only as we consolidated each evening and started opening up the club more and more, that we started a Bowie/Roxy night.' Once established, the Rum Runner had jazz-funk/rare groove, featuring a lot of American imports, on a Monday; Tuesday night was the Bowie/Roxy Music evening with the odd punk track; Wednesday hosted parties; Thursday was a less extreme version of the Tuesday evening and then Friday was a less extreme version of the jazz-funk set and Saturday was the 'dance' night, which was closest to the disco style of Studio 54. Such was their enthusiasm for this new enterprise that the Berrow brothers continued to make regular visits to New York in order to buy the latest cutting-edge records on vinyl and stay ahead of the game.

The Tuesday night soon became the focus for fans of electronic pop and also disenchanted punks. 'There was a lot of disillusionment going on at Barbarella's,' explains the six-foot-four older brother, Paul. 'At a certain point I think the girls started to get a little tired of having beer thrown all over them at punk gigs and I guess once the intellectual side of it started to fall away, the appeal became less. So the girls came pretty quick and, naturally, the boys followed. The club used to hold close to a thousand people. It was a big place and we packed it out.' The Rum Runner's growing reputation as a watering hole for alternative spirits was the reason why punk refugees John Taylor and Nick Rhodes turned up one late afternoon in 1979 with their locally recorded tape. 'I'm not saying what they played me was great, but what it had, was an aesthetic,' recalls Paul Berrow. 'Or at least it had the beginnings of an aesthetic which appealed to me personally. And it was quite musical. I remember some of Nick's synth lines were very catchy. The voice wasn't so much the thing that was interesting, to be honest with you. What happened was – this sounds like a really silly little story but it's the truth – we were standing in Studio 54 at the bar – I remember exactly where we were – and they'd been playing a Gino Soccio track. The evening had just begun, so all the lights started to come down and then the dancers used to start pouring out from the musicals and go hang out at the club and enjoy themselves. So the evening was just getting going, it was a great vibe there, and Rod Stewart's track "Do Ya Think I'm Sexy?" came on and then there was a George Duke track. So I turned to my brother Michael and I said, "You know, if we can find an English act for our label idea that can get that dynamic – Anglo-Saxon with the kind of Soccio, George Duke rhythm section – it's a magical formula without a doubt, that cross-genre sound in there somewhere." So when we got back we went about looking for a musical act with a good musical sensibility. We like really good songs within an interesting musical context with a little bit of weight. That would sum up our sensibility, really. Then John and Nick walked in and to their credit they had what we'd been looking for – far from fully formed, but you could tell that the attitude was there.'

Although it's hard to imagine the two young Brummies locking into a vision of Rod Stewart-mixed-with-George Duke, Duran Duran did have a 4/4 disco beat and the bacchanalian celebrity playground of Studio 54 certainly fitted with their own ambitious, glamour-tinted vision. John Taylor says, 'Paul [Berrow] and Nick and I took an instant liking to each other, and started making big plans.' 'Nick and I were like a couple of twins,' says the risk-taking strategist Paul Berrow. 'We were really thick during those early years, getting the show focused, making the right decisions. We were glued to each other in that period.' Rhodes himself describes the Berrow brothers as 'young, hip and smart. When they mentioned a management deal we thought, "Sure, let's keep talking." We were thrilled that someone was interested in us.' Effectively the Rum Runner became Duran Duran's new HQ. 'We gave them the environment and the facilities to realize who they were,' explains the well-heeled, forward-looking Paul Berrow. Rhodes was also hired as DJ for the princely sum of £10 a night, although that rose to £25 when he started packing the place out: 'We were all really into the dance scene back then. I had two turntables and worked hard on learning about rhythms, tempos and empty spaces. I began to figure out what worked with an audience rhythm-wise, what the crowd would respond to. In fact, sometimes I'd deliberately try to empty the floor to see what didn't work. I'd have to say that DJing was a very important element in my career. I used to be quite good at mixing. I always remember that Bowie's "John I'm Only Dancing" fizzled out very well into a mix of Roxy Music's "Both Ends Burning". What I used to like doing was filling the dance floor with three popular songs and then putting something else on that none of them knew, and it was so packed they couldn't move so they had to dance to it. And that's the way of breaking music in clubs.'

Nick Rhodes's DJ sets in the Rum Runner featured neon-lit songs by Kraftwerk and The Human League, along with the cathedral-like miserabilism of Joy Division and the works of the Thin White Duke. He'd also throw in a few old favourites such as Lou Reed's 'Walk on the Wild Side'. The Birmingham scene was about a year and a half behind events in London, where a Welsh ex-punk Steve Strange had hooked up with cockney drummer Rusty Egan to work the door at their own club nights, originating at Billy's in Soho in autumn 1978. 'All punks who were also closet David Bowie fans turned up,' writes Strange in his autobiography, *Blitzed!* 'Soon it became a regular event known as Bowie night.' Although it had a capacity of only 250, the 'Bowie Nights' made an immediate impression on metropolitan nightlife, with photographer Derek Ridges describing it as 'like walking into a Hieronymous Bosch painting: furtive but lively, with a dedication that's never been equalled since'. On 6 February 1979 the pair opened a new, much bigger club at a wine bar in Covent Garden called the Blitz. Steve Strange paraded outside in a variety of outfits, including a long leather coat and jodhpurs, while Boy George manned the 'cloakroom in his white Kabuki make-up and kimono'. On the dance floor, Rusty Egan's DJ sets pioneered the mix of electronic pop, Bowie and Roxy Music that Rhodes was starting to experiment with in the Rum Runner. A new club scene was developing in a way that had never happened before in the UK and Duran Duran had not only caught up with it before the movement went overground, but they'd eventually prove to be opportunistic and ambitious enough to capitalize on it.

But that was the future. For the moment the band's constant line-up changes continued at breakneck speed, as John Taylor recalled in 2003: 'Straight away Alan Curtis skipped town, thinking getting involved with two nightclub owners meant he would end up in pieces down a city alleyway.' 'Alan Curtis left a note, saying he'd left,' explains Michael Berrow. 'I don't think he liked Paul and me. But that line-up wasn't happening. It wasn't right.' This was followed by the departure of singer Jeff Thomas. 'The job was given to me to tell him he was no longer in the band,' remembers the quieter younger brother. 'He carried himself very well, a little bit like Bryan Ferry, he had that sharpness about him. But it just didn't work with him as the singer. I remember thinking, "God, how can I tell him?" I had a sleepless night over it. When I told him, he looked at me and said, "But Michael, does that mean I can't come in the Rum Runner any more?" That shows how seriously he took the band. We were all so ambitious and gung-ho about everything, plotting the future, that I'd just never realized Jeff Thomas must've seen it as a bit of fun, a hobby.' Although Duran Duran were once again without either a singer or a guitarist, the Berrow brothers didn't lose faith. 'They didn't have a full line-up, but Nick's very convincing,' laughs one of the band's oldest friends, Mike Caddick. 'A lot of the vision is his idea. He had a very strong sense of what he wanted them to be like.' Others weren't quite so convinced. John Taylor recalls, 'I remember being at Hawkins Wine Bar one Friday evening talking to George O'Dowd – this is before he became Boy George. Someone overheard me talking about my band and asked what the band was called. To my reply he responded, "Duran Duran ... are they still going?" '

Duran Duran's next move was to advertise for a 'livewire guitarist' in the *Melody Maker*. Up in Newcastle, a nineteen-year-old who had just returned to the UK after playing hundreds of gigs in a covers band across Europe picked up the music weekly and flicked through the back pages. Andy Taylor says, 'There were twenty ads and it was a bigger ad, so I thought they must have more money, a good sign.' Taylor arrived like a walking rock'n'roll cliché, complete with a guitar and amplifier slung over his shoulder. According to Roger Taylor, 'He was the loudest person I've ever met in my life. He came dressed in these dunga-rees and this pair of cowboy boots.' The guitarist's first impression was that 'there was a structure. You walk in a room and meet people and I just knew they were on the same wave-length as me. We started playing around and it sounded like a band but it didn't sound like anybody else. I said, "Where's the singer?" and was told he was on holiday. But of course they didn't have a singer.' Two days after returning to Newcastle, Andy Taylor was offered the job.

'We were actually looking for a guitarist that was more in line with Phil Manzanera or the whole Bowie/Roxy sound,' affirms Paul Berrow. 'That's what we were playing in the club, and that's what we were after. And when I say we, I mean collectively all of us – Nick, John, everybody was looking for that guy.' But when the energetic, rascally faced Andy Taylor appeared, the first thing that struck Paul Berrow was that 'he was a rock guy really, from another world to the rest of us. He was in jeans, more early 1970s rock I suppose, not the glam rock side of it. There were doubts, I think Andy knows that. Nick in particular was thinking, "Oh God." He's a bit of a snob when it comes to rock. Nick's not rock at all and the wit was streaming out of him on the issue of what Andy was wearing. But we gave it a go. Nick wasn't wrong, the guy did not look like a member of Duran Duran, not by a long shot, but he was a very, very talented guitarist who added a lot of balls to the sound which, certainly from our side, was obviously necessary. Especially if one was to break America, and we were very cognizant of the American market. We travelled there a lot, so our commercial antenna was tuned very firmly on that country, for all the obvious reasons. Everyone knows that to be significant on this planet, you have to break America, and in 1979 the only British band who had become successful there were Queen. You have to scratch your head a bit after that. So Andy felt right.' 'I liked Andy immediately,' reveals John Taylor, who appreciated the Geordie's practical skills as well as his high-octane guitar playing. 'We knew how to match lip-gloss and eyeliner but he knew how to change guitar strings and he could also get a Ford estate van started if it broke down on the motorway.' According to the band's resident conceptualist, Nick Rhodes, 'We wanted someone who could play atmospheric stuff like Pink Floyd's Gilmour, who had the power of Mick Ronson and was funky like Carlos Alomar [Bowie's most celebrated rhythm guitarist].' Now that he was 'in', Andy Taylor resolved to reinvent his look. 'They were quite blatant. They said, "We're poseurs. We want to be a good-looking poseur band." I said, "Good," because I like dressing up and I love wearing makeup. It freaked the rest of the family, though, when I dyed my hair.' 'Put it this way, Tuesday night at the Rum Runner must've been something of a culture shock to Andy,' laughs Paul Berrow. 'But to his credit, he's a plucky lad, he rolled with it, adapted swiftly, he was hungry, he listened to the band and the advice he was given, toed the line, changed his style, and did a great job.'

Andrew Arthur Taylor was born on 16 February 1961 in

Cullercoats, a fishing village near Newcastle with a population of 300. He has one brother, Ronnie, and two younger sisters, Anne and Lynette. In 2004 he explained: 'My grandfather had a fishing business, my grandmother was a fisherwoman, and my dad, Ron, did the fishing until I was about six or seven, when it really got difficult as a living and he changed to carpentry.' The family grew up in a three-storey house behind the Crescent Club in Cullercoats, which has long disappeared to be replaced by a car park. Andy and his immediate family lived on the ground floor, his grandparents occupied the middle and the attic was used to store all the fishing gear.

When Andy Taylor was not much past the toddler stage, the young prodigy would enthusiastically strum his father's guitar until one day the former fisherman was forced to sell it. At the age of five, Andy was bought a plastic one to make amends and within a couple of years he'd graduated to an old acoustic guitar given to him by an old friend of Ron's. He would spend hours in the attic with a book called *Hold Down a Chord*, which accompanied a BBC series. That way he learned all about finger-picking and the basic chords. 'Dad was great – he always encouraged me. When he got home from work he'd always be on at me to practise because he thought something might come of it. He was a big music fan and used to buy everything. I also had a cousin who gave me copies of *Sgt Pepper* by the Beatles and Jimi Hendrix records.' Sadly, there was personal tragedy just around the corner for this vital, animated pop fan and his supportive father. 'My mum packed her bags and left when I was eleven years old. I knew it was going to happen, but it was really sick and horrible. I came home from school and she was gone, so my dad looked after me. He was fantastic. I was the only one at school without a mother, and I grew up young.'

Although he passed his eleven-plus and started at Whitley Bay Grammar School, Taylor was expelled after a year. 'I was a little naughty bastard, basically. I was a disruptive element in the class. I had decided I wanted to play guitar and earn a living out of it. This is the late 1960s. I still can't spell properly and I write in capital letters without joining the letters up because I didn't pass my English "O" level.' Andy's brother Ronnie remembers, 'Andy was quite tough at school. He was very clever, artistic and always interested in music. I can remember when he went along to the careers officer with my dad. He told him he wanted to be a pop star – Dad just rolled his eyes in embarrassment. During the last years at school he just seemed to give up. He wasn't interested – he was more keen on his music.'

Inspired by the likes of AC/DC, Queen, Mott the Hoople, the Stones and Jeff Beck, Andy Taylor's musical obsession intensified and he started going around to a neighbour, Dave Black, for guitar lessons. 'Dave was four or five years older than me and really good. I was forever knocking on his door and asking him questions. He taught me so much stuff and then he helped me get my first gig with a club band.'

A friend of Black's was in a group called the Bandits and they needed a guitarist – the tutoring neighbour suggested Andy: 'It allowed me, as opposed to leaving school and having to go down Swan Hunter [a shipyard in Newcastle] or the likes, to be playing in the clubs and making £40/£50 a week,' he recalled to the *Newcastle Evening Chronicle* years later. 'Places like Consett, after they closed the steelworks there, I remember playing it before and afterwards, and the difference with the people was really, really sad. Our generation, when we grew up on Tyneside in the mid-1970s, watched it fall apart, watched everything closing down, the fishing industry, the docks, the shipbuilding, everything just shrunk away to virtually nothing. I think only one in ten kids when I left school got an apprenticeship.' There was not much of a music scene. Working men's clubs offered one of the few venues to play in. 'I was making a living playing the guitar and that, for me, was all I ever wanted to do.'

Taylor's horizons broadened even further when he started playing and singing at hundreds of gigs across Europe. He performed twenty-eight concerts during one month in Germany, humping his own gear and sometimes driving as many as two to three hundred miles a day with his cover-band comrades. The tireless eighteen-year-old also appeared at air force bases and clubs as his travels blurred across France, Belgium, Holland, Sicily. A ten-week residency at a beach club in Greece was followed by 'a bloke in Luxembourg owing us £2,000, which was a lot of money at the time'. However, when Taylor and his mates went to collect, they were held up at gunpoint – by the police!

Aside from cutting a single with punk band Motorway, entitled 'Teenage Girls', most of Taylor's work consisted of cranking out audience-pleasing classics, so when he returned to Newcastle the scrawny rocker decided that he was not only 'tired of agents trying to rip me off' but he also wanted to do something 'original'. By the time Andy Taylor searched through the *Melody Maker* adverts in early 1980, he'd already played over 600 gigs professionally.

Once he joined Duran Duran, the young guitarist moved down to Birmingham, often crashing at the Rum Runner or staying at John Taylor's house ('his mother would always leave a cheese sandwich with brown sauce on for us to eat when we got back from the Rum Runner') and making a bit of money by cooking burgers at the club. The band continued to rehearse, despite the fact they didn't have a singer. According to Andy Taylor, he immediately knew what his role was in this new electronic rock hybrid: 'They wanted the metal sound of the guitar but they wanted to keep it funky and danceable and also wanted Eno in the background. They had a concept I totally related to and I could see totally what my role would be in that, which was to make the noise and to keep the edge on it. We slotted in and about four weeks later we met our new singer.'

Simon Le Bon was told that Duran Duran were looking for a front man by his girlfriend, Fiona Kemp, who was working as a barmaid at the Rum Runner. It was May 1980 and the twenty-two-year-old, from the London suburb of Pinner, was in Birmingham studying drama at the university. When Le Bon arrived the first person he saw was Roger Taylor, who was outside painting a wall, followed by the languorous Bowie-freak, Nick Rhodes. According to Le Bon, 'I'd been told that Nick was a bit of a weirdo, so I was surprised by just how together he was. He did look weird, though. He had a pink glazed cotton jacket and purple trousers on. And blond hair – very, very blond hair. And he had makeup on – but it wasn't as good as it is now.' As for Rhodes's first impression of Le Bon: 'This chap turned up in pink leopard-skin trousers, brown suede jacket, dark glasses and pointed boots. He said his name was Le Bon, and I thought, "No, he can't be called Le Bon." But the moment I saw Simon, I decided that he had the right attitude – he just exuded attitude. And I thought, "That's it. I just hope he can sing." He was like a camp actor, something out of British 1960s films. But there was something about him that was really great. He could quote things from almost any Velvet Underground song and he arrived with his book, which was this scrawny-looking thing with the most perverse lyrics in it. People just don't give him credit for his lyrics, maybe because some of them are so pretentious. But all I ever wanted Duran Duran to be, more than anything else, was a surreal pop group. Before I heard him sing a note, I told everybody he was in the group.' The indolent-sounding but opinionated seventeen-year-old Warhol fan and the less talkative Roger Taylor told the others about this guy they'd met with 'bleached orangey hair and black shades', arranging an audition a few days later. Rhodes says: 'We were looking for a singer who was a cross between Lou Reed and Iggy Pop and David Bowie mashed into one. We didn't think Simon was exactly that. He sounded awful, like a choirboy, but then I wasn't much of keyboard player myself at the time. At least he was original and he got four out of five notes in pitch.' Le Bon himself has admitted, 'When I joined the group I was a god-awful singer but I was determined to do something about it.' Twenty-five years later, the weaselishly intelligent Rhodes argues that Duran Duran's management were concerned about Le Bon's singing abilities and at one point favoured a guy called Guy Oliver Watts. Whatever the truth of this, Berrow insists he regarded the six-foot-two-inch Le Bon as a 'swashbuckling, confident bloke and that's what you want in a rock star who's going to go and sell music in America'. He adds, 'Simon had a wonderful, natural sense of melody. That was absolutely crystal clear. Michael and I actually left the room and listened in reception. They were all up in the top bar rehearsing and there was a small opening where the sound was coming through which we'd found from experience was a good place to listen. And it was immediately clear that Simon was a natural. Melodies were just coming through that doorway, amongst all the thrash that was going on – good thrash, but you know what it's like.'

On that first afternoon, as the band started to jam, Le Bon listened through a couple of times to one of Duran Duran's embryonic tracks and within half an hour he'd slotted in the words and vocal line to 'Sound of Thunder', which would later appear on their self-titled debut album. While Le Bon's lyrics at the time were pretty abstract, that didn't faze a band whose previous front man had written lyrics about enigmatic swimmers and the linesman at Aston Villa football ground. Andy Taylor recalled to journalist Gordon Barr: 'Simon came in with this book of poetry and kept coming up with these ideas and melodies. We were like, "This guy doesn't even know what his potential is." There was an innocence to it all.'

Also there that day was the genial godfather of the local music scene, Bob Lamb, who observed how the new band line-up appeared to gel almost instantly – musically, visually and on a personal level: 'He was the missing link. Mike and Paul asked me what I thought and I said, "He's got to be the one." There's something about him, he's a very charismatic guy. He had this almost Elvis-like persona which was great for that band. I'm sure they were certain too. They got on very well, immediately made a connection. John and Nick were very glamorous boys for their age and as Simon was also a cool guy, they got on immediately.' John Taylor apparently discussed the trancy, electronic funk mantras of Simple Minds with the new singer and the pair admired each other's trousers. As for Le Bon, he was intrigued by Duran Duran's lanky, effusive bass player. 'The first time I saw John, he was this speccy geek with nicotine-stained fingers, trembling with fear at the prospect of having to meet people. He wore glasses, yellow pointed shoes and jeans with a stripe down the side. And his name wasn't even John. It was Nigel. He was a Nigel with glasses, poor sod. I remember staring at his face and slowly realizing that he was rather beautiful, exquisite in fact. I mean, this was the best-looking guy I'd seen in years, maybe my whole life.' Le Bon was also sensitive to a razor-edged sense of ambition in the band. 'It scared me a little bit at first, that they had such drive and motivation. I came out of the punk scene, so I was used to street cred, doing things for the sake of art. I remember John saying to me, "Street credibility, Simon? We've got about as much street credibility as Chanel No. 5." They wanted to be the biggest band in the world.' For the moment he privately noted to himself that he'd try the band out 'for the summer' and see how it went.

Born Simon John Charles Le Bon on 27 October 1958, to parents Anne and John in Bushey, Hertfordshire, he's the eldest of three brothers (the others are Jonathan and David). His earliest memory was hearing the radio from his cot and being able to work out 'the musical development of it and the emotional impact it would have if it went to a different chord. I would anticipate that it would go to a particular chord next and it did.' Music also played a part in his first sexual fantasy, inspired by a Rita Hayworth film that had can-can girls in it: 'I dreamed I was climbing inside Rita Hayworth's dress until I was finally on her legs. I didn't know it was bad, I just knew it was good. The can-can music was very much part of the arousal. There's just a similar feeling to sex and music.'

Le Bon (he claims his family is descended from the Huguenots, a sixteenth-century group of French Protestants) comes from a show business background, as his grandmother was one of the original Tiller Girls, his mother's aunt once danced before the Queen with the famous Ziegfeld Follies and his grandfather was reportedly part of the respected Ernest Read Choir. Simon's mother wrote children's books, loosely based on his own childhood. 'I was quite needy as a child,' he confessed in 2004. 'I really needed a lot of attention, particularly my mother's attention. I was very much a mamma's boy and didn't like it when she went out. I'd be literally sitting by the window crying and waiting for her to come back, like a dog. But I survived, quite happily. I don't think I'm scarred by it.' Later Anne Le Bon ran an antiques company in Florida, as well as a successful catering business, while his dad worked as an executive for the London water board. Educated at West Lodge Junior in Pinner, Simon himself appeared in several amateur stage productions such as *The King and I* when he was seven years old. According to Le Bon, 'If you can imagine an English Teri Shields [the zealous mother and manager of child star Brooke Shields], that was my mum. She wanted me to fulfil her ambitions. She was a brilliant singer who got married to my dad at seventeen years old and had me at eighteen. When I was a little boy she put me in the choir at Pinner parish church and I later did my first – "O for the Wings of a Dove" and "Ave Verum".' Le Bon developed a public outer skin at an early age, also appearing as 'the boy with a dirty shirt' in a famous TV advertisement for Persil washing powder, and posing for knitwear patterns in a women's magazine. He even did a series of Maxwell House coffee adverts in France. When he was thirteen years old, Le Bon made his professional debut at the Cambridge Theatre, London, where he played the part of one of Tom's friends at Rugby school in *Tom Brown's Schooldays*.

Le Bon sang on his first vinyl record at the same age, performing 'He Shall Feed His Flock' with church organist and choir supervisor Mr Turvey. Eventually the young protégé gave up the choir as his mother Anne was concerned that if he continued to sing as his voice broke, it could cause permanent damage. He'd also started getting into rock music, especially Genesis's *The Lamb Lies Down on Broadway*, David Bowie's *Aladdin Sane*, *Let It Bleed* by the Rolling Stones and the electronic soundtrack to Stanley Kubrick's cult movie, *A Clockwork Orange*. Later he became a massive fan of the Doors, in particular the dark charisma of their front man, Jim Morrison. The broadly built youth had a more physical interest too: sailing. It started after a visit to the Norfolk Broads as a schoolboy when he became 'fascinated by the water' and would sail a dinghy on a reservoir near his home in Ruislip each Sunday. He also spent most of his summers in Poole, Dorset, slicing through the water in small-keel boats.

Meanwhile, not only had Le Bon been a voracious reader since he was a kid (one of his favourites was the *Tales Of Hans Christian Andersen*), he wrote a lot too, contributing several of his own poems and stories to the school magazine. From the age of twelve, Simon Le Bon attended Pinner Grammar School, where he occasionally attracted trouble. 'I gravitated towards the naughty boys at school. But it was a problem for me, because they regarded me as a bit of a poof. I was a middle-class kid with a proper upbringing.' As a teenager he experimented with drink and drugs but was put off by watching his friends turn into drunks and speed-freaks by the age of sixteen. He's also described himself as a 'late developer … It was quite a difficult time. I was, in fact, the last guy in my school to be wearing short trousers. I was the last guy to get hair around my balls. I was the last guy to get a big dick. Actually, no, that's not true. Some of them never got big dicks. I was one of the last guys whose voice broke. My voice didn't even break, it just slowly changed over a period of four or five years. I was still speaking in a squeaky high voice at fourteen and fifteen. So I had to struggle quite a bit. I'd get beaten up occasionally and I wasn't very good at fighting. But I was a good laugh.'

Even as a kid he was 'interested in girls, big time. There was never a point in my existence when I wasn't obsessed by some girl.

My first obsession was with a girl called Alison. She was two or three years older than me. I was about eight and she was my first crush. I stalked her. Can you imagine being stalked by an eight-year-old? But girls didn't get into me until I was in Duran Duran. The ones who were interested in me were never the ones I was interested in. That's part of growing up, though. You learn to be realistic with your attractions or you make your feelings felt so that the object of your affection knows you're interested. Unrequited love is really the domain of the young, I think. We are always touched by unrequited love stories because they remind us of our own youth.' After leaving school with six 'O' levels and two 'A' levels in art and English, Le Bon worked as a hospital porter at Northwick Park Hospital, Harrow. He proved to be an unsqueamish attendant and developed a fascination with the life-affirming power of witnessing death and the dark side of life at close hand: 'It had a profound effect on me. I saw severed limbs, dead bodies and people badly hurt. But there was a good atmos-phere. It was the will to survive. The tenacity of people took me by surprise.' Aged twenty, the directionless adventurer went to a kibbutz in Israel, where he tried his hand at driving tractors, lumberjacking, tree surgery, orange picking, looking after chil-dren and, of course, chatting up Israeli women. 'I went with my girlfriend, we split up, I fell in love with an Israeli soldier girl and I started writing songs.'

Le Bon returned to the UK and enrolled in a drama course at Birmingham University (having been turned down for places at RADA and Bristol's Old Vic school) but soon felt disillusioned by the insular, self-indulgent atmosphere. Nicknamed Simon the Poser by his sneering classmates, he was the 'only bloke who wasn't afraid of making a fool of himself', at dancing and improvisations: 'I got really drunk at a party where there were a lot of drama queens and I realized I didn't really fit in. It was just another institution.' The beefy drama student was still in his freshman year when he auditioned for Duran Duran. They weren't actually his first band as he'd had a few short-lived experiences – singing in a punk act, Dog Days, when he was seventeen, and he'd briefly joined Bolleaux, who specialized in a pub-style R&B. He also tried out an electro-punk group called Robostrov before settling on Duran Duran. The night it was decided Simon Le Bon was in, the band printed up tickets for their first date at the Rum Runner club. They gave themselves about six weeks to get a set together. As John Taylor later confessed, 'There's nothing like a delivery date to work towards.'

Le Bon: *'I thought it was a hobby thing. Then I realized they meant business. Real business.'*

John Taylor: *'"Planet Earth" and "Girls on Film" were the sum total of what we knew at that time. We wouldn't have been able to play "Johnny B. Goode" if we'd wanted to.'*

Simon Le Bon: *'In this band we've always been very optimistic. I fight very strongly against bitterness and being jaded. Even as you grow up, you've got to find a freshness in the way you look at things.'*

Japan's former manager Simon Napier-Bell: *'Duran Duran came along and stole David [Sylvian]'s image. Every one of them copied David's looks, so you had five David lookalikes. Then they very sensibly went off, and instead of making esoteric Japan music, they recorded good, old-fashioned, four-to-the-floor disco music. They got the hits with the Japan look.'*

John Taylor: *'The band is like a box of Quality Street – everyone is somebody's favourite.'*

Simon Le Bon: *'I was a very boring individual before I was in a pop group. Music was my means of breaking out, of developing a kind of individualism and an idea of what I'm capable of and what I'd like to do.'*

On 16 July 1980, Duran Duran's classic line-up earned £50 by making their live debut at the Rum Runner, walking on stage to 'Tomorrow Belongs to Me' from Liza Minnelli's cult film, *Cabaret*. Although no doubt entranced by the seedy voyeurism expressed by the film at the height of glam (it came out in 1972 and was based on Christopher Isherwood's books *Goodbye to Berlin* and *Mr Norris Changes Trains*) and David Bowie's more recent exploration of Berlin culture on 1977's *"Heroes"*, the song's banner-waving wasn't an auspicious start. John Taylor says, 'We never considered the politics of it, being an Aryan anthem as such, and we upset a few people that night.' Looking back Le Bon commented, 'I think it was harmless but it did all get very silly. Factory Records were using fascist and futurist graphics, you had Hazel O'Connor goose-stepping around and the Skids put out their album, *Days in Europa*, which had a controversial Olympic poster as a cover. Which no one would get away with now.' Duran Duran also wore their disco influence on their rolled-up sleeves by trying out a version of the throbbing, sexually charged 'I Feel Love' by Donna Summer, which had taken electronics on to the dance floor at Studio 54. But the real thrill for the band was playing their new songs, opening with 'Night Boat' and also including 'Late Bar', 'Girls on Film', 'Sound of Thunder' and a very early version of 'Tel Aviv'. Le Bon also sang Jeff Thomas's lyrics to 'Ami à Go Go', while some of the other songs, such as the John Taylor composition 'Secret Success', have faded into obscurity. Duran Duran played further local shows at the Cedar Ballroom (19 July) and Holy City Zoo (22 July) before focusing on a two-month writing period, broken only by one further show at the Rum Runner on 6 August.

Anchored by Roger Taylor's compact, unshakable drumming, Duran Duran's songs rapidly took shape in this frantic period of creativity with John Taylor also proving himself to be an intuitive talent. He's very much a character who lives emotionally in the moment, which makes him a natural, expressive musician. Although Rhodes has always been quick off the mark to communicate the band's vision, John Taylor's talkative intensity and drive are just as vital in defining the spirit of Duran Duran. He is the sensitive, charming, ad-libbing pop star to Rhodes's more controlled Pop Art, platinum-haired alter ego. Although they share a love of simple and uncomplicated aesthetics, one senses it emotionally, the other intellectually. That also makes him a bit of an enigma. 'John's the sensitive one in the band,' says Paul and Michael's younger sister, Amanda Berrow, who in the early days travelled with Duran Duran, running errands and looking after their clothes. 'He's a very loving man and he really needs to be loved. He's very insecure and I could see really early on that he would direct his feelings inward. He was always beating himself up.'

In Andy Taylor they'd found a musician who could splice

together their rough, undisciplined mixture of punk energy, disco rhythms and analogue electronics into a strong, solid, cohesive structure. What's often overlooked, because they are polar opposites in the band, is the creative relationship between Nick Rhodes and Andy Taylor. The guitarist freed Rhodes to play the role of ideas man that he so clearly revels in. It didn't matter if his suggestions were completely off-beat because they now had a guy who could make musical sense of it all, enabling them to focus in on something good and hone it quickly. Not only that, but on a pure musical level Andy Taylor developed a way of playing around Rhodes's synthesizer patterns, enhancing and strengthening the melodies. 'In the beginning that worked because as we wrote the songs we'd all be pitching in and experimenting. Later that didn't seem such a good way of writing and today I tend to write my guitar parts around people's voices.'

Although the puckish guitarist valued Rhodes's input, he was blown away by the raw ability of Simon Le Bon. He noted that Le Bon wrote the lyrics easily and quickly for 'Girls on Film', after being given the first version. 'People often read him in the wrong way. But there are very few people on this planet ever who have written so many beautiful melodies as that man has.'

Le Bon is an underrated talent, largely because he often comes across in the media as somewhat pompous and cocky. He has the air of someone who appears to love himself just a little too much. In reality, one suspects that he's rather more complex. Perhaps he's always wanted to be perceived as a brooding, sexual being like his hero Jim Morrison and that encourages him to be either crude or a complete show-off. But his manner is, as Rhodes has described, more like that of a camp actor. Quite simply, he was always just too 'luvvy' to be heralded as a New Wave Lizard King. As for the arrogance and coldness, it seems to be more of a personal barrier than elitism. One senses that there's a lot going on in Le Bon's head and emotionally under the surface, but he doesn't give much away. That makes his moods unpredictable. Duran Duran's official photographer for many years, Denis O'Regan, has encountered the singer's changeable state of mind. 'Simon can appear very sweet, full of energy, a very physical presence. He can also seem abrasive and off-hand, perhaps more than he intends to be. He'll seem over-the-moon about seeing someone, fling his arms around them and so on. And then, for no apparent reason, you can sense that he's cooled off and it feels like there's an invisible barrier there. I think underneath there's a very sweet and loyal man but he's always swayed between these different characters for as long as I've known him. I had a conversation with John [Taylor] recently and he told me that after twenty-five years or so he's only just finding out what Simon's really like. He said that he's finding things under the surface that he really likes and he didn't realize were there before.'

In fact the singer has claimed, 'It took me about a year before I felt accepted in Duran Duran.' Amanda Berrow confirms that 'Simon was a bit of an outsider but he almost removed himself though. He was about the only one who wasn't working at the club and I perceived him as isolating himself. He's a charismatic man but with that there's this aloof quality. But he had a lot to prove. He wasn't a great singer, so I guess he had a certain amount of insecurity that he chose to hide. He was kind of an actor playing a part as a front man in a band.' In the early days, the two non-Brummies, Le Bon and Andy Taylor, shared a flat in a 'poor area of Birmingham', going out for a curry when they could afford it. According to the singer, 'Andy is very sensitive, though he doesn't show it to a lot of people.' The action-packed guitarist is a very emotional, energetic character who can often frustrate those around him by being completely contradictory. He thrived in Duran Duran's gang mentality but, like Le Bon, also felt out of step with the others. What is in no doubt, however, is that both Le Bon and Andy Taylor earned the respect of their colleagues very quickly and that clearly inspired the band. Within two or three months of the pair joining, Duran Duran had written all of their debut album, including a new version of 'Girls on Film' with a Le Bon lyric. Rhodes said in 1981: 'The thing which makes us all work well together was that we are five very different individuals. We all have strong personalities. Sometimes this fact means that there's a lot of tension between us, because we all have conflicting ideas. But that only seems to make us work better.'

The Rum Runner provided the environment where the five lads could work, absorb influences and ideas, earn some money and discuss the future. Andy Taylor worked in the kitchen, Roger used to do a lot of the cleaning – including polishing all the mirrored walls – and Nick Rhodes's Tuesday-night DJ slot meant that he still didn't have to get his hands dirty. The louche Le Bon has also boasted, 'All my memories of the Rum Runner are to do with shagging each other's girlfriends up in the warehouse in the dark.' 'The club was the centre of all the activity,' says Paul Berrow. 'It was a big family. They rehearsed upstairs and downstairs they could listen to all these different times and genres of music being played – a fantastic environment for developing a repertoire of songs and styles. You could literally pop downstairs and stand at the bar for half an hour and listen to the best sounds coming from all over the world.' John Taylor agrees: 'Back then the Rum Runner was divided into different rehearsal areas [Dexy's Midnight Runners and the Beat also used to rehearse there] and they gave us one of the rooms at the back. The bass-line in "Rio" is an example of how that club influenced us, with the jazz-funk bands that played there on a Monday night.' The band also sat around in the bar discussing their future at great length. According to Roger Taylor, 'We actually spent more time talking about what the band was going to sound like, how big we were going to be and where we were going to play when we were famous than actually rehearsing together. We had some really big ideas. We were just so positive about everything that it had to pay off.'

Duran Duran continued to record their demos at Bob Lamb's studio, often fleshing out ideas that had begun at the Rum Runner. 'Their parents used to bring them to the studio with their keyboards in cardboard boxes,' remembers Lamb, who observed their working methods at first hand. 'Nick and John were the driving force and a bit of Andy – that lively Geordie spirit. Nick's sequencing was the core, the pulse, and the song usually came from something Nick put in. He was quite ahead of his time, actually. Roger would add those drum-beats and Simon threw some words on there. It was very much a group thing and they wrote very fluently. In fact, Simon would write there and then, as he didn't always have a lyric. I used to have this platform bed and he would get up and lie there, sprawled out with his book of lyrics, just writing words. Songs like "Planet Earth" and all those early tunes seemed to come together almost effortlessly.' Lamb also adds, 'They were influenced by Japan, who were just starting to cross over – the pop thing and the arty glamour thing. That was their influence. I don't think they ever saw themselves as completely a pop thing.'

John Taylor, Nick Rhodes, Andy Wickett and David Twist had seen Japan 'very early on' at Barbarella's, where the band's singer David Sylvian performed behind a curtain of peroxided hair which often completely covered his face. His thin-hipped swagger was backed up by the rest of Japan, who were trashy devotees of eyeliner, glitter and low-slung guitars. 'We liked Japan because they looked like the New York Dolls and we were interested in anything resembling the Dolls,' smiles Twist. 'Although they were a lot more disco than the New Yorkers.' At this stage Japan had released two albums – *Adolescent Sex* and *Obscure Alternatives* – of sleazy rock-funk with some half-obscured signposts to the more electronic area they went on to explore in the early 1980s . Their immediate impact on Duran Duran was two-fold: Japan's fretless bass-player Mick Karn played with a completely untutored style that fascinated John Taylor and further encouraged him in his mission to push the instrument to the front of the mix as opposed to blending it in to the point of invisibility. That was, after all, the standard approach in most rock bands, but it didn't appeal to a fame-obsessed wannabe pop star like John Taylor. Not only that but aside from Japan's singer, Karn was easily the most charismatic figure on stage, which could never be said of fellow rock bassists John Deacon (Queen), Bill Wyman (Rolling Stones) or John Entwistle (the Who). Also, Japan's cross-dressing look, explained by Sylvian as a 'technique of passive confrontation with authority', mirrored Duran Duran's own fascination with image and inspired them to experiment further. Portrayed by Japan's manager Simon Napier-Bell as 'a cross between Brigitte Bardot and Mick Jagger', the young Sylvian claimed he would encourage his bandmates to shop 'in the tattiest women's boutiques we could find'. He also made it clear, and Rhodes duly noted, that it wasn't 'fancy dress' or playing 'a part, just for one night'. Sylvian claimed he felt 'confident' wearing makeup whether he was on a bus in Lewisham or on stage. While the androgynous Londoner eventually ditched his makeup box in the mid-1980s, to this day Rhodes rarely leaves his house without at least a touch of mascara or a dab of foundation.

According to Mike Caddick at Swordfish, 'Nick and John were obsessed with Japan and the day [December 1979] Japan's *Quiet Life* album was delivered to the shop, they couldn't get into town so I had to drive back in later to give them their records. They couldn't wait any longer. By that time Japan had changed quite a bit and were clearly into the whole Roxy style, as were Nick and John. But yes, Nick in particular started buying a lot of Japanese imports – artists such as Yellow Magic Orchestra, Ippu Du, Akiko Yano and so on.' Rhodes has made no secret of his enthusiasm for the sensitive, slightly abstract approach of Japan's keyboard player, Richard Barbieri, especially on *Quiet Life* and the next two albums, *Gentlemen Take Polaroids* (1980) and *Tin Drum* (1981): 'Barbieri came up with great ideas, great ways of presenting things,' he says. In the early 1980s Japan embodied some of the art-pop, electronic aspirations of Nick Rhodes, though less so for the other members. On their albums they traded in ideas stylishly assembled from the likes of Roxy Music, Bowie and Velvet Underground (*Quiet Life* even includes a cover of 'All Tomorrow's Parties' from Velvet Underground's debut album) and presented a new European cool, slightly withdrawn emotionally but still a world apart from the cold, machine-based sounds of their Futurist contemporaries. Japan's ambient synthesizer songs are stylistically echoed by Duran Duran's darker moments, from early tracks such as 'The Chauffeur' (*Rio*) to 'Winter Marches On' (*Notorious*) and the whole Arcadia spin-off project. However, there is an argument that Duran Duran were exploring these areas first in 1978, when Japan were still dolled up and rocking out on *Adolescent Sex* and *Obscure Alternatives*. In fact, the Devils album *Dark Circles* is full of melancholy, Ultravoxian balladery and atmospheric introspection.

Japan's former manager Simon Napier-Bell claims that, in 1980, 'members of Duran came day after day and begged Japan to produce them'. Although David Sylvian denies this, the softly-spoken and underrated Richard Barbieri does remember 'Nick Rhodes and John Taylor hanging round outside our gigs sometime in the very late 1970s and early 1980s. It is true that at one show they gave me a tape with a view to us producing them. The demo tape had "Planet Earth" and "Girls on Film" – I've still got it at home somewhere, actually.' In response Nick Rhodes asserts, 'It's possible that Richard Barbieri has a tape that we gave to him but I think it's more likely we wanted to do a gig with them rather than asking them to produce us. I certainly don't remember any conversation about that.'

Musically Japan's most commercially significant influence on Duran Duran dates back to April 1979, when Sylvian and his comrades played around with disco beats and sequenced electronics on their collaboration with Giorgio Moroder (and early 12"), 'Life in Tokyo'. Stephen Duffy remembers, 'Nick and John were completely obsessed with "Life in Tokyo" and wouldn't stop talking about it. This was around the time I left the band.' The track wasn't a complete stylistic one-off as a slightly toned-down dancey approach runs through Japan tracks such as 'European Son' and the song 'Quiet Life', which became Japan's first hit single in 1981. However, they didn't pursue this direction any further. Kajagoogoo's Nick Beggs, who later got to know both Nick Rhodes and various members of Japan (in fact Mick Karn did the artwork on Kajagoogoo's second album), argues that 'Duran Duran did embrace that whole "Quiet Life" thing. "Planet Earth" and the sequencers sound just like it. I know Nick denies it, but it's true.' However, the tone of 'Planet Earth' is completely different to 'Life in Tokyo', which still retains an esoteric weirdness. Even at their most commercial Japan are full of doubt and detachment, whereas Duran Duran imbued their songs with a pop-loving *joie de vivre* and fundamentally changed the spirit of the music, as Sylvian himself recognized when he spoke to *Sounds* in summer 1981: 'A couple of bands have taken things from us and adopted them but their attitudes are different, so the end result isn't the same.'

It is true that to this day the platinum-haired Nick Rhodes does bear a striking resemblance to David Sylvian *circa* 1979/80 and these bizarre (Jean) Cocteau twins have also shared an interest in French poets, Andy Warhol and art movies. 'I think it's fair comment that we all noticed a similarity between Nick Rhodes and David Sylvian,' says Barbieri. 'We objected to it at the time, but it's all part of growing up and developing your own style. If as a group we've inspired someone to do something, that's fantastic. Mind you, when I saw him on the Brit Awards recently, Nick Rhodes still looked like he could've been in Japan!' However, Rhodes had been experimenting with bleached hair, makeup and Roxy-styled clothing since he was sixteen years old, so it seems a bit unfair to accuse him of stealing the look from Sylvian. After all, Warhol had cultivated an image of straw-haired 'otherness' for decades before either of them, and if anything, they both plagiarized him. In many ways Rhodes is also the anti-Sylvian – he's an assured character with a very strong sense of himself, while the former Japan singer is an eternal worrier who went on to explore a more spiritual sensibility on beautiful solo albums such as *Brilliant Trees* (1984) and *Secrets of the Beehive* (1987).

Everyone rips each other off in pop music and many acts steal from the same sources, so the role played by Japan in Duran Duran's development should not be exaggerated. But in a strange twist of fate, the two bands briefly worked side by side in late summer, 1980. Duran Duran arrived at AIR studios in London to record 'Girls on Film' (featuring Michael Berrow on sax!) and 'Tel Aviv', and just down the corridor Japan were putting the finishing touches to their *Gentlemen Take Polaroids* album. Although Rhodes met Japan's singer at the session, he argues that a rather more famous rock couple made a bigger impression. 'Paul and Linda McCartney were working there and at the end of every day they used to stick their heads around the door and say, "Goodnight". It was really surreal.'

Within weeks of completing the twenty-four-track recording, Duran Duran were beginning to attract attention of their own. This was initiated by Paul and Michael Berrow, who had signed the band to their own production company, Tritec Music. Named after the Rum Runner's triangular themed bar, Tritec financed Duran Duran (they estimate they'd spent £30–£40,000 before the group were signed) and looked after management, publishing and merchandising, with the brothers effectively owning all of their recordings. A man of great vision and energy, Paul Berrow started calling around all the A&Rs at the major labels, using their next gig at the Hosteria Wine Bar on 16 September 1980 as an early showcase. 'I remember some record company people coming down to that,' says record store owner Mike Caddick. 'It looked very impressive; they had searchlights scanning across the stage.' In fact Duran Duran were one of the first bands to use moving lights at their shows, which allowed them to try things other than the static, criss-cross beams of their contemporaries. The band were all dressed in matching suits bought from a shop called Metropolis that Paul Berrow had discovered in London, although this was the only time they wore them. Roger Taylor's mum, for one, was impressed by what she saw that night: 'We used to say to Roger, "This is ridiculous – you're going to end up doing nothing." We were disappointed with him. Then he came home one night and said he was playing this gig with Duran Duran at a local wine bar in Birmingham called the Hosteria. I decided to go along to see what he was up to. A couple of my friends from work came along with me for support. My husband Hughie refused to go. When I came out I couldn't believe it. I was really bowled over.'

Meanwhile, Paul Berrow had also contacted Dave Ambrose, who had made his name as the man who had signed the Sex Pistols' publishing, but had only just started as A&R manager at EMI Records. 'Paul rang up and I was the lucky one who picked up the phone,' he grins. 'Paul said, "Do you want to hear this band, Duran Duran?", and that's how I got to know them. I went to see them and decided that this was the one.' Ambrose remembers watching them at the Holy City Zoo, which Duran Duran played on 22 October. 'They were a bit rough, actually, they weren't totally together then, but they had "the idea" and I thought "the idea" was fantastic. You could see the audience forming even then. They already had lots of pretty girls in the audience, lots of people dressing up. It was a big, celebratory splash of colour and had a sense of style.' Bob Lamb also recalls, 'before "Planet Earth" was a hit, I was pretty well convinced that they were going to happen. You know when you see a band and you just know that they're going to crack it. One of the reasons being, you go to a Duran gig – because I used to do out-of-front sound for them as well – and the place would be full of girls, models, real stunners everywhere. And the dressing room would be full of strange, beautiful people. This is before they'd cracked it.'

In reality Duran Duran didn't have much of a following in Birmingham, but the Roxy/Bowie circuit had spread rapidly in the last two years, first in the Romulus, then the Rum Runner, and the Hosteria Wine Bar was another favourite hangout. Boy George, who used to visit his Aunt Teresa in Birmingham at the weekend, was a regular face in the Romulus with Martin Degville, who later became the singer in Sigue Sigue Sputnik. He'd been a local character since the mid-1970s when he walked the streets of Birmingham with a startling, massive white quiff and a Bowiesque pale blue suit. In the years that followed kids from the local council estates would throw stones at him as he strolled past with a big stick and high heels, 'like some mad Chinese guy' as one friend remembers. 'He was the best-known local freak around at that time,' says Mike Caddick. 'You couldn't miss him. He was fearless.'

Local clothes designers Jane Kahn and Patti Bell kitted out many of the young Bowie fans who frequented Romulus and the Rum Runner. They'd originally sold vintage stuff to punks from their Hurst Street shop, but by 1980 they were better known for their ruffled shirts. Patti Bell was friendly with Degville, Boy George (who used to crash at her place) and Pete Burns, another eye-catchingly flamboyant cross-dresser who would come from Liverpool to buy fabric off her. This colourful mix of designers and poseurs had strong links with London, with Degville setting up a store in Kensington Market and Jane Kahn moving down there when she started going out with Tok, a mime artist in the dance troupe Shock. Ideas were swapped back and forth with the London scene, which still centred on Steve Strange's Blitz Club. In fact, as far as Patti Bell is concerned, 'By that time very similar things were happening in Birmingham and London. The difference was Birmingham had bigger and more elegant places to hang out in.' Nick Rhodes remembers, 'I'd started out DJing on Tuesdays at the Rum Runner and then ended up doing it on Fridays too. The thing is it would be absolutely packed and the club held at least 500 to 600 people. There would be queues around the block. We had to operate a door policy and my girlfriend at the time, Elayne, used to decide who could come in. She was absolutely the most exquisite creature you've ever seen and some nights she'd be dressed from head to toe in see-through plastic.'

Although there was a vibrant scene in Birmingham, recently launched 'style' magazines such as *The Face*, *i-D*, *Zig Zag* and *New Sounds New Styles* initially focused on London's pioneering Blitz Club. They described Blitz as the cultural home to the Cult with No Name, otherwise known as the Blitz Kids, or later the New Romantics. After Mick Jagger was turned away from the door one night – Strange claims because the club was already over its 350 capacity – the sense of era-changing, youthful exclusivity took the UK media by storm. The tabloids had a 'shock-horror' field-day with Blitz's bizarre-looking crowd, consisting of Pierrot clowns,

Restoration fops, girls in bell-hop suits, boys dressed as geishas, Russian Cossacks, pirates and gangsters with painted, androgynous faces. You'd even find the odd Boadicea and Carmen Miranda. For a moment, the Blitz was at the heart of British fashion. PX, a small clothes shop in Covent Garden, was the coolest shop in London as it was effectively the Blitz Kids' 'house designer' and nights out at the club inspired the work of students at the nearby St Martin's School of Fashion, including Blitz regular, John Galliano.

Ever alert to the latest trends, the movement's spiritual guru David Bowie dropped by the Blitz in 1980. He played out his role as godfather to the scene by hiring Steve Strange and some of his cohorts for the video to 'Ashes to Ashes', which appeared in the autumn of that year. But when Nick Rhodes went there for the first time, he wasn't impressed: 'I just thought, "This is no fun at all." It was a complete bunch of poseurs, very manicured and not vibey at all. It was a friendly scene at the Rum Runner and people really cared about the music.' 'The atmosphere in Birmingham was friendlier,' agrees Patti Bell. 'It wasn't as back-biting and competitive as the Blitz, although Degville could be quite bitchy about John Taylor, or Nigel as he called him. He'd make remarks about John's "vile hair" and "National Health glasses". Roger Taylor was the cool one. All the gay boys liked him. The first time I met Nick Rhodes he had eye-kohl and enjoyed dressing up, just like everybody else did at the time. I used to think he was quite posh, a bit of a snobby git. Then I got talking to him and he wasn't, he was all right. We became good friends then and we'd go out with Nick, Jane and Tok from Shock.'

Boy George snipes in his autobiography *Take It Like a Man* that Steve Strange 'lorded it on the door, making us wait while he turned away some poor freak from the sticks. I felt sorry for some of them, they'd spent so long putting on their makeup and lampshade hats. Steve Strange was superior ... and we resented his self-appointment as the king of the weird. His nicknames were Wally Weird or Nobby Normal.' Jon Moss, the drummer in Culture Club, who finally broke into the charts with 'Do You Really Want to Hurt Me' in autumn 1982, described the bitchy, ugly side of the Blitz in *The Face*. 'Smear stuff on your face; tacky, dirty, everything falls apart. Nice exterior, very dressy, but underneath it's dirty. There was no spirit, no faith, no religion. Ungodly. The Blitz thing was like walking into Hell, it was like Berlin in the 1930s. When I go to Hell, that's what I expect it to be like.' In fact Bowie had already nailed the scene's back-biting desperation with 'Fashion', the follow-up to 'Ashes to Ashes'. In November 1980 he told the *NME*, 'The song and video are to do with that dedication to fashion. A gritted-teeth determination and an unsureness about why one's doing it. But one has to do it, rather like one goes to the dentist and has the tooth drilled. It's that feeling about fashion which seems to have in it now an element that's all too depressing ... Yes, I must say I felt it when I was in London. I was taken to an extraordinary place by ... Steve Strange? Everybody was in Victorian clothes. I suppose they were part of the new New Wave or the permanent wave or whatever.'

As PX's frilly shirts hit the High Street, the scene held on to its alternative roots for a while in Strange's next clubs, Hell and Club for Heroes, before it died in the tacky purgatory that was Camden Palace in 1982. Nevertheless, by that time Blitz had proved itself as a breeding ground for new groups, including Visage. Formed by Steve Strange and Rusty Egan, they recruited various members of Ultravox! and Magazine, along with Midge Ure from the Rich Kids to form this New Romantic super-group. Visage's 'Fade to Grey' reached number eight in December 1980, complete with a disco-type beat and a girl talking seductively in French to lend it a voguish European feel. The band sounded as if they were enjoying themselves on their self-titled debut album as ex-Ultravox! electronic wizard and 'Fade to Grey' co-composer Billy Currie recently told *Q* magazine: 'Me and the guys from Magazine were all in our late twenties so there was a sense of urgency, even desperation in Visage. But there was also a real feeling of freedom for everyone. After being in these very heavy bands, Visage was fun.' Unfortunately Strange's weakness was that he took the project and himself more seriously than was actually warranted. As *The Face* commented in 1982: 'He obviously wanted (though perhaps not consciously) to be high camp, like Marlene Dietrich, but everybody outside his charmed circle insisted on treating him as low camp, like Gary Glitter.' Spandau Ballet, who started playing at the Blitz in late 1979, were guilty of even greater Blitz-inspired ludicrousness than Visage. They espoused a kind of mutant Mod ethic, presenting fashion and music as an expression of working-class aspiration. So far so good, but they looked absolutely terrible in yards of tartan, pin-striped trousers, headbands, sashes and shawls.

Spandau Ballet's combination of image, Malcolm McLaren-inspired 'pop manifesto' and their Blitz connection did, however, catch the attention of *Sounds* journalist Betty Page, who decided to write an article on the band. Over in Birmingham, John Taylor happened to be glancing through the magazine when he spotted the feature: 'There was an article in one of the music magazines, in *Sounds* actually, about Spandau Ballet and the headline was, "Enter the New Romantics". I read it and thought, "Wow." From the article it sounded like what they were doing in London, we were doing in Birmingham. They had the idea of playing European funk, whatever that means, with punk attitude but slicker. I called the writer up and said, "Hey, we're part of this New Romantic movement you're writing about," and she came to Birmingham a few weeks later and did a big piece on us. Then we put that line about New Romantics in "Planet Earth" as well, which just goes to show you how opportunistic we have always been.' Le Bon agrees: 'We jumped on the bandwagon. We got our feet in the door as quick as we bloody well could. We needed something to give the band a sort of personality – and it worked.' Nick Rhodes now insists that lyric was loaded in irony. '"Like some New Romantic looking for the TV sound." I mean come on, we were having a laugh. And when we did the video for "Planet Earth" we got some friends to do that ridiculous New Romantic dance. What you have to understand is that humour is brutal in Duran Duran. It's all day, every day.'

Even at this early stage, the two bands were very different. The exuberant John Taylor was happy to discuss the potential teen market with Page and outlined the band's all-inclusive, bright, positive attitude: 'The last thing we're ever going to do is sing about the bad times.' 'We want to be the band to dance to when the bomb drops,' added Le Bon. This was in stark contrast to Spandau Ballet, who encouraged a sense of elitism among their following by performing only one-off, 'secret gigs' in unusual locations such as the Scala Cinema in London, HMS *Belfast*, Blitz and even a two-week residency at San Tropez's Papagayo club. Members of Duran Duran went to check them out when they staged a show in the tropical foliage of Birmingham's Botanical Gardens. The venue looked great but Nick Rhodes was sour in his assessment. 'I remember when Spandau started getting all that publicity, I went to see whether they really were cornering the disco-rhythm market. Of course, thank God, they were useless.' Andy Taylor was just as dismissive. 'When we first went to see Spandau Ballet, we said, "We're going to slaughter them, they haven't got the songs we've got, they can't play as well as we can, they may be from London, but we're going to slaughter them." And we did.' For the moment, Spandau Ballet stole a lead on Duran Duran, scoring a Top Five hit in December 1980 with 'To Cut a Long Story Short'. John Taylor recalls: 'We rushed out and bought a copy, brought it back to the club, played it, no problem, you know, we've got them licked.'

Tritec and Duran Duran toyed with the idea of releasing their own independent single as a cool way of launching the band. They recorded versions of 'Planet Earth' and 'Anyone Out There', shot a promo video at the Cedar Club in Birmingham (it's a hidden extra on the *Greatest* DVD and is a priceless record of the dandified times) and printed up five thousand record labels, but the idea was scrapped as they decided the best option was to kick-start their career on a major label. Le Bon says, 'John's idea was, "We want the cars, we want the girls and the money. We've got to have hit records." ' In the meantime, the DJ Peter Powell started playing this early 'demo' version of 'Planet Earth' on Radio 1 and Betty Page's article in *Sounds* ran before the band inked a record deal.

Tritec and Duran Duran did, however, decide to keep up the momentum by forking out £12,000 to secure a support slot on Hazel O'Connor's fifteen-date tour of the UK in autumn 1980. Michael Berrow mortgaged his house to raise the money. 'I didn't feel that it was risky at the time,' says the shrewd but personally low-key investor. 'It was obvious to me that Duran Duran were going to go all the way. I had to do it because we had absolutely no money. The club was supporting the development of the whole thing, which was quite a strain on our resources. I remember Bob Lamb still hadn't been paid for some demos – these were the ones we were hawking around record companies. He came to the club and said he wanted his money now. The only money we had was in the tills, so it was all in change. He said, "Right, I'll take that." So we loaded up these bags full of change and got them to the car.

Then Bob said, "It's OK, I just wanted to make sure you can pay me." Then he helped us load it back into the tills. It was all or nothing.' As for the experience of playing their first tour, Duran Duran are certain of their value. Rhodes recalls, 'It did us so much good. It meant we played everywhere from Manchester Apollo to the Marquee, tested them out, learned how to win an audience. Like Chris Spedding said to me, "If you rehearse nine days a week you become very good at rehearsing; if you play nine dates a week, you become very good at playing live." ' Bowiesque, female android O'Connor had scored a Top Five hit in August 1980 with her jerkily futuristic 'Eighth Day' single (from the movie *Breaking Glass*) and was a much-hyped star at that time. Now based in Ireland, she asserts, 'The Berrow brothers had a lot of faith in the band. They didn't have a record deal at the time, so the tour had to be done on a budget. They'd have one hotel room every night. John Taylor told me that they'd draw straws to see which of the two would get the room. The rest of them had to sleep in the van. They were nice lads. We'd all get together for a cup of tea in the hotel. I got on well with Simon. We had a few intense conversations about how to look after our voices. He also got up on stage with me at the Dominion Theatre in London and we did Bowie's "Suffragette City" together. My audience was OK towards them, but this was around the time of *Breaking Glass*, so it was a kind of punk, post-punk crowd. So, they did get a bit of gobbing and abuse. I remember Simon in his little frilly shirt being spat on. Mind you, back then, the crowd would spit at everybody whether they liked them or not! I wasn't too sure about their image, all that big, floppy New Romantic stuff, but I used to nip out during "Planet Earth" and watch them.'

During the O'Connor tour, Duran listened to offers from both Dave Ambrose at EMI and Roger Aimes at Phonogram. The former was absolutely certain that he'd unearthed a very special group. 'Sometimes when you're dealing with people you sense a power that is more than you. I found it quite intimidating when I met them,' he gushes. 'When you feel that power from a load of people and that singleness of mind, you become almost in awe of them in a strange kind of way. They're bigger than you, without a doubt. They were in control; no way was it the opposite way around. They were absolutely certain of where they were going, so it was a bit of a treat really. Too often it's the complete reverse.' Ambrose was so determined to sign them that when they set off in support of O'Connor, he went with them in the back of their Winnebago. 'Not for all the dates, but for quite a few,' chuckles the intrepid, tenacious A&R man. 'That was pretty tricky because we were negotiating while I was on tour. We thought we had signed the band but there were other forces at work, in fact other offers were coming through while we were on tour and the band were finding it very difficult to talk to me. But it was fine, I'd just get on the phone to raise the offer and that would happen.' According to the methodical, thoughtful Rhodes, 'We had massive arguments about where we should go. Roger Aimes at Phonogram offered us a better deal but we liked Dave Ambrose. I mean you're talking about the guy who discovered the Sex Pistols. Phonogram meant business, they were crushed when we went to EMI and I often wonder what would have happened if we'd signed with them instead. But it was instinct that led us to EMI rather than the extra £50,000. And we were patriotic, we thought, "EMI, English company, the Beatles" ... we loved Kate Bush too.' Dave Ambrose describes EMI as 'the last great English company. It was great fun going to work at EMI Records because when you got to the offices in Manchester Square you'd see the Union Jack flying above the building and that was always very uplifting. So, I was really into it and I can understand Nick feeling that way too. I didn't know about Phonogram offering a better deal. I had a suspicion but I assumed in the end that they just dropped out. I'm very flattered that they went to EMI. I think the reason it worked was that everyone from marketing to international, the video department, everyone came down to the gigs, everyone was very enthusiastic.' EMI effectively licensed the album off Tritec, who owned the band's recordings and publishing, for a £42,000 advance. Each band member was put on a £50-a-week retainer.

A month after finishing the Hazel O'Connor tour, the freshly signed Duran Duran performed at the Venue in London, which was being hired out by Rusty Egan to showcase New Romantic bands. Tim Dry, one half of Tik and Tok, and also a member of the dance troupe Shock, was at that 12 December 1980 show. At the time Shock were regular performers at the Blitz with a style of performance that was very much of the times – yes, we're talking robotic dancing! Forget the clichés though, this could be pretty surreal stuff, as Betty Page describes in her review of their Lyceum show in 1981: 'There seem to be new dance troupes emerging from rehearsal studios as fast as the Lycra can bind them but Shock are still, for me, the most visually and aurally stimulating of them all. Their newest and best piece to date has Tik, dressed in Oriental threads, reading an excerpt of poetry while girls dressed up as the Brides of Dracula danced around the prostrate body of "dead" robot Tok, who is later resurrected and begins to play a geometric glass violin ...' Tim Dry, aka Tik, explains how he first came across Duran Duran: 'Yes, I saw them at the Venue and they were good fun. I already had a Birmingham connection. I knew Jane Kahn because she'd started going out with Sean (Tok!), so me and Sean used to go up to Birmingham and stay at Patti Bell's house. One day Jane said, "You've got to meet this band from Birmingham." When I met them, Simon Le Bon was probably the most down-to-earth of the lot. He didn't actually dress very well and there was always a sense of, "Wow, I've landed myself doing this, what a great time I'm having." He was very unpretentious about everything. Our house band at Blitz was Spandau Ballet and to be perfectly honest, I think we all liked Duran Duran a lot more. Spandau were very precious in a way. The thing we liked about Duran was they just wanted to be pop stars and that was it, pure and simple. You've got five good-looking guys writing pop songs, whereas with Spandau it was always like, "We're so hip." It was very insular. Rusty Egan was very open-minded so he would play Duran along-side Kraftwerk and Bowie at the Blitz. It all suddenly opened up a bit. This New Romantic thing seemed to start in London but it was also happening in other cities as well. As Shock we did a gig at Leeds Warehouse and the cloakroom attendant was a guy called Marc Almond. And there was Duran Duran in Birmingham. But what set them apart was they wanted to be pop stars. I remember reading a Gary Numan interview in 1979, and he said, "Well, we've had Bowie, we've had Bolan, but since then there hasn't been an actual pop star and so I'm here to fill the gap," and he did. Duran also had that shameless desire to be successful and what's wrong with that? The thing about pop music is that there's a joy involved in it too – you're giving joy to people, so it's never just about making money. It was very reassuring because we'd had all that grim, social awareness punk thing and Duran suddenly arrived saying, "Hey, we're pretty, we're glamorous, let's go." And everyone said, "Yep!" So there was Numan, Adam Ant and then Duran Duran …'

John Taylor: '*As far as I'm concerned, music doesn't exist before the Beatles. From that moment on, pop became packaged with carefully designed sleeves and album cover photographs. In pop music, the photograph is important. I probably wouldn't be in this business if it was just playing an instrument.*'

John Taylor: '*I remember two things about recording "Planet Earth". Staying in a horrible hotel in Fulham, where I got very sick, and John Lennon dying.*'

Nick Rhodes: '*See when we started we were just five men in a boat rowing out to sea but Spandau got a motor boat and roared past us out into the middle. Now they've run out of petrol and we've got our oars, we're rowing past them all and they're just sinking.*'

Andy Taylor: '*John lives and breathes for being the bass player in Duran Duran.*'

John Taylor: '*Of course we slept with the models in our videos. Everybody sleeps with everybody in this game.*'

In late 1980 Adam Ant filled the pop vacuum and ended years of cult obscurity by reinventing himself as a flamboyant, sex-obsessed pop insect who ruled the charts for the next nine months with an intensity not witnessed since T. Rex in the early 1970s. He painstakingly assembled an image that alternated between tribal brave and swashbuckling pirate, while incorporating elements from the cult movie *A Clockwork Orange*, the French Revolution and Lord Byron. 'I still maintain, none of the ideas are mine,' he declared. 'The only people who are absolutely original are geniuses, and they're very rare.' When pressed he could think only of Salvador Dali and the playwright Joe Orton.

Adam Ant controlled every aspect of his career (just as Numan had done a year previously): the music, stage shows, record sleeves, T-shirts, posters, stickers, backstage passes, videos and so on. It was his vision and he followed through with an absolute dedication to every detail. From December 1980 through to the autumn of 1981, Ant scored Top Five hits with strikingly inventive 'warrior' pop songs such as 'Antmusic', 'Dog Eat Dog' and 'Kings of the Wild Frontier', before switching to a 'dandy highwayman' for chart-topper 'Stand and Deliver'. His run of form ended in typically flamboyant style with the ludicrous 'Prince Charming', which summed up the New Romantic philosophy in the unforgettable line: 'Ridicule is nothing to be scared of.'

Although Ant's regular change of image, complete artistic control and unabashed mimicry followed a similar path to Gary Numan, they were stylistically very different. While the doleful, alienated synthesizer pioneer explored the darker side of life, Adam Ant focused on optimism, youth, imagination and sex. In December 1980 he told the *NME*: 'If you don't think you're special, if you don't have personal pride and integrity and self-respect, then spiritually you're dead. Pessimism is unforgivable. And when things are down you've got to get up, there's no point in giving in. Kids need something to tide them over, something they can have fun with. All they need is hope.'

In addition to machine-gunning an exhilarating sequence of great pop singles, Adam Ant provided a constant flow of new images for the likes of *Smash Hits* (which had been rapidly growing in popularity since its launch in 1978, peaking at 500,000 in the early 1980s) and girls' magazines such as *My Guy* and *Jackie*. Ant argued that pop music is historically all about teenagers discovering sex for the first time: 'Even the word rock'n'roll is black slang for fucking. A lot of kids who come to our concerts are just beginning to find out what it [sex] is all about. There's a sense of danger and excitement in it.' Dressing up was all part of this experience: 'It amazes me how much people really look forward to going to a fancy-dress party. You get the straightest girls – butter wouldn't melt in their mouths – going as vamps with suspenders, the lot.' Although Adam Ant's colourful mutiny against mediocrity was short-lived, his celebration of sexuality, pop, youth, individualism, escapism, artistic control and presentation-rather-than-originality was a massive influence on the tone and style of the UK music scene in 1981. He set the stage for a group of good-looking, larger-than-life characters – rather like a cross between 'the Monkees and Kraftwerk' as Rhodes so eloquently put it – to stake their claim as the Next Big Thing.

At the start of 1981 Duran Duran worked on their self-titled debut album in Red Bus, Utopia and Chipping Norton Studios. The six-week sessions were helmed by producer Colin Thurston, whose impressive credits included engineering David Bowie's *Heroes* album and co-producing The Human League. Essentially the song arrangements were very similar to the band's demos and live shows, although a little more detailed. As an engineer-turned-producer, Thurston's focus was to make the sound of the album as good as possible. 'I think the biggest difference from the Bob Lamb demos was actually the vocal,' considers the band's A&R man, Dave Ambrose. 'Colin did a very good job at holding all that together. I think it's fair to say there were times when I was a bit worried about Simon's voice. He sings quite high in places and pushes himself too hard and that enthusiasm makes him either sharp or flat. Singers do that, they get too excited, go tearing up that note and sometimes it doesn't work. Simon did tell me he had doubts himself but he was just learning what his voice could do.' In fact, Colin Thurston claims that at the start of the session he was actually asked to 'audition' the inexperienced Le Bon to make sure that his voice was strong enough for the album: 'There was some talk of getting another singer in, so Simon came down, we had a run through and I let them know he was fine, he got the job.' Dave Ambrose reckons he 'heard a whisper of something like that going on', before adding, 'There were a few moments when it looked a bit tricky but you know, as far as I was concerned Simon was the lead singer and that was it.' Paul Berrow dismisses Thurston's story as 'complete nonsense', pointing out that Duran Duran were already signed to EMI with Le Bon as the front man. According to the band's well-spoken and authoritative-sounding manager, 'The real story is this. We'd just done the deal, everything was going great and Simon, being the bright and bouncy character that he is, was full of enthusiasm and he started partying a little too much. A lot too much in fact. He was working with Colin Thurston in the studio for a week and he was not delivering. Dave Ambrose said to me, "We're all a bit worried about Simon." So, we all sat down together, band and management, and I was given the task of being the bad guy. I told him, "If you don't get your act together there is an inevitability that you won't make it." That was how I phrased it. I said to him that he had to look after his voice, stop smoking, stop partying every night, otherwise he was destroying the goodwill of the band, the support of his parents – he was letting everyone down, basically. He was read the riot act and he took it like a man. He got on with the job; we didn't have another problem. Simon has never held it against me and we're still friends.' Whatever the truth is, in the end Le Bon threw himself into the songs on the first album, creating a distinctive style that is often a triumph of courage over technical ability. As Nick Rhodes once put it, 'There's a certain energy that comes from pushing things to the maximum, which suits Duran Duran in many cases.'

By early 1981 the band had completed their debut album and their search for a wider audience began in earnest. After supporting the Sweet at the Lyceum on 4 January they recorded their first Radio 1 session, which at the time was a crucial stepping stone towards pop success. Over the course of the show, the DJ Richard Skinner aired a total of four songs from their debut album: 'Sound of Thunder', 'Anyone Out There', 'Friends of Mine' and 'Careless Memories'. On 2 February 1981, the finished version of 'Planet Earth' came out on 7- and 12" (featuring an extended mix of the A-side) with artwork designed by Malcolm Garrett of Assorted Images. Garrett had made his name in 1977 by pioneering a modern, art school approach to graphic design, demonstrated by his sleeve for the Buzzcocks' punk single 'Orgasm Addict'. Initially introduced to the band by EMI, for the next five years Duran Duran embraced him as the designer for all of their single and album covers, T-shirts, tour programmes and posters, so that every visual element of the band was co-ordinated and given a very distinctive, instantly recognizable twist. The 'Planet Earth' single also featured one of the group's best B-sides, the infectious 'Late Bar', which was a big live favourite in the early days. Both sides of the 7" are wrapped around instantly catchy hooks, with 'Planet

Earth' also propelled by the kind of handclapping, funky sway that Bowie employed so effectively on songs such as 'The Secret Life of Arabia' (*"Heroes"*) and 'Fashion' (*Scary Monsters and Super Creeps*), although it lacks the weight of those songs. Instead 'Planet Earth' spins on an axis somewhere between Japan and Kim Wilde's trashy, synthesizer anthem 'Kids in America', which also came out in February 1981. In fact, it shares a bubblegum pop sensibility with the latter single that has aged better than the neo-classical melo-dramas of Midge Ure's Ultravox ('Vienna' reached number two in early 1981) or the pomp of Spandau Ballet ('Musclebound' was their second Top Ten hit in April of that year).

Although Blitz founder and DJ Rusty Egan argued that 'Duran Duran arrived right at a pivotal time – everyone was looking for something and they delivered in every area,' not everyone was an instant convert. *Smash Hits* reviewer David Hepworth was left cold by this mechanized debut: 'If all these New Romantics really mean what they say about the music only being a part of what they're all about, then why don't they send the synthesizers back to the shop … This would then leave their days free to pursue the important business of life – like running up new jodhpurs and scanning maps of Germany for snappy song titles.' *Sounds* reviewer Valac Van Der Veene was more encouraging: 'Sci-fi space lyrics warbled by an appealing voice, bouncy mid-Blondie bass-lines and firm rhythms from drummer Roger Taylor provide a tempting taster from their soon-to-be-released album.' However, Le Bon was quick to dismiss the idea that 'Planet Earth' has a science fiction theme. 'It's not really got much to do with that,' he argued. 'The fact is that at one point I just had this idea of what it would be like if you were coming in and seeing this planet for the first time. In my head was also the idea of being born, but at an age and with the kind of mentality where you can actually see what's going on. It's all about waking up, really.'

Duran Duran were disappointed that the song missed the Top Ten by two places, but that was enough to gain them a slot on *Top of the Pops*. In February 1981 their dandified, overdressed perform-ance successfully registered them in the minds of a young, adolescent audience as part of the much-hyped New Romantic movement. Some of the clothes for that TV appearance were made by *Guardian* journalist and former St Martin's fashion student Judy

Rumbold: 'Stripped to their underpants, the raw material looked unpromising – their physiques ranged from hod-carrier to jump-jockey – but we took their inside leg measurements and discussed, solemnly, the kind of knickerbockers they would be requiring. It had to be knickerbockers, for this was New Romanticism at its peak, when it was normal for big blokes to go out dressed in their mum's frilly blouse, muscular calves emerging from billowy pantaloons. They would, we assured them, look fabulous. But all that frilly shirt stuff never suited poor Simon Le Bon. He was entirely the wrong build for it. Although the effect he was after was that of a gaunt, swashbuckly bandolero, he always looked more like a scrum-half who had blundered absent-mindedly into his mum's washing line.'

In case anyone still wasn't sure of their foppish credentials, Duran Duran's accompanying promo video was a riot of dyed hair, lip-gloss and shirts with gigantic ruffles, all styled by Patti Bell on a £500 clothes budget. 'They did look good in the clothes and little girls liked camp men, didn't they?' reflects Bell. Her friend 'Gay John' was one of the dancers in the video and helped her out with the band's gear – 'The frilly shirts were a killer to iron, it took about an hour to do each one,' he laughs. Directed by Australian Russell Mulcahy (who also worked on the grandiose video for Ultravox!'s 'Vienna'), the first Duran Duran promo features such moments as Le Bon dancing on an upside-down crystal pyramid dressed in the prerequisite jodhpurs; a frizzy, orange-blond-haired Nick Rhodes pouting at his keyboard while wearing the frilliest shirt ever created, and James Dean lookalike Roger Taylor getting his kit off – well, his shirt at any rate. For all its obvious flaws, the video helped 'Planet Earth' to top the charts in Australia and Portugal. The song was also a big hit in Sweden.

Within a year the band were distancing themselves from their first visual statement. John Taylor no longer pinched clothes from one of his girlfriends at the time, Roberta Earl Price, and confessed: 'I look at the "Planet Earth" video, or the frilly shirts, or the makeup, which isn't that long ago, and think, for crying out loud! At first I didn't want anyone to be put off by the fact that I had deep cherry lip-liner on. Now, if they don't buy our records because we haven't got all that stuff on, I'm not interested. Compared to what Steve Strange and Spandau Ballet wore, we looked like poor old boys from "oop north" who couldn't quite afford all the gear. It was like a Foster Brothers version of PX.' In fact Taylor had needed convincing about the necessity of doing a promo video in the first place. 'I was like, "What the fuck is this about?" "Well, John, this is going to save us going to Australia. We've got a hit record in Australia and we need television presence over there, but we don't have to go there." That was how we got to do "Planet Earth". None of us really understood. Simon perhaps got it, probably because it had been explained to him a little more fully, but that whole concept of a video, I didn't really get it, it was certainly at odds with the whole punk ethic.'

The same night that Duran Duran recorded their *Top of the Pops* performance, they also played at the Sundown club underneath the Astoria in London's Charing Cross Road (it's now called the Mean Fiddler). This was one of a series of dates that included half-hour sets in various Top Rank venues around the country as part of Peter Powell's Radio 1 Roadshows. The idea had been thrashed out with live agent Rob Hallett, who'd taken on the responsibility of booking Duran Duran's gigs after seeing them support John Cooper-Clarke and Pauline Murray at the end of 1980. 'The theory behind the Top Rank shows was that Duran Duran sounded better live than they did in clubs because they had a bigger, rockier sound than some of the other bands,' says Hallett. 'The highlight was obviously London because I remember us all running back to the venue after their first *Top of the Pops*. Everyone was off their heads by the end of the night. Right from the start I realized that Duran Duran were going to be a lot of fun.' *Sounds* journalist Betty Page was at the Sundown gig to witness how the youthful art-pop pretenders had progressed: 'Duran bounced on stage through dry ice sporting a few more ruffles and sashes than before ... but a very polished sound evolved, along with an overtly confident approach and impressively thought out appearance. Andy Taylor has toned down his tendency to romp about like an axe hero but his chunky rockin' guitar still dominates proceedings. That, readers, is the bugbear, the nagging worry. Duran claim to merge disco with rock and achieve a new hybrid, but observers whispered that icky phrase that is an anathema to most: "They're just a rock band!" ' In a quick vox pop, Page was told by a 'disillusioned pirate', 'That's the closest thing I've seen to Heavy Metal for ages.' Duran Duran were too conventional to be embraced as fellow outsiders by London's snooty

New Romantic crowd. However, as Page also pointed out in the closing lines of her piece, the band were already setting their sights far beyond the dance floor of the Blitz Club: 'The two enormous mega-trucks outside the stage door confirmed the fears. Balletomanes were not amused but Duran Duran don't seem to need them.' The Rolling Stones' former manager, Andrew Loog Oldham, was also there, observing that it was a 'career-breaking' moment: 'The group were on that exciting tightrope and it showed. The drummer was real and as opposite to the group as Charlie Watts was to the Stones and it worked. They were hungry young pups with a view to a kill.'

As 'Planet Earth' charted, articles on Duran Duran appeared in *The Face*, *i-D* and *New Sounds, New Styles* (which was designed by Malcolm Garrett). They also launched themselves via a campaign of endless interviews and photo shoots with pop and teen magazines including *Smash Hits*, *Mates* and *Patches*. John Taylor threw himself into this with characteristic gusto, befriending magazine editors and offering his services at every opportunity: 'Not once at that time did I think, "No, I don't want to do that," or, "Perhaps it will not be good for our career" or better yet, "We want our music to be taken seriously." No, I wanted fame, first and foremost.' In 1982 the pontificating Rhodes used 'pop art' as a way of explaining Duran Duran's initial relationship with the media: 'Andy Warhol once said that he never read his press but he always weighed it and if it was heavy, then he knew everything was OK. I kind of went along with that regime for a while. I thought as long as people were talking, it was good. Then I realized that when I wanted to talk seriously about some aspect of Duran Duran or life in general, people already had so many preconceived ideas about me and the band, and I found that pretty depressing.'

Duran Duran's suspicious guitarist Andy Taylor has accused EMI of exploiting their looks – particularly those of the band's bass player – claiming, 'We didn't realize the capability and cynicism of the machine around us.' There's no doubt that Duran Duran's courting of the teen press undermined their credibility in England, but the whole spirit of the band was to get stuck in, take any opportunities and ask questions later. That gave them an edge over some of their rivals. The fiery, contradictory Geordie also ignores the fact that John Taylor and Nick Rhodes dreamed up Duran Duran's aesthetic after poring over pictures of their own glam rock heroes as kids. In the early 1970s, David Bowie, T. Rex and Roxy Music used to appear in teen magazines alongside clean-cut heart-throbs such as Donny Osmond and David Cassidy. The pair's fascination with photographic image endured when they started reading music inkies such as *Melody Maker, Sounds* and the *NME*. 'John Taylor was very aware of how to look in a photograph,' says former *NME* lensman Denis O'Regan who first started taking pictures of Duran Duran back in 1979. 'He knew whether something was looking right or not. He also had an amazing knowledge of photographs. John's only five years younger than me but I was amazed when, at our first meeting, he confided, "I used to look out for your shots in the *NME* when I was at school." He could even tell me the specific pages on which certain shots appeared.' According to the image-conscious bassist, 'Each of us had a distinct style, even though as a band we all wore similar uniforms. Andy had the edge, he was the guitar-swinging, beer-drinking bandolero, a working-class hero. Simon Le Bon was born to play Romeo, he was the pop star Shakespeare would have invented. Nick was cast as the "outsider" and Roger had the most traditional appeal, a rugged James Dean look coupled with a super no-nonsense attitude. If he had been an actor he would have been cast as the "reliable leading man" type. Me? I had purple hair, wore makeup, swung a guitar, and played up the romantic image more obviously than any of them.'

The ever watchful O'Regan also observed how various egos in the band were immediately vying for attention now that Duran Duran had scored a Top Twenty hit: 'I found Simon more difficult at the beginning. He didn't trust me. There was rivalry between Simon and John in those early years over who was the biggest heart-throb. I think Simon felt that as the singer and front man it should be him. Sometimes it was amusing to watch all of them try to outdo each other in photos.' John Taylor agrees: 'Me and Simon used to clash terribly, because I thought, "I started this band, it's my band." And Simon would think, "Well, I'm the singer, I'm the leader of the band." Subliminally we both used to clash. And we were all tremendously competitive over women.'

Music and sex have always gone hand in hand in Le Bon's sensual world: 'Girls. Absolutely gorgeous girls were the reason for forming the band. It was an excessive time, from every possible point of view. I was never particularly great with girls at school, so when the band took off I just went crazy, I really did shag myself senseless. The same went for John. We used to compete for girls and John usually won. He was a man transformed. To see him in action was incredible. He could charm the knickers off anyone.' In contrast to the carnally driven singer and charmingly hedonistic John Taylor, the more cerebral Nick Rhodes has always claimed he was a little above all this hardcore rutting: 'I think Simon dealt with most of the sex-crazed groupies. John and Simon were definitely going for records at the time. Olympics groupie records. But it all seemed a little too risky and seedy to me. They never came looking like pages out of Italian *Vogue*.' Andy Taylor, who had been on the road since he was sixteen years old, also had other things on his mind. 'It's funny, I remember being in a dodgy mini-cab one night with Andy, Nick and John,' laughs Rob Hallett. 'The rest of us were talking about the girls we'd met and Andy was going on about how we should get advice about getting a pension.' By the end of 1981, the guitarist had started seeing a pretty local Birmingham girl called Tracey Wilson. They'd met when Duran Duran visited a hair-dressing salon which was run by her brother Mitchell. Andy Taylor recalls, 'Tracey used to cut my hair. A fabulously cute, really sweet lady – nothing like me, and no interest in the music business at all. I was getting my hair cut three times a week and she didn't want anything to do with me. The only woman who ever said she wanted nothing to do with me. Six times I asked her out before she said, "Yes".' The quiet, security-loving Roger Taylor was the other band member who had recently settled into a long-term relationship. He'd fallen for a spiky-haired girl called Giovanna Cantone who used to model photos for the Wilson salon and also worked on the door at the Rum Runner.

Meanwhile, according to Simon Le Bon, in the early days Duran Duran were so hungry for the big breakthrough success that John Taylor wouldn't sleep on a Monday night because he couldn't wait to see where they were in the charts on the next day. April 1981 was therefore not a happy month in the Duran Duran camp when their second single, 'Careless Memories', stalled at number thirty-seven. 'The second single was a mistake, or was it, I don't know,' shrugs Dave Ambrose. 'I think in a way it was the marketing people's fear that the band was getting too commercial too fast. I don't like to say "cheesy" but that was the worry. But "Careless Memories" didn't get any airplay, which was a bit scary. It didn't lock in.' Built around a moody, strobing sequencer pattern created by Nick Rhodes, 'Careless Memories' is a lot darker and tougher-sounding than 'Planet Earth', falling somewhere between the Cure's 'Primary' and Blondie's 'Atomic'. Le Bon's vocal injects just enough turbulent energy into the ultra-dramatic lyrics – 'fear hangs a plane of gun smoke drifting in our room' – to pull the whole thing off.

Duran Duran promoted the single with their first ever *Smash Hits* cover, but the magazine's reviewer Mark Ellen was not won over by the polished post-punk sound of the A-side: 'Sensibly side-stepping the over-ploughed "sensitive" disco field (Spandau etc.), the persuasive force of the ten-ton drum sound is not lost on this lot. Buried beneath layers of silk finish is a construction so stagger-ingly basic you wonder if their punk roots don't extend back to the Dry-Ice Age.' The accompanying promo also undermines Duran Duran's video-age visionary status somewhat. Directed by Perry Haines and Terry Jones, who showcased their talent more effec-tively by founding *i-D* magazine, it's a folly of New Romantic pretension featuring an uncomfortable Le Bon at his most hammy. 'I believe that is the worst video we've ever made,' declared Rhodes not long after. 'It did nothing for the song. It was done in a very "Habitat" manner. I'll never forget the painting on the wall – it was the most hideous-looking thing I've ever seen.' Haines did redeem himself with the band members by taking them to the Plaza, the Anthony Price-owned store on London's King's Road, immortal-ized in Roxy Music's single 'Trash'. According to John Taylor, 'Our love affair with Anthony Price suits began that day.'

Despite the 'Careless Memories' setback, Duran Duran forged ahead by releasing their self-titled debut album on 15 June 1981. Peter Powell again proved to be a loyal supporter by airing four tracks on a Radio 1 session and the *Record Mirror* were sufficiently impressed by the LP to list it at number three on their 'Albums of the Year' chart. *Sounds* described the album as 'an incredible, mature debut bristling with prospective hit singles', while in America, *Trouser Press* enthused, 'an extraordinary album filled with classic songs'. Not everyone was convinced and Duran Duran were snubbed by some of the other synthesizer-based acts who were around at the time. Ultravox's diminutive Scot, Midge

Ure, was an outspoken critic and Martyn Ware, founder of the Human League and Heaven 17, reveals, 'We saw them as a glamour puss band and were kind of snotty about them. We thought they had no sense of originality or art about them and regarded them more as a glossy pub band.' In stark contrast, Gary Numan was an early supporter. 'I loved "Planet Earth" when it came out. I really liked the song and the whole package looked great. I thought Simon Le Bon's voice was very distinctive, in a good way. It's instantly recognizable and that's like striking gold for any pop group. It's much more important than being technically a great singer.' Twenty years later Courtney Taylor of the Dandy Warhols also came out as a fan: 'If you go back to the first record, they smoked everybody, and they still smoke everybody. It's incredible! Disco bass-lines, Japan textures and mixed by the guy who did the Iggy Pop records.'

Opening with the sound of Paul Berrow's Nikon camera, *Duran Duran* is full of melodic, dance-floor synthesizer pop delivered with youthful flair and the odd arty twist. At times it shares an affinity with the disco-rock explored by Blondie on 'Call Me' (another Giorgio Moroder production) and Japan's *Quiet Life* is also a reference point, although vocally it's very different. In contrast to David Sylvian's guarded introspection, Le Bon launches himself at the songs – a bull in the rather delicate world of Roxy and Bowie-influenced electronica. Twenty years on, Rhodes's analogue synthesizers sound warm and organic on the dreamlike 'Night-boat', 'Tel Aviv' and 'To the Shore' and despite the rockist accusations there are no guitar solos. Quite the opposite: Andy Taylor's work is melodic and punchy throughout. He adds real weight to the verses on 'Friends of Mine' before it breaks into one of Le Bon's ultra-catchy choruses, and the jabbing riffs on 'Girls on Film' give the track a subliminal power. Duran Duran's rhythm section mixes together the styles of Moroder, Mick Karn and Chic, with John Taylor's bass playing proving to be an underrated highlight. Duran Duran are also enthusiastic and adept plagiarists on every track. Several moments are reminiscent of early Ultravox!, especially the cathedral-like intro on 'To the Shore', the 'Hiroshima Mon Amour'-styled drum machine on 'Night Boat' and their mixture of strings and electronics on 'Tel Aviv'. John Taylor enjoys a playful reference to Bowie's 'Ashes to Ashes' in the bass-line for 'Anyone

Out There', Simon Le Bon's banshee yelp on 'Nightboat' is curiously like Siouxsie Sioux and the ghosts of Gary Numan haunt some of the icier textures. 'It's one of the most honest albums ever, in my opinion,' argued Rhodes in 1982. 'I know because I was a fifth of what made it. There wasn't a thing on that album that was contrived. We worked so hard and wished and prayed and put everything we had into that record ... All our musical ideas from when we were fifteen or sixteen years old.' Although Le Bon's glory-or-be-damned approach occasionally ends in a defeated whine, more often than not his gift for pop melody breathes life into the artificial sounds. As for his visual song titles and cryptic lyrics, they work with the music but rarely make much sense on closer inspection. 'I was quite fascinated by how Simon's mind worked, because he seemed to write about the most ridiculous things,' ruminated Rhodes. 'We may wish Simon had never written some of his lyrics but there are very few songs that we've been embarrassed by. People don't listen to lyrics while they're dancing anyway.' That said, many fans picked their way through the nebulous, ambiguous phrases, constructing their own meanings. As a thirteen-year-old, award-winning author Andrea Ashworth had found an emotional escape from the violence of inner-city Manchester through reading books and listening to Duran Duran records. She recently described her connection with the band in an article for the *Guardian*: 'Duran Duran poured out music we could dive into and flounder extravagantly about in, gesturing at great depths, raving, not drowning. The lyrics were polished, arty crosswords, blessedly obscure, so you pondered them as long – or as little – as you liked. The music was turbulent but buoyant, urging elation and anger, frustration, insouciance, conquest, sometimes all in the same song. It let you write words such as "chiaroscuro" and "euphoria", "epiphany" and "solar plexus" in your diary.'

Although Duran Duran's audience was predominantly female that didn't mean that they were all permanently in a state of adolescent hysteria, bellowing their lungs out as the band's electronic pop whooshed through their home stereos. Many were at least as forward-looking and experimental as the boys, losing themselves in Duran Duran's noir-funk while dreaming of their own creative futures. Among the girls in trilbies and silver lipstick were Gwen Stefani, Kylie Minogue and D'Arcy from the Smashing Pumpkins.

Meanwhile, on 29 June 1981 Duran Duran kick-started their eleven-date *Faster than Light* tour at the Brighton Dome. For the band, this was a real eye-opener as they were faced by this young, mostly female audience for the first time. According to John Taylor the band started playing their first song, 'Sound of Thunder', when the curtains opened and they were greeted by 'screaming, screeching kids stretching out for a touch of us ... this was not an audience, this was pandemonium. It threw us off guard; we had some trouble hearing ourselves above the level of noise that was coming at us on to the stage. Between each number the noise did not cease, it increased! It was impossible to communicate with these people! In fact the communication had already taken place, these kids were fanatic, they had become obsessed, with us! What had happened?' Le Bon adds: 'People often say, "Weren't you disgusted to be followed by those kind of people?" And I always felt no, because young people have very good taste in music. They're the ones who can choose anything. They have no hang-ups, they have no inhibitions, they can take whatever they like. So I felt that it was quite a compliment to be chosen by them.'

Although their agent Rob Hallett was disappointed that not all the venues sold out, there was enough hype around the gigs to start a short-lived 'national fashion'. Le Bon says, 'Headbands, yes. That started at Newcastle City Hall. Roger took a towel and put it round his head. I thought, "That's pretty odd, a bit Jimi Hendrix," so I did one as well. It was a tea towel on the head. It caught the mood.'

On 13 July, two days after the tour ended, Duran Duran released their third single, 'Girls on Film'. This time they had a single that was all over Radio 1 and, third time lucky, they broke into the UK Top Five, staking their claim as one of the biggest new bands of 1981. Hazel O'Connor met up with them on *Top of the Pops* as the band celebrated and invited her back to their hotel in St John's Wood: 'One of the band members was really snotty with the waitress and Paul Berrow was like, "For fuck's sake, you're sounding like the nouveau riche." I don't know, maybe when that level of fame happens you don't have time for the niceties.' In the wake of 'Girls on Film', the *Duran Duran* album peaked at number three and went on to spend 118 weeks on the UK chart, selling 1.6 million copies worldwide. Twenty-odd years later, Franz Ferdinand claim it's one of the songs the band listens to before they play a gig, because 'it makes you feel glamorous'. Simon Price in the *Independent on Sunday* recently summed up the song's stylish appeal: '"half Chic, half Sex Pistols". That, from the outset, was Duran Duran's mission statement. The latter half of it, of course, was somewhat delusional. But with the Chic acknowledgement, Le Bon, Rhodes and the three Taylors were spot-on. What Chic did was to borrow the romance and opulence fetishized by Roxy Music – all that "Baby Jane's in Acapulco, we are flying down to Rio!" stuff – and apply it to populist black funk as opposed to art school rock. What Duran Duran did was to borrow it back, with interest (specifically, Nile Rodgers's trebly guitar chops, imitated by Andy Taylor on countless occasions, most memorably just before the chorus to "Girls on Film" kicks in). By combining these elements, Duran made populist-yet-art-school rock-funk, and in so doing, matched the musical and cultural mood of the 1980s perfectly.' Of all the band's early tracks, 'Girls on Film' is Duran Duran's most successful fusion of Chic, Roxy Music (*circa* 1980's *Flesh and Blood*) and punky New Wave pop.

Although the song's lyric is ostensibly about the exploitation of women in advertising, no one explained the concept to Godley and Creme, who were hired to shoot the accompanying video. Instead they were instructed to film scantily clad *Penthouse* models in fish-nets, heels and wet T-shirts (soaked with champagne, naturally). The directors also story-boarded pillow-fights, mud-wrestling, a model in a nurse's uniform and – during one scene – a girl's nipple, rubbed with an ice cube. According to international playboy-in-waiting John Taylor, 'My memories of it are not that great. I remember being a bit embarrassed about it. You have a bunch of guys around and put a nearly naked girl in the room with them and it turns them all into idiots. You know, five guys tripping over each other trying to get their attention. It wasn't a great experience for any of us really.' 'I went and bought the "Girls on Film" video, for obvious reasons,' smirks Gary Numan. 'Even though they were younger than me, Duran Duran seemed to know so much more than me about good living. They were already so well groomed. They were hanging out with models and living the ultimate pop star fantasy life. That's when I realized, "Oh, that's what I should be doing!" They definitely had an influence on my lifestyle,' says the singer who upped sticks in 1982 and moved in next door to actor George Peppard in West Hollywood, LA.

The idea for shooting the luridly sexual 'Girls on Film' video (which was banned by the BBC in England) originated from trips Paul and Michael Berrow had been taking to America while setting up the debut album for release. They observed that many US clubs had video screens that would either show old movies or musicals and in some cases the Playboy Channel, which was just taking off at the time. There was also a new initiative called Rock America, which distributed pop promo videos around US clubland. 'We did that video strategically,' says Paul Berrow, 'because to be blunt, America was thinking that Duran Duran were a gay band. So we put about 1,000 tapes out across the States in all the hard-assed bars, so that these guys could watch the long version of "Girls on Film" while having a cold beer. Duran Duran are high-testosterone males and we showed it.' As Dave Ambrose recalls, 'It was very provocative, the first semi-pornographic long-form video which really shook everyone up in the clubs. And that's what started to break them in America.'

Although it had very little impact at the time, a new cable TV channel, MTV, also started screening 'Girls on Film'. The station had been launched on 1 August 1981, and for the first few months it was broadcast only in New Jersey, Texas and Florida. It was so underground it had the freedom to play pretty much anything. ' "Girls on Film" was a great opportunity for us to get some press,' says one of MTV's founders, John Sykes. 'The video was something that could never be played on broadcast networks, but we could play it on MTV. So it brought a lot of people over to cable and MTV, to not only discover the cool new bands but also this art form that was not yet ready for prime-time television.'

Although US chart success was still over a year away, the 'Girls on Film' video is the moment when Duran Duran's relationship with America really started. Until that point even their Los Angeles-based label, Capitol, were not prioritizing them. Their debut album had come out in summer 1981 without much of a fanfare, as no one outside the main cities such as New York, LA and San Francisco had even the slightest interest in synthesizer pop or New Romanticism. Quite the opposite, in fact. Angus Margerison, who worked in EMI's international department at the time, remembers, 'Even at Capitol it really was a case of, "You sure these guys you're sending over aren't faggots, 'cos they sure look like it to us." It was a world long before anyone had heard of political correctness and there was a lot of resistance at the label to a group of English pretty boys in makeup. It was only when they saw "Girls on Film" that certain people at Capitol realized that Duran Duran were not actually gay.' Doreen D'Agostino, who was 'national publicity manager' at Capitol, recalls, 'The "Girls on Film" video gave them a little notoriety. Older writers were shocked by the ice cube on the girl's naked breast. But in the hip clubs people were like, "Hey, it's art!" '

Shortly after filming the sensationalistic 'Girls on Film' video, Duran Duran headed off to Europe for a date at Ancienne Belgique in Brussels and a promotional trip to the Capitaine Video Club in Paris. A quick glance at their passports revealed the band's musical insecurities. John Taylor recalls, 'When Duran Duran really started moving and we started playing overseas, we all put "managing director" instead of "musician" on our passports. There was always a fear we weren't "musicianly" enough and we were tremendously afraid of playing and performing.' EMI forked out £9,000 on publicity and another £2,000 on ferrying Duran fans from the Rum Runner over to Paris, ensuring there would be a crowd. However, Simon Le Bon experienced an early embarrassment in his career when he tripped over some wires during the band's performance and fell flat on his face in front of the entire French media. A few days later, they played their first date in Sweden, where they were already enjoying pop success, and followed that with a gig at the Paradiso Club in Amsterdam. The first date of their North American tour was at the Spit Club, Long Island, on 16 September 1981. Over the next month they played eighteen club dates, usually to 200–300 people a night and sometimes a lot fewer. According to the unworldly art school dreamer, John Taylor: 'I was such a baby. At JFK airport I couldn't fill in the address bit on the immigration form. I put "Holiday Inn, Long Island". The guy said, "I guess if we need to find you, we'll put out an APB for a faggot with purple hair" … I didn't sleep for the whole four weeks. It began with the television and you know, you wanted to watch all thirty channels at the same time and then you got this breakfast menu and you wanted to order everything for breakfast and from then on it was these limousines and clubs and girls. You just wanted to consume everything that was offered; it was just a dream really.' Nick Rhodes used one of his favourite albums as a reference point for his new experiences: 'Lou Reed's *Transformer* became a reality the first time I came to New York City in 1981. It was during Duran Duran's first world tour, when I was nineteen and too young to get into most of the clubs we played. It came as a real culture shock. The biggest shock of all was having potatoes for breakfast or jelly for dinner, being served on the same plate as the meat. "New York Telephone Conversation" and "Walk on the Wild Side" from *Transformer* started to make sense …' The tour included cities such as Detroit, Chicago, Boston and Washington, plus two Canadian dates on the itinerary: Toronto and Montreal. The ultra-professional Duran Duran attended every radio station interview and local TV promo without complaint. 'They worked bloody hard,' says their almost paternalistic manager, Paul Berrow. 'Total dedication from every-body, day and night, seven days a week. Anything that moved, on the phone, brainstorm, move on it. The guys were fantastic. People used to take the piss out of us for us being like a military operation. Well, if being organized is military then it was, but it never felt like that inside. It was just that everybody surrendered to the needs. There was no "I don't want to go and do an interview" going on … it was just unheard of, it just didn't happen.'

In New York and Los Angeles it was as if five lads from England had been body-snatched and replaced by glamorous aliens. Suddenly freed from the snobbery of their own country, they were perceived as an exotic, arty, underground band and attracted a cool, beautiful-looking party crowd in these major cities. Rob Hallett remembers 'Lots of gorgeous models hanging around', at the Roxy in Los Angeles. 'Even in the early days of travelling around the world, Duran Duran always seemed to have all the local models backstage. Someone called the local agencies and lots of attractive women appeared.' In New York, Duran Duran met Andy Warhol. The former window-dresser and *Vogue* graphic artist noted in his diary: 'They all wore lots of makeup but they had their girlfriends with them from England, pretty girls, so I guess they're all straight but it was hard to believe.' Le Bon recalls, 'Andy Warhol had a real crush on Nick. And Nick, at that time, looked like a young version of Andy Warhol. So it's quite funny, really. New York was an incred-ible place at the start of the 1980s. You had all these amazing nightclubs. The Peppermint Lounge. Studio 54 was still going.

There was the Paradise Garage. There was Danceteria. It was incredible. You'd go to clubs and run into Billy Idol and Johnny Thunders, and all kinds of people were just out. Debbie Harry. And the whole scene was still there and it was out, and it was about having fun.' Youthful sex Olympian John Taylor was impressed by the straw-haired, mannequin-like artist with the ghostly complexion: 'Andy Warhol was a sweet man. Very kind to us actually. The first time Duran Duran went to New York, Doreen D'Agostino, Capitol's then press agent, thought Andy would like us and arranged for us to visit the Factory. Andy took polaroids of us and asked us to sign them, and he gave us signed copies of his book, *From A to B and Back Again*. We met Andy a number of times over the next few years. I remember one New Year's Eve when Duran played live on MTV from New York's Savoy Ballroom, standing at the bar with Andy afterwards, he said, "You should be the singer." I remember thinking, "I bet he says that to all the boys." ' Doreen D'Agostino recollects Warhol and Rhodes regularly hanging out together in the DJ booth at Studio 54 and Paige Powell, who was the assistant of the pop art icon, affirms: 'Andy really liked him. He was attracted to originality and Nick exuded that.' 'I don't know how anyone could dislike Warhol,' said Rhodes of his art-fop sugar daddy a couple of years after this first meeting. 'I think he's one of the most down-to-earth people I've ever met.'

Of greater significance to the band's immediate commercial future was a visit to MTV's New York office, which at the time consisted of three rooms staffed by sixteen people. According to drone-voiced schmoozer Nick Rhodes, 'I remember when we first went to MTV, they had a little office in Manhattan and we soon got to know everybody there, from the people that owned it, to the, you know, tea boy, on first-name terms. We were thinking, "What a great idea, a music television show." ' Duran Duran's charm offensive was also spearheaded by John Taylor: 'I think the kind of videos we then delivered were a direct result of those conversations. We were the first band to really give them something that was a turn-on to the viewers because it was colourful, real and fun.'

Back in the UK, Duran Duran booked a session in London's Townhouse and recorded a new song, 'My Own Way', as a breathless, string-led response to their first experience of America. Le Bon's lyric even includes directions to the Peppermint Club in New

York. Rhodes hated it. 'It was the only time we actually sat down and said, "OK, we've got to write a hit single." That was only released as a single in England. Biggest mistake of our career. Ever. We'll never do it again.' Released on 16 November, 'My Own Way' reached a respectable number fourteen, enjoying an eleven-week run of the chart. Although the B-side, 'Like an Angel', is one of their weaker early efforts, 'My Own Way' is far from being a disaster. Dave Rimmer in *Smash Hits* wasn't sure if it was 'funk, futurist, Euro-disco or mid-'70s art rock. I can't decide whether I like this or not. The chorus is a winner though.'

By the autumn Duran Duran had received a Gold Award recognizing 100,000 sales in the UK of their debut album and they were starting to displace a burnt-out Adam Ant in the pages of *Smash Hits*. But Duran Duran were not the biggest new pop group of 1981: that crown belonged to The Human League, who came out winners as the Best Newcomer at the British Rock and Pop Awards at the start of 1982. Formerly an innovative but commercially unsuccessful cult act, singer Phil Oakey had split with founding member Martyn Ware and reinvented the group as an 'electronic Abba'. He led the sound with his own deadpan baritone, sweetened by the sound of two girls he'd discovered in a Sheffield nightclub. According to Oakey they set out to make 'an album full of singles. We've moved away from textures to tunes. It's tunes every time.' The result was *Dare!*, featuring a title and artwork ripped off from a cover of *Vogue* and packed with great pop songs, including 'Sound of the Crowd', 'Love Action', 'Open Your Heart' and of course 'Don't You Want Me', which topped the charts at the end of 1981. As Michael Bracewell wrote in *GQ*, '*Dare!* was the final summation of all the boys and girls who lived out their dreams of Roxy Music glamour and fashion-magazine style through provincial nightclubs and Saturday-afternoon shopping trips in the rain.' The Human League loved pop music and wanted to sell as many records as possible: 'I wear makeup because people will listen to our records more if I wear makeup or if I've got a silly long haircut on one side,' announced Oakey. 'It's a gimmick and if that's necessary to make people listen, then that's what you've got to do. The more people you can actually get to the better.' *Dare!* was not only a fully realized pop gem but it also shone in the context of The Human League's previous experimentation. The album came across as a

Bowie-like reinvention rather than a last desperate bid for fame and success. It was cool, credible and forward-looking, refining a new sensibility where artists employed new technology to play around with that age-old convention, the four-minute pop song. Or to put it another way, irony was 'in'; pop was 'in'; rock was most definitely 'out'. 'I don't hang out too much with other musicians,' declared ABC's Martin Fry in early 1982. 'I tend to shy away from conversations about plectrums and things.' In this atmosphere, Duran Duran's foot-on-the-monitor-style guitars and traditional band dynamics made them outsiders. Not only that, but The Human League didn't play to a mass of screaming, fainting teenage girls. As journalist Sheryl Garratt writes in her article, 'Teenage Dreams': 'One of the most important things about most teeny groups is that almost everyone else hates them.' At least Adam Ant had enjoyed some notoriety as a punk act with a taste for S&M clobber to counteract his teen-idol status and T-Rex had already released several albums as an underground, hippy-psychedelic act. Although they'd been heavily featured in the style press, as far as the serious British music media were concerned, Duran Duran didn't have a history to fall back on and the backlash stung a confused and crestfallen John Taylor: 'I'm into pure pop. I'd much rather be a pop star. We've been getting a lot of slagging for attempting nothing more than pure entertainment. But that's so hypocritical because what about Adam Ant? What about Funkapolitan? They're no different but they don't get slagged off because that's all fun for the feet not for the head so it's supposed to be OK ...' That said, Duran Duran were perfect for *Smash Hits*' gossipy, humorous mix of myth-making and the mundane (questions about toenail clippings and hair dye jostle with colourful, glamorous serenades of pop star high life) and they were also fixtures on Saturday-morning kids' TV, which was hugely important in driving record sales. The band also appeared on *Jim'll Fix It*, with Simon Le Bon fulfilling the ultimate pop fantasy by turning up at a teenage girl's classroom dressed as a knight in shining armour and then whisking her away from her school desk and off into the sunset.

All this ensured that they ended 1981 on their own high with December's *Careless Memories* tour, which consisted of seventeen sold-out dates, including three at the Odeon in Birmingham. Neil Tennant, still a few years away from forming the Pet Shop Boys, reviewed their Hammersmith Odeon show in *Smash Hits*: 'Duran Duran are of course the standard bearers of the scarf-and-head-band-wearers. The pretty-ish boys from Birmingham bounced into view looking just like pop stars … but the searchlights and the scarves and the smoke couldn't hide the dullness of much of their set. Duran Duran are at their best with good tunes and they ain't got a lot of them. A new song like "Last Chance on the Stairway" has the same hollow ring as old faves like "Careless Memories" and "Faster than Light" [B-side to "Girls on Film"].' This lukewarm critique contrasted with the more upbeat tone of *Melody Maker's* Steve Sutherland, who was one of the few writers to recognize Duran Duran's growing importance. Duranmania was in full, rampant bloom outside the Sheffield City Hall on 10 December. The journalist observed how the band were 'scratched, mauled, buffeted, bruised, surrounded by dozens of small screaming girls who're just desperate to love them to death … As if by divine intervention, little miss sweet sixteen in frilly blouse, decorative headband – y'know, the full New Romantic regalia – chooses this morning to cease her doe-eyeing, take a deep breath and stumble forward. Her arms slap around Nick's shoulders, pulling his painted head towards her and their lips meet for a brief moment. She reels, swoons, her eyes roll back and she hits the floor in a dead faint, just like so much meat. "Oh Christ," groans Nick. "That's never happened before." '

John Taylor: *'In my youth, fresh out of school, Birmingham and my parents' clutches, I was a hedonistic little fucker. I accepted everything. The work, the hotels, the constant travelling and bickering, but I did it from behind a curtain of drugs and alcohol. I may have lost something of myself, but doesn't everyone?'*

Andy Taylor: *'John likes flying on Concorde. He's just the perfect jetsetter really. Jet Set, that's his name. I'm Rock Star and he's Jet Set.'*

Andy Taylor: *'He's got very big feet, John. Possibly one of the biggest pairs of feet I've ever seen.'*

Andy Taylor: *'I can remember my first cheque for £1 million. I was only twenty-one. Fifty per cent went to Mrs Thatcher but even still.'*

Michael Berrow: *'It was the time. There was a freeing up for some parts of the country, not for everyone of course, but there were opportunities for many people. Maggie was in charge and we all subscribed to that kind of sensibility.'*

Nick Rhodes: *'I don't understand these groups who claim they don't want to be successful. It's an attitude, isn't it?'*

According to Nick Rhodes, 'When we started the *Rio* album in January 1982, we were all terrified of the success of the first LP and we thought, "How on earth are we going to top that?" ' Over the next six weeks the band focused on defining their own New Wave style, rather than making another record crammed with their youthful influences. Although *Rio* was once again produced by Colin Thurston, initially they demoed some of the material in Birmingham with their old friend, Bob Lamb. ' "Save a Prayer" sticks in my mind because they first did that here first,' remembers the ex-Steve Gibbons drummer of the pretty, lullabying electro-ballad. 'I remember driving around afterwards with that beautiful synthesizer line still in my head.' Duran Duran also worked on an early version of the atmospheric composition 'The Chauffeur' with German sound engineer Renate Blauel (who later married Elton John) before moving to the bigger studio at AIR on Oxford Street to complete the album.

As the record progressed, John Taylor usually crashed at Rob Hallett's flat in Kilburn. 'It was the hottest bachelor pad in London,' recalls the band's agent. 'John was the best-looking man in Britain and got the most amazing girls. I hung round for the leftovers.' However, Taylor's makeup and dyed hair still confused some of the more conservative people in Mayfair, London. 'We had a routine which involved going to the clothes shop, Ebony, in the day and in the evening we'd be at the Embassy Club,' says Hallett of their nocturnal visits to the members-only drinking establishment. 'But we never picked girls up there and we couldn't figure out why. We were normal guys, we were always on the lookout. We asked one of the blokes who worked there and he was like, "What, you want to meet girls! We thought you were gay." '

As for the duo's habitual trips to Ebony in daylight hours, they often ended up with the lanky, trilby-wearing bassist being followed by fans. On a Saturday afternoon in early 1982, John Taylor dropped by to see the store's in-house designer John Kay, who was responsible for the jet-black, pseudo-military garb that the band experimented with for a while. By the time he was ready to leave, the shop was completely surrounded by screaming kids and so the police were called to drive the pop star away to safety. What they didn't know was that before arriving at the store John Taylor had already been shopping. 'There were a few trips in to town with John to buy drugs,' remembers the band's hedonistic ally, Rob Hallett. 'I was doing as much coke as they were. It gave you that feeling of invincibility. It was "Fucking hell, we can take on the world!" '

'John does everything very intensely and he got into drugs a lot more deeply than some of the others,' asserts the band's officially appointed observer, Denis O'Regan. 'Andy Taylor indulged heavily too, but it didn't affect him in the same way. The thing with Andy is that he's always been a big drinker.' A self-confessed extremist, Taylor's constitution was already becoming legendary but when he wasn't drinking 'lightweights' under the table, he retreated to a more restrained lifestyle with his girlfriend Tracey, who 'wasn't at all into the partying and hedonism', says Hallett. On 16 February 1982 Andy Taylor celebrated his twenty-first birthday by downing a skin-full with Simon Le Bon at the Rum Runner. During the course of the evening he told the singer that he intended to propose to Tracey, who was lying ill in his flat. Andy Taylor remembers, 'There were lots of girls in my life. They used to last three weeks before I got fed up with them, but gradually Tracey was the one I felt most comfortable with.' When the guitarist crawled in at four in the morning and asked her if she wanted to get married, she initially told him not to be silly. The next morning Tracey woke up, realized that it hadn't been a dream and said, ' "Yes!". It's just about saying to a girl, "I'm willing to keep you for the rest of my life, how about it?" ' declared Taylor. 'Me, you know, nobody else. And it's a big thrill to know that someone would say "yes" to that, especially when you both know about all the crap you have to go through in the rock business and me going away all the time. But all I ever wanted was a family, a nice house and a car.'

Meanwhile, the life-loving, in-the-moment personality of the band's well-built, egotistical provocateur Simon Le Bon was skilfully summed up by *Smash Hits*' Ian Birch in an article published in early 1982: 'He knows what he likes and enjoys it all with lip-smacking relish. Le Bon is supremely confident and will roguishly stir a situation to keep everyone on their toes. He lets his imagination gallop in the hope that he'll encourage everyone else to follow suit. He loves food and positively bellows with delight at the prospect of fresh asparagus in a French sauce.' Although a man of Epicurean appetites, the energetic singer didn't indulge in drugs to the same level as John and Andy Taylor. 'I don't think Simon cared for it much, really,' opines the coterie's photographer, Denis O'Regan. 'I think he was a bit dismissive of it. He's too much of a keep-fit type of guy to get sucked into it.' Le Bon himself insisted in 1998: 'I wasn't as bad as some. I mean, I enjoyed myself but I never actually lost control. I don't think I've got a particularly addictive personality, so the coke was there but it wasn't central. And I should add that it was mainly coke.' The singer also had a couple of relationships in 1982, revealing in March of that year that his girlfriend Anna 'is a fashion designer, painter and runs a motel at the moment in Florida. She and my mum are running two nearby motels in Florida. They're both very adventurous people. Just like me!' A few months later he met up with eighteen-year-old, English-born model Claire Stansfield, a six-feet-tall, long-legged, Amazonian figure who spoke fluent German and was raised in Toronto, Canada. She settled in London for a couple of years, studying drama and sharing a flat with another actress/model, a larger-than-life, vivacious Australian girl called Virginia Hey who would later go out with John Taylor.

In spite of all these distractions, Duran Duran had to finish the new album by the end of March because they were already booked to start an Australian tour on 15 April. Sandwiched between the recording sessions and the tour was a video shoot with Russell Mulcahy (who'd worked with them on 'Planet Earth' and 'My Own Way') in Sri Lanka, which Le Bon was already talking up in interviews in early 1982. The future-predicting front man insisted, 'I take video very seriously. I see it as an artform. Most people see it as a promotional device. I draw two main parallels with video. The first is with the film industry in the 1920s when talkies first came about. Videos are the "talking pictures" of today's music industry. The second is with stereo. Pink Floyd's *Dark Side of the Moon* was the first real stereo record. I want to make a visual *Dark Side of the Moon*.'

The exotic location of their latest shoot was suggested by Duran Duran's mission controller Paul Berrow, who'd just spent Christmas there and viewed it as an 'escapist, poetic and interesting place to make a video'. Former film student Marcello Anciano wrote the story-boards, treatments and art directed all of Russell Mulcahy's promos at this time. 'The thing with working with someone like Russell is that he had loads of visual ideas but he didn't have the time or perhaps he didn't put in the effort to arrange those visual ideas into any coherent form that could actually be put into production. So often the two of us would listen to the music, come up with ideas, have a conversation and I would try to formulate Russell's fantastic images into a clear whole that would make sense.' Anciano flew to Sri Lanka with Mulcahy and video producer Eric Fellner (who would later set up Working Title Films, responsible for producing the likes of *Four Weddings and a Funeral* and *Bridget Jones*) to check out locations, although he recalls at that time the Aussie director was interested in doing 'more of an *Apocalypse Now* type of thing. I think the only thing that remained from that idea was the reverse shot of John Taylor coming up in the water in "Hungry Like the Wolf".' Anciano remembers carrying around Le Bon's lyric sheets during the trip but doesn't recall speaking to the singer prior to going to Sri Lanka. As for the budget, EMI agreed to £45,000, but only on the basis that the band filmed three videos for the money.

Backed up against the video deadline and with the album still unfinished, four band members flew to Sri Lanka to shoot 'Hungry Like the Wolf', 'Save a Prayer' and parts of 'Lonely in Your Nightmare', leaving the band's resident control-freak Nick Rhodes to make some last-minute tweaks to the LP. Refusing to leave London until the job was completed, Rhodes and the album's engineer-producer Colin Thurston stayed up for forty-eight hours solid. The platinum-haired Warholian then sat rigid for sixteen hours on the plane to Sri Lanka with a copy of *Rio* playing in his headphones, wondering, 'What's wrong with it, something's wrong, there's a mistake.' He arrived sweating inside the 'black leather ensemble' he'd been wearing in London and looked around in vain for a waiting limousine: 'This little sort of flatbed truck pulls up, with this charming little Indian guy, who says "Mr Rhodes?" And I thought, "Oh no!" I said, "Well, how far is it to the hotel?" Thinking, "I've got to have a nap." He says, "Oh, it's about five hours?" And so we were driving through Sri Lanka, in this flatbed truck, with this album in these headphones, me dressed like that.'

On landing in Sri Lanka, a homesick John Taylor felt almost as disoriented as Rhodes and wondered what on earth he was doing there. 'I thought, "What has this got to do with pop music?" The first day I was there it was awful – I hated it. You're totally cut off, can't phone home. Then you go out to the beaches and it's mind-blowing – just like the Bounty adverts.' Marcello Anciano adds, 'Considering that we were in a real Third World country, they got into the spirit of it really fast. They were real troopers about it all. I mean this is before tourism hit Sri Lanka, so it was pretty primitive.' He says with a laugh, 'One of Russell Mulcahy's skills as a director is that he's incredibly charming and he can get you to do anything.' Both band and crew stayed in crumbling, beautifully time-worn Dutch colonial guest houses which used to be the residencies of the old European ambassadors. According to the shoot's eloquent story-boarder Anciano, the rooms were 'enormous' with a giant bath tub in the centre. 'They were extraordinary, stunning spaces but falling apart so these wonderful baths didn't have any plugs in them or any water.' The crew also experienced some unusual equipment problems. As there is already a huge film business in India, the producer Eric Fellner decided to hire everything locally. Modern, up-to-date equipment arrived right on time and everything looked perfect. However, when they put one of the camera cranes on the tracks it immediately buckled. On closer examination everyone realized that the Sri Lankan hire companies had copied them from a catalogue, so they looked identical to the real thing but they didn't actually work.

'Anyway, we'd organized it all,' continues the chatty Anciano, who would later make his own name as a video director by shooting over 500 videos, including Berlin's famous 'Take My Breath Away' promo clip. 'Then Paul Berrow came in the day before the shoot, looks at all the models in the swimming pool and goes, "I think we should have nudity in the video." I'm like, "Paul, we've got to get the right kind of models. I suggest that you do this another time." We had high-class models with us, not the kind who do stripteases! I seem to remember Nick was very interested in the black girl who was covered in tribal body paint in "Hungry Like the Wolf".' Rhodes wasn't so keen on some of the other exotic creatures in that video. According to the green-eyed, pale-skinned nineteen-year-old, 'I was sitting down in a restaurant when we were filming the final scene for "Hungry Like the Wolf" and there's this snake charmer sitting down with a little pipe, turban on, basket in front of him ... So I went up to him and said, "Watcha got in there, eh?" He taps the basket and these two cobras come wriggling out.'

Shooting at breakneck speed on a relatively small budget, almost inevitably the occasional continuity error crept in, such as

Le Bon's hair changing colour during 'Hungry Like the Wolf'. The singer was supposed to have blond tips put in but instead his heavily gelled, spiky mane ended up a vile, brassy yellow, which shocked the locals when Le Bon's hat flew off as he attempted to negotiate his way through a low doorway: 'This huge crowd of Sri Lankans all stepped back and gasped when they saw my bright yellow hair. They had never seen anything like it.' Anciano is convinced that they filmed the famous elephant scenes for 'Save a Prayer' in the same spot where Spielberg shot his action adventure *Raiders of the Lost Ark*. 'I think we were using the same animals,' says the man who witnessed one of the elephant keepers drawing a knife on the crew because he wanted more cash. That was swiftly smoothed over and the on-set japery continued: 'As a joke someone in the crew recorded a playback of an elephant, God knows why, and they played back this tape and it turned out to be a mating call. Roger's elephant heard this and ran down this river with Roger still on it – there was no seating; he was just holding on to his ears. I looked around at Paul Berrow and I could just see these eyes flashing in horror as we lost sight of them.' The director Russell Mulcahy also wanted a scene where the elephants sprayed water over the band, and as a result Andy Taylor swallowed some of the fouled liquid and fell ill: 'I'm riding on elephants and swimming in the water they pissed in,' revealed the guitarist. 'I got really sick with a virus. That's my memory of making those videos. I used to hate doing them anyway and John and I used to get drunk and hide.'

In order to film some of the most spectacular scenes in 'Save a Prayer', the shoot relocated to Anuradhapura, which is the holiest Buddhist city in southern India. It's a very beautiful and atmospheric area, scattered with the ruins of ancient temples, monasteries and palaces. However, the day Duran Duran arrived to shoot there coincided with a meeting between all the more militant Buddhists in Sri Lanka, who were calling for Westerners to be banned from the country. 'And here we are, shooting this Western, decadent pop video, prancing around with half-naked girls and all that stuff,' recalls the droll Anciano. He's still amazed that they managed to get away with it. 'Some of these people were threatening to kill Westerners for being on the sacred sites. You're not allowed to put your back against the Buddha statue in

Anuradhapura, that's out. Police can arrest you for that sort of stuff. And here we were filming in front of a four-thousand-year-old statue and having to do it really secretly and then get out of there as quickly as possible.'

The image of the long-limbed, cotton-suited John Taylor strumming a six-string guitar on a beach would subsequently have a potent effect on the band's female audience, but one shot the young fans didn't get to see was set up inside a huge tent in almost the same spot. 'There was a spectacular sunset with these fantastic fishing boats silhouetted against it,' says Anciano with a grin. 'And we said, "We want it really opulent, like the Arabian Nights inside this tent." They did a fantastic job, except that right in the middle they'd put a hookah and they were using real smoke, if you know what I mean. So we shoved all the band into this tent and went away to set up this very elaborate shot. We came back and when I walked in there, the tent was thick with smoke and the band's eyes were completely wasted and I'm like, "Russell, I don't think we can shoot this." '

As the surreal video shoot ran over schedule by a day, there was still more to do as Duran Duran rebooked a last-minute flight to Australia later that evening. They were filming in a café when Paul Berrow suggested rerouting their electrics into the main grid in order to illuminate the interior. 'We plugged it in and we blacked out half of the region,' cackles Anciano, 'and then Paul's shouting in this pitch black, "We've got to go in two hours, we've got to go ..." We had to quickly get the shots, bundle them in a car and I think they had to delay the plane in order for them to get to Australia on time. It was real seat-of-the-pants-type stuff.' Although this would prove to be an era-defining video shoot, the vampirically pale Nick Rhodes confessed: 'I've no desire to go there again. It's probably the most beautiful paradise country in the world but it's a little too primitive for me. I tend to get nervous with no TV, magazines and so on ...'

After landing in Australia, Duran Duran continued their relentless drive towards global success by playing six sold-out dates, despite Andy Taylor collapsing from pyrexia, a tropical fever brought on by the water in Sri Lanka. The guitarist keeled over at the Horden Pavilion in Sydney on 21 April 1982 and was very run-down for the rest of the tour. On doctor's orders he had an oxygen mask at the side of the stage for the remaining dates, in case there was a problem. The Australian trip was followed by five shows in Japan, consisting of three dates in Tokyo and concerts in Osaka and Nagoya. The band were pursued by hordes of girls everywhere they went. Rob Hallett recalls Duran Duran singing Joan Jett's 'I Love Rock'n'Roll' as they were 'chased by fans in twenty or thirty taxis! They loved it. On another occasion they were surrounded by girls in this shop; I mean it looked like a crowd of thousands, and the shop had to put its shutters down. When the police arrived they shoved us in these cars and the girls were banging on the windows, smashing everything.' Not surprisingly in such an overheated, sexually charged atmosphere, the band's libidinous singer was having the time of his life: 'In Japan all I was interested in was finding women. So I'd go to the clubs where Western models would meet and I'd take them back to the hotel. I spent all my time either in the club or in my bedroom bonking. It was all front. You grab your balls, close your eyes, swagger up to the woman of your choice and just go, "Hi, baby." That's it.' Born shopper and gadget-lover Nick Rhodes was also indulging himself. 'I've done very well for myself. I went shopping for electronics in Hong Kong, clothes in Japan and junk in Manila.' Not that Duran Duran were multi-millionaires just yet. 'We haven't struck it rich,' explained John Taylor, sounding for a moment more like his old Nigel self. 'We plough it all back in, we really do. We just believe in reinvestment, in business.'

Duran Duran's ambitious plan to create a pioneering full-length video album consisting of the best songs from the first two albums meant that they still had more promos to shoot. This time their chosen location was Antigua in the Caribbean. According to the impish Andy Taylor, first of all he made sure the hotel was on the beach and then he just lay there until someone called him. 'That's when I really started my video avoidance phase. I don't know why it intimidated me so much, but the camera being bunged up my nose, it used to really frighten me.' 'On "Rio", I came up with the ideas,' explains Anciano. 'Well, it wasn't so much ideas, I just gave Russell a load of really poppy, high-gloss colour photographs. Really bright, vibrant colours. Silks against white backdrops. Paul and Michael were avid sailors, so they wanted a boat. Simon and the boys like good-looking girls, so they got good-looking girls. That was my role – getting it all together so that everyone was happy in a form that fitted the budget.' Just as, musically, Duran Duran were fashioning a new sound that didn't linger for long in atmospheric backwaters and cut straight to the chorus – an approach typified by the track 'Rio' – their fashion sense was sharpening too. Gone was the foppish dandyism of the New Romantics, to be replaced by their favourite Anthony Price suits. 'You don't really want to be on a yacht wearing a frilly shirt and a samurai jacket,' laughs Tim Dry of Tik and Tok. In retrospect, Nick Rhodes argued: 'It's easy to look at the "Rio" video and say, "My God, it's like a Martini advert, there they are in their lilac suits, swanning away"… for us, it was like, "Wow, we can get the record company to pay for us to go to the Caribbean islands and make a video?" Of course we were going to go, we were kids. You'd never make a video like that now, but for the times they reflect, they were very much in context. The funny thing is that it looked like we were having a great time, but it was appalling. There wasn't one of us who didn't lose our lunch on that shoot … God, I hated that boat. Wrecking my Anthony Price suit with those dreadful waves splashing everywhere. Really! Tie the damn things up and serve a couple of cocktails on them. They're best tied up, just like women.' Le Bon agrees: 'We portrayed a James Bond fantasy – John making a beach landing in combat gear, me in a white tuxedo in the boat, with the phone and wearing flippers. We were just making arseholes of ourselves in the Caribbean. The boat thing was the closest we got to that superstar affluence thing, but I don't think it was elitist. It was like, "Hey, look at this! This is fantastic!" And it was something nobody had seen.'

The 'Rio' video's 'high gloss', ultra-real vision of pink and blue telephones, body-painted models, huge bouncing balls, banana skins and Nick Rhodes pretending to play saxophone on a raft is certainly one of the defining videos of the 1980s, although it is so stylized and over-the-top it's hard to take the playboy campery too seriously as a symbol of rampant, right-wing Thatcherism. Nevertheless Boy George argues in his autobiography, *Take It Like A Man*, that 'the champagne-swilling, yacht-sailing Duran Duran touted playboyeurism and new pop superficiality. Suddenly it was OK to be rich, famous and feel no shame. Some saw it as a natural consequence of Thatcherism.' Duran Duran certainly expressed a mood in the country at that time and they painted it in the lurid colours of a fashion spread in a magazine. However, the Tory leadership was contributing to an increasing division between the 'haves' and the 'have-nots', later summed up by Harry Enfield's grotesque Loads-of-Money character. As a result, lines were also drawn culturally. In music, Paul Weller and Billy Bragg marked their territory on one side. Duran Duran, standing in line on the 'Rio' yacht wearing their Anthony Price suits, belonged to the other. But while Martyn Ware of Heaven 17 is not exactly a fan of the band – ' "her name is Rio", for fuck's sake, how can they be concerned about their artistry?' – he argues, 'Duran Duran's ambition was an issue because it was in the middle of Thatcherism, which was obviously a disaster zone for many people in this country. But I can also understand the escapist thing. They saw themselves as pure entertainment without self-consciousness and I wouldn't criticize them for that.' Inspiration for the band's luminous, over-the-top imagery came from America, fashion magazines and most of all pop music – the likes of Marc Bolan, Bowie and Roxy Music had all indulged in glamorous, both-ends-burning lifestyles. In fact musicians have always been society's excessive fantasists and cash-burning bankrupts of tomorrow. Plus, as Stephen Duffy noted in 2003, it's all to do with perception. 'Duran Duran were decadent in public, and had decadence twinned with the Thatcher era. I'm sure Johnny Marr was just as decadent but nobody wrote about him.'

Duran Duran also expressed the aspirations of a new generation, many of whom were not 'Thatcherite' or at least would never admit to it. Youth in the early 1980s began to travel more than their parents had – in fact, it wasn't unusual for many teenagers to be the first to go abroad in their immediate family. Britain was becoming a less parochial place for millions of young people and as the world opened up, greater choice went hand in hand with consumerism and creativity. There was an explosion of ideas in fashion, design, graphics, magazines, club culture and pop music. Duran Duran's 'Rio' video is flawed, silly and smacks a little too much of keeping up with the Joneses (hey, my yacht's bigger than yours!) to be held up as great 'pop' art, but it does have a sense of vibrancy and fun to it that captures this change. Just as many social observers have described the crossover from the 1950s to the 1960s as a switch from black-and-white to colour, the 1980s became a super-real, almost garish riot of graphics and design, driven forward by new technology and street culture. From John Galliano to Acid House and Lycra, Britain lost some of its four-walled intro-spection, and for better or worse, as the 1980s switched to the 1990s, Morrissey's world of cold tea and deserted seaside towns was already starting to feel like the bitter-sweet taste of nostalgia for many people.

Duran Duran's glowing travelogues are one thing, but less successful is Simon Le Bon reciting lines of Shakespeare in the other Antiguan promo clip for the album track 'Nightboat'. Sat on the quay, the former drama student mumbles through Mercutio's 'Queen Mab' speech in *Romeo and Juliet*. It's one of those moments in the band's career when they seemed to revel in a wind-up. In fact, when you stand back and strip it all down, Duran Duran have always acted above their station. Sometimes they pull it off, but on this occasion, Le Bon's Shakespearean quotation is most definitely a culturally 'un-good' moment. Much better is their promo for the moody, atmospheric 'The Chauffeur'. Taking the photographs of Helmut Newton as their kinky but elegant inspiration, Duran Duran commissioned director Ian Emes to make a sexy black-and-white 'short'. He filmed various beautiful women, including Billy Idol's girlfriend Perri Lister, as they're transported by limousine from the ornate hotel rooms and grand apartments depicted in Lang's most famous images to a multi-storey car park, where they meet up and 'dance' together.

Meanwhile, on 4 May 1982, Duran Duran released their fifth single, 'Hungry Like the Wolf', and reached number five for the second time. The salivating, sexual imagery of the lyric was not to everyone's taste, with Dave Rimmer at *Smash Hits* pointing out that 'the wolf of the title appears to be a character who haunts women – charming'. The singer claimed the Doors' Jim Morrison as an influence on the song's lyric: 'He was the Lizard King, the animal spirit god. That idea meant a lot to me and I tried to get it into my music. While we were standing there wearing Anthony

Price suits and lip-gloss, there was this writhing, scaly thing inside us. That image thing was just a decoy. You had to package yourself in a way that people were prepared to accept.' Clearly they'd already travelled a long way from the passive androgyny of New Romanticism where boys looked like girls and girls looked like boys. After the laddish 'Girls on Film' video, the imagery and subject matter of 'Hungry Like the Wolf' were also provocative, especially the moment when Simon Le Bon is filmed searching for a girl in a tropical jungle to the sound of panting and orgasmic wails. As for the song, it's one of Duran Duran's best, built around Andy's Taylor's rough-edged guitars, a striking, popping sequencer marshalled by Rhodes and another great melody line courtesy of their singer. In fact, the band won an Ivor Novello for the composition in 1983.

A week after the new single, Duran Duran released the *Rio* album, which climbed to number two in the UK. The first striking thing about the album is Patrick Nagel's cover art, featuring a Latin girl with a big, cherry-lipsticked smile, raven-black hair and great big earrings. Paul Berrow had come across Nagel's work in *Playboy* magazine and the band felt that it was right for the album. Nagel's style is a glamorous combination of magazine illustration, Japanese woodblocks and Art Deco styling, described by critics as 'fantasy realism ... bold, dark lines shape perspective out of flat, cool colours and stark white spaces'. The original *Rio* drawing used to hang in Paul Berrow's office at the Rum Runner, until one night the band stole it on their way to *Top of the Pops*. After that they took it in turns to hang it up in their own houses and apartments.

'*Rio* is a very bright, fast album,' declared Nick Rhodes in 1982, summing up the breathless seven-song sequence that begins with the title-track and runs through to 'Last Chance on the Stairway'. There's only a last gasp for air with the arrival of two atmospheric 'slowies' at the end: 'Save a Prayer' and the limo-noir of 'The Chauffeur'. 'Rio' is a great opener, expressing the band's excitement after gorging themselves on America a few months earlier. Le Bon says, 'People always go on about how money-based, two-faced and backstabbing America is. And it is like that. LA's the biggest jungle I've ever been to. But there are also some very nice things and "Rio" is a celebration of them. America can be colourful, open and honest.

So instead of calling her America, I called her Rio.' In fact it was John Taylor who came up with the name 'Rio' and everyone liked it because it caught the 'more optimistic' tone of the LP. Le Bon agrees: 'The word looks great, sounds great and makes people think of parties, rivers – it's Spanish for river! – foreign places and sunshine.'

The new album witnessed a band working brilliantly within their limitations, creating a sound later described by Nick Rhodes as 'elegant punk'. Le Bon's vocal melodies are as simple and colourful as the cover art, with bold lines marking out every track; John Taylor's dexterous bass playing complements Roger Taylor's solid, no-nonsense drumming (aside from the occasional flamboyant flutter) and Andy Taylor increasingly flexes his muscles on the harder-edged 'New Religion' and, of course, 'Hungry Like the Wolf'. Although *Rio*'s production is sparser than their debut, there are still some cool little touches. 'Last Chance on the Stairway' opens to the sound of a cigarette being lit and a voice going 'cheers', followed by clinking glasses, party noises and some taped train station ambience. Rhodes created the strange opening to 'Rio' by throwing small metal rods on the strings of a grand piano and later there's the sound of birdsong. Rhodes's girlfriend at the time, Cheryl, giggles at the start of 'Hungry Like the Wolf' and as for 'The Chauffeur', it's not only a stand-out moment for its unlikely combination of electronics and ocarina (a simple oval-shaped wind instrument with finger holes and a mouthpiece) but there are also insect noises, a weird narration about grasshoppers and keys rustling at the end. According to the languid Rhodes, 'There are a lot of silly little things on it. That's our own game, if you like. I think the second album has got Duran Duran stamped all over it. It sounds like us – I don't think it sounds like anybody else.'

Steve Sutherland at the *Melody Maker* grasped the nettle with both hands and wrote one of the most positive reviews of the band's career: '*Rio* is the true culmination of the much misunderstood New Romanticism – energetic, proud, enthusiastic, joyous; something to escape *fully* into. It cultivates the class that makes Roxy great, it encompasses almost every trend and rhythm going, embraces everything from funk to Thin Lizzy and still sounds unmistakably like Duran Duran; an unashamed new breed of rock band, the unrivalled masters of melody. If there's a catch, it's that – honest to God – *Rio* is so good and defines such an exuberant majesty, where the hell do they go from here?' Others, however, remained unconvinced. *Smash Hits* scribe Fred Dellar was initially impressed, writing, 'the first three tracks – the singles "Rio" and "My Own Way", and the marvellously melodic "Lonely in Your Nightmare" – had me jotting down theories about the new golden age of pop. Then the quality swing meter began gradually slipping back. By the time the last song, the 1978 vintage 'The Chauffeur' dragged itself off the turntable it was apparent that the Le Bon squad had delivered yet another well-dressed but not totally satisfying album. Third time lucky? Could be. Could be.' *Sounds* recognized that Duran Duran's new slimmed-down sound had effectively shed the skin of the art-fag crowd: 'Frankly they used the entire futuro-romantic caboodle like any astute business mind would, skimming the surface but never diving in. Clever boys.' The *NME* remained unmoved: 'What they've done is spin out the formula, quite efficiently. Another soft, seamless package of pop-dream preferably for the very young and innocent. It's a sweet lumpy pudding of a noise.'

Rio has since been listed at number sixty-five in *NME's* 100 Greatest Albums of All Time and ranked number ninety-eight in *Q's* All-Time list but although it is a famous 1980s pop album, the LP has never been revered like ABC's *Lexicon of Love*, The Human League's *Dare!* or *New Gold Dream* by Simple Minds (all released within a year of each other). In fact, when you shine a light on it, *Rio* is far from perfect. Lyrically, it's full of Le Bon's most obtuse tongue-twisters ('New Religion' is presented as 'a dialogue between the ego and the alter ego'), although there are rare moments of clarity, especially when the singer sums up the album's high spirits in one line: 'No time to worry cause we're on the roam again – hold back the rain.' His vocals are also sometimes a leap of faith – instantly recognizable, but if only he'd sung the chorus of 'New Religion' a little better. The reason why *Rio* has successfully ascended the all-time lists is through its striking, back-to-back pop melodies, the best of which is 'Save a Prayer'. Featuring Nick Rhodes's moody keyboard line, Le Bon's bitter-sweet whine and a plaintive guitar solo courtesy of Andy Taylor, the song was recently summed up by Moby, in *Q* magazine, as 'a perfect hybrid of electronic, conventional and pop elements'.

As a call to arms *Rio* is pretty intoxicating, even if all we're talking about here is a headlong rush into hedonism, fashion, art and the 'video age'. Unfortunately Duran Duran's visual travelogues had one immediate side-effect back in the summer of 1982, as Andy Taylor contracted another illness in Antigua and the band were forced to postpone their June-scheduled European dates until September. This meant that their first port of call after releasing the *Rio* album was America. The tour was a huge £100,000 investment consisting of twenty-five club dates that stretched from the Peppermint Lounge in New York to Calgary, Alberta. Although they were still a long way from crossing over into mainstream success in the States, the band continued to do everything they could to promote themselves. John Taylor summed up the mood in the camp: 'Too many bands think the music scene ends at the English Channel and they seem quite happy in that knowledge. We have never thought that way. We really do believe in old-fashioned sweat and toil.'

Rio's spirited pop had little to do with New Romanticism, but the term clung to Duran Duran in the States, where the Cult with No Name was regarded by the media as a short-lived 'triumph' of packaging over content. Steve Strange seemed to confirm this perception when he launched Visage in New York by riding a camel into the city. As a result Duran Duran possessed a cultlike cool in LA, New York and San Francisco, but they were frozen out by the US hinterlands. However, by the summer of 1982, British acts were scoring individual pop hits that included Flock of Seagulls' 'Wishing (If I Had a Photograph of You)', Kim Wilde's 'Kids in America', Soft Cell's 'Tainted Love' and The Human League's 'Don't You Want Me', although none of the artists were establishing themselves as huge, arena-filling, long-term prospects. Duran Duran aspired to be the new Rolling Stones in America – a decadent rock band rather than a disposable pop moment. As John Taylor so eloquently put it, 'The Human League may sell a lot of records, but they'll never play Madison Square Garden. I think we will.'

While 'Don't You Want Me' blasted out from US radio, Duran Duran set out their stall as a live act with Sylvie Simmons from

Sounds flying over to see their open-air show in the Greek Theatre, Los Angeles on 27 July. Although observing that the venue was 'not as packed as some of those of earlier British visitors and certainly not as packed as they deserved ... the performance was almost flawless as performances go. The music had a confidence and a levity and a sensuousness that so many of the British visitors had been lacking and wasn't the usual note-perfect/tedious reproduction, cute immobile clothes-horses you might have expected.' Although very few people in America recognized it yet, Duran Duran were much more suited to the US marketplace than most of the other English bands. They had a rock'n'roll guitarist; by now only one of them was still wearing makeup at all hours of the day and, most importantly of all, Duran Duran viewed themselves as good, old-fashioned entertainers. Le Bon declared, 'Because of the kind of stigmatism that punk rock gave to show business, a lot of the new bands attached a certain uncoolness to putting on a show. We are showmen! We move a lot basically because all of us are deeply physically affected by the music we play. I mean, I can't keep still. I like the beat and I like to dance.'

When the headlining part of the tour finished, Duran Duran had a few days off before they set off as the support act for one of their favourite bands, Blondie. Andy Taylor grabbed this moment to marry his fiancée Tracey Wilson. The wedding was held in Los Angeles' famous Chateau Marmont Hotel, a castle-like building rising above Sunset Strip which had opened as luxury apartments in 1929. It's a very Duran Duran type of place, with the atmosphere of an English stately home that had once made it a favourite LA retreat for Hollywood stars such as Errol Flynn and Greta Garbo. The Chateau Marmont also has a darker reputation. In March 1982 the actor John Belushi died from a drug overdose in one of the hotel's bungalows around the swimming pool and one of Duran Duran's favourite photographers, Helmut Newton, was killed at the age of eighty-three after losing control of his Cadillac while leaving the hotel's car park. This glamorous location – which also contains a piano once owned by country star Gram Parsons – played host to a happier occasion when on 29 July 1982, Duran Duran gathered together, dressed in top hats, wing-tip collars, cravats and pearl-topped tie pins. The service itself was conducted by a dean from a nearby university. Andy Taylor: 'Why do I love Tracey so much? She understands me. She is very religious and she goes to church a lot. She's a Catholic. She's like my angel – she lights candles for me when I'm on the road to keep me safe. She reads the Bible and overcomes things. And I fancy her as much now as when we met – she's beautiful. Without her, I'd be a raving lunatic, for sure. I might have ended up like Keith Richards or someone, you know, because I'm an extremist, so I either go one way or the other.' 'I wouldn't describe Tracey as religious,' says the band's original travelling 'mum', Amanda Berrow. 'She was more spiritual. She's quite a wise one, very connected and intuitive. She knows who he is and she loves him.' Reportedly the wedding gifts included a porcelain saki set from Simon Le Bon and a light shaped like a French cigarette packet, courtesy of Nick Rhodes. Rob Hallett remembers that 'it was a great party and Roger and me were later thrown out of the Roxy for wrestling'. Meanwhile, the married couple set up home in an old English townhouse in Wolverhampton with their Jack Russell, Charlie.

In the summer of 1982, Nick Rhodes also met his future wife, Julie Anne Friedman, while working on remixes of tracks from the *Rio* album for US radio. The LA studio he'd been working in held a yacht party in the band's honour and the way Rhodes tells it, Roxy Music's *Avalon* album was playing as he spotted a 'beautiful' pair of legs on a couch and wanted to see who 'was attached to the other end'. Julie Anne has described Rhodes 'awkwardly' introducing himself. To begin with she wasn't sure about a man who wore more makeup than she did and was also several inches shorter. But they talked for a while and by the end of the party Rhodes and Julie Anne were so taken with each other that over the next few weeks they were rarely apart. Rhodes cooed, 'High cheekbones, dark eyes and legs that go on for ever seem to be the right credentials, and she's intelligent with a very dry sense of humour.' Born on 9 March 1960 in Des Moines, Julie Anne Friedman had grown up with money (her family owned shares in the Younkers department store fortune) and was a well-educated, sophisticated six-foot model who was used to getting her own way. It wasn't long before Rhodes had introduced her to Andy Warhol, with the dry-as-a-bone diarist noting on 23 August

1982: 'The Duran Duran kids came by and brought some bigger and taller girlfriends.'

The couple were together when Duran Duran flew to Kansas City to start the twelve-date tour supporting Blondie. For John Taylor the high point of these shows wasn't on stage, it came after their New Jersey concert at Meadowlands when he met up with two of his heroes: Nile Rodgers and Tony Thompson from Chic. After bonding in the bathroom over a line of "Charlie" they all went clubbing together in Manhattan. The tour ended at the JFK Stadium in New York, where Le Bon sat and watched the head-line act: 'I was in the press box, front row, with all these journalists behind me. And then this guy knocks me on the arm and hands me a mirror full of cocaine and this steel snorter! It really was that blatant. Everyone was using drugs back then, mostly cocaine. You couldn't go anywhere without being offered whatever you wanted.'

At the end of August Duran Duran returned to the UK, where the alluring *Rio* highlight 'Save a Prayer' climbed to number two in the chart. This melancholy, wistful song describes a character who is hoping to lose himself in an almost dreamlike 'one-night stand' where the lovers 'see the world in all its fire'. Le Bon says, 'For me, the physical world is a spiritual thing. I don't have to have mysticism because I think we are already surrounded by this most incredible, wonderful thing. I don't need an external being called God because I have everything I need right here. I live in the moment. I love simplicity.' As the song glided into the charts, some of the band members started living in their parents' homes again, as they hadn't found the time to buy their own flats or houses. For twenty-year-old Nick Rhodes sleeping in his bedroom back at his mum and dad's house must have felt surreal after his experiences in America. But events took an even more bizarre twist when the phone rang one afternoon. His mother called up to him, 'There's a Michael on the phone ...' It was Michael Jackson, who wanted to discuss the idea of a collaboration. It never came to anything in the end.

In the autumn Duran Duran set off on a month-long European tour, playing to an audience of 'gay skinheads' in Stockholm, Sweden and then travelling across Finland, Denmark, Netherlands, Belgium, France and Germany. Everything was going fine until they arrived in Munich, where Roger Taylor was hassled by a local in a club called the Sugar Shack. The situation turned nasty, the guy took a swing at the drummer and the band's security had to wade in. A highly emotional John Taylor hadn't even been at the club but when he found out he completely 'lost it' and punched his fist through a glass partition in his hotel room. As a result, when Duran Duran walked on stage in Lisbon, Portugal, a few days later to play their first ever arena shows (a mind-boggling achievement given the size of the market) a band-aged John Taylor had to watch from the wings while a session musician took his place. 'It must have been a very humbling experience for him,' says Paul Berrow.

John Taylor made sure that he was fit for the sold-out twenty-five-date tour of the UK that followed a week later, which featured a line-up augmented by saxophonist Andy Hamilton. The concerts included three in London and four in the Birmingham Odeon at the end of November. As a 'thank you' to all the local fans who had supported the band, Duran Duran also decided to do a 'secret gig' at the Rum Runner. They released hundreds of customized balloons announcing the show, but either the Duran Duran fans in Birmingham town centre that day thought it was a spoof or they were too young to go to a night-club. As a result, the band only played to about twelve people that night! The Birmingham Odeon gig on 30 November featured another unannounced surprise when art house robots Tik and Tok came on as special guests. 'I made the stupid mistake of standing too near the stage during one song and I actually got pulled into the audience,' recalls Tim Dry (Tik) with a wide grin. 'The other thing that happened was Simon asked if we wanted to do something during Duran's set. So we thought, "How about if we come down on wires from the ceiling during 'Planet Earth' without telling any of the other band members?" So Sean and I got fitted into these ball-tightening harnesses and sure enough, we lowered ourselves from the ceiling with the band not knowing what's going on and three thousand people in the audience staring up in the air.'

In the UK Duran Duran scored their fourth Top Ten hit when 'Rio' reached number nine. At the same time they celebrated their first American chart success when the *Carnival* EP crept into the US charts at number ninety-eight. Featuring the remixes of 'Rio', 'Hold Back the Rain', 'My Own Way', 'Hungry Like the Wolf' and 'New Religion' that the band had completed with former Joe Jackson producer David Kershenbaum, *Carnival* also came out in Spain, the Netherlands, Japan and Taiwan. However it was particularly important in encouraging US club and radio DJs to play Duran Duran, mostly for the first time. Paul Berrow had stayed out in America to 'work' the new mixes by motivating and hassling Capitol's radio plugging department and finally this dynamic, driven approach was starting to pay dividends. Yet the most significant breakthrough occurred at the rapidly growing cable station MTV. Les Garland (senior executive vice-president, MTV) recalls, 'We had our weekly meeting to hear new music on Tuesdays – back then it was a fledgling industry and we'd get maybe ten videos a week and everyone would gather and sit through them all. I remember our director of talent and artist relations came running in and said, "You have got to see this video that's come in." MTV wanted to break new music and "Hungry Like the Wolf" was the greatest video I had ever seen.' As the station's audience expanded, record store owners found themselves selling boxes of Duran Duran records in areas where the radio still wouldn't touch them. Fans then started requesting these local stations to play 'Hungry Like the Wolf' and, combined with the efforts of Capitol and Paul Berrow, slowly but surely the track picked up momentum on the US airwaves. In early November Capitol rereleased *Rio* with some of the new Kershenbaum mixes, followed by a third pressing of the album containing a retooled version of 'Hungry Like the Wolf'. For three dramatic months at the end of 1982, MTV and Duran Duran fed off each other in a completely new symbiotic relationship and by 3 December 'Hungry Like the Wolf' had climbed to number three in the American charts. John Taylor says, 'The success was totally unbelievable for us, because we sort of watched it from across the channel.' That changed when they flew over to New York for MTV's New Year's Eve Rock'n'Roll Ball on 31 December, with Duran Duran performing an hour-long set to 8 million viewers. The year couldn't have finished on a higher note for the band, as they also won Best Group, Best Album and Best Single (not forgetting Le

Bon's awards for Most Fanciable Male and Best Male Singer) in the *Smash Hits* Awards. 'You might as well call it *Duran Hits*,' said a slighted Boy George.

CHAPTER SIX

Simon Le Bon: *'It was a hilarious time. We had fabulous, much-publicized love affairs with a string of obscenely beautiful women. Passionate times ...'*

Anthony Burgess, author of *A Clockwork Orange*: *'The essence of pop stardom is immaturity – a wretched pseudo-musical gift, a development of the capacity to shock, a short-lived notoriety, extreme depression, a yielding to the suicidal impulse.'*

Simon Le Bon: *'I believe the word "fuck" means love. It's being misused and it's a good word.'*

John Taylor: *'I've always been the most available member of Duran, because the other guys have either been married or going with someone very seriously.'*

John Taylor: *'We were definitely built for speed. Sometimes it felt like we were in a space capsule or something. We were anything we wanted to be. We behaved any way we wanted to behave.'*

At the start of 1983 Duran Duran received three awards at the British Rock and Pop Awards: Best Album (for *Rio*), Best Group (they polled more votes than the next five nominees put together) and Simon Le Bon won Best Male Vocalist. The only dark cloud on the horizon was that the British tabloids were beginning to turn Duran Duran into some kind of tacky soap opera. 'We like to call it Duranysty,' explained Rhodes in his dry slow drawl. 'And I think you lose your mystery, you kind of break a spell. English love to see Americans succeed, they love Hollywood and they flock to movie openings, but they cannot bear to see an English person succeed. Maybe it's to do with us being a race of peeping Toms, more interested in private lives than public careers.' In the early 1980s, *The Sun*'s editor Kelvin McKenzie pioneered pop gossip in the newspapers by launching the 'Bizarre' column, written by journalist John Blake. *The Sun* was read by one in twelve of the British population, giving Duran Duran massive exposure as a colourful, glamorous young band on their way up. The exotic locations of their videos added a splash of sunshine to the pop pages and their photographs provided some attractive eye-candy. At first John Taylor played along, quipping his way through interviews and arriving at airports with a series of beautiful women: 'Being a rock star is like putting a sign in a window, "For Sale",' said the wisecracking jetsetter. 'I did an interview with *Penthouse* and they said, "What's your idea of a great woman?" I replied, "Someone who could tie me up and whip me and make great bacon sandwiches." It's part of playing to the gallery.' Love it or loathe it, pop trivia and scandal began to fill the papers in a way it had never done before and it was so successful for the tabloids that when Robert Maxwell took over the *Daily Mirror* he immediately set out to hire Blake. This started a crazy bidding war with *Sun* proprietor Rupert Murdoch. Blake, who eventually transferred to the *Daily Mirror*, told *Time Out* magazine: 'It was ludicrous. They were offering me Porsches, jobs in America, you name it. I doubt if either of them had read a word I've written. It was just these two inflated egos bidding for some object they wanted to possess.'

The trouble was that in this competitive atmosphere, John Blake exaggerated and distorted any vague tittle-tattle about the band into sleazy headlines. The public understood that Duran Duran were complicit in this arrangement – they'd wanted to be famous, after all – but there's a point when the brand becomes tarnished by over-exposure. Duran Duran's story was blown up, cropped and converted into a series of dramatic 'exposés', boosting record sales but increasingly portraying them as egomaniacs and male bimbos – silly playboys living absurdly lavish lifestyles, imprisoned by the screams of even sillier teenage girls (who don't know better anyway) and apparently hated by almost everyone else. They didn't enjoy much support from the music press, the style media had moved on to cover fresher, more underground trends and the tabloids loved to play up Duran Duran's rivalries with other bands. This encouraged fans of Duran Duran and Spandau Ballet to split into clearly segregated groups in the school playground, although it was actually Culture Club who seemed to take the greatest pleasure in dissing Duran Duran at every opportunity. In 1983 Jon Moss declared, 'Duran Duran reflect what people can't have in life. We reflect what they can have.' As revenge one Duran fan invented a story in *The Sun* that Boy George had punched her outside EMI Records and left her lying battered in the road. She retracted it only after Culture Club threatened to sue for libel. Even ex-Sex Pistol Johnny Rotten joined in the sport, sneering, 'And as for you poor little cows who buy Duran Duran records, you need serious help 'cause those people are conning you. Making records for people just because you think that's what they want. To me that's fascism.'

Meanwhile, Nick Rhodes had started work on his first musical project outside Duran Duran. He'd been approached at one of Duran Duran's favourite watering holes, the Embassy Club, by Christopher Hamill (aka Limahl), who used to work there as a 'bus boy'. Rhodes was having a quiet drink and minding his own business when 'this two-toned, spiky-haired guy came along. I liked what he was saying and it reminded me of Duran Duran before "Planet Earth".' Nick Beggs, the blond-haired fretless bass player in Kajagoogoo, takes up the story: 'Limahl met him at the Embassy – he'd actually stopped working there by this time, but he was still going down there and schmoozing. Limahl was always a great networker, very well connected because he was in London and the rest of Kajagoogoo were still in Leighton Buzzard. I think Nick must have been taken with the way Limahl looked, which was quite striking. Strangely enough what he came up with later with the band was comparatively refined. Limahl gave him a demo and Nick got back to him a little while later and said, "This is really good, let's talk about it."'

A proper meeting was arranged in the Embassy, this time attended by Rhodes and his girlfriend Cheryl – described by Beggs as 'a very cute girl, very sweet' – Paul Berrow, Limahl and the bassist. 'He looked exactly like Nick Rhodes,' laughs Beggs. 'Big hair, makeup, smoking a cigarette in a very kind of French Parisian café style. He talked in a very intuitive way about business and then spoke passionately about music. I really trusted him.' Rhodes took the demo to EMI who, like all the other major labels, had already rejected the band. 'Nick made them listen to it again and they changed their minds,' explains Beggs. 'There's no doubt about it, we were signed because of Nick Rhodes. And we hadn't even written "Too Shy" at that point.'

Initially Kajagoogoo approached Alex Sadkin and David Bowie's right-hand man Tony Visconti to produce the album, but they both declined. In fact Visconti announced, 'I'm a living legend and I'm not going to work with that lot!' Beggs recalls that Paul Berrow, who signed Kajagoogoo's publishing to Tritec Music, suggested Nick Rhodes as a co-producer with Colin Thurston. 'I thought, "What a great idea,"' says Beggs. 'They said, "We'll do it under a pseudonym – we'll call ourselves Bill and Ben the Production Men" and off we went to Chipping Norton where Duran Duran had also done some recording. At the weekend we'd do these demos at Manchester Square studios and sometimes Nick would hang out with us. He was a very good ideas man. He had a very intuitive way of working that always seemed to lead us to the right conclusion and he was able to cut through over-complicated ideas, which is what we tended to do. He made us see things in a stripped-down way, a more pop way. "Too Shy" had a slightly jazzy guitar solo in it and he didn't like it, things like that.' While Kajagoogoo were pretty lightweight and never the coolest band in the world, Rhodes's pop instincts were confirmed when 'Too Shy' reached number one in the UK in February 1983. At this point he still hadn't scored a chart-topper with Duran Duran! The song also reached number one in seven other European countries and, aided by MTV, peaked at number five in America. Their debut album *White Feathers* followed in April and included a second UK Top Ten hit, 'Ooh to be Ah'.

Although the other band members ribbed Nick Rhodes about his contribution to another act's number-one single, they didn't have to wait long before Duran Duran reached the summit of the UK chart. On 19 March the band released the Beatlesesque 'Is There Something I Should Know?' and watched it debut at the top of the charts, which wasn't a weekly event back in the early 1980s. The band also released their self-titled video album on VHS, Beta and Laserdisc, featuring their latest promo flick. Filmed in a Battersea studio, it's made up of easy-on-the-eye, abstract images of staircases, silhouettes, red pyramids and a child with a bouncing ball. The band are dressed uniformly in blue shirts and white ties, a visual nod to both the song's Beatle-type guitars and the comparisons to Beatlemania which Duran Duran had inspired in the media. At one point Le Bon looks as if he's walking through a stage set of giant hair follicles while the others dress up as backing singers in grey military uniforms and mime the line, 'You're about as easy as a nuclear war.' This lyrical clunker has a certain humorous charm, like listening to a Les Dawson piano recital.

To say this was a 'hot' period for Duran Duran is something of an understatement. They were number one in the UK with a song that combined an ultra-catchy, jingly-jangly guitar riff with a classic Le Bon chorus. It was as refreshingly poppy as anything they've recorded before or since, utilizing a new co-producer on the track, Ian Little, whose previous credits included assisting on Roxy Music's *Avalon* album. Over the next few weeks they lip-synched 'Hungry Like the Wolf' and 'Is There Something I Should Know?' on BBC TV's *Oxford Road Show* and appeared on *Top of the Pops*, the *Kenny Everett Video Show* and *Riverside*. Their US status was confirmed when they were chased by packs of delirious teen fans after arriving in New York to perform 'Hungry Like the Wolf' and 'Girls on Film' on *Saturday Night Live*, the country's most influential entertainment programme. Andy Warhol joined them in the studio and filmed a sequence about Duran Duran for his cable TV show while they were rehearsing. He later joined Simon Le Bon and Nick Rhodes on MTV, where they presented the station with a *Rio* gold disc as a 'thank you' for helping them break America. The band were also in America to promote their first 'Video 45' featuring 'Girls on Film' and 'Hungry Like the Wolf' and had lined up a 'video-signing' in Times Square on the same trip. This event witnessed a new level of hysteria as Duran Duran were mobbed by a reported 12,000 fans, forcing the New York Police Department to send in mounted cops to deal with the crowd. In scenes that truly were reminiscent of Beatlemania, the British act were smuggled out of the back to safety.

At the end of April *Rio* was awarded platinum status in America, recognizing sales of 1 million units. Eventually it reached its highest US placing of number five in June 1983. The album remained in the American charts for over two years (129 weeks), contributing to global sales of around 5 million. Duran Duran also released the

'Rio' single on 11 March and watched it peak at number fourteen. In a cute marketing move, they repackaged their debut album for the US market, featuring the new single, 'Is There Something I Should Know?'. The ploy worked – the single peaked at number four in June, and in its wake they celebrated a second Top Ten album. Duran Duran weren't the only UK act in the chart. The so-called 'Second British Invasion' was at its height and on 16 July 1983 the American Top Forty contained no fewer than eighteen singles of UK origin.

Over a year after completing the *Rio* album, Duran Duran realized that they had to get back into the studio. The only problem was that it was no longer possible to record in either London, New York or Los Angeles. Rhodes recalls, 'Things were getting pretty hectic. I mean, the daily papers were getting so persistent, I couldn't go anywhere. I went to a restaurant one night and they were waiting outside! It was getting a bit much. We'd have been prisoners if we'd stayed.' There was also the small matter of the Inland Revenue, as they faced a monumental tax bill if they remained in the UK. The immediate solution was to escape from the high-pitched hysteria and follow the likes of the Rolling Stones into tax-exile status. So, in summer 1983, Duran Duran and their management hired a mobile studio and installed it in a chateau on the French Côte d'Azur. 'They had this fantastic, fuck-off mansion,' remembers Marcello Anciano. 'I mean massive. And outside was a twenty-four-track studio, twenty-four hours a day on call and there were two *cordon-bleu* chefs.' The band immediately caught some flak from the tabloids. John Taylor told *The Times* in 1995: 'We were recording in the south of France and pretending we were the Rolling Stones when we were only making our third record. We'd just barely moved out of our parents' homes. We didn't know anything about tax years but our managers did and that's why we were there. And that really began a negative roll of publicity.' Maybe so, but the move to France did allow Duran Duran to escape some of the mania surrounding them. 'It was a very relaxed atmosphere and a bit of a break for them,' recalls O'Regan, who took pictures of the band picnicking in the grounds of the mansion. 'I went into Cannes once with John Taylor and he didn't attract too much attention. I'm not sure how well-known they were in France at that time.'

'The South of France was brilliant fun,' enthuses Anciano of the

Bacchanalian atmosphere he encountered on his arrival. The video-maker spent a couple of weeks with the band, joining Simon Le Bon on a trip to Cannes where Russell Mulcahy was shooting a promo for Elton John's 'I'm Still Standing': 'When we got there, Simon went off with Elton for a chat and got him absolutely pissed – this was when Elton was a complete fiend. A few hours later we all said, "All right, we're going now," and we went back home to the mansion. The next time I saw Russell he said, "What the fuck did you do to Elton?" Apparently, Elton had come back from the bar and then proceeded to do these elaborate stripteases in front of the camera, rolling around on the floor naked, then running off, changing into the most outlandish costumes, coming back and doing another extraordinary striptease. All the time he was demanding that the camera continued to run on – and it was all Simon's fault.

'Another time we were in Cannes for the film festival and Simon says, "Let's go sailing." So we got this small two-man catamaran and set off. Except that it was pretty blowy outside and suddenly the wind took us and we just hurtled across the bay. I mean Simon was a pretty good sailor and I'd sailed quite a bit as well, but we were frantically moving all these ropes and we just went "crash" straight into this enormous Arab-owned gin palace. We scratched the side of this boat and leaning over the side of their boat there were these guys with guns, cocked and pointed at Simon and me. We're going, "What the fuck?" Simon's shouting, "Sorry, sorry, we didn't mean it." Anyway, we managed to tack away and of course the wind just sent us hurtling straight back in.

'The other weird thing was that about half an acre from their mansion – although we were in a state of mind that was a little altered, shall we say – there was a film set on the grounds. Andy Taylor and I discovered it one night when he'd decided that the thing to do was to see who could roll the largest joint, and Andy rolled this huge, fuck-off thing. So then we set off for a walk at night, and halfway across a muddy field we came across this film set – an enormous sixteenth-century French street, falling apart on this land. That's my memory of Duran, I shared all these surreal, almost dreamlike moments with them.'

Duran Duran had decided on a change of producer for their third album, hiring Alex Sadkin (previous credits include Robert

Palmer and Grace Jones) and Ian Little to work with them in the south of France. The band had recorded *Rio* at a rate of knots, but this time around the situation was very different. The new sessions began tentatively and then collapsed into a slow crawl. John Taylor remembers: 'I didn't know my head from my arse by the time we came to starting that album. We'd worked *Rio* until we were blue and we had no new material.' He was also still living up to his fun-loving image. According to Le Bon, 'Every night John would go into Cannes and get completely shit-faced and we usually didn't start work until four o'clock in the afternoon the next day. If we managed to get an hour and a half's work down we were lucky.'Apart from a raw, edgy demo for 'Union of the Snake', a track called 'Seven and the Ragged Tiger', which remains unreleased, and various embryonic ideas, the band didn't achieve much on the French Riviera.

Band and management decided to relocate to an island in the Caribbean, where there would be fewer distractions, so in May 1983 Duran Duran began five weeks of recording at George Martin's Air Studios in Montserrat. There were some successes, such as recording 'The Reflex' with the help of a couple of bottles of John Taylor's birthday champagne, but the band hated working there. Rhodes complained, 'The studio kept falling to bits and the tape machines weren't running at the right speed.' Even the amiable Roger Taylor was unimpressed by the new environment: 'When we got there it was, "Oh God! Montserrat!" But it's just like anywhere else. I mean, all we've done is record, play pool, swim and play table tennis – we could be in Birmingham or anywhere.' Amanda Berrow arrived there for a holiday and sensed that 'Something had changed ... The band had been very self-contained and laddish at the beginning. Now there were growing egos, a growing sense of "What's in it for me?". I think Andy Taylor was possibly more boisterous about it but they were all going through it. And part of that division was quite natural. They'd all got into their women and that causes a separation. They had their nearest and dearest with them and the atmosphere was noticeably different. Simon's Claire was there and she was good fun, I liked her and she was quite an interesting character, if not a bit challenging. But, you know, it was Nick who really took on a lot with Julie Anne. They were complete opposites. She was exciting, feisty, vibrant but also volatile. Nick's such a cool, calm person, very pleasant, and I think she stirred him up a bit. But maybe in the end he took on too much.' 'After a couple of years of the "All for one and one for all!" mentality, wives and girlfriends come along,' opines her brother, Paul. 'At first it was military – videos, tour, album, tour – but what do you do when you get there? Get a girl-friend – and a demanding one, almost certainly – and then the whole entity changes. The band comes together for just work and goes away again to a new set of friends. There is conflict among the merry men.' Such is the lifespan of a band, as John Foxx (who left Ultravox! after three albums) explains: 'The band thing is a phase – like being in a gang. You can't really be part of a gang all your life. It begins to feel undignified and it stunts your growth, unless you want to be a teenager for ever. Some do. Some don't. The benefits of being in a band are *Gestalt* – where the whole is greater than the sum of the parts, a very powerful experience – and working in a closed society with people who have the same aim. Of course, the aims almost inevitably diverge as you all grow.'

As work continued on the new album, long-term supporter, *Melody Maker*'s Steve Sutherland, flew over to Montserrat for a progress report. He arrived there to discover that Rhodes had a studio tan of 'deathly white, Roger is bronzed but sluggish, Simon's casual and chipper, John's brown but bored and Andy spends much of his time studying form for the local crab races'. After Duran played him 'eight new songs in various states of disarray', Sutherland commented, ' "Union of the Snake" is possibly the next single; a hard, heady funk track with a characteristically infectious melody. "The Reflex", likewise, is sharper and more brutal than anything they've recorded before – a terrace anthem enticed on to the dance floor. The title track, "Seven and the Ragged Tiger" has already taken up permanent residency in this hack's memory. With its Cockney Rebel-ish acoustic lilt and rousing chorus, it could well be the album's "Save a Prayer", a concert sing-along favourite … this is truly popular music, music that encourages participation, a celebration.' Marcello Anciano also remembers 'Seven and the Ragged Tiger' as a 'fantastic' track with 'a really honest lyric about the stuff that had happened to them'. Michael Berrow enthusiasti-cally agrees: 'The song "Seven and the Ragged Tiger" is a big hit for them – it has a classic Simon melody, a great song – at the time

I think they probably felt, "This is too easy, it can be better." It was quite raw to begin with. A reaction to the success. Much more of a self-deprecating style, brilliant chorus, maybe it's the next thing they'll release once all the demons have been expunged. They'd be silly not to. It's a classic Duran Duran single.' His brother Paul has a different memory. 'I seem to remember the feeling in the band was that it was a bit twee – a bit nursery rhyme.' This view is confirmed by Nick Rhodes, who says with his usual self-assurance, 'I didn't like it. I thought it was too naïve and throwaway. I've always enjoyed Simon's more obscure lyrics.' Parts of this original idea were adapted into a new track, 'The Seventh Stranger', and Duran Duran used the title for their next LP, much to Rhodes's chagrin, as he still only refers to it as 'the third album'. 'It seems to me like the name of a kids' book, not so much the Famous Five, more sort of piratey,' said Le Bon in 1983. 'It's an adventure story about a little commando team. The "Seven" is for us – the five band members and our two managers – and the "Ragged Tiger" is success. Seven people running after success. It's ambition. That's what it's about …'

Meanwhile Nick Rhodes's health took a dramatic turn for the worse while they were recording in Montserrat. He'd already complained that the sun was burning him 'like toast' and a bout of food poisoning hadn't improved his mood. At a time when he was stressed out by the deathly slow work on the album, Rhodes collapsed, unable to get his words out properly as his heart began to race faster than normal. It's a condition called 'paroxysmal tachycardia' (or 'fear of impending doom') and medical assistance was immediately called for. Rhodes was taken to a bigger island close by and to his obvious relief doctors informed him that the situation was not life-threatening. 'It's very common, apparently,' he later explained, 'but it's really scary when it happens. I went to see a specialist and asked him if I was having a heart attack and he said, "No, don't be daft!" He said I might never get it again in my life, or it might come back next week, but not to take notice of it, cos it'll never do me any harm. It was just a little bit scary.' Doctors told Rhodes the attack was not influenced by lifestyle and that it was more likely to be a hereditary quirk. After asking his family, he discovered that one of his cousins had gone through a similar experience. Whether it was this incident that caused a change in lifestyle or not, at the ripe old age of twenty-one, Rhodes 'pretty much gave everything up', except for cigarettes and vintage red wine. Amanda Berrow remembers, 'It was a serious incident; we were all worried and Nick was obviously concerned about it because he got a grip on his life after that. He started taking his health seriously.' According to Marcello Anciano: 'Nick was no angel in terms of the excesses but he had that heart scare and that freaked him out. I think it just sobered him up really fast and he became a very different person. In the early years Nick was the creative artist who wouldn't talk to anyone, who would come up with genius ideas out of the blue once every few days and you'd go "Fucking hell, where did that come from! Oh, Nick, hi!" It was only when he sobered up that he became a proper person, at least whenever I was around. Before that it was like, "Nick, hello, anyone there?" That's what he encouraged. He wanted to create this sense that he was this artistic alien who has fallen among men.' Michael Berrow's recollection of the incident was that 'Nick was really ill there. I heard it was a tropical fever but maybe some of the partying had weakened him. I never got the impression that he was as excessive as others in the band, but he was quite small and frail-looking in those days. He's just not a physical kind of guy, so maybe it did affect him more than the others. It is true, now that I think about it, he did change his lifestyle after that experience and looked after himself a lot better. I always enjoyed talking to Nick, but he did play the weird "alien" thing a bit. And he could be a bit of a whinger.' 'The thing with Nick, it was difficult to tell whether he was on drugs or not,' adds O'Regan. 'He's always been that persona, which is a little out of the ordinary.'

On 19 July Duran Duran escaped Montserrat by flying home to play two shows, supporting Dire Straits at a Prince's Trust concert in London, which would be attended by Prince Charles and Princess Diana. The following day they were performing at their own headlining charity event in aid of MENCAP. Duran Duran were mobbed at the airport, although just how many fans were there depended on which newspaper you read, estimates ranging between 250 and 2,000! Still jet-lagged, the 'Fab Five' were then whisked to the Grosvenor House Hotel on Park Lane, where they posed for photographs in the street. Their arrival dominated the newspaper headlines on the following day, as the tabloids gushed,

'Love and Duran Mania' (*Daily Star*); 'Durandemonium – It's Just Like the Screaming Sixties as Fans Mob Fab Five' (*Daily Express*) and 'Dramatic – Beatle-Style Mania as Princess Diana's Favourite Group Fly in' (*Daily Mirror*).

Unfortunately the group were exhausted and under-rehearsed as they took to the stage at the Dominion Theatre, London. The hour-long set was plagued by technical disasters, including John Taylor's bass, which he claimed had been de-tuned by a box of chocolates someone had thrown from the crowd. He subsequently confessed, 'I played horrendously as we were under-rehearsed. I spent the thankfully short set trying to tune my guitar. Whenever I would get real nervous, I would keep retuning my guitar, thinking it was out of tune, when really I was playing the wrong notes.' Duran Duran then met the royal couple for a relatively 'informal' chat. After watching Simon Le Bon throw himself around in a wild attempt to draw attention away from the ragged calamities occurring behind him, Prince Charles apparently commented, 'I never knew you had to be so fit.' Nick Rhodes says, 'They chatted about Montserrat. They seemed to know quite a lot about us – they'd obviously been briefed well. Diana looked great. Really pretty. They were very nice. Very human, actually. Prince Charles liked our "gear" – "I rather like your gear," he said.' Staunch royalist Andy Taylor beamed, 'I love the royal family. When we met Diana and Charles at that charity do, they were sparkling.' Early editions of the *Daily Mirror* on the following day read 'Diana's Delight'. Later, they changed their minds to 'Diana's Let-Down'. Le Bon recalls, 'The Di thing was a bit naff. It was something your mum and dad liked, so there was a part of me that bristled at it. Every time we opened the dressing room door, there she bloody was – under the table trying to get an autograph. It was like, "Can't your husband keep you under control?"' In January 1997 an IRA informer confessed there had been a plan to kill Prince Charles and Princess Diana at the concert, but luckily the explosive wasn't planted.

Duran Duran's troubles continued the next day at the fundraising MENCAP show in Villa Park, Birmingham. The idea had been to finish the *Rio* campaign with a one-off hometown gig but as the band didn't want to make any money off it, partly because it would have caused a complication with their tax

Andy Taylor dreams of Madison Square Gardens while Roger and John look on, 1980.

Simon Le Bon – the New Romantic Elvis, 1981.

Duran Duran in full Rum Runner regalia, 1981.

Nick Rhodes reveals that the *Daily Mirror* just can't make up their mind about the band's 1983 charity gig: was it a 'delight' or a 'let-down'?

John Taylor relaxes backstage on the US *Sing Blue Silver* tour, 1984.

Living in their limousine: Andy and Simon ghost through the streets of New York.

Andy Taylor adds some rock 'n' roll attitude backstage in America.

John Taylor in transit between their limousine and Duran's chartered aircraft on the *Sing Blue Silver* tour.

Roger Taylor in full shy, sensitive, brooding mode.

RIGHT: Nick Rhodes, the indestructible Captain Scarlet of Pop, plays the role of 'the outsider' in New York, 1984.

John Taylor having the time of his life, 1984

Warren Cuccurullo on stage, 1986.

arrangements, everyone agreed it should be a charity event. Their agent Rob Hallett had worked at a home for mentally handicapped children when he was a teenager and suggested they could do the show in aid of MENCAP. He then approached the charity with the idea and they were delighted, especially as Hallett estimated that the event could raise as much as £80,000. However, the first problem he encountered was booking the support acts, as Culture Club, Eurythmics and the Thompson Twins all said 'no' – they wouldn't support Duran Duran. In the end, Hallett settled for Robert Palmer and Prince Charles and the City Beat Band, but neither were going to pull in many fans and both had to be flown in at great expense from overseas. Worse still, on the day itself only 18,000 people turned up, which was well below expectations. This was pre-Live Aid so the whole concept of a pop band playing an outdoor gig was a bit of a novelty and perhaps their fans just weren't sold on the idea. Hallett realized that the show wasn't going to cover all the costs, let alone make a profit. Duran Duran and their management decided to make a donation of £5,000 to MENCAP but the charity didn't cash it. The next day MENCAP's secretary general appeared on breakfast TV claiming that 'No one knows where the money is.' According to Simon Garfield's *Expensive Habits: The Dark Side of the Music Industry*, MENCAP did accept the accounts were correct twenty months later and as a gesture of good faith Duran Duran made a second, larger donation. Apparently the original cheque for £5,000 is now mounted alongside a photo of Duran Duran in a glass case at MENCAP's head office. What had started out as a homecoming charity event that would please their fans and fill the newspapers with some positive press ended up as a damage-limitation exercise. Andy Taylor was later extremely outspoken in his criticism of Paul and Michael Berrow's handling of the event, which suggests that this was one of the first moments when a spark of discontent ignited between band and management.

Meanwhile, John Taylor must've thought it really wasn't his day when the twenty-three-year-old sports car freak took his beloved Aston Martin for a spin, only for it to break down after travelling all of 400 yards. 'John's classic cars were always breaking down,' laughs Mike Caddick from Swordfish Records. 'There was always something wrong with them, like doors

getting stuck or bits falling off.' When he finally arrived at the
Rum Runner after-show party, the bassist started chatting with
Duran Duran's support act on that day, the suave, power-suited
Robert Palmer. Taylor was a fan of Palmer's *Clues* album and the
pair discussed the idea of working on a project together, which
ended up being The Power Station a year later. The line-up for
Duran Duran's first 'spin-off' band also included Chic's drummer
Tony Thompson, whom John and Andy Taylor had met up with
for a second time in France that summer. Thompson was playing
drums for David Bowie on his *Serious Moonlight* tour and the trio
bonded 'in the toilet', where they talked about collaborating on
an extra-curricular project. The seeds of further division in
Duran Duran had been sown.

Before jetting off to their next destination, Duran Duran were
all over the papers again that weekend. Most of the tabloids now
focused on the relationship between Simon Le Bon and Claire
Stansfield, circulating rumours that the pair were about to
announce their engagement. The headlines were either a bit of a
tease – 'Secrets of Sexy Simon' (*Sunday Mirror*) – or in the case of
the *Sunday People*, effusively romantic, as they declared, 'Prince of
Heart-Throbs – How Duran's Star Found His Own True
Princess'. Back in 1983 the highly visible Le Bon complained, 'We
certainly do not pander to the daily press any more. We know only
too well how they use you. All that stuff before we left England,
with pictures in the papers of rings on fingers. Dear oh dear! It's
silly. It makes it all seem very light when actually it's quite a strong
personal thing.'

Although the original plan was to go to Nassau in the Bahamas
for the next stage in recording, Duran Duran made it clear they
were not setting up their HQ on 'another bloody desert island',
so in August the band decamped to Sydney, Australia. Le Bon
says, 'Oh my God, did we have a good time.' In 1984 he
described his nomadic existence in poetic terms. 'It's like being a
stream of water... you're not vulnerable the way you are when
you have a fixed abode.' John Taylor was more confessional about
his lifestyle, accepting that it was a form of escape from obligation or accountability: 'Being a musician is a great job if you have
intimacy issues – or even issues with responsibility, because you
don't stick around long enough. You're always on the move, so

that constantly gives you excuses not to deal with something.' 'If you go into a city and there's thousands of screaming girls outside your hotel room, life's weird to begin with,' explains a sympathetic Anciano. 'When you're living an extreme life all the time, the fact that your recreation is big doesn't mean anything – because everything is big; every gesture is big. You had big holidays, you had big affairs, you did everything in an extreme way.' John Taylor agrees: 'Have you seen the movie *24 Hour Party People* where the Happy Mondays went to the Bahamas? Sydney was like that.'

Aside from exhausting Sydney's nightlife, Duran Duran recorded and mixed *Seven and The Ragged Tiger* in 301 Studios. One further delay of their own making was that as the songs continued to mutate and morph into different versions, they had to discard many of the original rhythm tracks. It was a frustrating, time-consuming process that tried the patience of the band's temperamental bass player, who was desperate to get the album finished: 'I was sharing an apartment with Alex [Sadkin] and one morning I remember him coming to me saying, "We've changed the chords to a song, you have to play bass on it again." I smashed the shower door because I just wanted the fucking thing finished. That's why I decided to go away and do The Power Station.' 'John does get affected by things,' divulges Denis O'Regan. 'Whereas Simon can control his emotions, John's more intense and at times self-destructive. He can surprise you. You'll be having a conversation and everything will be fine and then suddenly you'll notice that he's growing quietly angry about something. He'll pick up on things you've said and he'll want to know what you meant by it.' To add to the chaos, Duran were also forced to abandon their rooms in the city's top hotels because management objected to herds of teenage girls milling around the entrances day and night. Even on the other side of the world, they had no private life. 'You go to a restaurant and it's in the paper,' grumbled the band's introvert, Roger Taylor, to one visiting British journalist. 'You can't scratch your bum in public.'

John Taylor sounded emotional when he spoke to the UK press from Australia: 'It's like a nightmare at times. We've been here for eleven weeks and that's the longest I've been in one place for three years. I've got a flat in London that I've spent only ten nights in and

I bought a house in the country that I've only been in once.' He also bellyached, 'You can't buy decent clothes in Australia.' Le Bon came across as 'homesick' but philosophical. 'Whatever happens we're an English band and wherever we go, we're waving a Union Jack. People think that internationally we're completely successful, which just isn't true. That's what we're working for. That's why we spend so much time out of England.'

It wasn't just the fragmented lifestyle that was taking its toll, as tensions simmered over the direction of the album. According to the methodical Nick Rhodes, 'I thought the thing was never going to get finished. Everybody was pulling and tugging in different directions. To me, that album, more than any of them, on the surface of it, there's a lot of pretty songs on there but then underneath there's this sort of not quite controllable hysteria.' Rhodes worked fifteen-hour days alongside Alex Sadkin and Ian Little, fine-tuning, polishing, layering and ultimately creating a very detailed, technology-based record: 'I'm the one who was there for every second of everything recorded on that album,' he declared.

Although there's some fine melodic guitar playing on *Seven and the Ragged Tiger*, very little space was left in the mix for Taylor's usual cut-and-thrust. By Rhodes's own admission back in 1983, it was always tough trying to incorporate their contrasting visions into one band. 'It's a hell of a job, it really is. Andy and I are the polar opposites in the band. Basically I am much more abstract and into obscurer artistic things and Andy is much more into rock guitar.' However, he insisted that Duran Duran had got the balance right on the new album: 'Somehow we get on great and things mesh. Andy's guitar playing on the new album is far and away the best work he's done. The guy is actually an astounding guitarist – he can play anything from your blackest rhythm guitar right through to the noisiest heavy metal chords you've ever heard – but what he does on this record is a lot more melody than anything else.' However, the Geordie livewire disagreed: 'It's my least favourite. It took seven or eight months to record, which was just too long. The LP involved a set of compromises; we were too careful. It was like we were saying, "Hey guys, we've made it to the top now, so let's be careful now and not spoil it." The album just went too far in the other direction for me, with less and less guitar and I wasn't too happy about that.' John Taylor also felt that the guitarist had been 'underused'.

New technology played an important role in changing Duran Duran's sound. Nick Rhodes had bought a Fairlight sampler from a factory in Australia, offering him the chance to record noises, stretch them, mix other sounds into them and so on. Given that Rhodes was already keen to create a more sophisticated pop album full of exquisite minutiae and multiple textures, the sampler arrived at a perfect time for him to see through his vision. 'I've had a lot of fun with the Fairlight so far,' he enthused in 1983. 'I've spent days in the studio which I shouldn't have, just playing with it, just merging sounds together, then sequencing them, cutting them off, making them as long as you like. You can get remarkable results from the most ridiculous things. We have this sort of tube in the studio for a vacuum cleaner. Somebody went in there with a drumstick and ran it down this tube. It didn't sound like anything I'd ever heard before.'

As a result, *Seven and the Ragged Tiger* is crammed with instruments and effects, such as the 'thunder' sound in 'New Moon on Monday' which is actually Rhodes tearing up some newspapers. It's intricate stuff and works beautifully on the electronic-based instrumental 'Tiger, Tiger' and moody finale, 'The Seventh Stranger'. There's also a new richness and sophistication to the rhythms. Roger Taylor preferred working with Alex Sadkin, as the pair worked on a more natural sound as opposed to the machine-like, rigid beats of the first two Duran Duran albums. This organic feel is supplemented by percussionists Rafael de Jesus and Mark Kennedy and some funkier playing by John Taylor to create a more exciting, dynamic foundation for the songs. But the album's flaw is a lack of real punch and power. Instead, the more up-tempo tracks such as 'Of Crime and Passion' and 'Shadows on Your Side' sound like musical panic attacks, communicating a sense of clock-watching insomnia, hysteria and a certain red-eyed lunacy. Although arguably a true reflection of what was happening in the band at that stage, this frenzied, chaotic bluster isn't as potent as the simple interchanges on *Rio*.

By autumn 1983, there was no time for further debate. In fact Duran Duran were still mixing the album's first single, 'Union of the Snake', right up until the last minute, leaving themselves only twenty-four hours to write, record and mix one of their best B-sides, the moody electro-carousel of 'Secret Oktober'. The video for 'Union of the Snake' was shot on 35mm film near Sydney, which was another innovation at the time. However, Duran Duran's desire to pioneer new visual styles was sometimes thwarted by the time-consuming size of their operation. In the 'Union of the Snake' video, Simon Le Bon was reinvented as a leather-clad road warrior, scrambling across sand dunes with a red sky behind him *à la Mad Max*. The only trouble was, it was identical to the look that Gary Numan had adopted for his *Warriors* album and single a few weeks earlier. By the time 'Union of the Snake' appeared, the synthesizer star had already graced both *Top of the Pops* and *Smash Hits* in black leathers and bleached hair. Not only that, *Smash Hits* had also published a four-page article showcasing the apocalyptic *Escape From New York*-style stage set Numan had constructed around the image. 'I don't know whether this is true,' says Numan, 'but I've been told that Duran Duran saw the "Warriors" video when they were in Australia and went, "Oh, no," because I'd beaten them to it. But they probably had the idea at the same time as me. I mean, all I had to do was fly my band to a place in Shropshire where they were all measured and fitted up for the leather gear. Then I flew them back and the outfits were delivered in a week, ready for *Top of the Pops*!'

In the 'Union of the Snake' video, Le Bon follows a 'bell-girl' dressed in a scarlet uniform down to a bizarre subterranean world where Nick Rhodes poses with a map and a joker juggles dice. Some of the imagery is redolent of the early-1970s sci-fi movie, *A Boy and His Dog*, where a nuclear holocaust leaves a desolate underground world serviced by androids and people wearing clown makeup. In 'Union of the Snake' there's also a bird-man, parrots and a vampish female. Essentially road-warrior machismo pays a visit to a court of foppish New Romanticism and decides to get the hell out of there. The video is slick, escapist nonsense, but the sense of scale gives an impressive account of Duran Duran's fortunes at this point. It's the stuff of a committed Bowie fan, writ larger than any of his earlier followers had been able to attempt, including Gary Numan. As video-age pioneers (by 1984 *Billboard* magazine estimated that the US music industry spent $60 million on video clips) they even managed to spark off a short-lived controversy when the promo flick was sent to MTV a week before American radio stations received their edit of the single.

Duran Duran might have ruffled a few feathers but 'Union of the Snake' was another massive hit, reaching number three in both America and the UK. Nevertheless, the band's failure to secure the top slot in their home country was interpreted by some critics as a sign that they'd passed their peak. Even the band themselves felt that they'd lost some of their focus and hadn't set the release up properly. 'It was terrible,' said Le Bon in 1984. 'We'd got to the point where we thought we could release a fart and it'd go to number one. We simply rested on our laurels and we were wrong.' To a fickle, young audience back in the UK, Duran Duran were starting to get a bit too big for their boots. Despite the ever supportive Peter Powell broadcasting a Radio 1 special on the band, there was a growing perception that they'd become aloof, arrogant globetrotters and as a result the atmosphere around the release had perceptively altered since the colourful excitement of 'Is There Something I Should Know?' Perhaps it was the song itself too, a slower, bulkier track armed with special effects and lacking the streamlined suss of the *Rio* hits. At the time it didn't feel strong enough to relaunch the band, although 'Union of the Snake' has aged surprisingly well. There's a sense of substance and weight to the track, which in retrospect makes it one of the highlights of *Seven and the Ragged Tiger*.

Meanwhile the final preparations for the worldwide release of the new album included a lavish photo shoot for the album's cover, merchandising and tour programme. The idea centred on using a real tiger but as there weren't any big cats in Sydney, the band flew one in on a private jet from Melbourne. UK-based sleeve designer Malcolm Garrett was also brought to Australia, where he met up with a photographer and assistants, who had just stepped off a flight from America. The Sydney Public Library was chosen as the location for the shoot, which on the day itself was surrounded by Duran Duran's entourage and crew, plus local journalists and TV cameramen and, of course, an audience of fans and passers-by. In the middle of all this hubbub was the poor tiger. When the smoke bombs started going off, the animal was so spooked that the original concept had to be abandoned.

According to the band's quick-witted court jester John Taylor, the tiger 'wasn't into it – I think he must've been a Jam fan'. Oddly enough, this was the second time the band had given up on using a tiger as part of the album's promotion. 'We were going to shoot a promo in the lakes in Kashmir,' says Paul Berrow. 'We got as far as doing scouting for angles and locations there. Russell went, Eric Fellner, myself. We wanted to do it with the Himalayan mountains in the background, all the snow peaks. We were going to build an underwater platform and get this tiger to run right across the lake so that it looked really surreal and Daliesque. It would have been great, really something, but Andy Taylor didn't want to travel or something. He didn't fancy the idea of going to India. They'd had enough of all that.' Rhodes recalls: 'I think our management felt like they had an open chequebook. We used to call Paul Cecil B. De Berrow, because he was always travelling off to exotic locations, but we felt that we'd done all that. The delusions had started.'

In the end, only the eye of the tiger made it into the corner of Malcolm Garrett's caramel-coloured artwork. It's a small detail on a desert map that suggests there's a secret code to be broken, an Indiana Jones-style quest for some hidden meaning. Essentially, it's a visual representation of Le Bon's soul-searching on the album through admittedly ambiguous lyrics. On *Seven and the Ragged Tiger* he seems to be pushed and pulled in hundreds of different directions at once – a gambler in 'I Take the Dice', living according to pure instinct like a child in 'The Reflex', dragged by a passionate undertow in 'Of Crime and Passion' or attempting to escape by changing identity ('The Seventh Stranger'). Superstition, the lunar tides, sex and guilt all take him to alternative places in this 'summer of madness'. Almost every song portrays someone in a manic, slightly deranged state, including 'Union of the Snake' ('there's a fine line drawing my senses together and I think it's about to break'); 'I Take the Dice' ('try to remember again and again what it is that I recognize'); 'Shadows on Your Side' ('with everybody to say that you're having the time of your life when your life is on the slide') and '(I'm Looking for) Cracks in the Pavement' ('if I had a car I'd drive it insane'). He also seems to be on the run, as if haunted by an accusatory past that's about to catch up – 'kill that light, it's so bright and you're shining it in my eyes'; 'you got me coming up with answers all of which I deny'; 'something on my mind breaking open doors I had sealed up before' – and the album's opening line, 'you gone too far this time'. There are 'clouds on your shoulder', 'shadows on your side' and 'the storm is about to blow'. The album's spookiest image is arguably 'bride of wire – how disguise so easily cracked'. No wonder the album ends with a man-with-no-name fantasy of riding off into the sunset, as Le Bon sings, 'I'm changing my name as the sun goes down in the eyes of a stranger.'

On 21 November 1983 *Seven and the Ragged Tiger* became Duran Duran's first number-one album in the UK. It also got as high as number eight in the States, where within months the LP was awarded platinum status, recognizing 1 million sales. *Smash Hits* loved the album: 'The arrangements are water-tight, the melodies are razor-sharp and every number is drenched with the mystique of a James Bond theme. A classy concoction, it should ensure that they'll be around for quite a while yet.' However, most of the reviews were scathing on both sides of the Atlantic, with America's *Trouser Press* assassinating *Seven and the Ragged Tiger* as 'a sorry collection of half-baked melodies, meaningless lyrics and over-active studio foolishness'. *Sounds* magazine went even further: 'I feel pity for Duran Duran. It's as if "Seven and the Rancid Ravings" is so assuredly awful it breaks new ground in badness ... the only true reaction you can have to it is: all those words wasted! All that expense thrown away! *Seven* is more redolent of illness – a nervous disorder of people near to cracking up – than it is of just being an amusingly dreadful recording.'   An eternally optimistic Nick Rhodes argued that 'time will be very kind to our songs' and consoled himself with the knowledge that two of his favourite albums, David Bowie's *Low* and *Berlin* by Lou Reed, had been described as 'an act of purest hatred and destructiveness' and 'a gargantuan slab of maggoty rancour' respectively. Of greater concern was that after fantastic first-week returns in the UK, sales of the LP began to dip a little faster than anticipated. EMI became increasingly concerned when the album's second single, 'New Moon on Monday', stalled at number nine in the UK, although its Top Ten slot in America illustrated that Duran Duran were reaching bigger numbers overseas. Although the track is livened up by a characteristic, sky-scraping Le Bon vocal on the chorus, the production on 'New Moon on Monday' is too ornate to make it a classic Duran Duran single. The video was just as over-elaborate. Despite some beautiful shots of a medieval town in France, all it seemed to illustrate was that the band had more money than sense. A few years later Rhodes admitted, 'That video was really awful. When the director dresses up as the blind man, you know you've got a catastrophe on your hands.' Dave Ambrose at EMI was beginning to worry: 'The budget for *Seven* ... was terrifying and when the first two singles didn't really take off, I started getting very anxious. The sound was different, you see. They'd decided they wanted a different producer and they got Alex Sadkin in. I knew Alex well. He was a real perfectionist and a really good engineer, but he had no clue about songs whatsoever. But it was those days when a great band could have someone like Alex, a kind of producer-engineer, and as long as they kept their heads together, they'd get some great sounds and it would work. But underneath all that there are some insecurities that come out when you've got unlimited budgets. You can end up over-mixing and it can all take a terribly long time.'

CHAPTER SEVEN

John Taylor: *'I'll give you excuses to trash a room. One is that construction work is going on and they didn't tell you. Two is that the curtains do not close properly. And three – because you're a star, baby!'*

Nick Rhodes: *'That's the Chrysler building [in New York]. I'm going to buy that one day.'*

Simon Le Bon: *'John said in an interview that he needs a good cry and a cuddle. Sweet. I don't need that. I was brought up not to cry.'*

Nick Rhodes: *'There are things like "Save a Prayer" that I can play in the middle of World War III with my eyes shut.'*

Slash, Guns N' Roses: *'John Taylor was the quintessential fucking pop star – and he only played bass, so he wasn't too complicated.'*

Simon Le Bon: *'There was supposed to be one hotel in Los Angeles where you could order drugs on room service but we never found it. Try as we might. There was a lot of it around and we were able to handle it, for a while.'*

Duran Duran's *Sing Blue Silver* tour opened at the National Indoor Sports Centre, Canberra, Australia on 12 November 1983, the first of eight shows around the country. These were followed by a sequence of UK shows in December that included two nights at Manchester Apollo, back-to-back concerts at the National Exhibition Centre in Birmingham and five sold-out nights in Wembley Arena. To create a new, classier look for the performances, they hired the set designers who had worked with Roxy Music on their stylish, understated *Manifesto* and *Flesh and Blood* tours. The new configuration included six columns at the back (which on closer inspection were inflatable, making them easy to transport), a barrage of cutting-edge lighting effects and an overhead video screen displaying close-ups of the band. As the cameras zoomed in on John Taylor's grinning face the audience would erupt into deafening screams, ignoring what was happening on stage. Operated by the tour video director, Wendy Childs, the screen became integral to the pacing of the show in a way that had never happened before. In contrast to the sweeter subtleties of the *Seven and the Ragged Tiger* album, Duran Duran were a tougher, heavier prospect live. Roger Taylor: 'The guitar is a lot more upfront. We go for more power and everyone projects a lot. It's basically a rock show. We're not a synthesizer band.' Andy Taylor ranted to the rock magazine, *Kerrang!*: 'A lot of music pisses me off because there's no guitar, which means a lot of the human energy and excitement is lost. We get compared to Depeche Mode – I mean, come on. We don't just drone on, twiddling knobs. I've got to jump around and pull shapes, attack the guitar, not only hear but see the power.' After a year of frustration in the studio, Andy Taylor played like a man possessed, driving the sound with massive, dive-bombing riffs, especially on powerful versions of 'Union of the Snake' and 'Careless Memories'. He was also guilty of the occasional mischievous and unplanned embellishment, confessing: 'Live, I used to tear it up and play things that just weren't on the record. Then I'd get a bollocking in the dressing room afterwards.' 'He gave energy to the show,' says Marcello Anciano of Taylor's splenetic performances on the tour. 'And part of the energy is that he has a lot of anger. And he will find anger in anything and everything.'

The tireless and opportunistic guitarist also found time during the first week of the UK tour to launch his own Rio Restaurant and Wine Bar on Whitley Bay's seafront, near his hometown. His business partner Graham Jenkinson had met Taylor on a boozy night out seven years earlier when the seventeen-year-old AC/DC fan 'was going around boasting that he'd just drunk ten pints'. The pair believed the restaurant was a licence to print money, but the Duran Duran connection turned out to be more of a hassle than anything else. Rio was plagued by young fans ringing up from America and reversing the charges. Jenkinson wasn't too impressed, either, when the band themselves dropped in for a meal. 'They were filming for the kid's TV show *Razzmatazz* up the road in Newcastle and they all came in with their managers and people. There were about fifteen of them. They had their meal and then they didn't pay the bill! I was dead miffed.' Over the next three or four years Jenkinson saw a lot more of Andy's brother Ronnie than his famous business partner and in the end bought him out for £30,000 – only £5,000 more than the original investment.

When the British dates of the UK tour ended in London, on 23 December, John Taylor for one enjoyed a relatively 'normal' Christmas with his girlfriend, ex-Bond girl Janine Andrews. 'I knew Janine before John did and then suddenly she entered their solar system,' says Denis O'Regan of the *Octopussy* actress, who played a member of the all-female cult who live on a floating palace in India where no men are allowed. 'I must admit I was a little horrified because it meant John was off the list for having fun on the tour. Janine came out to see John on some of the dates and they had quite a fiery relationship. When John gets worked up you do know about it, he's very transparent and open. I seem to remember they had a few spectacular blazing rows and hotel rooms were destroyed. They were engaged during the tour but there was one night when John knocked on my door and handed me this £10,000 engagement ring and said, "Can you look after this, she's handed it back to me." ' He adds, 'There would always be tensions when the band's girlfriends were on the road because they were concerned that the boys had been up to something and of course, they'd always deny it.' Bizarrely, although John Taylor and Janine Andrews had met in Australia, they were born three miles from each other in Birmingham. 'We're both very down-to-earth and spend Christmas at each other's mum's and dad's,' he told Neil Tennant of *Smash Hits* magazine. 'The papers go on about my "Page Three Girl" but it's got nothing to do with any jetsetting. It's not like that at all.' Fantasy and mundane reality collided on Christmas Eve 1983. Pop star, Bond girl and Aston Martin sports car flashed through the streets of ... Birmingham to pick up some chicken bhunas from a local curry house. The door of the classic car jammed and they were left on the street holding their meal until some lads from a nearby disco gave them a hand.

On 17 January 1984 Duran Duran played the first of seven

Japanese dates at the Sendai Sports Centre, followed by three nights at the massive, 12,000-capacity Budokan, which was originally built for the 1964 Tokyo Olympics. 'Simon attacked me in Japan,' recalls Denis O'Regan, who was hired as the official photographer on all of the *Sing Blue Silver* dates. 'He'd drunk a bottle of tequila – I think he's only drunk it once since and the same thing happened – and it was just after a minor earthquake, so I went up to his room to see what everyone was doing. And he just attacked me. I'm six foot but Simon's bigger than me and we're knocking over the TV set, furniture is sent flying and we fell through the unopened door of a private suite. The occupants weren't impressed. Then it all faded away, but I felt all this pent-up anger inside me and I thought I heard someone saying "shut up" and complaining about the noise. So I kicked their door down and it was these poor Japanese people inside who didn't have a clue what was going on. Later Simon apologized and Andy rang me up to say that the band were paying for the damage. I've never seen Simon like that before or since. He doesn't explode when he's angry, he's quite controlled, but the hysteria around them was unrelenting. The band were being chased around the whole time. In Japan it was very odd because there would be girls running after their limo and hundreds around the stage door, yet inside the venue all the security guards had to do was stand in front holding a tape. No one crossed that line during the concert.'

Duran Duran were also surrounded by fans on their North American tour, which commenced at the end of January. According to the waifish, bottle-blond Nick Rhodes, 'When we weren't on stage we had to hole up in the hotel and couldn't go out. Sure, it was a golden cage but still a cage. There were always hundreds and hundreds of people outside the hotel, and we had to go through the kitchens to get away. I can say that I am very familiar with the kitchens of all the world's hotels.' Another favoured escape route was through underground car parks. In New York, where they were staying at the Berkshire Place Hotel, fans outside staged a vigil, screaming and singing until four in the morning, which understandably upset the other guests. The surrounding streets had to be blocked off from traffic and barriers were also erected outside the hotel. This meant that the other guests had to prove they were staying there in order to get past the hastily arranged 'checkpoint'. Not surprisingly, Duran Duran were not welcome everywhere, especially in luxurious hotels with lots of residential clients.

Over the years the band's fans have come up with some inventive ways of getting closer to their idols, such as hiding under tables or locking themselves in a wardrobe backstage until the band arrived. One girl successfully negotiated her way to their dressing room by disguising herself as a medic. Duran Duran have also provoked strange, extreme behaviour such as a piqued, upset obsessive peeing on the floor at an after-show party because John Taylor wouldn't speak to her. More seriously, on one occasion in Paris a girl pulled out a knife and handed it to Nick Rhodes because she wanted him to stab her in the heart. He gave her back the blade and left quickly. Worryingly for the band, emotional and uncontrollable girls used to jump in front of their limousines, risking life and limb as panicked drivers sometimes instinctively put their foot down on the accelerator. Meanwhile, Simon Le Bon has received gifts that range from teddy bears to poems and X-rated polaroids, but the strangest object that he's had thrown at him while on stage was a beautiful, 'glittery' thing that arced towards him 'flashing in the light'. Le Bon thought about catching it but decided to duck at the last moment. 'So I moved my head out of the way, the thing whizzed past and landed on the stage near the drum kit. And at the end of the song, I turned around to go and have a look and see what it was. And it was a fucking hunting knife that somebody threw at me. Amazing. I've still got it at home.'

The wall of noise and hysteria that surrounded Duran Duran and at times imprisoned them also gave the impression that the band were more successful than they actually were. 'To get to the really massive volumes you have to have ongoing sales right across America,' explains Michael Berrow. 'But all the makeup and New Romantic thing was off-putting for a lot of people in the States. They were like, "Hell, I'll be damned if I'm going to buy into that!" ' Although their record sales were never in the same league as, say, those of Madonna or U2, Duran did compete with the world's biggest acts in generating revenue from other areas. As Dave Rimmer writes in *Like Punk Never Happened*, 'True fans don't just buy records and concert tickets. They buy videos, posters, watches, badges, T-shirts, scarves, tour programmes, fan club specials, bags, books, magazines, board games, dolls and indeed just about anything that the merchandising minds can dream up.' 'Duran were breaking house records in 1984,' recalls Michael Berrow. 'I seem to remember at the LA Forum in 1984, we did over a million dollars in merchandising on each night.' 'I went backstage on the US *Sing Blue Silver* tour and there were suitcases of cash,' reveals Marcello Anciano. 'No one really knew what kind of scale of revenue merchandising could bring in and Duran were one of the bands who led the way with that. I think the only other people who were doing that level of business were the Rolling Stones.' The band's franchise was not only incredibly lucrative, but it also took on a slightly surreal quality as they developed it to include collapsible Japanese opera glasses, phone cards and even Duran Duran batteries.

They may not have been eyeball-to-eyeball with some of their rivals in terms of album sales but the ambitious synthesizer-rockers played to an impressive 554,000 people on the North American stage of their *Sing Blue Silver* tour. Opening in Calgary, Canada, on 30 January 1984, over the next seventy-nine days they performed fifty-one gigs and travelled 18,000 miles, many of them in their private Viscount aeroplane. 'It was a bit "bling",' laughs Rob Hallett. 'I wouldn't say it's the norm but logistically it was a lot easier. You could get the band on to the next destination that night without having to go back to a hotel and try to wake them up the next morning.' They also travelled short distances in a convoy of limousines, an image which is strikingly portrayed in their *Sing Blue Silver* documentary film. As the long black cars ghost across wide open plains and through the neon streets of cities at night, the scenes are a cool flashback to the smoked-glass glamour of the David Bowie documentary, *Cracked Actor*, screened by the BBC in 1974. David Buckley writes in his Bowie biography, *Strange Fascination*, that the 1970s film 'contains images as haunting and mesmeric as any David Bowie song'. Duran Duran, as ever, were assembling and playing around with visual ideas as much as musical ones.

That said, the tone of *Sing Blue Silver* is very different. While Bowie was a gaunt, skeletal figure rendered paranoid by cocaine,

Duran Duran were on an adrenaline-charged 'voyage of discovery', playing to new audiences in arenas across America. They threw themselves into the shows, filling every inch of the stage – Andy Taylor whirled around in tight spins, throwing 'shapes' in a fetching red kimono as he thrashed the life out of his guitars; a tousle-haired John Taylor alternated between enigmatic smiles from the back of the stage and sprints to the front wearing the full-bodied, Cheshire cat grin of a 'dedicated good-timer' (*San Diego Union-Tribune*); although Simon Le Bon lacked the natural predatory magnetism of Jim Morrison or INXS's Michael Hutchence, he played up to his audience and had enough power to have fun with it; Roger Taylor provided a very powerful, solid platform for the sound and still looked like a rebel film star, while Nick Rhodes camped up the Eno comparisons by posing in a bizarre, Spanish matador-type outfit in front of a work station consisting of various synthesizers and a 'futuristic' computer monitor.

Meanwhile, the perception of Duran Duran as an all-conquering British export was strengthened when they appeared on the cover of *Rolling Stone* magazine under the headline 'The Fab Five?' This was quite a coup as *Rolling Stone* has a long-standing reputation as a serious and influential US publication, famous for its maverick rock writers Hunter S. Thompson and Lester Bangs. Unfortunately the writer James Henke concentrated his piece on the moment when Simon Le Bon sneezed and the buttons popped off his black, silver-studded trousers. As a result the singer is caught in his underpants, prompting Henke to observe: 'It was not, frankly, a particularly awe-inspiring sight, not a slob, just chubby legs, a little bit of gut.' He also disclosed that Le Bon's bandmates used to call him Lardo and that his 'tortured singing and klutz dancing were at times an embarrassment ... halfway through he stopped dancing and raced over to the side of the stage for assistance – the buttons had popped again'.

Nevertheless, they had made it on to the front of *Rolling Stone* and they had the cover-star egos to go with it. 'Duran Duran were huge in 1984 and that was starting to really change them,' says Denis O'Regan. 'It's difficult on a big tour, as there are various pressures and distractions. They were making loads of money and it did go to their heads. A band becomes strange on tour. They can think the world revolves around them because when they're on tour it really does. They all loved hotels and they were spending an absolute fortune. Nick in particular just loves hotels. The fact that he's being waited on and that he's at a spot in the city where everyone will come to him. He was very happy to hold court in his suite and he'd work up these huge room service bills. Of course, he'd have to have Cristal champagne and hotels always overcharge for everything. I remember a famous discussion between Nick and John about who had the biggest hotel bill, and it was something like £40,000 – and this is twenty-odd years ago. Andy Taylor loves hotels too. He's a bit of a nomad, a gypsy in his existence. He doesn't seem to need a base. I think he would like to live in a hotel the whole time.' 'I remember regularly paying hotel bills of £20,000–£30,000 for a weekend,' confirms Michael Berrow. 'They probably had a couple of rooms each. Nick always had at least two rooms, although he'd sometimes take over the whole floor. But it's very difficult to talk financial sense in that kind of atmosphere. Everywhere we went, you had to shut the door to stop the screams. Duran Duran always packed a big punch. They were big in everything they did and there was literally this huge noise around them all the time. It's hard to explain what that's actually like.'

Some of the personalities in the band were exaggerated to almost cartoonish proportions by this over-indulgence. Andy Taylor's rock'n'roll instincts ripened on tour. 'He's one of the few old party monsters that we still have left,' says Marcello Anciano of the five-foot-seven-inch guitarist, who was still rakishly skinny with the physique of a jump jockey back in 1984. The avuncular video collaborator remembers Taylor getting 'hammered' in a New York hotel with the Rolling Stones' rock gargoyle Keith Richards. Anciano claims that 'Richards turned around to Andy and said, "I've got to go to bed, I can't take any more." Andy is unique. You need these kind of rock'n'rollers.' Yet, for all his excesses, Andy Taylor was always very professional on tour. 'Andy can drink, he can take drugs and he'll drink you under the table,' says Then Jerico's Mark Shaw, who worked with him in the 1990s. 'But he's always up in the morning. He's always had this work ethic which gets him through. You'd be absolutely plastered with him and then the next morning he'd be up. He's got a phenomenal constitution, like a rhinoceros.' He was also the tour's resident court jester, as Denis O'Regan recalls: 'I seem to remember it was at Andy's instigation that the two of us climbed over adjoining hotel balconies and strolled through John's room while he was "entertaining" a friend.'

Andy Taylor was beginning to style himself a little differently to the other band members. His hair was a dead ringer for a Davy Crockett hat and increasingly he hid his bloodshot eyes behind shades, as his ghostly white visage told a story of another night without sleep. 'The thing is with Andy, he's got such a bad image of himself,' says Shaw, who is best known for the 1989 Then Jerico hit 'Big Area'. 'He doesn't think he's a pretty lad, so his thing is not to smile in pictures because he doesn't like his teeth. And he doesn't like his eyes, which is why he always wears shades all the time. I walked into his room once and he was in bed with shades on. He doesn't like shopping either. He's very comfortable in his long black leather coat and that will do fine for him. I've seen him standing around at home in his coat and slippers, just kind of ruminating ...'

At the other end of the spectrum, Nick Rhodes was threatening to complete a transformation from androgynous weirdo into a cross between Sue Ellen from *Dallas* and *Dynasty*'s Krystle Carrington – big hair, pink lipstick and a slightly vacant, other-worldly expression which was apparently due to Asian flu. Perhaps not surprisingly, many Americans assumed that this anaemic-looking, slightly built, borderline drag queen was gay. In 1984 Rhodes asserted in his slightly camp, tranquillized voice, 'I never minded being thought of as homosexual. I'm sure a lot of people still think I am. I never thought things like that mattered. It's like, why? But no, I've never shagged a man. When we get to the Midwest and I'm standing next to a few truck drivers discussing life, things can get interesting. But I have always believed in indi-vidualism and I believe that you should always stick your neck out, because it's always worth it.'

The idiosyncratic twenty-one-year-old was joined by his tall, dark-haired girlfriend Julie Anne on several dates of the US tour. 'Julie Anne was a lot more worldly-wise than he was,' affirms O'Regan. 'She did come on tour for a bit but to be honest, I don't think Nick had much choice in the matter.' According to the newspapers, Julie Anne's parents weren't happy when she told them of her plans to go on the road with Duran Duran. However, they apparently changed their minds after spending some time with Rhodes. 'We found him to be hard-working, goal-directed and talented,' declared her father, Bill Friedman. Rhodes had several key obsessions on the tour, especially the look of the stage set and the band's overall visual presentation. 'I'm horribly particular about colours,' he divulged. 'The arguments I've had with lighting designers about shades of magenta ...' The son of a toy shop owner also developed a habit-forming interest in the video games *Galaga* and *Asteroid*, which he played before every show (Rhodes's enthusiasm for *Space Invaders* dates back to hours spent on a machine at the Rum Runner). As an equally solitary pursuit, the self-styled arty voyeur started assembling a collection of abstract-looking polaroids which were actually pictures of flickering, random images on American TV sets. He was initially inspired when watching television in his hotel room during the tour and 'all of a sudden the picture became distorted and all these strange shapes appeared. I pulled out my camera and photographed it. The result was really fascinating.' After that he'd deliberately play around with the controls until he created 'a beautiful or odd shape'. The immediacy of polaroid film was also an important part of Andy Warhol's aesthetic and his cultural guru often took pictures of the famous people who came to meet him, including some of Duran Duran. By 1984 the pair were spending quite a lot of time together, with Denis O'Regan coming across them quite by chance in New York's One Fifth Bar in New York. 'The thing that struck me was how much alike they looked,' says O'Regan. 'Nick set out to be what he has become. He loves that lifestyle, maybe more than the music. He's met the people he wanted to meet. He's non-stop, he's always out there, he doesn't hide away in a corner and I find it amazing that he's got so much time for everyone. He is hugely knowledgeable in that "arty" area and people really like him, they find him to be very good company.' The porcelain-like, Max Factored keyboard player often featured in Andy Warhol's dairies, with the artist noting a few months earlier, in August 1983: 'Nick Rhodes of Duran Duran came to the office and he brought his girlfriend, Julie Anne. He's twenty and she's twenty-three. He was wearing twice as much makeup as she was, although he's half as tall.' Warhol later mischievously told one reporter that his feelings for Rhodes went beyond the norm. 'I love him, I worship him. I masturbate to Duran Duran videos.'

As for Simon Le Bon, in 1984 he was a fun-loving Elvis looka-like with a long, bleached, spiky Sting haircut. Although his face doesn't have the vivid, sculptured lines of a young Elvis, he was skinny enough on the US tour to suggest he could have been a pouting English cousin. Buoyed up by the realization that this was Duran Duran's 'moment', the twenty-five-year-old grasped it by giving some of his career best performances, matching even Andy Taylor's frenetic energy levels. Off stage, Rob Hallett describes him as 'a big kid. Everything was happy and jolly at all times with Simon. Duran Duran were at their peak and he loved every second of it.'

Yet the singer was also a great moderator and diplomat while the band were on tour. 'Some people were starting to get fucked-up,' says Marcello Anciano. 'The excesses were too much, but they were not willing to give up that lifestyle. Simon held it together. He can be a great diplomat when he wants to be. If someone walked out of a meeting, he would continue that meeting and then work out how he would call back the other band members.' 'Simon was the moderating influence in the band. He's a lot calmer than John or Andy,' reckons Denis O'Regan. 'Nick is calm but he's more confrontational. He's less willing to accept someone else's point of view or in pacifying another person. Simon's the one who would see more than one side of an argument.'

According to John Taylor, who was living on the edge of his nerves throughout the tour, 'The difference between me and Simon is that he dives into the rock'n'roll business pool, swims about, gets out, dries off and goes away, and I can't. I'm like a twenty-four-hour breakdown. Simon is like this free spirit who runs around, but I need other people to help me function properly.' The delicate-featured, foppishly fringed twenty-three-year-old was a charming but vulnerable character during the American trip. He lived for being the bass player in Duran Duran and would freak out if a string broke and knocked him off his groove. But off stage he was just as intense – a quiet, scarred pop cavalier who dealt with his shyness and insecurities by transforming himself into a simple rock'n'roll hedonist: 'Cocaine was literally given to me on a plate every day,' he confessed years later. 'I was able to be this pin-up guy twenty-four hours a day. Especially useful after midnight.' 'John's an emotional, sensitive guy,' says one of his closest friends at the time, Rob Hallett. 'People were aware that he was doing a lot of coke, maybe too much, and everyone was saying to him, "Hey, John, you should slow down a bit." Marcello Anciano asserts, 'John is such a nice guy, he really is, but he did have problems. He was getting into drugs really heavily. He seemed troubled. There's this self-destructive streak in him and the drugs were part of that. It was like he was saying to himself, "I can't be having a good thing, so therefore I'm going to fuck it up somehow." ' Accounts of John Taylor's self-destructive behaviour on the tour include kicking in a TV set and being taken to hospital after punching a lightbulb. The bassist himself confessed to *Smash Hits*, 'In San Francisco I did my foot in. I got twenty stitches from dancing on broken vodka bottles. I had to go to hospital and have seven injections. It gives you an awful feeling. It's like your body leaves you and you have to keep breathing deeply to stay OK. I felt as if my soul was pinned to the ceiling. It's the worst I've ever been.' Apparently this incident occurred after an argument between John Taylor and his fiancée Janine Andrews, although friends insist they don't believe that he then performed a self-mutilating jig on the shattered glass and argue that it was more likely he cut his foot open as he ran to comfort his girlfriend. However, Duran Duran's manager Paul Berrow does accept that it wasn't an isolated event and that the volatile, brooding pop star was showing signs of finding it 'extremely hard to adjust to being a global icon – understandably, as it does take a bit of getting used to. But he knew that Michael and I were ruthlessly intolerant of anything that would threaten the integrity of the band. Apart from that one time with Simon on the first album, John was the only other band member that we had to sit down and talk to. We sat down as a team and he responded very professionally.'

'This is typical John Taylor at the time,' suggests Marcello Anciano. 'They had a big deal with Coca-Cola to sponsor the tour and the band went to the head office in Atlanta. John got up on stage and said, "I prefer Pepsi myself." It was gob-smackingly like,

"What the fuck are you trying to do, John?" ' Michael Berrow recalls: 'Coca-Cola put in $2 million to sponsor the US tour and there were competition winners there and about 3,000 employees. After John said that, the whole place went completely silent. I don't think you were allowed to say the words Pepsi-Cola in the building, let alone announce them on stage! You could've heard a pin drop. I don't think John knew what he'd done. He's got that kind of sense of humour and the air he was breathing was pretty heady at the time.'

The one band member who seemed unchanged was Roger Taylor. In fact, even his mother Jean told one magazine, 'He hasn't changed that much. He is still very placid.' Nevertheless his experiences with Duran Duran had transformed him from 'the quiet one who sat in the back of the class who nobody really noticed' into an international pop star. This had probably saved him from his own conservative nature, and by his own admission his lifestyle was the 'opposite of what everyone expected of me'. He was also drawn to the other members of the band because they were all outgoing characters who were capable of taking him out of his natural self-absorption. In fact Froggie (he was given the nickname after a scuba-diving holiday in the Caribbean with John Taylor) often broke through his shy manner with dry, tell-it-as-it-is humour. He certainly wasn't ignored by the rest of the band, with Nick Rhodes recently declaring, 'When Roger said something it was listened to. He has always considered things carefully. He's very measured. He'd make a great poker player.' However, although the charisma of his bandmates had the added bonus of drawing attention away from him in the media, by 1984 the band's success had reached a level where he no longer felt comfortable. 'I'm not that happy with being a public figure,' he confessed to *Modern Drummer* later that year. Their rootless travelogue – from the south of France to Montserrat and then Australia, followed by a world tour – was unsettling and he had the added burden of being considered by the rest of Duran Duran as 'the rock'. So far, he'd successfully kept all dark thoughts at bay and remained supportive of the others, but this also meant that he didn't really have a way of dealing with his own accumulated angers and frustrations.

For the moment Roger Taylor's emotions remained under the

surface and Duran Duran continued on their journey across America. On 28 February, they were awarded two Grammys, for Best Short Video (for the 'Girls on Film', 'Hungry Like the Wolf', video 45) and Best Video Album (for the *Duran Duran* video album). However, the band weren't there to receive the awards as they were already committed to performing in Pittsburgh.

On 14 March, Le Bon challenged Andy Taylor's status as the band's practical joker by faking a dislocated elbow and completely fooling band, crew and management at Worcester Centrum in Massachusetts. Five days later, Duran Duran reached the zenith of the tour when they achieved their dream of performing at Madison Square Garden in New York. Not only that, but the 20,000 tickets for the first night sold out within three hours, and by the night of the second show, that too was crammed to capacity. Andy Taylor babbled with enthusiasm in the bright lights of Manhattan, informing *Melody Maker*'s Steve Sutherland that 'It's the dream you have when you're a kid. I think it's the most prestigious gig in the world – everyone's played there who's ever existed. It's brilliant,' he exclaimed, his mind whirling as he reeled off a list of celebrities the band had been ligging with since their arrival in the 'Big Apple'. They included Carly Simon, Liza Minnelli ('we sang her happy birthday and she started crying and hugged us all'), Ronnie Wood ('he knows all our names. I mean, imagine!'), Eddie Murphy and Al Pacino. As for the show itself, Sutherland writes, 'The screaming's so loud, I'm suffering vertigo, my hearing's impaired and my balance is going. It's a cliché, of course, but over here everything is bigger if not better, screaming included. The show itself is bolder than ever, tanked up and tuned to the audience's taste ... If Madison proved one thing, though, it's that Duran are now unashamedly an American band working to American standards. I can't see the British love affair lasting at this rate. This over-the-top stuff doesn't pass for fun where I come from, it passes for insecurity. Still the show, as a show, is stunning.'

The following day Sutherland visited Andy Taylor's room at 4.30 p.m. to discover that the pasty-faced guitarist had only just woken up. In the detritus of the night before, Taylor 'picks up a bottle of Jack Daniel's with about a quarter-inch of fetid liquid in the bottom, makes to raise it to his lips, thinks better of it and sets about opening a beer instead'. Sutherland pursued an increasingly disgruntled line of questioning about Duran Duran's Stateside showmanship, but Taylor remained unabashed: 'People like stars in America. It's the American way. Everyone's a star in LA, you know. Spandau Ballet aren't playing Madison Square Garden. We are.'

The final US dates included two nights in Oakland, California, where Russell Mulcahy filmed the concert sequences for Duran Duran's own movie *Arena* and the tour ended at San Diego Sports Arena, California. Andy Taylor, for one, was desperate to get home to his seven-months-pregnant wife, whom he hadn't seen in five weeks, but he had an unexpected shock at British customs on his arrival. The exhausted, emotional guitarist was strip-searched as Tracey was forced to wait outside: 'These guys told me to take my clothes off and they body-searched me for drugs. It was horrific. I was standing there with nothing on and I didn't know if they were gay or not or if they were getting some kick out of it. They looked everywhere – and I mean everywhere. They said, "Bend over. Have you got anything up there?" God, I hated it. I just felt sick.' By the time he'd got through customs, Tracey had gone back to their flat in London with Roger Taylor and his wife Giovanna. 'They were all petrified,' he explained. 'They thought I'd been busted.' The next day Tracey and Taylor drove back to their farm in Shropshire: 'I've never been so pleased to get home in my life. It wasn't just being arrested, it was the whole strain of being on the road. Staying in hotel rooms away from the woman I loved. We went straight upstairs and made love. It was wonderful. And little things mean so much – like getting into your own bed, having your own slippers and things. And I could wear old comfy clothes that I couldn't wear in public. I thought if that's what being a rock'n'roll star is really all about, you can keep it, Jack.'

Duran Duran had just finished the tour as 'The Reflex' hit the shops on 16 April 1984. It shot to number one on both sides of the Atlantic, giving them their biggest hit so far. The song's huge, exuberant chorus expressed Duran Duran's original sense of live-in-the-moment optimism and revitalized the *Seven and The Ragged Tiger* album, driving sales a full five months after release. The single version of 'The Reflex' is actually a remix by Chic impresario Nile Rodgers, whom Duran Duran had approached after they'd heard his production on the INXS track, 'The Original Sin'. He opened the song up with some great hooks that were half-buried in the frenzied original. Rodgers recalls, 'I got the track and listened to it and I picked up on this obvious little hook thing, "tra-la-la-la, tra-la la la". I went, "Wow, that's the record, I could make a loop out of that." And then I came up with the "Fle-fle-fle". I sent it to the guys; they loved it, they thought it was fantastic. After I'd sent it to them they called me from the tour bus. I still remember the sorrow in Nick Rhodes's voice: "Nile, we've submitted it to the record company and they hate it, they said you've made us sound too black." Anyway, the guys fought for it, they released it and it shot to number one.' 'That's true,' said Rhodes recently of the band's stubborn determination to get the remix released. 'Capitol really didn't want to put it out, but we all dug in our heels.'

Rodgers's revamped, bubblegum classic had a huge impact on Duran Duran's career, but he did come in for some criticism for working with a so-called 'Thatcherite' pop band. He retorted in *Everybody Dance*, 'Musicians have always made lots of money. Talking about it in a cynical way is what Chic used to do all the time. I can work with anybody with a great sense of humour. Duran are working-class guys, from places like Newcastle and the Midlands. If these guys didn't make it as rock stars, what would they be doing? These are guys who got a break and were crucified for their success. If I'd never worked with them, I could still appreciate where they are coming from. I liken it to a lot of what Chic was trying to do.'

As Duran Duran celebrated, *The Sun* ran a two-part exposé of the band's fondness for cocaine. It was only a matter of time before the story broke, especially after an intoxicated, rambling, saucer-eyed John Taylor famously appeared on kids' TV with DJ Mike Reid a few months earlier. 'A guy who used to work at the Rum Runner spilled the beans on the whole coke thing,' remembers Bob Lamb. 'It was no big deal, really, but it was great for the newspapers. He told me beforehand what he was going to do and I think he figured that it wasn't going to do Duran Duran any harm.' Quite the opposite, in fact, as according to Nick Rhodes what actually happened was that sales of 'The Reflex' were starting to drop off, 'but after the drug story broke they picked up again and the single went back up the chart'. The only people who were upset by the drug revelations were the band's families. 'There are a lot of people who don't talk to them now and some who've started talking to them because of us,' said Rhodes in 1985. 'When they walk around the corner to get a Sunday roast, somebody always says [he affects a crabby tone], "We hear your son takes cocaine." '

CHAPTER EIGHT

Simon Le Bon: *'I love denim but Nick would kill me if I wore it on stage.'*

Nick Rhodes: *'Pretentious? I should jolly well think so.'*

Roger Taylor: *'I am a worrier, I want to please everyone all the time, I guess.'*

Nick Rhodes: *'We all said, "Thank God it's not called 'Octopussy'"'* and wrote this song.'

Nick Rhodes: *'I would have loved to have lived when they used to wear those hideous things that came to the knee and the big socks and painted beauty marks.'*

John Taylor: *'Fame was like walking into a very loud and noisy room, and staying there for five years.'*

Buoyed up by the success of 'The Reflex', Duran Duran and Nile Rodgers hooked up again, this time working side by side in the studio for the first time. According to Roger Taylor, the band had discussed the idea of the Chic maestro producing their next album and wanted to give him a trial run. By the end of the session Rodgers was declaring, 'It's a marriage made in musical heaven.' In stark contrast to the slow progress of *Seven and the Ragged Tiger*, the ideas for 'The Wild Boys' came together very quickly. 'It happened in ten minutes,' grinned Andy Taylor during a filmed interview for the *Arena* project. 'Nick turned on his sequencer and we were off. It was all very spontaneous.' Once the band had delivered the original idea, Rodgers fattened it up into a heavy, funky, special-effects extravaganza. John Taylor declared,

'It is the best thing we have ever done. We are getting more meaty. We are moving towards a rougher sound.' 'We have changed a lot,' concluded Andy with a satisfied grin, his eyes hidden behind Ray Bans. 'We wanted to be more abrasive. "Wild Boys" is the first song we have recorded that has captured the energy and power we have live. I think we have found the right format that works for this band.'

No doubt influenced by Frankie Goes to Hollywood's 'Relax', which was a number-one single at the end of 1983, 'The Wild Boys' works because it's full of flashy, almost gimmicky samples, but they're bolted into a very solid rock track. The song's metal-like structure can carry the technology with ease, as opposed to the quirky, over-complicated trickery on the poppier *Seven and the Ragged Tiger*. 'The Wild Boys' also features one of Simon Le Bon's bravest vocals. The whole song is pitched at a level where he's straining for every note, and who can forget the 'wild boys always … shine' kiss-off at the end of the chorus. It's theatrical, over-the-top stuff which demanded an equally ambitious video to go with it. In fact, this truculently aggressive composition is the only song Duran Duran have written specifically for the accompanying visuals. Russell Mulcahy had acquired the rights to the William Burroughs story *The Wild Boys*, and wrote a treatment for a feature film based on the book. Duran Duran recorded the song to go with the movie and planned the video as a 'taster' for the project. However, like so many phantom Hollywood blockbusters, the movie never went into production. 'Russell would never have got it made,' explains the director's writing partner, Marcello Anciano. 'It's a real homoerotic, alternative kind of book. I showed the treatment to Simon and then he wrote "The Wild Boys" based upon the ideas from the treatment and the notion of the Burroughs book. He hadn't actually read it at that time. To be honest, I don't know what he would have made of it! Then he wrote the song and Russell did the video based on all the ideas for the film. He shoved them all into a five-minute clip.' As a result, 'The Wild Boys' is a big-budget mini-film rather than a standard promo flick. Not only that, but the only way this sci-fi epic could be financed by Duran Duran was as part of their own bigger project: the concert movie *Arena*, which they worked on in tandem with 'The Wild Boys' during a ten-day shoot at Shepperton Studios, not far from

London. The band themselves were gob-smacked by the scale of the set. Le Bon recalls, 'I remember standing in the enormous studio and there were about twenty guys about to jump off trampolines and come out of the walls!' One of the ideas that Mulcahy and the band were keen to explore was the concept of a performance conducted while 'under threat' and, as a result, the set designers built a torture-windmill that Le Bon was strapped on to as he sang the track. When the blade of this bondage machine wheeled around, the intrepid front man was periodically dunked in freezing cold water. Unfortunately, at one point, the mechanism jammed and he was left under water for a few minutes, during which time he was only able to breathe through a straw. Given the number of people around, it wasn't a life-threatening situation, but it's to his credit that he didn't panic and make the situation far more serious. As for the other members of the band, John Taylor was tied up, Messiah-like, on a derelict car; Andy Taylor found himself hoisted up on a strap and left dangling as he fought off various bizarre, fantasy creatures with his guitar; while Roger Taylor flew around in a James Bond-style jet-pack. Nick Rhodes had the least physically adventurous role and is merely caged with his keyboards, wearing a jacket that he'd made for himself after rejecting the one he was originally given. John Taylor had also made a minor adjustment to his costume, adding a red silk sash, as he wanted to 'soften' the band's new, overtly macho look. As the various band members played out their roles, Mulcahy orchestrated images of school desks being blown in a dust-storm, scavenging 'wild boys' somersaulting through the air while carrying torches and geyser-like blasts of flame shooting up as if the whole place was about to blow.

It's intriguing to speculate as to what would have happened to Duran Duran if they'd pushed on ahead and recorded a new album that year with Nile Rodgers. Like Trevor Horn, who came up with another Frankie Goes to Hollywood corker, 'Two Tribes', in June 1984, they were pushing the technology of the time while retaining a rock edge. 'The Wild Boys' is bright, chunky, futuristic and rhythmic, seemingly satisfying both sides of the camp – Rhodes and Andy Taylor – and all points between. However, a new album was never on the agenda. Not only had they got to shoot the video, but the schedule demanded that they finish filming the *Arena* project.

As Nick Rhodes put it: 'Everyone was on good terms. Everyone was pleased with "The Wild Boys", but then we did a film of the tour, which was the last thing in the world we wanted to do, and ended up hating it.'

Director Russell Mulcahy had already captured the band on stage at the dome-shaped stadium in Oakland on the US tour. In fact the building's circular rim of windows allowed them to shoot footage through the glass from a helicopter. More live material was later filmed at a specially arranged 'freebie' show in the Birmingham National Exhibition Centre, where tickets were given away through various newspapers. In addition to the conventional rock concert element, Mulcahy wanted to spice up the visual side, constructing a fantasy set for 'conceptual' scenes, which were then linked together to create a bizarre storyline while the band performed on stage. Some of these world-within-a-world, alternative scenes took place around a pyramid, described by Le Bon as an 'overgrown Zumarian temple with chrome robots having erotic encounters by a pool of fluorescent green water. There's also a fluorescent Rollerball game with *Mad Max*-style outfits in which everybody pulls off each other's clothes. Like the "Girls on Film" video, it uses the idea of an erotic joke with a stylized violence.' Although the singer boasted to *Smash Hits* that it was going to be 'the greatest live video ever seen', *Arena* falls well short of that. The visuals switch from concert to a 'sub-plot' involving the original character Durand Durand from the *Barbarella* movie (once again played by Milo O'Shea), attempting to take his revenge on the band for stealing his name. However, this back-and-forth technique kills any sense of 'live' atmosphere and the final product is mostly an unwatchable folly, as misconceived as Michael Jackson's 1988 fantasy *Moonwalker* or Prince's *Under the Cherry Moon*.

Not only were they disappointed with the final outcome of *Arena*, some of the band members were becoming concerned about the cost of these lavish projects (they'd spent around £1 million in total on 'The Wild Boys' and *Arena*). Although Paul Berrow insists that they recouped all of the money through TV rights, it was a jaw-droppingly large project for a band to take on. It wasn't just the massive sets, but *Arena* also utilized dancers, choreographers, stuntmen, actors, extras, a full film crew and accountants and lawyers who were needed to budget and control it all. At the centre of all this organization was Tritec Music. Housed in a swish office in Soho, which by Paul Berrow's admission was 'a symbol of how well we were doing', by 1984 Tritec employed over thirty people, including publishing managers, a merchandising team, roadies, an accounts department and the people running the fan club. As a result, the sums of money now being made and spent in Duran Duran's name ran into millions, which started to concern Nick Rhodes and Andy Taylor – the control-freak and the wary worrier. 'Andy's a deeply intelligent man, but he didn't go to school very much,' says Mark Shaw. 'So that makes him very, very sensitive and he always thinks someone is trying to rip him off.' A naturally explosive character, Andy Taylor was fired up against the business structure that had grown around Duran Duran. He needed to escape and, as it happened, he'd already been handed the keys to the getaway car.

'Let me see, one day we were recording "Wild Boys" with Nile,' recalled the guitarist over a decade later. 'Then we had a day off and John and I went in the studio with Tony Thompson and Bernard Edwards to do the rough tapes for The Power Station's "Get It On" – then there was some time off. Then more work on The Power Station in between doing promotional work for Duran Duran. We were whizzing about all the time and I was literally living out of a suitcase.' Although it didn't have a name at the time, John and Andy Taylor's side-project, The Power Station, had become a reality almost immediately after the end of the *Sing Blue Silver* tour. Frustrated by the amount of time *Seven and the Ragged Tiger* had taken, and disappointed by its synthesizer-domi-nated sound, the pair had vaguely discussed the idea of collaborating on a more aggressive, funk-rock project during their Sydney, Australia, sojourn back in 1983. Even the heavier 'The Wild Boys' hadn't satiated their appetite, as effectively that had already stalled as a 'one-off' and, in any case, the single was being launched with the kind of budget normally associated with a new Michael Jackson album. 'Andy and I had finished our third album,' explained John Taylor in *Everybody Dance*. 'It was a bitch and we were out there wrestling with our lives. It was like being on a really out-of-control racehorse, whereas we had been used to being on the donkeys at Paignton. We decided we weren't being heard, so we wanted to do a side-project as soon as we got the touring done. We didn't know what it was going to be.' They called up Chic's drummer Tony Thompson and reminded him of a conversation they'd had with him on David Bowie's *Serious Moonlight* tour the previous summer. Thompson agreed to work with them, but he also suggested Chic's bass player Bernard Edwards come along and produce the sessions. John Taylor had never met Edwards before and found him a very mellow character, the opposite to Nile – who was the party animal.

The first track they worked on, T. Rex's 1971 hit, 'Get It On (Bang a Gong)', was originally going to feature John Taylor's short-lived girlfriend, Bebe Buell, on vocals. The pair had met at an LA soirée in the Hollywood Hills on the *Sing Blue Silver* tour. 'It was all quite glamorous and sweet and we were drinking champagne and I think there were other naughty things going on,' says the former 1970s *Playboy* pin-up. 'He just grabbed me and kissed me; it was divine.' Given that Bebe Buell's previous conquests include Mick Jagger, Jimmy Page, Todd Rundgren and Stephen Tyler from Aerosmith (she's Liv's mum), she wasn't fazed by Taylor's lifestyle: 'I'm sure he was shagging his head off. He was having the time of his life.' She wasn't quite so taken with some of his other appetites, however, revealing, 'He was a McDonald's freak – we'd always have to stop off somewhere for a Big Mac.' Their fling didn't last for long, and the idea of Buell singing on the track was soon abandoned. At this stage the project was still a bit of a laugh – a self-indulgent, vibey release from the intensity and scale of Duran Duran. They toyed with the idea of getting a series of guests vocalists, including Mick Jagger and Bowie, involved, and then John Taylor thought of Robert Palmer, who had seemed enthusiastic about the idea of working together when they'd talked at the MENCAP concert in 1983. The skinny bassist sent Palmer a rough instrumental tape that the band had been working on in Paris and the super-smooth blues lizard wrote some words on the plane, then walked into the studio and recorded his bit with characteristic gusto. According to Tony Thompson, 'Robert came in, sang the track "Some Like It Hot" and then asked us what else we had. Then he did "Get It On", and we said, "To heck with Jagger. This is it! It's kind of a Chic funk foundation with a Duran Duran, rock'n'roll top and R&B feel courtesy of Palmer." '

The album was assembled in pieces with basic tracks recorded in London and Paris, followed by overdubs and embellishments at The Power Station studios in New York, hence the band's name. Palmer worked on most of his vocals in Nassau, where he was living at the time, writing lyrics to fit the existing music. Although the band were rarely all in the studio at the same time until late in the sessions, both of the Taylors did spend a lot of time with Bernard Edwards and Tony Thompson in New York. John Taylor says, 'It was only when I started hanging around Manhattan studios and working on The Power Station album that I started thinking of myself as a musician, and compared myself to other musicians and not in a good way either!' Not only was the insecure bass player worrying about his lack of technical ability, but the drugs were taking their toll, too. He told Daryl Easlea: 'I was so fucked-up at the time, I would suggest Bernard played it [my part]. He would always say, "You got to keep playing, don't ever stop playing." ' When Palmer walked in to the new sessions he discovered a non-stop party in the studio with the likes of Mick Jagger and Herbie Hancock often dropping by. Andy Taylor later confessed to *Goldmine* magazine: 'There was a lot of hanging out going on. We used to hang out down in the Village at Beebop and get whacked, do Power Station and fuck about. We were really living it up, spending $500 a night, just doing stupid things. It was just a massive party the whole time. I don't know how we got any work done, it was great.' 'In New York, quite a few people used this bogus bike messenger service,' recalls *Smash Hits* journalist Peter Martin. 'They would deliver drugs in photo sheets with twenty-three different types of coke in it. The clients had a "catalogue" and ordered over the phone. At the time it was considered a very good assignment to get a "Duran" trip.'

However, these cocaine-imbibing rock superheroes were spending their money faster than it was coming in. 'I think Andy has done all right financially, but he doesn't have as much as he should have,' reckons his old friend Mark Shaw. 'He's one of these lads who will always have cash in his pocket because it's a northern thing, it's what you do. But Andy will spend all the money in his pocket. If you say you haven't got any money, he'll give you £50 just like that. So I think the combination of his northern pride and his naïveté means he's got a bit of a funny relationship with money. He always thinks he's being ripped off but he's also very generous. And there are lots of hangers-on who will take advantage of that.' However, the guitarist was thrilled to be able to pay off the mortgage on his dad's semi and buy him a big BMW with a personalized number plate. As the funds flowed in and out, the two Taylors took up semi-permanent residence in the city's swanky Carlyle Hotel on Madison Avenue for a few months, sending the total cost of The Power Station album to over $500,000 – an astonishing amount twenty-one years ago. Opened in the 1930s, two suites at the hotel can cost as much as $10,000 a night in 2005, not including restaurant and bar bills. So, as they rubbed shoulders with politicians, diplomats and royalty (the Reagans were often guests and Prince Charles enjoyed staying there) they were forking out $50,000–$70,000 a week in today's terms. They also took on the relatively minor expense of flying Roger Taylor and his drum tech over on Concorde and then paying for a week-long stay at the hotel. The Duran drummer eventually played on the album after a luxurious five-day wait. According to John Taylor, the laid-back Bernard Edwards was keen that The Power Station wouldn't cause a rift in Duran Duran and so the producer encouraged this jet-set commute.

John Taylor was in need of a stable, thoughtful mentor at that time, and who better than the man who had inspired him all those years ago as the creator of the bass-line to 'Good Times'? The young heart-throb had fallen into a dangerous cycle of reacting to self-doubt, restlessness and insecurity by bingeing on drugs. He wanted to grow up but realized that his fame was a 'freeze period. You almost stop growing in some ways because you're pampered and there's a certain way you're treated.' For the moment, the twenty-four-year-old decided he should burn himself out while the going was good and, inspired by his new experiences in New York, he bought a beautiful apartment on the Upper West Side. According to the visiting *Smash Hits*: 'Fifty per cent of the wall space is glass, the rest is all black and chrome and resembles the nerve centre of *Star Trek*'s USS *Enterprise*.' Taylor moved in at the end of 1984, boasting that his apartment had the 'best view' of Central Park to the east, skyscrapers to the south and the Hudson River to the west. 'I can walk the streets of New

York like nowhere else,' he enthused. 'England became so claus-
trophobic for me that it was driving me mad. I just couldn't
handle having fans outside my house twenty-four hours a day.
Sometimes I wanted to scream when I opened the curtains and
there were thirty faces pressed up against the windows. And two
days after I bought a car somebody took a knife to it and carved
it up.' 'The New York apartment was fantastic,' recalls Denis
Regan. 'It was the only tall building in the area and he had one
half of one floor so he had views on three sides. John enjoyed the
American way of life. He took to it and found it more laid-back
in some ways. And I think he started to find England a bit
insular.' Ironically, his neighbour was Duran Duran's big rival
Boy George, who recalls in his autobiography, *Take It Like a Man*,
that John Taylor paid him a visit one evening brandishing a
Power Station tape: 'Marilyn called it the battle of the superegos.
I was off my head and more braggy than usual. I can't speak for
John. To liven things up Marilyn flipped on some hardcore gay
porn. John blushed as Rick Humungus potted a piece of trade on
a pool table.'

While the Birmingham-born pop star was enjoying the freedom
of New York, Roger Taylor had decided it was time to tie the knot
with his makeup-artist girlfriend, Giovanna Cantone. On 27 July
they married on a 'stiflingly hot' day at the Capo Di Monti church
in Naples, Italy, and then set off on a honeymoon in Egypt.
However, when they moved into a large house in the Maida Vale
area of London, it was a disaster. 'All the papers kept printing my
address,' declared the aggrieved drummer. 'There were kids out
there before I'd even moved in. I'd just bought the house, the "for
sale" sign was still up and I went round to see it – and there were
kids sitting on the doorstep.' On one occasion he'd returned home
to discover a love-struck fan had broken in and left a note on his
kitchen table. In contrast to some of the other band members,
Roger Taylor was less attached to Duran Duran's nomadic lifestyle:
'It's good to go back to a nice cooked dinner when you've been on
the road, living on club sandwiches and beefburgers. My life
changes radically when I'm not on the road. I don't think I could
maintain that touring lifestyle all year round.' Roger Taylor was
laying the foundations for his future. Although he was still attracted
to the irrational madness of Duran Duran – after all, it had coaxed

him out of his shell in the first place – at home he felt much more certain and secure about himself.

Andy Taylor hadn't been able to make the wedding because he was concerned about travelling when his wife Tracey was almost due to give birth to their first child. Eventually their 6lb 5oz boy, Andrew James Taylor (aka Bear), arrived on 20 August 1984. 'All the nurses were looking at me instead of my wife,' he joked. However, two days before the birth he did find time to nip down to the wedding reception of the newly hitched Nick and Julie Anne Rhodes. 'It was a bore,' he said with obvious mischief. 'No, it was pretty. Very pretty. It must have cost him a lot of money.' 'Everyone was so high, I'm surprised Andy can remember,' laughs Rob Hallett. 'But it was a bit stiff and pretentious – string quartets and all that sort of stuff.' The couple tied the knot in a civil ceremony at London's Marylebone Register Office, where Rhodes arrived in a simple dark grey suit (plus pink carnation) and his new wife wore a 1940s-style white skirt suit with matching wide-rimmed hat. His ex-girlfriend Elayne Griffiths, the 'exquisite creature' who had worked the door at the Rum Runner a few years earlier, was the 'best man' (she also later had a daughter with Duran Duran's producer Alex Sadkin and Rhodes was named as the child's 'godfather'). Royal and *Vogue* photographer Norman Parkinson, a man Rhodes clearly admired, recorded the day for posterity: 'Norman is lovely, he's still fantastically there, very intelligent and still totally into what he's doing,' enthused the twenty-two-year-old non-musician. 'I'd like to end up like that and for people to say, "Now there goes a fine old chap." ' For the reception, Rhodes changed into a pink and white silk taffeta suit complete with top hat and tails, while Julie Anne made her grand entrance in a long, snug-fitting lavender and white lace dress designed by Anthony Price. On her wrist, the tall, dark-eyed bride displayed a sapphire and diamond bracelet which was a wedding gift from her husband. In addition to Nick and Julie Anne wearing matching pink lipstick, the latter continued the vibrant colour scheme with her flowered headdress. London's Savoy Hotel hosted the reception in true Art Deco style, and almost everything on view was also pink, including live flamingos, a salmon and roast lamb dinner, the champagne and, of course, the flowers. According to the press, seventy-five of the bride's friends and family members flew in from America for the event and among the total of

219 guests who were screamed at by the crowd of tearful fans outside were the actor Michael Brandon, Linda Gray (best known as Sue Ellen from *Dallas*), Steve Strange, Tik and Tok and all of Duran Duran. When asked about his thoughts on his son getting married at such a young age, Rhodes's father only replied, 'I'd rather not answer.' At the end of the evening, the bride's family retired to their $425-a-night suite, and the next day Nick and Julie Anne Rhodes left the UK to spend three weeks sailing around the Greek islands in a private yacht. They also visited the Acropolis in Athens, which Rhodes described as 'a real bore – it looked like Birmingham Town Hall'. After such opulence, the band's self-appointed dandy sounded a little piqued when it was Roger Taylor's wedding, not his own, that was voted Event of the Year in the 1984 *Smash Hits* poll: 'It's a bit weird. I wonder why Roger's wedding got more votes than mine?' Roger's reaction was typical of the bloke. 'Event of the year?' he said, shocked. 'Was it? That's ridiculous. I tried to make my wedding a low-key event, but I suppose it got quite a lot of press. That's ridiculous.'

Nick and Julie Anne Rhodes set up home in a three-storey Victorian mansion in Gilston Road at the edge of the Boltons in south Kensington, London, which they bought for £500,000. According to Julie Anne, London was a compromise because her husband wanted to live in Paris and she preferred New York. When they purchased the property it was not much more than four walls containing a long-neglected interior, so they had the whole place gutted and then collaborated with several designers and architects, including Alan Bayne – one of the guys who had designed the *Sing Blue Silver* stage set for Duran Duran and Roxy Music's 'comeback' shows – to create their own 1930s-style, Art Deco dream home. At the time, Rhodes was obsessed with the period, naming his favourite novels as F. Scott Fitzgerald's *The Great Gatsby* and *The Last Tycoon*: 'I think it's something to do with my fascination for the lost generation. I like that 1920s and 1930s period very much.' When completed, the features in their new abode included an elegant staircase with brass banisters that were apparently identical to those in the Savoy; breakfast tables dating back to 1927; a marble hall floor with a design replicating a Russian constructivist painting; a beautiful Art Deco piano from the 1930s and a small 'whirlpool' that had been sunk into a natural stone floor and faced a mirrored wall. Rhodes's study contained work by Andy Warhol and an up-and-coming New Yorker, Keith Haring, although most of his growing art collection was too valuable to display and was kept in storage. This included a 'small' Picasso that he'd bought with his American Express card while on holiday in the south of France and drawings by his hero Jean Cocteau.

At the age of twenty-two, this convivial host and raconteur had not only succeeded in transcending his own working-class roots but, in addition, Rhodes had found a way of living out his 1930s fantasies in the late twentieth century – he was married to an American beauty; the couple lived in a sumptuous Art Deco house where he could hold court as if it was his very own luxury hotel; and, as a non-driver, he'd successfully fashioned a lifestyle where he was chauffeur-driven everywhere. Rhodes had followed his art-loving hero Bryan Ferry (who famously appeared in a white tuxedo by a swimming pool on the cover of his 1974 album, *Another Time, Another Place*) into a whole new social stratosphere where his dry wit and upbeat nature made him a popular figure. However, he did sometimes come across as a ludicrous, dandified eccentric. Steve Strange writes in his book, *Blitzed!*: 'Nick always put on a show ... I remember once I was skiing in Gstaad with Nick and Julie Anne Rhodes. This was at the height of Duran Duran's success and Nick was complaining that he couldn't get over the fact he was being recognized all the time. I turned around and said, "Nick, if you took your makeup off while you were skiing no one would take any notice of you." ' In his own way Rhodes was being as excessive as his bandmates but this was more Ferryism than Thatcherism – a glam fantasy planned in his head in the mid-1970s and made viable by Duran Duran's success in America. However, it all looked just a little too perfect as Rhodes described nights of placid domestic bliss with his young wife, playing Scrabble ('we have two dictionaries because Julie, being an American, spells things differently') as they were sleepily observed by their cat, Sebastian.

It remained to be seen how long this film-set fantasy would last but, in 1984, Rhodes's dream year also included his first – and so far only – art book and exhibition. Opening on 27 December 1984 and running for two weeks at the Hamilton Gallery in London (it was also shown in galleries in New York and Tokyo), *Interference* was a cherry-picked display of the polaroids he'd taken while on tour in

America. Although the press turned out in force, Julie Anne attracted more attention than the framed abstract photographs when she made an entrance at the show's Christmas Eve preview, wearing a backless dress that was open past her hips. Apparently this was the year of gentlemen taking polaroids, as Rhodes staged his exhibition a few months after David Sylvian's *Perspectives*, which consisted of photographs taken by the introspective singer while staying in hotel rooms around the world. Sylvian's semi-hallucinogenic images were achieved in a different way (he scratched them with a pen), but both he and Rhodes openly acknowledged Jean Cocteau as the inspiration for experimenting with other artforms. Sylvian dedicated his *Perspectives* book and exhibition (also held at the Hamilton Gallery, which had played host to Mick Karn's sculptures a year before) to the French poet, photographer and film-maker, while Duran's keyboard player enthused to *Smash Hits*: 'He's just one of the most original people that ever lived. Yes, I suppose I would also like to end up like him, to be remembered for being creative in lots of different areas.' Rhodes was certainly affected, but then didn't Brian Eno once say that David Bowie was at his best when he was at his 'most pretentious'?' It's also striking to observe that in the early 1980s, even so-called 'teen' pop stars talked about relatively obscure French poets, a subject that has yet to surface in *Heat* magazine. Despite Roger Taylor setting out to dispel the mystique – 'a lot of people see the wrong side of Nick and you could find him very pretentious, but he's actually quite straightforward' – Rhodes discussed pop artists such as Sonja Kaminski, Roy Lichenstein, Andy Warhol and Robert Rauchenberg with *Smash Hits* and revealed that he'd started painting, drawing and had recently tried his hand at silk-prints. Not only that but, like any twentieth-century art-fop with a strong visual sensibility, in 1984 Rhodes expressed a hope that he'd soon be able to work on some of his own film projects. A massive fan of directors such as Federico Fellini, Buñuel and Alfred Hitchcock, this lifelong movie buff revealed the outline of one self-penned script as 'an abstract storyline – a little tale of vanity involving two ladies and a man, sort of arty *Dallas*, with lots of debauchery'. He later commented, 'The concept stemmed back to a phase I went through of writing everything down. Every thought, every idea, even every dream. I found that I was forcing myself to wake up in the middle of a dream just so I could write it all down. I got into a dreadful state about it. But lately I've been working so hard I haven't had the time to dream.' Twenty years later, Rhodes has still yet to write or direct a movie, although he insists, 'I write every day. It's something that I want to focus on when I have the time.' According to one friend, the prolific scribbler keeps an 'Ideas Box' containing hundreds of suggestions for films. Every now and again, he has a spring clean, picking out the ones that have been made by other directors while they collected dust in his imagination.

As for Simon Le Bon, his world was opening up too but in a very different way: the daring, all-action adventurer wanted to sail around it. Le Bon says, 'I like getting out, I like sports – sailing is a big part of my life. A few hours at sea gives you a great perspective. Life becomes very simple.' In the summer of 1984 the singer spent a couple of months with his brother Jonathan, Duran Duran manager Michael Berrow and other friends on a yacht in the Mediterranean. They also 'island-hopped' in the Aegean and raced in the Swan World Cup in Sardinia, where they were placed sixth out of seventy-one boats. It was during this trip that Le Bon met the American racing veteran Skip Novak, who would later captain the Duran Duran star's own yacht, *Drum*. Already at this stage, *Smash Hits* savoured reporting some of the dangers as they detailed Le Bon (nicknamed 'Salts' by the magazine) getting 'bashed on the head by a "clew" ' and noting that 'whiplash from a sail left a foot-long weal on his back'. 'Try explaining that to your girlfriend,' laughed Le Bon. 'I got hit by a rope. Yeah, sure.' The ocean-loving buccaneer was also planning to buy a house, although in stark contrast to Rhodes he wanted something 'inconspicuous – I'm not into great displays of wealth'.

Le Bon and Rhodes were together again as Duran Duran's representatives at America's MTV Video Awards on 14 September, where they presented an award for Best Female Music Video to Cyndi Lauper for the track 'Girls Just Want to Have Fun'. Duran Duran also released the *Dancing on the Valentine* video EP, containing promos for 'Union of the Snake', 'The Reflex' and 'New Moon on Monday'. This was followed by 'The Wild Boys' single, which peaked at number two in both America and the UK, spending over three months in the British charts. Le Bon's singing on the track prompted Midge Ure to dismiss it as 'pathetic' and even his A&R man, Dave Ambrose, admits, 'When I first heard the vocal, I thought, "Can I cope with that?" But it was so effective and it became part of his style.' In a smart marketing move, the single was included on their new *Arena* album, which came out in November 1984. Including a studio track on a live LP was hardly one for the purists but it fuelled sales to their highest levels yet. *Arena* reached number four in America and six in the UK, where the LP spent thirty-one weeks on the charts. Andy Taylor was especially happy with the performance of the album: 'I hope that it's a reflection of our ability to play live. We played to at least a million people on the world tour and some of them obviously liked us. *Arena* broke us in both Italy and Germany!' In fact 'The Wild Boys' is Duran Duran's only number-one single in Germany. Despite *Arena*'s commercial success, like most live albums it failed to seduce an implacable, indifferent media. *Rolling Stone* awarded the LP two out of five, arguing that 'listening to *Arena* is like watching TV with the sound turned down: you have the feeling that some vital element in the presentation is missing ... When the band finally kicks into a headlong version of "Careless Memories", it's a firecracker too late to rescue the project from its static somnambulism.' The *Sing Blue Silver* documentary video and *Arena* concert film (containing an extended version of 'The Wild Boys' promo) also came out at the end of the year on VHS, Beta and Laserdisc. At the suggestion of Paul Berrow, an hour's worth of concert footage was edited from the project and retitled *As the Lights Go Down*. This was broadcast by MTV, HBO and ITV, who also showed *Sing Blue Silver*. Perhaps not surprisingly, 'The Wild Boys' won Best British Music Video Award at the following year's Brits.

Meanwhile, on 25 and 26 November, Duran Duran attended the Band Aid recording of 'Do They Know It's Christmas?' at Trevor Horn's Sarm West Studio in London. Bob Geldof had gathered together the cream of 'New Pop' for the session, including Duran, Spandau Ballet, Wham!, Boy George and, er, the curmudgeonly Paul Weller. The song successfully raised a substantial amount of money for the victims of famine in Ethiopia when it went straight in at number one in the UK. John Taylor declared, 'The whole thing serves a dual purpose – it can raise a lot of money and I'm really proud of it because it's a celebration of British pop music. I've always wished that something like the Beatles' "All You Need is

Love" could happen now.' The musically insecure bassist had actually recorded his part a couple of days earlier, as he felt that 'playing in front of all these posers would be a bit unnerving'. As for Duran Duran's singer, he later joked to *Deluxe Magazine*: 'I remember the *News of the World* said, "Simon Le Bon Wept to Feed The World". They thought I was crying in the video, but I probably had some of John's coke stuck in my eye, haha!'

Light-hearted, laddish rivalry now defined the relationship between Duran Duran and Spandau Ballet and in Christmas 1984 a one-off *Pop Quiz* special pitted the young millionaires against each other. *Smash Hits* also reported that the bands had recently spent two nights 'trying to drink each other under the table' while filming a TV show in Dortmund, Germany. In his excellent book, *Like Punk Never Happened*, Dave Rimmer describes a scene around this time in San Remo, Italy, where Duran Duran were due to appear alongside Spandau Ballet and Frankie Goes to Hollywood. As Nick Rhodes wandered around taking photographs of everyone, Spandau Ballet's drummer John Keeble laughed, 'Don't bother with that, Nick. They're bound to be crap, just like your book.' Meanwhile, standing on a table in the centre of the room, Andy Taylor and Nasher from Frankie Goes to Hollywood dropped their trousers to prove who had the bigger 'chopper'. Effectively, these groups had formed a clubby, jetset elite who were as much part of the 'rock establishment' as Elton John or the increasingly mainstream David Bowie. After a few years of extravagantly weird (or weirdly extravagant) British pop music, by the middle of the decade the frisson had almost completely gone. Culturally there was something new in the water too. AIDS, the 'big disease with a little name', as Prince phrased it, was the central issue of the time. Combined with horrific images of starving children in Africa, the effect on youth culture was to turn against the decadence personified by Duran Duran. 'Their success was built on all the wrong things: fashion and the vacuous nature of materialism,' argues Michael Berrow. 'Other sensibilities had to take over.'

Duran Duran's year of high living and dreams-made-flesh wasn't over just yet. They still had one major card to play before the changing cultural climate caught up with them. Nick Rhodes and John Taylor approached James Bond producer Cubby Broccoli at a Michael Caine party and asked him if Duran Duran could compose the title-track for the next James Bond movie. 'I think we had a number-one single at the time,' explained Rhodes. A few months later, the idea had turned into reality and John Taylor found himself playing host to John Barry, the man who worked on the music for Bond films such as *From Russia with Love*, *Goldfinger* and *You Only Live Twice*, which had provided hit singles for Matt Monro (1963), Shirley Bassey (1964) and Nancy Sinatra (1967). It was agreed that the new writing team should first meet up at the bassist's Knightsbridge flat in London – a typical 'pop star pad', described by *Smash Hits* as 'a long, light room, dominated by a white grand piano and giant metallic TV/video console. The walls are lined with photos of females with dodgy footwear, whips and not many clothes.' According to John Taylor, after a few hours of sitting at the piano and drinking, one thing became clear: 'Barry hated most of us and most of us hated him. It was a real show of fucking egos.' Paul Berrow claims that Simon Le Bon actually wrote the lyric and melody line in his apartment in Paris. 'We were drinking a 1957 armagnac and he strummed it in about thirty minutes.' John Taylor credits the song's producer Bernard Edwards (who was of course also working with him on The Power Station at the time) for pulling all the different elements together; in particular for the way he handled a full sixty-piece orchestra on a three-minute pop song.

Duran Duran weren't just 'clashing' with John Barry. They weren't really talking to each other and it was a job getting all the band into the studio at the same time. 'There was a lot of in-fighting,' recalls Marcello Anciano, 'and so many little dramas. You just thought, "It's not really about this; it's not really about the girl-friends, it's about something a lot deeper," but of course they couldn't actually deal with it properly. If you're a star from that young an age and you get that level of adulation, it's very hard to see clearly.' 'Simon was really obnoxious at this point,' remembers ex-*Smash Hits* scribe Peter Martin. 'He was going through his self-important phase.' Andy Taylor later admitted that he couldn't bear to be in the same room as the singer around the time of 'A View to a Kill'. Although Le Bon had the ability to be a great diplomat when he wanted to – and that was exactly what Duran needed at this stage – too often there were other distractions. He either missed the warning signs or he chose to ignore them. Marcello Anciano also detected an unspoken tension between Andy Taylor and Nick

Rhodes. 'My feeling is that Nick and Andy's differences had a lot to do with character. In other words, Nick's sense of elitism and Andy's sense of being slighted. I love Andy but he has a huge chip on his shoulder. They would never admit it to each other, at least I've never heard them talk about it. But I think that kind of frisson happened because of their sensibilities. Nick is very much the Andy Warhol kind of elitist artist, whereas Andy is a rock'n'roller who wants to get down and dirty – sex, drugs and rock'n'roll.'

The festering atmosphere in Duran Duran was mostly expressed through absences rather than any open battles. Andy Taylor's unhappiness was more transparent than the others' but Rhodes, for one, was not prepared to get involved in a shouting match. The keyboard player told *Smash Hits*: 'I hate it when people rush around me, screaming and shouting. It's the same as being nervous. It's just a waste. I try to eliminate all waste feelings. Obviously I have faults and anxieties like any normal person, but I always try to rationalize things. I like my state of mind and I hope I can keep it like this. Placid is the word.' Rhodes's calm state of mind suggested a fair and balanced outlook but, although a quick thinker, his scholarly manner was usually founded in his absolute conviction that he was right. That undermined his ability to negotiate a solution that would make everyone happy. Not surprisingly in such a fraught situation, even the Atlas-like Roger Taylor was starting to feel uneasy. He'd always supported the majority opinion, but he was acutely aware that the spirit in the band had changed. Although he still wasn't fully acknowledging or expressing his own needs, the drummer's sense of dissatisfaction was creeping up on him. As for John Taylor, the self-eviscerating star was still fluctuating between the hedonistic thrill of living out his fantasies and feeling disillusioned by the mega hype surrounding Duran Duran. He felt so drained by the experience of recording 'A View to a Kill' that he'd lost all enthusiasm for the project. 'The Bond single and all that entails – premieres, parties and things – is gonna be a real drag,' said the soul-weary bassist.

There was no time for John Taylor to recharge his batteries. His life was still turned up to eleven as The Power Station's first single, 'Some Like It Hot', climbed to number six in America in May 1985, a full three months after its release. It's a feverish, anthemic track with a salsa feel which Robert Palmer credited to the 'non-stop partying'. 'Some Like It Hot' was less successful in the UK and stalled at fourteen. In March 1985, the self-titled *The Power Station* album came out, reaching number twelve in the UK, where it spent twenty-three weeks on the chart. In America, the LP followed 'Some Like It Hot' up the charts and passed over 1 million sales during its slow ascent into the Top Ten. In a *Rolling Stone* article, the magazine focused on the disparate identities within the group, expressed through their contrasting dress sense: 'The dapper, well-groomed Palmer looked like he'd wandered over from Wall Street. His three-piece suit and Club Med suave contrasted sharply with the pop-star androgyny of the Taylors, who were wearing what appeared to be knee-length dresses.' The magazine's reviewer David Fricke accepted that 'The Power Station has its occasional successes, particularly when Thompson and John Taylor – a far tougher bassman than his dreamboat looks suggest – lock up the beat. In the hit single, "Some Like It Hot", the closest this album ever gets to a model Duran–Chic hybrid, Thompson's bold wallop and Taylor's agile boom bubble like hot lava. Meanwhile "Communication" surges with the same confidence, topped off by a dynamic pop melody and some of Palmer's least mannered singing.' Despite Fricke's concluding assertion that the music is encased in a 'drab, metallic production', at a time when many of their contemporaries were experimenting with gated drum snares, The Power Station managed to stomp louder than anyone else. They achieved this partly through using elevator shafts as echo chambers. Andy Taylor plays a major role in creating the colossal sound, which is heavier than anything Duran Duran had recorded up to that point. Robert Palmer is in command of the horn-led material (courtesy of Lenny Pickett) and adds his own additional power and thrust. In addition to 'Some Like It Hot', the T. Rex cover 'Get It On (Bang a Gong)' possessed enough commercial suss to seduce US radio and achieve the band their second American Top Ten hit (it reached only twenty-two in the UK). 'Go to Zero' sounds slinkily restrained, 'Murderess' is stiletto-through-the-heart pulp-funk, 'Communication' offers a lighter, poppier transmission after an awakening blast of horns and 'Lonely Tonight' achieves an urban, neon-blues feel. Less memorable is the over-refined ballad 'Still in Your Heart', but the album's true nadir is a cover of 'Harvest for the World' which Andy Taylor sings with Palmer. Nevertheless, the pair did go on to record 'Addicted to Love' together, along with Bernard Edwards and Tony Thompson, so that effectively Robert Palmer's US number one featured the Power Station line-up minus John Taylor. 'Before working with this lot I must admit I was turning into a bit of a crooner,' confessed Palmer in 1985. 'This has set me back on the rails and I want to continue in a similar, strong direction.' Andy Taylor must have felt that he was a magic talisman, as he'd scored American Top Ten singles with three different projects. If anything, this fired him up even more: 'I'm going to get old one day and I won't be able to do this any more, so now I've got the chance I might as well milk it. But even when all this does disappear I'll be happy. I've got a fantastic wife, a healthy kid and loads of money.'

In March 'The Reflex' was named International Hit of the Year at the Ivor Novello Awards, but there was no sign of Duran Duran getting together to write another one. As The Power Station performed 'Get It On' and 'Some Like It Hot' on *Saturday Night Live* in America, Nick and Julie Anne Rhodes relocated to Paris, where they were joined by Simon Le Bon and later Roger Taylor. While Le Bon claimed he would have been happy to take some more time off, Rhodes wanted to make a 'delicate' album in stark contrast to the thundering riffs of The Power Station. The keyboard player insisted that Arcadia (the band are named after the Latin phrase *'et in arcadia ego'* from Virgil) wasn't a direct response to Andy and John Taylor but because he was 'bored' hanging around waiting for them to return to the fold. Freed from the internal tensions within Duran Duran, this was also a particularly happy period in their lives. Rhodes recalls, 'Arcadia was actually a great time for Simon and me, because we managed to escape from the craziness. We fled to Paris, which became our sort of second home.' Nick and Julie Anne were in the first flush of marriage and were able to enjoy their time together without the constant hassle and pressure surrounding Duran Duran. Not only that but by the spring of 1985, Simon Le Bon had fallen in love with Yasmin Parvaneh, a nineteen-year-old model who had already graced the covers of American and British *Elle*. Born in Oxford on 29 October 1964 to an English mother, she inherited her olive skin from her Iranian father. As a child, she was strong-willed and determined, but also very shy. When Yasmin was seventeen she was spotted by an agency scout and initially worked as a hand model. Two years later, Simon Le Bon spotted a picture of the elegant teenager in an agency portfolio while working on 'The Wild Boys' video and managed to get hold of her number. At first she thought it was a joke and hung up on him, saying that she'd rather date Rod Stewart. He persisted, sending her roses every day for a week ('It was a really rock star thing to do,' said Le Bon) and eventually Yasmin agreed to a second conversation. 'We spent over an hour on the phone,' he recalled. 'She told me that she smoked Marlboro Reds and drank Glenfiddich. We arranged to go on a double date with some friends of mine to the première of *Indiana Jones and the Temple of Doom*. So I turned up at her tiny flat the next day with a carton of cigarettes and a bottle of whisky, which we drank half of on the way to the cinema.' This was back in June 1984, and the papers printed the story, 'Duran star falls for top model Yasmin'. At the time Le Bon had responded: 'I'm just sick of remarks like "Simon's cheeky two-timing antics." It's really hurtful to Claire, because it makes her look such a fool. I hate the fact that my private life is not private.' The papers also ran stories of him with 'mystery blonde La Fox' at the Cannes Film Festival in summer 1984. In fact, even for casual observers, headlines such as 'Le Bon's Belle' and 'Simon's Secret Lady' had become familiar tabloid fodder over the previous two years. Perhaps not surprisingly, given his reputation, Yasmin played hard to get. Le Bon remembers, 'We went out for two weeks and then lost touch. Why only two weeks? She wouldn't fuck me. I couldn't figure for the life of me why not.' However, he courted her again in spring 1985, with Paris forming an ideal romantic back-drop. 'The fires of passion began to burn in a big way,' confessed Yasmin a year later. 'She has a beautiful flame burning inside her,' he told one writer. 'She's a very pure girl.' As for Claire Stansfield, according to Denis O'Regan, 'Simon really liked her but she just wasn't "the one".' The young model moved to California where her father lived and launched a successful career as an actress. In the 1990s she appeared in *Frasier, The X-Files, Twin Peaks* and played the sorceress Alti in *Xena: Warrior Princess*.

Understandably, Le Bon was in high spirits as work continued on Arcadia's *So Red the Rose* off and on in Paris. Although the final product was later described by one US critic as 'the world's most pretentious album', what the media didn't realize was that at the

John Taylor tries out one of Patti Bell's ruffled shirts: Nick Rhodes and Roger Taylor look on, amused, 1980.

New Romanticism is white-washed into the famous *Rio* imagery, complete with John Taylor's trademark trilby, 1982.

Picnic in the south of France as the band avoid work on their third album, 1983.

Simon Le Bon topless during a photo session for *Cosmopolitan* in New York.

John Taylor pouts for a *Cosmopolitan* cover shot, 1984.

Duran Duran vs Spandau Ballet on BBC's *Pop Quiz*, 1985.

Nick Rhodes hangs out with his cultural guru Andy Warhol in a New York nightclub, 1986.
Julie Anne looks on.

Three get ready: Rhodes, Le Bon and Taylor still together as Duran Duran battle on, 1988.

Warren Cuccurullo (third from left) was a full-time band member from 1989 to 2001.

The classic line-up reformed and walking the streets of Putney, London, 2003.

The 'Fab Five' backstage at the NEC, 2004.

John and Roger Taylor – back together at last, 2004.

Simon Le Bon backstage at The Brits with wife Yasmin and daughter Amber.

Simon Le Bon happy to be back in front of a sold-out crowd at Wembley Arena in 2004.

time *So Red the Rose* was one of the most expensive albums ever made. The outgoings on Arcadia even dwarfed the kind of bills racked up by The Power Station. Michael Berrow confesses, 'It was over a million pounds and that's just to make it. The videos and marketing cost hundreds of thousands on top of that.' Over the years Rhodes has lived 'for several weeks at a time' in some of the world's most luxurious hotels, such as the Carlyle Hotel (New York), Chateau Marmont (LA) and the Ritz (Paris). However, arguably his finest hour was spending several months in the Plaza Athenée, Paris, in 1985, where Arcadia took over the entire floor. To be fair, he usually wasn't alone: 'Simon also had one suite, Roger had one [he joined them after finishing his week with the Power Station] and Alex Sadkin. Then there was the security guy and some of the people who played on the album like Andy Mackay of Roxy Music, the percussionists Rafael de Jesus and David Van Tieghem, Masami Tsuchiya and so on. We opened all the doors so you could wander right through from one end to the other.' In the end Rhodes bought an apartment in the city, but he wasn't prepared to give up hotel living just like that. His new place was close enough to the Plaza Athenée for him to order room service from the hotel. 'Nick was the worst for hotel excesses,' says Rob Hallett. 'It all got a bit silly, like insisting that rooms were painted a different colour, that sort of thing.' The nouveau socialite lived this rarefied lifestyle in the city's restaurants and nightclubs with the likes of Grace Jones, Sting, Carlos Alomar and Pink Floyd's Dave Gilmour, who all guested on the album. Often suffering from bouts of insomnia, he could be found scribbling ideas for songs on matchboxes and tissues while holding court in a club at 3 a.m.: 'The most alarming one to me was when I put my hand in my pockets one day to actually blow my nose on this tissue and I looked in horror and I sneezed into my other hand because it had musical notes and chord patterns written all over it. It was a song on the Arcadia album.' Rhodes was also spotted at tables in Paris with his friends Sean (Tok) and Jane Kahn, whose bizarre, heavy makeup and half-shaven heads inevitably attracted glances from the more conservative diners. 'I think Nick really liked Sean and they are quite similar in some ways,' reckons Tim Dry (Tok). 'They're quite quiet and introverted but they play outside the box. What I found interesting is that there's a bit on the Arcadia video where Nick has actually become Sean from Tik and

Tok. He's got the dark hair and dark eyebrows. It was just funny seeing Nick, who was this perfect blond, becoming this perfect raven-haired, dark-eyed, goth character.' Rhodes says, 'I used to change the colour of it every few months. It was a real sort of religious routine. And it had been blond for so long. I thought, "What's the most radical thing I could do with it?" It seemed to be to make it negative, which in this case was black.' Le Bon also dyed his hair black for the Arcadia project, partly to fit the music, which he described as 'ethnic, almost gypsy in style', but also to trick English tourists: 'I was living on rue de Rivoli in Paris [he too had moved into his own apartment] which is like a sanctuary for Englishmen – you can walk upstairs and have bacon and eggs and baked beans for breakfast – and I'd get followed in by thirty tourists. And it occurred to me that my most recognizable point was my blond hair and when I dyed it black I didn't get followed so much.'

The costs of Arcadia rocketed beyond their accountant's wildest nightmares as recording sessions at Studio de la Grande Armée in Palais de Congrès went on and on, driven by an obsession for detail shared by Rhodes and producer Alex Sadkin. The atmosphere was more relaxed but the constant polishing of elements that surely no one else would notice, let alone care about, must have been crushingly dull for the other musicians. Roger Taylor confessed he missed the other members of Duran Duran: 'I miss them quite a lot, actually. When we're all together, getting a bit serious, they – especially Andy – always used to come up with a wisecrack and break the atmosphere. Musically, as well, they always provide a friction.' On another occasion he said, 'It would be boring if we were all doing the same thing. If we were like Nick, we'd sound like some obscure Brian Eno album.'

Much to Roger Taylor's relief, Duran Duran regrouped briefly in spring 1985 to shoot the video for 'A View to a Kill'. They hired the Eiffel Tower for the princely sum of £20,000 and played out their schoolboy James Bond fantasies for the directors Godley and Creme, who'd previously worked with them on 'Girls on Film'. However, the band later admitted to *The Face* that this rendezvous was 'punctuated by arguments, breakdowns and tears'. 'Even my mum's worried now,' laughed Roger Taylor, disguising his disappointment. 'Every time she rings up she says, "Are you going to split up?" ' He insisted that the band was going to get back together in September, but there was a sense of regret in his voice as he talked about the old times in Duran Duran: 'We'd get ten pounds a week, we didn't have apartments but we seemed very happy. Now we're all millionaires, got everything we've ever wanted, but sometimes we don't seem as happy as we were.' Yet while they sniped behind the scenes, the band continued to have humungous hit singles. In the summer of 1985 'A View to a Kill' gave them another chart-topper in America and it was held off from the top slot in the UK only by Paul Hardcastle's anti-war novelty single, '19'. As for the James Bond première, it wasn't a drag after all for John Taylor, who arrived on the red carpet with the Danish model Renee Simonsen. She was the latest in a procession of beautiful women that this 'buoyant, voluble sensualist' and 'engaging, self-indulgent, little boy charmer' had been seen with over the previous four years. They had recently included *Playboy* cover girl Virginia Hey, who had played a 'warrior woman' in *Mad Max 2* and during her relationship with Taylor invited the cameoing pop star to appear as a character called 'The Hacker' in a sci-fi TV movie, *Timeslip*. 'Virginia, yes, she was a totally mad Australian girl who didn't stick around for long,' laughs Denis O'Regan. Over a decade later she became a cult icon by playing the blue-skinned, slap-headed psychic alien Pa'u Zotoh Zhaan in the television series *Farscape*. However, in contrast to his other short-lived flings (he'd also reportedly dated ex-Shalamar singer Jody Watley and actress Diane Lane, who later married Christopher Lambert), John Taylor's relationship with Renee Simonsen almost survived the rest of a turbulent decade. 'I met Renee after seeing her picture on a poster,' revealed Duran Duran's Delphic poster boy. 'She won the "Face of the '80s" competition and I became obsessed with her. I would go on and on about her to the girl I was engaged to at the time. Then I got her phone number from a friend and called her up. She wasn't the slightest bit interested.' Eventually he was able to win her over and by the end of 1985 they were engaged: 'Renee has helped me cool down a bit,' he declared. 'She's my total opposite, so she balances me out ... even though she has to fight to do it.' According to Rob Hallett, 'John's New York apartment had two beautiful things in it. One was a parrot. No cage. Just a parrot on a perch that wouldn't stop talking. The other one was John's girlfriend, Renee Simonsen. She wasn't interested in rock music at all. In fact before she met John, I'm not sure that she'd even been to a rock concert. Renee was a lovely girl, very down to earth. Her personality was like that of a dead normal girl who's working behind the counter at Woolworth's. They seemed to stay in a lot and order pizza. Well, you would, wouldn't you!' However, given John Taylor's lifestyle, it was an understandably volatile relationship. 'She didn't like all John's excesses,' affirms Hallett. 'She wasn't interested in that world at all.' Boy George confirms this: 'A friend and I would find John's girlfriend crying in the hallway. We'd bring her in and give her a cup of tea and get all the gossip. John's apartment was the most rock'n'roll place I'd ever seen.' When Peter Martin from *Smash Hits* paid John Taylor a five-day visit, he observed: 'Boy George and his friends were going ape-shit on heroin at the time; they had the whole London crowd over at his flat. Me and John crashed a party of theirs. We went in and Boy George was trying to fill himself up from a tap – he thought he was a kettle, which I thought was very creative of him. It was a gang of clubby, post-New Romantic people all on smack. John was quite horrified. He was quite happy in the coke/being Axl Rose-type scenario, but suddenly it was getting a bit dark.' John Taylor agrees: 'My apartment was a beautiful place to go mad in. George and I both lost part of our minds on that twenty-seventh floor. Fame was having its way with us. There was a courier service that would bike around bags of pot with little flags of the country it came from on the sachet. At Christmas they did party bags – that was useful.'

The immediate demands of The Power Station's schedule in 1985 meant that John Taylor continued to bullet through life at an artificially accelerated rate. As a result, he didn't have the time, opportunity or inclination to enjoy some of the 'toys' he'd spent hundreds of thousands of pounds on. While recording The Power Station album, Duran Duran's prettiest star had splashed out on one of the most famous automobiles of the decade: a gull-winged, futur-istic-looking DeLorean, otherwise known as the car in *Back to the Future*. In the early 1980s the entrepreneur John DeLorean was arrested by the FBI on suspicion of trafficking cocaine (he was later cleared of all charges) and Taylor decided to buy one of the sporty machines as a soon-to-be-defunct rarity. Rather like his classic Aston Martins, the DeLorean was pretty unreliable. It looked great, but the windows leaked and the engines seized up, so it's doubtful that John Taylor enjoyed many happy hours on the road cruising in it. Although he ultimately made a big loss on the DeLorean, the bassist confessed that his biggest extravagance was 'the third Aston Martin, which I never actually drove. It stayed in storage for two years before I sold it for a lot less than I paid for it. It's ridiculous, but it's what boys do. I've never been a saver and I don't invest wisely – it's not the way I was brought up. I spend it as quickly as I can by buying the biggest toy I can afford.'

Meanwhile Taylor had set off on a short break when, on 20 June, Robert Palmer backed out of The Power Station tour at the last minute. 'It's all been a bit of a trauma,' he confessed in 1985. 'It was a complete surprise. I was going on holiday at the time and had to come back and decide if we were still going to do the tour … he told us he was running overtime with his album. It was rather strange, since three weeks before he said he'd do it.' Andy Taylor suggested Paul Young as a replacement, but he wasn't available. The guitarist then came up with the idea of hiring Michael Des Barres, the singer in Silverhead and Chequered Past, a rock band that included Sex Pistol Steve Jones, who would later have numerous bizarre Duran Duran connections. Des Barres also co-wrote the track 'Obsession', which had been a big hit for Animotion earlier that year. Eighteen days after he'd received the call-up from The Power Station, Des Barres told one journalist, 'I'm absolutely in space. What happened was, two and a half weeks ago, I was in Texas with a friend of mine (*Miami Vice*'s Don Johnson) to make a movie. So the phone rings and it's … the Power Station's representative … Then it just whirl-winded. It's like being cast in a movie as a major rock god. It's fantastic. I was born bubblegum … I've always had a bubblegum brain.' Des Barres proved to be an animated, enthusiastic front man who was arguably better equipped at hyping up arena audiences than the more mannered, gravelly-voiced Robert Palmer. His friendship with Don Johnson also subsequently led to The Power Station guesting on an episode of the flashy TV cop show *Miami Vice*.

The new Power Station line-up made their live debut at the Ritz, New York, on 1 July. This was followed by gigs in Merriweather, Raleigh and Toronto, before the Taylors met up with the rest of Duran Duran for the American Live Aid concert, which was set to take place on 13 July. In the week of this globally televised event, 'A

View to a Kill' was top of the US charts; The Power Station's 'Some Like It Hot' was at seven and the rock-funk album from which it was taken had reached number fourteen in the album chart. This was an impressive achievement at a time when Spandau Ballet were entering into legal action against their record label, Chrysalis, for failing to 'honour its contract and promote the group as agreed' because they still hadn't broken the States. Yet at the height of their success, it was the first occasion the various members of Duran Duran had all been in the same place since March, when they'd shot the video to 'A View to a Kill'. Not surprisingly, the rehearsal for Live Aid was 'fraught'. On the actual day itself The Power Station came out early at the JFK Stadium, Philadelphia, and played two songs, 'Get It On (Bang a Gong)' and 'Murderess'. It was an instantly forgettable performance, completely overshadowed by some of the acts such as U2 and Queen, who grabbed the world's attention that day. An under-rehearsed Duran Duran took the stage later that evening, performing 'A View to a Kill', 'Union of the Snake', 'Save a Prayer' and 'The Reflex'. 'When we did the Live Aid show I noticed that John and Andy were behaving differently on stage from the way I had remembered,' recounted Le Bon a few weeks later. 'They looked shocked to see me up there singing rather than Michael Des Barres. It's hard to say how the two camps will blend together. It could work very well or it could be a real mess.' The worst moment in Duran Duran's set occurred when Le Bon hit the wrong note in 'A View to a Kill', exposing the frailties of his voice to the biggest TV audience of his life. Not surprisingly, he has described this as the 'most humiliating' on-stage howler of his career. As Duran Duran's listless, self-absorbed performance swiftly faded into obscurity, what no one realized was that this was the last time the so-called 'Fab Five' would perform together until their much-hyped reunion shows nineteen years later.

Scheduling meant that the band were separated immediately after Live Aid as John and Andy Taylor continued The Power Station's US arena tour for another six weeks. Aside from seeing Nick Rhodes, who 'guested' at one show by walking on stage carrying a broom and then pretended to sweep the set, there was very little contact between The Power Station and the other members of Duran Duran. Worse than that, as Andy Taylor batted off questions about how he felt as a family man on the road – 'I think it's easier for a man to leave a baby than for a woman' – the relationship that really suffered on the tour was his friendship with Duran Duran's bass player. According to John Taylor, rather than this being a celebratory period as The Power Station album climbed to number six in the American charts, 'I just wanted to crawl into a hole and die because I'd lost control of Andy completely. We exchanged maybe twenty words a day towards the end. We were burning the candle and it was not a great time for me. Halfway through the tour, it had lost its lustre.' By the final dates the boozed-up Duran Duran duo usually set off into the night with different sets of friends and hangers-on. Orchestral Manoeuvres in the Dark supported The Power Station on these dates. 'I saw more of John than anyone else really,' says OMD's Paul Humphreys. 'I got to know him on the tour and we did quite a bit of partying. I expected there to be a lot of cocaine on that tour, but I must admit I was surprised by the level of abuse! I didn't see much of Andy Taylor. There seemed to be lots of alternative parties going on and I always ended up at the ones with John. He's a lovely guy; I really like him. We got on really well. There were quite a few nights on the tour when there would be a knock on the door and I'd already gone to bed and it would be John, "Is the party in here then?" But there's a level where it all becomes destructive because it's night after night and I had a sense that maybe John was partying too much. You can get into a routine with that drug where you start to panic if you don't have it with you. I thought there would be a night where the band couldn't actually perform but they did keep going.' 'You're a very, very young man given an awful lot of power and the tendency for human beings is to abuse it,' confessed Andy Taylor in 2004. 'Not just to other people, but to yourself. You can get self-destructive and then you look in the bank and go, huh!'

Meanwhile Simon Le Bon was sailing off into stormy waters of his own. In 1984 the singer and the Berrow brothers had jointly spent $1.35 million on a seventy-seven-foot maxi-yacht, which they named *Drum*. It was the largest ever one-piece completely moulded floating structure ever built, making it a staggering 23 per cent lighter than any boat of a similar size. It also boasted a revolutionary new keel design. They christened it *Drum* as its bare hull was being towed from Cowes to Hamble, where it was due to be fitted out. An excited Simon Le Bon leapt on board and remarked on the incredible sound the yacht made as it sliced through the water. One of the boat builders overheard him and said, 'Just wait till you get it in the Southern Ocean, then it'll really sound like a drum'. However, after that million-dollar outlay, the trio felt that the yearly $40,800 insurance payments were too high and they decided not to insure it. Their collective dream was to sail the yacht for the 27,000-mile Whitbread Round-the-World Race, a very demanding and dangerous challenge which immediately drew some fierce opposition from some of the other band members. 'Simon's decision to sail the *Drum* around the world was hugely divisive,' says Denis O'Regan. 'I don't think the other band members particularly objected to him owning a boat, but it was the fact that he was risking his life. I didn't hear Simon's side of the story but, rightly or wrongly, it caused a complete split in the camp. And it undermined the relationship that various band members had with their management too, because both Michael and Paul Berrow were heavily involved in the *Drum* project.' According to the physically unadventurous Nick Rhodes, 'None of us wanted Simon to do the boat thing. We thought it was a complete disaster. It's not very rock-'n'roll, is it? The whole thought of orange cagoules was very displeasing to me aesthetically,' he added as a dry pay-off. The keyboard player did set sail on *Drum* just the once, when Simon Le Bon invited him on board during a trip to Mustique. Other guests included Mick Jagger, Jerry Hall, Nick Kamen and David Bowie, but it wasn't long before some of the A-listers were left feeling decidedly seasick. Twenty years later, *Drum's* original co-owner Paul Berrow remains unrepentant about his decision to race the yacht with Le Bon on board. 'The boat caused a bit of a problem because Simon went sailing and it all seemed to be my fault. But you know, Simon was a grown man who wanted to realize his dreams. He should be allowed to do it without blaming the management for having planted the idea in the first place. Simon is an adventurous guy. That's why he's still a mate of mine. We're outdoor-type people. It was a fresh challenge and the quality of camaraderie was similar to the early days of being in a band.' His brother Michael chimes in agreement: 'I don't think the others understood that we were all just doing something that we really liked. We all enjoyed sailing, everybody needed a break, we wanted to have some time off. OK, so they were right to be worried. Andy and Nick were very concerned that it was dangerous and as it turned out, they were absolutely spot on there.'

In June 1985 *Drum* had won the Round-the-Island race, coming in only six minutes behind the record, and then on 21 July the yacht raced in the Seahorse Maxi Series at Cowes. Although it was fifth over the line, *Drum* took first place on points. Three weeks later Simon Le Bon, his younger brother Jonathan and both of Duran Duran's managers were among the twenty-four-man crew led by Skip Novak (who revealed, 'Simon's a bloody good toilet cleaner') as the *Drum* set off in the 600-mile Fastnet Race around Britain's coastline. They intended this to be a serious run-through for both boat and crew, in preparation for the upcoming Whitbread Race. However, the Fastnet had its own dangers, most horrifically in 1979 when seven boats sank and fifteen crewmen drowned after being hit by violent storms. History threatened to repeat itself when on 11 August *Drum* sailed into a force-nine gale three miles off Falmouth on the Cornish coast. Le Bon had just finished a four-hour watch and had gone below. He was just about to fall asleep when the boat turned over. What he didn't realize was that the *Drum's* keel had completely sheared off: 'Rick, who was sleep above me, fell out of his bunk, and I thought, "Oh, there's Rick; why is he lying there?" Then I was thrown out of the bunk. I heard a couple of bangs, and then the boat went over sideways! I couldn't believe it. I thought, "Goddamn it, this thing is still going over." Rick said, "Come on" and he moved quickly towards the hatch. At that moment, two heavy sails – which take six men to lift – fell on us. We humped and shunted our way along underneath, kneeling. I've got bruises all over my legs. Suddenly I saw this patch of blue, and then we realized, "God, the boat's upside down!" We were so disoriented. We had started crawling up before we realized we had turned turtle.'

Le Bon and five other men were able to breathe in an air pocket underneath the hull, although it was already thick with petrol fumes and hydrogen chloride gas: 'It was horrible, messy and smelly in there but there was no panic, just very clear thinking. We realized at that time we would be much safer staying inside there and not trying to get out. We dealt with it. That was all. In my head I just said, "Look out for brother Jonny. Look after all the guys but especially Jonny." I imagined that he and the others were outside sitting on the hull.' Three minutes after the boat went down, an automatic radio beacon went off after being activated by the seawater. A Royal Navy helicopter arrived on the scene around twenty minutes later, dropping an expert diver, thirty-two-year-old Petty Officer Larry Slater, into the water: 'I helped them one by one and pulled them through the hatch,' recounted the Navy frogman. 'They had to swim for the light. I don't know how long they could have held out – perhaps an hour. There was a lot of oil in the water in the hatch and the fumes were pretty toxic.' Le Bon recalls, 'That was the hardest thing. Rigging was hanging down from the deck. All the lines were trailing, just like a Portuguese man-of-war, a big jellyfish with all those things, floating. That's what it looked like. The wires and ropes were like trying to fight through spaghetti. My right thermal legging got caught around the lifeline but I pulled it free and came up towards the surface. I started to breathe too early but decided at the last minute, "No, don't do it yet: there's still water there." ' On the surface, Le Bon discovered that all twenty-four sailors were safe, including his brother. They were taken to safety and 'on reaching land the first thing I did was I trod in a cow pat, a big brown pancake. And do you know what? It made me so happy. It was warm. It squashed through my toes!'

Before the news was broadcast on TV, Le Bon's parents were tipped off about the accident by a mystery phone call. Simon's mum, Anne, admitted, 'Ever since we realized Simon wanted to sail, we had been bracing ourselves for something like this. Neither Simon or Jonathan knew if the other was alive. The hardest thing for me was knowing that both boys were in pain for each other. They are very close.' As for Le Bon's girlfriend of a few months, Yasmin had been waiting for his arrival with her parents in Cowes. After watching the rescue efforts on TV, she left for the six-hour drive to Falmouth and met up with Le Bon and the other crew members at a local hotel. Understandably, Simon and Yasmin's relationship intensified after having to face the possibility of losing each other so early on. In the immediate aftermath, they were both still on a high, making an almost cartoonishly happy pair as Le Bon related his seafaring tales, dressed in a skull-and-crossbones T-shirt and 'toying with his sailor's bandanna'. Yasmin purred, 'I love dangerous things.' 'Like me,' added her boyfriend with a smile. John and Andy Taylor heard the news of Le Bon's near-fatal accident while still on tour with The Power Station. The guitarist complained, 'Fucking right I'm worried about the boat. It's sort of tinged with rock star lunacy. That boat sinking is just a reflection of what happened to Duran Duran. Too many things done quickly and you get there and you just trip over.' Nick Rhodes, who was in New York mixing the Arcadia album, also reiterated his opposition to the *Drum* project. However, the band's resident adventurer was determined that he would still participate in the Whitbread Race, in spite of the dangers. 'I'm going and that's it,' he declared. 'This hasn't put me off. It was such a freak accident. I mean, if you want to talk about fate, we went down by the biggest heliport in Britain. It was fated that we live and it's fated that we go ahead with the race. It's as simple as that. I'm not a person who gives a damn that much about what other people say. It doesn't stop me from doing what I want to do.' Le Bon and the Berrows got their way. Despite the concerns expressed by Andy Taylor, Nick Rhodes and John Taylor (Roger remained silent on the matter, publicly at least), on 28 September 1985, *Drum* set off from Portsmouth as part of the Whitbread Round-the-World Race following a $400,000 refurbishment. Although Le Bon wasn't on board for the initial leg, he planned to join the race in the new year once some of his work commitments were out of the way. This was, after all, the stuff of dreams. 'We were sitting in the Rum Runner about six years ago, talking about great quests,' explained Paul Berrow back in 1985. 'We decided on either sitting on the moon or sailing around the world in the Whitbread.'

In the short term Le Bon's dramatic rescue made him perfect chat-show fodder. As he told his life-threatening story to David Letterman in New York, Nick Rhodes, Alex Sadkin and Ron Saint Germain were a few blocks away, attempting to complete the mix to Arcadia's first single, 'Election Day', which had already taken a staggering nine weeks. When *The Face* paid Rhodes a visit in New York the magazine observed the self-styled renaissance man blowing $500 in five minutes on art books and illustrations of 1920s Paris in his favourite bookshop, Rizzoli's. Later that evening Rhodes dined at the Odeon restaurant, West Broadway, with Andy Warhol and the graffiti artist Jean-Michel Basquiat. The actors Michael Brandon and Glynis Barber – Dempsey and Makepeace – subsequently joined them at the table. A few days later the single mix was completed and 'Election Day' finally appeared in October 1985, reaching the US Top Twenty and peaking at number seven in the UK. Arcadia blew a whopping £300,000 on the gothically styled accompanying video, filmed in Paris by Roger Christian. Rhodes had initially met up with movie director Ridley Scott (the man responsible for *Alien*, *Blade Runner* and *Gladiator*) to discuss the idea of directing the promo flick, but he wasn't able to do it due to other commitments. As for the song itself, 'Election Day' is essentially a one-chord track with the vocal melody remaining the same throughout. However, there's a lot going on around that simple structure, including a short monologue by Grace Jones and a saxophone solo courtesy of Roxy Music's Andy Mackay. Le Bon described the song as being about a 'strong desire for freedom', a theme which Rhodes expanded on: 'It's about having to make a decision and taking a chance about something special happening so that it could be your election day.'

Arcadia's album *So Red, the Rose* was released worldwide in November, charting at number twenty-three in America, but only peaking at thirty in the UK. Clearly Arcadia's more 'esoteric' approach was out of tune with the majority of Duran Duran's fan base and the sales didn't justify the massive spend on the album. Paul Berrow blames the LP's relatively poor commercial performance on the intricate final mix: 'Arcadia was very indulgent and lost a lot of its energy because it was over-mixed. We were all really excited when I brought the rough mixes back to London and played it in the office. People were going, "Wow." EMI thought it was superb. And it got mixed and mixed and it emptied all the energy. So sad, that. A great disappointment to me because Arcadia could have been really good.' His brother Michael agrees: 'The demos were great and we completely over-mixed it and we all have to hold up our hands over that. We all got sucked into it. You know, "It's nearly there, maybe we could just mix that part again." Months later, you still haven't finished the album.' *Rolling Stones*'s analysis also focused on the fastidiously detailed production: 'The playing is so crisp and the production is so clean that Arcadia's limitations stand out so clearly: in the end, every speck of an idea is embellished and underscored, milked for more than its worth.' In 1985 an uncompromising Rhodes was adamant that he'd achieved exactly what he wanted on the LP: 'We chose Alex Sadkin for this particular project because he has the delicacy we really needed. This is a very subtle album which takes a lot of time to achieve and Alex is definitely the world's most patient man.'

For once reviews were more upbeat in the UK than they were in America with *Smash Hits'* Tom Hibbert enthusing: 'It's all finely crafted, there are some proper tunes and there's a couple of miraculous touches that make it almost jolly. A warmer and less clinical collection than anything yet attempted by Duran.' *Sounds* awarded the album four out of five: 'This is their *Tin Drum*, their *Low* (side two).' *So Red, the Rose* is a very pretty, ambient pop record, featuring some of Le Bon's sweetest melodies laid over the top of short-wave radio effects, layers of synthesizers, piano, violin, sax, guitar, ocarina and the sound of rain. Although the project was initiated by Rhodes and is the fullest realization of his vision, Le Bon responded with some career-best vocals (helped by the fact that the songs are written in a lower key) and a lyrical fluency that hints at real feeling within all the random images. The pair were particularly inspired on 'Missing', a song about a father who is haunted by his dead child. Rhodes created some genuinely beautiful music, as piano and acoustic guitar circle around Le Bon's ghostly lyric. The serene, Eastern-sounding 'Lady Ice' is another highlight, with Rhodes's obsession for ornate detail reaching such a level that Andy Mackay's instrumental solo is a composite of two separate recordings on oboe and lyricon. Dusky, Latin flavours filter through 'El Diablo', a fantasy song about selling your soul to the devil and buying it back again. Le Bon sounds spookily like Scott Walker, circa his 1983 album *Climate of Hunter*, on the brassier 'The Flame' (which also contains echoes of Duran Duran's 'A View to a Kill') and Sting, Dave Gilmour and Herbie Hancock all crop up on 'The Promise'. Rhodes explains, 'Herbie Hancock was just in Paris at the time we were recording and he popped into the studio a few times. He was there one night and we asked him if he'd like to play something. He said, "Sure", and he played the soft jazzy thing on the Fairlight with that flutey sound in the middle. I was watching him play and my eyes were popping out of my head. His hands were so fast.' 'Rose Arcana' is a short electronic instrumental influenced by 'Erik Satie and Stravinsky', while both 'Goodbye is Forever' and 'Keep Me in the Dark' feature the kind of moodily catchy choruses that epitomize the project. Rhodes and Le Bon had no plans to tour the Arcadia album, so they shot videos to five tracks: 'Election Day', 'Goodbye is Forever', 'The Flame', 'The Promise' and 'Missing'. 'I think the Arcadia videos got out of control,' says Paul Berrow. 'You could have made a movie like *Letter to Brezhnev* for the same price. I was ashamed.' For all the money spent on them, the gothic flamboyance of the promos is undermined somewhat by the lack of dynamics between Le Bon and Rhodes. They wander through various darkly fantastic, Cocteau-inspired sets (just watch his films *Orpheus* or *Beauty and the Beast* and spot the atmospheric references) with grim visages, as each successive single fared worse than the one before – 'The Promise' reached number thirty-seven in the UK and 'The Flame' only got to fifty-eight. Nevertheless, photographer/director Dean Chamberlain successfully portrays the dreamlike, enchanted tone of the song 'Missing' through his pioneering, open-shutter technique of 'painting with light'. An additional, non-album track 'Say the Word' later featured on the soundtrack to a movie, *Playing for Keeps*. However, the imaginative highlight of Arcadia's promo campaign was a one-hour MTV special on the project. The station agreed to Rhodes's request to build a completely white set around him and Simon Le Bon, including the chairs, background and floor, so that over the course of the sixty minutes, the New York artist Keith Haring was free to fill in the blank space. By this time Haring and Rhodes were not only good friends but they also shared the belief that art should be accessible to everyone, whether through a stunt on television or by working on paintings in the subway system, which is where many people first discovered Haring's work. What's not well known is the fact that Rhodes had already collaborated with some underground graffiti artists in Paris during the recording of Arcadia. The art enthusiast wanted to create some unusual photo-graphs for the project and so covered up 'this really swishy recording studio in Paris with boards', before leaving them to paint it. 'You can imagine the expressions of the studio owners when these guys in masks and carrying spray cans turned up. But we didn't do any damage.'

One noticeable absentee on the MTV special was Roger Taylor, who didn't appear in any of the videos and dropped out of the Arcadia promotion after suffering from 'acute anxiety' following three days of interviews for the project back in August 1985. Rhodes recalls, 'Roger was always in the shadows and at no time in the first five years did I realize how concerned he was about having to be in the limelight at all. He certainly wasn't volunteering information and I don't think he really knew himself that he had a problem until the Arcadia project. When we all split up he wasn't shielded by the four people in Duran Duran; it was just Simon, Roger and myself. There was a side of him that started to come out and we became quickly aware that he didn't like to be in the public eye and had become disillusioned with the whole thing. It was very difficult for us to deal with, but it kind of seems inevitable, looking back. Roger was only ever interested in playing his drums and spending time with Giovanna. He never cared about the rest of the stuff. In fact he actively disliked it all.' 'Roger didn't exactly have a nervous breakdown, but you could see it coming,' said Le Bon a few years later. 'He was developing agoraphobia and fear of confronting people and being confronted by them. That caused a big hole in our hearts.'

In December 1985 Roger Taylor confirmed that he was leaving Duran Duran: 'I'd been on a thousand airplanes but I didn't know how to get on one as an individual. I had to relearn life. I think I was just burned out by the whole thing. I joined the band when I was nineteen and our global success just got too much for me. I was a very shy kid. When I was little, if I saw someone I knew walking down the road I would cross over.' John Taylor had once described him as 'the ground that cannot be shaken', but perhaps he was just bottling it all up. Roger Taylor and his wife Giovanna moved out to a farm in Gloucestershire and left the music business completely: 'I had quite a bit of land and a few chickens and horses. We had children and lived the life of landed gentry for years. A bit *Spinal Tap*, I know. Everyone thought I had gone crazy and turned into a recluse, but I was enjoying a very simple life.' Roger Taylor did have tabloid reporters looking for him. One morning he was in bed and there was a knock at the front door. His wife Giovanna thought it was the postman, so the drummer grabbed her pink nightie and ran down the stairs. However, when he got there it was a journalist from *The Sun* who wanted to know why he had left the band. According to Taylor, 'I just shut the door on them but the next day on page five, there I was, unshaven and in a pink negligee.'

Duran Duran always left the door open if Roger Taylor wanted to return and he remained on good terms with the other band members. After all, Giovanna and Andy Taylor's wife Tracey were also close friends. In fact, it was John Taylor (already committed to an afternoon at hospital radio apparently), not the band's ex-drummer, who was the absentee when Simon Le Bon married Yasmin Parveneh at a register office in Oxford on 27 December 1985. The couple told everyone only the day before the ceremony. Le Bon explains, 'It was very quiet. Just basically a register office wedding – very straightforward and discreet – with a few friends and relations.' Afterwards, the reception was held at a country hotel, the Bear in Woodstock: 'My brother (David, the best man) made a two-second speech and my dad told a terrible joke.' Charley (Le Bon's long-standing nickname) and Pebbles ('she puts her hair up in a really cute little bundle with little bits sticking over her eyes' like Pebbles on the *Flintstones*) honeymooned in the south of France and Le Bon declared that this was a significant turning point in his life: 'The notion of responsibility is very important. I've become more health-conscious, more aware that my behaviour would have knock-on effects. It's not just about me any more. I mean, you can't carry on leading your life like some errant teenager.'

Nick Rhodes: '*I don't like looking back – I'm not very nostalgic but I wish we never had a lawyer or an accountant.*'

Simon Le Bon: '*I couldn't understand why they'd wanted to go. To me it was all going so well.*'

Nick Rhodes: '*I am still obsessed with Duran. I live it and breathe it. I have never known anything else.*'

Andy Taylor: '*When I was a kid growing up in Cullercoats, I wouldn't have believed I would have done cocaine. And I'm thinking, "Who did give me that?" And then suddenly you realize that it's someone who worked for you. And then you're thinking, "They're trying to control me." *'

Yasmin Le Bon: '*If any girl fans got too close and friendly, I would grab him by the balls and stand there holding them going, "These – they're mine." *'

Nick Rhodes: '*Although I'm vain enough to wear makeup, I'm not vain enough to carry it around with me.*'

The four remaining members of Duran Duran continued to live completely separate lives at the start of 1986. Simon and Yasmin Le Bon bought a modest house in Battersea, south London, to stay in while their new Chelsea home was being renovated. Although his new wife was pregnant (as was Nick Rhodes's partner, Julie Anne), the singer still insisted on fulfilling his new year commitment to *Drum*, which by then had sailed to Auckland as part of the Whitbread Round-the-World Race. On 15 February, *Drum* left the glittering harbour of New Zealand's largest city with Simon Le Bon on board. As soon as *Drum* arrived in second place at Punta del Este, Uruguay, in late spring, the Duran Duran front man flew straight home to be with his wife. However, with Yasmin's support, he stuck to his original plan and returned for the next leg a month later. Finally, on 11 May 1986, *Drum* crossed the finishing line in third place and a triumphant Le Bon set off on the UK chat-show circuit, including appearances on *Wogan* and TV AM. He also put together a book and video of his experiences, entitled *Drum: The Journey of a Lifetime*. The soundtrack included a new Simon Le Bon song, 'Grey Lady of the Sea'.

Over in New York, John Taylor was taking piano lessons after teaming up with soundtrack producer Jonathan Elias. The pair had met while working on Duran Duran's 'A View to a Kill' (Elias is credited as the provider of 'digital samples') and in 1986 they composed the soundtrack to the Mickey Rourke and Kim Basinger movie *9½ Weeks*, which also featured Taylor's first solo single, 'I Do What I Do'. 'I didn't want to sing,' he claimed when visited by *Smash Hits* in New York. 'But it looked like it'd never come out otherwise. I hardly want to push myself as a front man – I get enough attention from Duran as it is.' Released in March 1986, 'I Do What I Do' reached number forty-two in the UK, although it was much bigger news in America, where it achieved a very respectable peak of twenty-three. This was a lot better than the third Power Station single, 'Communication', and it was no surprise when John Taylor announced the dissolution of his rock-funk busman's holiday.

As for Nick Rhodes and Andy Taylor, at the end of January 1986 they briefly reunited to work on ideas for three new Duran Duran tracks at a studio in Los Angeles, where the latter was now based. According to Rhodes, 'Andy had a couple of weeks spare and I had too and we thought why not try out a few sounds as opposed to starting serious writing.' Three months later the keyboard player hooked up with John Taylor to do some more informal work, this time at Davout Studios in Paris. They expected the band's Geordie-axe-man-turned-Malibu-beach-bum to join them, but he didn't appear. The vagabond guitarist later revealed, 'When the lads wanted me to do the next album, which ended up being called *Notorious*, I didn't do it straight away. I couldn't stand being shut up in a room for three months going through the same old drivel again.'

Given that the four remaining members of Duran Duran were physically, emotionally and culturally in different places in the first half of 1986, the only area where they shared common ground appeared to be a collective determination to end their arrangement with Tritec Music. Termination letters from each of them arrived in turn at the Soho office, effectively giving Paul and Michael Berrow ninety days' notice before their involvement with management, merchandising and touring was severed for good. John Taylor claimed that they fired their managers because 'there was a lot of bad blood after the *Drum* fiasco'. Of course, it wasn't as simple as that. The Berrow brothers are born risk-takers who speculated to accumulate in the early days of the group. Like most investments in the music industry, it could have ended in failure, but their dynamic handling of Duran Duran's affairs contributed to a globally successful business that was turning over around $100 million at retail by the time of the break-up. Both men insist to this day that the deal they struck with the high-spirited unknowns back in 1980 was 'fantastic' for the band and that, in any case, Tritec Music's accounts were transparent and open to audit at all times. However, their relationship with some members of Duran Duran became tense when the now-famous rock outfit began to question royalty rates and percentages that they'd agreed to as teenagers. Once the internal bleeding started there were plenty of other catalysts to increase the flow: the 'divisive' boat issue; disputes sparked by the handling of the MENCAP charity concert; a battle for career control after five years of hands-on, 'paternalistic' management; plus the disorienting impact of ego-fuelled ambition, where everybody feels they're right because, after all, the 'seven' were now very successful, individual multi-millionaires. If you throw drugs, paranoia, insecurity, panic, Arcadia, The Power Station and Roger Taylor's defection into the situation, it was inevitable that the relationship was going to be sorely tested by the mid-1980s. In the end, only Simon Le Bon's friendship with the Berrows survived the fallout, especially after the brothers sold up to EMI, who effectively took over the deal with Duran Duran on the same terms. By then, the lawyers had taken over, ensuring that the rift was irreparable as direct communication between the two sides officially ended. 'It's a shame, what happened between the Berrows and the guys,' affirms Marcello Anciano. 'They all decided to get their own lawyers and their own agents, so you couldn't actually have a coherent conversation. It all just fell apart.' 'We'd sat in the Rum Runner in the early days, where there were a lot of discussions about the future,' remembers Michael Berrow, who went on to breed racehorses (his brother Paul 'got married, learned classical music and spent four and a half years building a yacht with a team of people'), 'and we all swore that whatever happened we wouldn't get to a point where we'd all fall out and only talk through our lawyers. And that's exactly what happened. If there's any question about where all of their money went, I'd really like to know how many millions they squandered on lawyers and accountants.'

What happened next was that Duran Duran decided to manage themselves. 'We put on a brave face saying, "Oh, we don't want a manager, we're going to deal with it all ourselves," ' explained Rhodes in 1998. 'I think it was a case of having been badly burned by the previous management, so the last thing we wanted to do was jump in the deep end with another manager we weren't sure about.' This outcome placed Duran Duran under enormous pressure, as they now had a global operation to run from their new London office, as well as trying to write the first studio album since 1983's *Seven and the Ragged Tiger*. 'It's hard work to keep a check worldwide with what's going on with your assets,' argues Marcello Anciano. 'Paul and Michael handled it so efficiently that, quite honestly, I don't think the band ever saw the kind of work that went in to breaking it. They just weren't party to it. They had no idea.' EMI were also concerned about the decision-making: 'The peak had been hit. They tried to take over their own career and manage themselves. We felt that trying to do it themselves was a mistake,' was the view of former Capitol EMI President, Joe Smith.

Nile Rodgers, who produced the *Notorious* album (his previous credits include Madonna's 'Like a Virgin' and David Bowie's 'Let's Dance'), summed up the new situation: 'They didn't have a drummer or guitarist, no management, and the record company had just fired the president. That's the album in a nutshell. Also, John and I loved to party and stay out every night.' The *Guardian* recalled in 1999 that *Notorious* was 'produced from the floor of the studio' by the Chic guitarist: 'I was smashed out of my mind, I can't remember all those songs. I was so high in that period – I think,

"Wow! How much coke did I do that day?" ' John Taylor corroborates this: 'I had a lot of good times with Nile. Everywhere was debauched, I didn't have to look in particular. It got to the stage with cocaine where I didn't even have to ask, it was always just there. I was drinking every day and taking cocaine every day, I didn't eat that much. I took drugs, that was my diet. I convinced myself it was cool.'

Le Bon set out to bring some kind of order to the chaos by bringing Andy Taylor back into the fold. He told the *News of the World* in 1987: 'When I came back from the boat race, I went straight to Paris, where we were supposed to meet up to record the new album. Andy wasn't there. The others told me he'd refused to come. "Don't worry, I'll sort it out," I said. "I'll phone him up, I'm sure he'll listen to me, I know I can do it!" ' Le Bon spent a week trying to get Andy on the phone. 'Impossible! I got his secretary, I got his manager, I got his bodyguard once. I even got his cleaner three times. But no Andy.'

For a while Rhodes, Le Bon and John Taylor continued to work in Paris with Nile Rodgers coming up with the new guitar parts. Then they heard a rumour that Andy Taylor was in the UK and the band's diplomatic envoy flew over to meet him. 'I went to his flat and I was feeling like, you know, this is my mission!' said Le Bon. 'We had a lovely evening with him and his wife.' Andy Taylor told the still hopeful singer that he was 'very worried' because Roger wasn't in Duran Duran any more and it 'simply wouldn't be the same'. The guitarist also voiced his concern about the management situation and the band's relationship with the record company now that they were dealing directly with Capitol EMI. 'Andy was very concerned that we were getting a shoddy deal,' Le Bon explained to the *News of the World*. 'I said, "Well, maybe it's not the best deal, but then we haven't made a record for three years now. So what can we expect? To be treated like John Lennon returning from the grave?" But Andy was adamant. "We've got to sort this business out before we make the record," he said. "And that's gonna take us a very, very, very long time." '

Le Bon was hoping to fly back to Paris with the guitarist, but he disappeared again for a few days, finally turning up in Bath. This time the other members of Duran Duran also came back to the UK, but the meeting ended up with Le Bon 'screaming at Andy and him screaming back at me'. The Geordie rock'n'roller made a vague promise of starting work in August but the time came and went. Then the band received a letter from Andy Taylor's solicitor threatening to sue them if they used the name Duran Duran. Le Bon recalls, 'Too many lawyers and accountants getting involved. It got quite nasty. It was quite difficult to make an album, going to lawyers mornings and laying down tracks in the afternoons. Thank God for Nile Rodgers: he held it all together.' Meanwhile, EMI had done a deal with MCA freeing Andy Taylor as a solo artist so long as he played on the *Notorious* album. 'So what happened?' exclaimed Duran Duran's front man. 'Andy bloody turned up! I mean, this was the last thing in the world we wanted by then. Suddenly the guy was in the country to play on the record. So we said, "Forget it! We've done it now!" And he said, "You can't stop me, I've got a right to." The bottom line is Andy just didn't want to be in the band any more so he simply fulfilled his contractual obligation, played on four songs and then off he went.'

So why was Andy Taylor so determined to leave Duran Duran? According to the leather-clad, be-shaded, former stick insect from Cullercoats: 'I would never have left if Roger hadn't. I know that. He left gracefully, but it was hopeless. It had got to the stage with Simon where we couldn't even stand being in the same room for more than fifteen minutes. We couldn't talk. By the end John was living in New York, I was here in LA and Nick was in Paris – that's how much communication there was between us. I saw people's lives getting destroyed and my own getting rocked a bit. I mean, I made a lot of money, blew most of it, made records the wrong way, used the wrong choice of producers, things that I regret. I know what cocaine can do to you. I know what drinking Jack Daniel's constantly will do to you. The strange thing is, I never even said, "Goodbye." When I went along to play those last few tracks on the album, I played alone.' In a series of interviews back in 1986, the estranged rocker also complained about the 'relentless whipping from the record company to keep coming up with it' and described his former bandmates as 'pathetic little boys' who were 'too old' to play in front of teenage audiences and 'took longer to put on their makeup than it did for me to tune my guitars'. He rounded on Nick Rhodes as the band's least proficient musician, sniping, 'I taught Nick the difference between a major chord and a minor chord. I couldn't get him all the way to diminished, but I did teach him the difference between major and minor.' The implacable Rhodes calmly responded, 'He wanted to do his own solo thing, to stand up in the middle of the stage and be a rock'n'roll hero, which isn't what Duran Duran is about.' He also had to sort out a distressed John Taylor, who 'was sort of ready to leave as well. I probably would have if I'd been sober. When I was out there promoting "I Do What I Do", if I'd really got my shit together I would probably have followed that up with another single and an album and then who knows? But Nick was in New York and we sat and talked. I don't know what drew me back and once I was back, then it was not an easy road, but I became one with the fight.'

As the workmanlike Rhodes held on to John Taylor and kept together what was left of Duran Duran, Andy Taylor continued to live out his adolescent rock'n'roll dreams in Los Angeles, where he got 'lost in the haze of celebrity because there you don't stand out in the crowd'. It had been a life-changing few months, during which his new manager Danny Goldberg had already scored a huge deal from MCA for his debut solo album, *Thunder* (which came out in 1987) at a time when many people believed he was the only genuine musical talent in Duran Duran. Taylor's attitude was, 'If the fools want to give it to me, I'll take it ... Well, it's going to pay for the party.' The guitarist had also hired the burnt-out, flat-broke former Sex Pistol Steve Jones to play on his record, putting him on a £50,000 retainer to sort him out. As he put it, 'I've got a big organ-ization, I've got loads of money, I can do whatever I want.' What Taylor didn't realize was that when he approached Terry Bozzio and Patrick O'Hearn of the band Missing Persons to work with him, he set off a fresh chain of events that would have an unexpected and long-term impact on Duran Duran's future. The bouffant-haired Missing Persons were a New Wave, Blondie-type act led by a former Playboy bunny from Boston, Dale Bozzio, and managed by producer/engineer Ken Scott, whose most famous co-production is his work on David Bowie's *Ziggy Stardust* album. Missing Persons sold over 500,000 copies of their US album, *Spring Session M*, back in 1982 but broke up four years later. When Taylor contacted Bozzio and O'Hearn, it alerted former Missing Persons guitarist Warren Cuccurullo, who realized that the Englishman with the permanent wrap-around shades and rock'n'roll attitude had no intention of rejoining his former band. As a result, this opportunistic New Yorker sent a tape of his work to the remaining members of Duran Duran with a note attached that read, 'I am your new guitarist.' At the time the band were somewhat nonplussed, as Andy Taylor had not yet officially left the band, but the truth soon began to dawn and they decided to try him out. 'I go into most situations with the utmost confidence,' says Cuccurullo. 'I felt that I didn't really have any shoes to fill. I felt that once I left, they'd have shoes to fill. That's just the way I do things!' In spite of his extrovert, persuasive personality, Cuccurullo didn't become a full-time member of Duran Duran for several years. Initially the band decided to hire the twenty-nine-year-old guitarist as a session player for both the *Notorious* album and accompanying tour. Born Warren Bruce Cuccurullo on 8 December 1956, in Brookyln, New York, he started playing drums when he was nine and moved on to guitar twelve months later. After leaving school, he worked in his father's Manhattan printing business for a while and earned some extra cash by giving guitar lessons. Initially Cuccurullo was a massive fan of Led Zeppelin, Jimi Hendrix, Cream and the Rolling Stones, but in 1973 he discovered the more avant-garde music of Frank Zappa. It was a turning point in Cuccurullo's life as he became obsessed with Zappa's music, travelling to gigs to see him play and submitting tapes of his own work to the left-field maestro. Gradually the naturally gifted and talkative guitarist started getting to know some of Zappa's band, including drummer Terry Bozzio, with whom he would later form Missing Persons. When he finally met Zappa face to face, the older man was amazed to discover that Cuccurullo already knew the guitar parts to every single one of his songs. They became friends and the youthful protégé began to mix with a very different crowd to his friends in Brooklyn: 'We went out for dinner with William Burroughs and Allen Ginsberg, the great writers, and Frank introduced me to Ginsberg, calling me "a guitar player". That was the first time anybody ever referred to me as a guitar player.' In December 1978, the twenty-two-year-old Cuccurullo joined Zappa's band, playing rhythm guitar on *Joe's Garage*, and two years later he started Missing Persons with Terry Bozzio and his wife Dale. By 1986, Cuccurullo had adopted a whole set of fresh influences, including David Bowie, Brian Eno, Peter Gabriel, Devo and other New Wave, synthesizer stuff including

Arcadia, as he was a big fan of their 'Election Day' single: 'I know my style was much better for what Duran Duran was doing than Andy's ever was. I was never a fan of Andy's guitar playing, I don't really know what he does. Obviously he left the band to play retro rock, whereas I'm more of an esoteric European, more compositional guitarist. I always thought that if I had been in Birmingham in 1980 and gone to the audition, I would have been in the band.'

Meanwhile, the slimmed-down Duran Duran released their 'Notorious' single on 20 October, revealing the trio's new funk sound. According to John Taylor, 'I think there were a lot of things that were successful about The Power Station that I wanted to bring to Duran. What I had going for me in the arguments was, "Hey, you guys had Arcadia, it didn't work. I did Power Station; it worked."' Later sampled by Puff Daddy, 'Notorious' illustrates the fact that John Taylor and Nile Rodgers had become Duran Duran's guiding creative force. The production on the single has all the discipline of a martial art, built around whiplash drums, horns and a jagged, hard bass-line. Le Bon sounds unfazed by the stylistic changes as he wraps a great vocal melody around the new structure, taking the single to number two in America and seven in the UK. Lyrically, it's a swipe at Andy Taylor ('who really gives a damn for a flaky bandit?' is aimed at the guitarist, who dressed as a Mexican gunslinger in his early solo promo shots) and the media, as Le Bon declares with real emotion, 'I need this blood to survive.' Although the single is one of their finest and proved that Duran Duran still had plenty of fight left in them, when the *Notorious* album followed in November 1986 it only got as far as number twelve in the States and stiffed at a very disappointing sixteen in Britain. They were still a major, platinum-selling act in America, where *Notorious* sold just over a million, but overall the physically shrunken band had lost two-thirds of their worldwide audience. Ostracized by a changing social climate, haemorrhaging band members and lacking a steadying, managerial structure, it was always likely that even a forward-looking, determined Duran Duran were going to experience a drop in sales, but the scale of their commercial crash still came as a shock. Although they'd been playing around with funk styles since 1979, some fans also found the new album's alienated, soul-weary groove to be lacking in impact compared with the mad-eyed, hysterical pop of *Seven and the Ragged Tiger. Rolling Stone* pinpointed the band's change in direction: 'On *Notorious* Duran Duran have forsaken what made them famous – a sort of baroque art-rock bubblegum – in favour of fey funk-rock. *Notorious* is by far the group's most consistently listenable work but, while it doesn't plunge to past depths, neither does it scale the giddy heights of irresistible hit singles like "The Reflex". In their search for musical maturity, the surviving Durans have lost a good deal of their identity.' *People Weekly* awarded the album a B grade, but felt it was very much a transitional rather than fully realized project: 'It makes for a wary listener, not knowing whether to want more substance or more fun. They're not mutually exclusive, of course, but Duran Duran has become the very definition of pop-music froth. It's hardly possible to renounce a reputation like that overnight and this album, often more interesting intellectually than musically, suggests they aren't sure how to go about it.' In the UK, *Sounds* awarded the album three out of five, arguing, 'The remaining trio have managed to concoct an album that is, despite the presence of Le Bon, tasteful.' The review ends with the 'qualified recommendation' that this is 'the best Duran album ever'.

Housed inside a black-and-white artwork, with a shot of the model Christy Turlington on the back sleeve, there are stylistic similarities with The Power Station, especially on 'Vertigo (Do the Demolition)' and 'So Misled'. However, fans of the Robert Palmer-led spin-off would have found the two albums completely different in tone. *Notorious* sounds a like a dreamlike retreat from the world rather than a hot-blooded, clattering rock-funk hybrid. Although the album opens with the fully engaged pop of the title-track, on the next song, 'American Science' (the only Duran Duran track to feature both Andy Taylor and Warren Cuccurullo on guitar), Simon Le Bon sounds lost in reverie as he sings 'all night she can two-step and sway', like David Bowie fading away on Quaaludes. 'Skin Trade' is the album's zenith, a timeless, elegant pop-funk track shot through with cynical insights into exploitation and prostitution, while 'A Matter of Feeling' is Duran Duran at their most minimalist and intimate, blending images of isolation and loneliness with a very pretty, oriental-sounding keyboard line. 'Hold Me', 'Vertigo (Do the Demolition)' and 'So Misled' are rockier, but they're still haunted by introspection and melancholy;

'Meet El Presidente' adds some Latin sunshine; 'Proposition' is blandly attractive and 'Winter Marches On' expresses the icy, frozen soul of the *Notorious* album. It's intense emotion expressed through sadness and simplicity – the winter after the 'summer of madness'. The less-is-more approach on *Notorious* works when everything comes together, as on the title-track, 'Winter Marches On', 'Skin Trade', 'American Science', 'A Matter of Feeling' and 'Meet El Presidente'. Drummer Steve Ferrone (of the Average White Band and Scritti Politti) gives the LP a powerful kick and the combination of Borneo Horns and creamy-voiced backing vocals adds some organic warmth throughout. But half the album sounds muted and hollow – not so much starkly beautiful as just missing something. John Taylor comments, 'My style has very much been formed as a result of the people I've played with, Roger and Andy and Nick, and finding a way to communicate amongst what they're bringing to the table. So you have the guitar player and drummer leave, with whom you've forged your style, and your style is suddenly out at sea, you know what I'm saying? So you have to adapt. I started playing with Steve Ferrone, but it just didn't work in the same way as it had with Roger.' Nick Rhodes now says, 'Roger is the anchor of this band and when he went, we didn't realize how much we were going to miss him. He has a unique style which is hard to find in drummers. Steve Ferrone was an amazing player but he wasn't as original as Roger.' In the end following The Power Station's direction was always going to be a false trail as Le Bon's voice lacks the fire or drive of a white blues singer such as Robert Palmer. It's more of a pop vocal with a deepening sense of melancholy attached to it and as a result some of the funk-rock moments on the album just don't catch alight. Le Bon says, 'There were certain areas where John was going like Sly and the Family Stone, where I could just about get my head around Michael Jackson. I wasn't going to do a bad impersonation of funk.'

The year ended with Simon Le Bon acting as best man at Bob Geldof's wedding to Paula Yates, while Nick Rhodes's wife and daughter joined him in New York, where the band were rehearsing for the upcoming *Strange Behaviour* tour in a US Navy airport hangar. On 23 August 1986, Julie Anne had given birth to the couple's first and only child, Tatjana Leigh Orchid Rhodes, and eight weeks later she became the youngest person to fly on

Concorde. Julie Anne remembers, 'In the early days of our marriage we used to have a family motto which said: "Have baby, have nanny, will travel", because we felt it was best for the family to stay together.' Less happily, Duran Duran's war of words with Andy Taylor kicked off again as news of Duran Duran's nose-diving record sales reached their former guitarist: 'I'm just glad I'm out of the way and off the sinking ship. Well, their records aren't doing too well, are they? Ha Ha!' He also described Simon Le Bon as fat and unable to sing in an article with *Guitar* magazine. 'It was completely shocking,' responded an exasperated but diplomatic Le Bon. 'Andy and I were the new boys, the last two to join, and neither of us was from Birmingham, so I felt very close to him. Then all of a sudden he's saying all these awful things about me. In his defence he said he was misquoted, but I find that difficult to believe because not even the most cynical journalist is likely to make that one up. I suppose he thought no one reads *Guitar* magazine; except musicians do. I mean, he's a lovely guy. He can just be very stupid sometimes and that was a prime example.'

Duran Duran released the excellent 'Skin Trade' as the album's second single, but it flopped, attaining number twenty-two in the UK and only thirty-nine in America. This tested the resilience of even the band's most self-assured optimist, Nick Rhodes: 'When we put out the *Notorious* album we thought, "Wow, we've got a song here, 'Skin Trade', that's probably the best thing we've ever written!" We put out "Notorious" as a single, which did extremely well and we thought, "Great, now we'll put out 'Skin Trade', it's going to do twice as well because it's a much better song." And we put it out and it bombed, pretty much. From that moment onwards, I never second-guessed anything.' Originally, the artwork was going to feature a 'tasteful' photograph of a woman's bottom, but EMI pulled the idea as they said WH Smith wouldn't stock it. The B-side, 'We Need You', a short, delicate composition with some elementary piano, courtesy of Rhodes, is the only song from the *Notorious* session to feature only the three full-time members of Duran Duran.

In early 1987, Nick Rhodes received further upsetting news, when his friend and long-term mentor Andy Warhol passed away after a gall bladder operation. Although Duran Duran continued to promote the album, one senses that for the moment the heart had been ripped out of the campaign. On 27 February 1987, the band appeared on the *Joan Rivers Talk Show*, followed by a slot on *The Late Show* during which they performed 'Meet El Presidente' and 'Skin Trade'. Back in the UK, Le Bon upset the BBC when he announced on *Saturday Superstore* that the real 'horror' of the *Drum* accident was 'seeing the cook's arse first thing in the morning'. His former bandmate Andy Taylor described this controversy as 'pathetic' and boasted, 'I remember being on there and throwing this cake at a *Grange Hill* kid and it landed him right in the mush. There were loads of complaints and we were banned for a while.'

Duran Duran's *Strange Behaviour* tour opened in Japan on 16 March 1987 with the line-up augmented by drummer Steve Ferrone, Warren Cuccurullo, a three-man horn section and two back-up singers. It was a very powerful, pumped-up sound that rejuvenated the band's spirits and allowed them to experiment with a cross-section of songs from their career, including Arcadia's 'Election Day' and 'Some Like It Hot' by The Power Station. The show's most striking visual innovation was the construction of a 'video wall' consisting of about forty TV sets which were lifted up on hydraulics. In addition to showing video footage, for 'The Wild Boys' a sequence of strobelike electronic flashes was followed by the sight of Simon Le Bon's face appearing on the televisions, as if it were a transmission beamed in from some Orwellian nightmare. Although this was an effective piece of technology-led theatre, the overall look of the show was sometimes marred by Le Bon's Vegas-like, tasselled jacket fashion disaster. His weight was also varying more than ever, so that sometimes he looked more like a pudgy-faced matinee Elvis than a prize-fighting pop star battling to save his career. Reassuringly, Nick Rhodes was a relatively unchanged, immaculately dressed figure half lost in smoke machine atmos-pherics, while a slightly chubbier John Taylor was particularly proud of two bolero jacket and vest combinations that he'd talked Anthony Price into designing for the tour: 'Ever since I was ten or eleven, I've loved military uniforms, especially ones reminiscent of the Napoleonic and Second World Wars. The fringes on the jackets add a touch of camp.'

As Duran Duran played six shows in Japan, including two nights at Tokyo's Korakuen Stadium, the ultra-picky Nick Rhodes exercised his 'extreme aversion' to 'brown and beige' rooms by ritualistically draping white linen sheets over the offending decor. In Tokyo he went a step further, going from room to room and picking furniture that he liked, which was then reassembled in his own suite. The amateur interior designer later claimed that the Japanese hotel owner loved his redesign so much that he left the room untouched after he checked out. Nevertheless, no amount of interior redecoration was going to disguise the changed atmosphere on the *Strange Behaviour* tour compared with that of *Sing Blue Silver* four years previously. Of the band's all-conquering, globe-trotting team only three band members and their agent Rob Hallett remained, and even then, it turned out to be *his* final Duran Duran tour. Some of the creative absentees included Russell Mulcahy, Marcello Anciano, Malcolm Garrett, Colin Thurston and, of course, the Berrow brothers. Denis O'Regan continued to work with the band on and off, but wasn't around on the new tour and Dave Ambrose moved over to MCA after the *Notorious* album. Even the production and road crew had changed, to be replaced by an all-American squad of managers and sound engineers. 'The whole thing was very, very different,' opines Hallett. 'The camaraderie had gone. It was all very slick – perhaps too much so.'

Meanwhile, on 29 March the band briefly returned to the UK to appear at the Secret Policeman's Third Ball, an Amnesty International charity concert, where they performed 'Save a Prayer' and 'Skin Trade'. Duran Duran initiated their European tour the next day at the Forest National, Brussels, followed by dates in France, Germany, Norway, Sweden, Denmark, Dublin and Belfast. In April, the band released 'Meet El Presidente', the third single from *Notorious*. It was the first time they'd included a CD single as one of the formats, but the track got stuck at number twenty-four in the UK and only climbed to number seventy in America. On 24 April they appeared on the last ever episode of *The Tube*, where their set consisted of 'New Religion', 'Meet El Presidente', 'Hungry Like the Wolf', 'Notorious' and 'The Wild Boys'. It was a spirited performance by a lean, hungry band, only lessened by Le Bon's wobbly vocals on 'Notorious'.

Commencing at Queen Hall, Leeds, twenty-four-hours later, Duran Duran played a five-date UK tour, including concerts in Liverpool and Manchester, plus two in Edinburgh's Playhouse. For

Nick Rhodes the shows offered a brief chance to spend some time with his wife and daughter. Although he'd occasionally fly them to shows around the world, he didn't take his family on tour with him and that meant long absences in 1987 as the *Strange Behaviour* road trip stretched on to a total of a hundred shows. After this brief sojourn in south Kensington (where the couple had bought an adjoining house and knocked through to connect both properties on the first floor), Rhodes set off again, this time for dates in France, Switzerland, the Netherlands, Germany, Austria and Switzerland, where Duran Duran appeared at the Montreux Pop Festival. On 15 May the band returned to the UK for a home-coming show at the NEC in Birmingham, followed by gigs in Brighton Centre, Empire Ballroom in London and three nights at Wembley Arena (18, 19, 20 May). *Smash Hits* reviewed one of the shows at Wembley Arena, focusing on a staged rant by Simon Le Bon: 'Tonight's set has obviously been very carefully worked out – mainly stuff from the *Rio* and *Notorious* LPs – and gradually builds to a climax with "Meet El Presidente", during which a pair of fascist-style banners descend on either side of the stage as Simon ascends a podium and starts pretending to be a mad dictator (quite convincing actually, apart from his pathetic attempt at an American accent).' Eventually this leads into a 'storming' version of 'Election Day'. Duran Duran's European jaunt concluded with dates in Spain and Italy where, on 8 June, their youngest member, Nick Rhodes, celebrated his twenty-seventh birthday.

The band's first full American tour since 1984 kicked off on 22 June in Philadelphia, followed by two sold-out shows in Madison Square Garden, where they were supported by Erasure. Although this proved that Duran Duran were not ready for the wrecking ball just yet, some of the other US venues were downsized on the tour, including the sizeable switch from the 16,000-capacity Lamar Park in Wyoming to 3,500 at the Welsh Auditorium. John Taylor confessed to the American press, 'It's a strange period for us. It's like a constant period of transition. It's very hard to stay on top, and right now we're not there any more. What we've got to do is get out and sweat, convince the entire world that this band will be around.' Despite these setbacks, the dauntless Le Bon argued that once the band were on stage, 'Suddenly life all gets very clear and everything falls into perspective. Sometimes I think beforehand that I'm not looking forward to it and I could do without it but as soon as the music starts it works. Time stops for two hours.' Their reduced record sales didn't immediately impact on their lifestyle, either. As Nile Rodgers puts it, 'Good times don't necessarily end; the supply did with Duran Duran. When we were travelling, you'd go to a hotel room and open up your little vanity case, you'd have Dom Perignon, Krug Rose or Cristal, vintage of course, an assortment of cocaine and that was just the standard travel kit for guys like us – Duran, myself and other people in the scene in those days. It was nothing spectacular, just a normal, average day on the farm.'

The *Strange Behaviour* marathon flowed on through June and July, including a performance of 'If She Knew What She Wants' with the Bangles at Irvine Meadows and a post-concert party thrown by Capitol Records after their Forum show in Los Angeles. Tragically, on 2 August, Nick Rhodes lost another close friend when the band's producer Alex Sadkin was killed in a car crash in Miami, Florida. Duran Duran's own headlining schedule finished with two sold-out shows in Puerto Rico and an appearance in a Texas amusement park on 10 August. Two days later they set off as 'special guests' of David Bowie on his North American *Glass Spider* tour. 'Let's just say that it's more of a double bill,' argued Rhodes at the time. 'It just happened that David and us were on world tours and we thought it would be advantageous to join forces. But let me just add that this is the first and only time that Duran Duran will go on tour before another act!' On 31 August, they played the hundredth and final show of the tour, a charity concert at the Beacon Theatre for the Association to Benefit Children. John Taylor sang the intro to 'The Reflex' and they performed 'Sweet Jane' and 'Walk on the Wild Side' with another one of their heroes, Lou Reed. The tour was documented in a behind-the-scenes video, *Three Get Ready*, which came out a few months later.

Although the tour was effectively over, the new year began with an appearance at the Hollywood Rock Festival, Rio de Janeiro on 8 January and they also played in São Paulo and Nassau Coliseum, Uniondale, Long Island. Now that the relatively straightforward logistics were behind them, they wisely decided to appoint a new manager, selecting Peter Rudge, who had previously worked with the Who and the Rolling Stones. The band's avowed control-freak, Nick Rhodes, declared in 1988: 'It's such a relief and a pleasure to have somebody who really cares about what you're doing and making sure that things go right. He cares about the kind of things I care about, which is the small print on the label and making sure that the radio station in Kansas City has the record on time – little things about which record companies can easily become complacent.'

Keen to build on the momentum of a hundred-date world tour, Duran Duran began recording a new album, *Big Thing*, at Davout Studios in Paris. They chose two very different producers for the project: Jonathan Elias, the soundtrack guy John Taylor had worked with on his debut solo single, and dance producer Daniel Abraham, whose credits included Madonna and Seal. According to Abraham, 'The original sessions were basically more like jamming/writing sessions in the studio, to come up with the material. The band at this point was still defined as Simon, John and Nick. We used a drum machine, Jonathan Elias played some additional keyboards and I played some guide guitars. Once the basic ideas were there, Steve Ferrone flew in to lay the drums and Warren Cuccurullo came in to play the guitar parts for real. Then Simon worked his vocal parts last.' Nick Rhodes claimed that the new material was fuelled by a more energetic, experimental attitude in the studio: 'We dispensed with the politeness of *Notorious* and we could scream at each other again. We like tension, we have disagreements. I think that's how we create.'

However, the Paris sessions rapidly split into two opposing factions. Although John Taylor had collaborated with Elias on film projects, he naturally began to ally himself with the more rhythmic approach of Daniel Abraham. Nick Rhodes gravitated towards Jonathan Elias, as they shared an interest in atmospheric elec-tronics. When Warren Cuccurullo arrived in Paris to play his guitar parts, he felt that he'd walked into a situation of 'total chaos and confusion'. 'I was sitting in the hotel not knowing whether I was going to the studio or not. It was a split camp. There was Nick and Jonathan, who were much more into soundscapes, and then there was this little French dance guy working with John. Simon was kind of in the middle of trying to work out a way between the two. I hated the location of the studio and I found it a very depressing experience.' Nick Rhodes asserts that the 'split' was more a case of 'convenience rather than warfare. It's true I did most of my stuff with Jonathan because he's a keyboard player. Also I like working late at night. So what happened was that John and Daniel worked together in the day, then there'd be a little crossover period. After that I'd work with Jonathan through the night and sometimes there would be another crossover in the morning. There were songs where we'd go off in completely different directions and that didn't always work out. If you can imagine, we'd be working away all night, and by the time John arrived the next day there were would be times when we'd completely changed the track. But Duran Duran has always been a very eclectic band and I think, with one or two exceptions, most of the songs worked out great.' The widest split in the camp was over mixes for the track 'Drug (It's Just a State of Mind'). John Taylor hated a house-influenced alternative version by Joe Dworniak and Duncan Bridgeman, which Rhodes and Le Bon insisted should go on the album. Taylor told *Goldmine* magazine, 'I nearly left the band; that album was finished over the argument about "Drug".' According to Nick Rhodes, he didn't feel the situation was threatening the future of the band, but he does concede that the bassist was right to argue for the original mix. 'There was this trendy, techno-house remix and I felt that it would give the album an interesting edge. But, looking back, it wasn't in the right context. The original mix fitted much better with the other tracks on the album and John was absolutely right.'

Big Thing was mixed at Soundworks in New York, where Le Bon escaped from the pressures of the music industry by falling in with Manhattan's fashion crowd. The elegant, chic Yasmin Le Bon was at the height of her career, gracing the covers of numerous fashion magazines, including American *Vogue*, and walking the runways of fashion shows in Paris, Milan and New York. She worked for Calvin Klein, Christian Dior and Karl Lagerfeld, becoming one of the original 'supermodels' along with the likes of Naomi Campbell, Cindy Crawford, Elle MacPherson and Christy Turlington.

Meanwhile, Duran Duran felt that the new album was one of the best things they'd done, and their instincts appeared to be confirmed when the first single, 'I Don't Want Your Love', rose to number four in America and was a Top Ten success in Canada. However, it only stumbled to fourteen in the UK. Featuring a guy called Chester Kamen on guitar rather than Warren Cuccurullo, the track is a wide-screen take on American funk. There is a European, dancey flavour in the beats, but essentially the mixture of rock, funk and electronics is a formula Prince made all his own in the mid-1980s. *Big Thing* followed on 18 October 1988, peaking at twenty-four in the States and only nine places higher in Britain. Although the album went on to sell just over 500,000 copies in America after spending three months in the Billboard Top Hundred, that was half of what they'd achieved with *Notorious*. Reviews were generally poor, with *Q* magazine describing *Big Thing* as 'sadly devoid of ideas ... clumsy and boorish', while *Smash Hits* concluded, 'the dumper beckons'.

As the commercial slide continued, Le Bon talked up the new songs as 'Duran Duran with rave music. There's acid house in that funk piano thing. I'd taken ecstasy before the whole acid house thing happened. I had it pharmaceutical grade once, made by a pharmacist there and then – I asked him, "Have you heard of this stuff?" "Oh, funny you should say that, I made some up today." It was intense ...' It might seem like a great idea when you're blobbed-out on an E, but it's not easy to incorporate funky dance music into pop/rock. There's a tendency for bands to over-simplify their songs into repetitive chants, and that's exactly what happens on the two weakest songs, 'Drug (It's Just a State of Mind)' and the title-track. At least with the latter, Duran Duran also experimented with some strident, anthemic power chords in the chorus, which raises it above the banal 'Drug'. Aside from chasing the mirage of dance floor highs on a rock record and arguably missing Andy Taylor's direct, catchy riffage, *Big Thing* is an underrated album. There's a breadth and sense of space to it after the coiled, funky *Notorious*. Not surprisingly, given the artistic push-and-pull between producers in Paris, the album is divided into two halves. The opening tracks are more rhythm-based and include 'I Don't Want Your Love' and its short-circuiting dance floor cousins, 'Big Thing' and 'Drug'. Thankfully Duran Duran delivered 'All She Wants is' to offset those disappointments. Not only referencing the synthesizer pop that used to pulse on the Rum Runner's dance floor (which by then had been pulled down by the council), 'All She Wants is' also mixes Prince's robo-funk with the more rigid, futuristic textures of electro. Further ornamented with Cuccurullo's Fripp-like guitars and sampled orgasmic beats, Duran Duran successfully rewire electronic pop history with an unexpected flair after almost completely abandoning synths on

Notorious. 'Too Late Marlene' is another highlight, a sweetly delivered ballad floating on airy synthesizers, while 'Do You Believe in
Shame?' is the best of the lot, a Depeche Modey, half-crooned
track that also echoes the kind of stately, restrained grandeur David
Bowie does so well on songs such as 'Fantastic Voyage' and 'This
is Not America'. A grieving Le Bon wrote the song after his 'best
friend' David Miles died from a drug-related accident in 1987:
'Remorse? God, yes …' said Le Bon a few years later. 'If only I had
called him up the night before like I said I was going to, maybe he
would have come out with me instead of his old junkie friends. I
still feel him with me. I dedicated a little bit of me to him when I
did "Do You Believe in Shame?" It finishes with the lines, "Do you
believe in love? Do you believe in life? Because I believe a little
part of you and me will never die." I think about him every day. He
was my very, very best friend.' It's a moving song lyrically and
features one of Le Bon's richest-sounding vocals. 'We were very
conscious to write songs that were in a good key for him,'
explained Rhodes, reprising the approach he'd tried on the Arcadia
album. 'When there were the five of us in the group, it tended to
be all of us shouting our opinions across. As a result, I don't think
the songs always ended up being in Simon's best interest. I think
we did well with these tracks because John, Simon and I kept in
mind that no matter how good a song is, it won't make it without
the vocals.' The final songs on *Big Thing* are the most cinematic,
flowing so easily from one to another that on first listen they're
impressionistic almost to the point of invisibility. You're left with a
sense of wide open spaces that is more striking than the details.
However, each track transmits its own tone and flavour with
repeated listens. 'Palomino' features whale song and campily exotic
imagery courtesy of Le Bon ('the scent of burnt sugar on her skin'),
'Land' has a very dreamy vibe which the band would later return
to on the last tracks of 2004's *Astronaut* and 'The Edge of America'
sounds heavily influenced by Peter Gabriel. The latter bleeds into
the long, instrumental workout 'Lake Shore Driving', which closes
the album.

On the day of *Big Thing*'s release, Duran Duran opened the first
of eleven dates on their *Secret Caravan* tour in the Metro Theatre,
Chicago. The idea was to play a series of club dates, giving their fan
base a chance to see them at closer quarters after the last two arena

tours. Warren Cuccurullo still took his place on guitar, but he felt frustrated and unhappy about the *Big Thing* experience, where he was essentially nothing more than a hired hand. He was itching to contribute to the writing of new Duran Duran material. There was a change on drums, as neither Steve Ferrone or David Palmer (ex-ABC) was available, so they brought in Sterling Campbell who, as a fourteen-year-old, was tutored by David Bowie's drummer Dennis Davis. According to pop culture academic Nick Rhodes, 'Playing at the Fillmore in San Francisco was so exciting for us because that place has so much history. I've read about it since I was ten years old and they only recently reopened it. We wanted to introduce the new album to people. Last time our live sound was very slick and polished; this one is much more raw and violent-sounding.' The tour did appear to reinvigorate some of their fans. One supporter, Anna Peters, eighteen, of Pasadena, explained, 'I was losing interest before because I wasn't quite sure if I liked their new style and image, and because two members were gone. But the fact that they're getting back to the club scene and getting more personal with their fans is getting me back. It's wonderful to see them in this close perspective.' Jennifer Chu, a fan from Irvine, seemed oddly resigned to the band's flaws: 'They used to look gorgeous but now Simon Le Bon is old and married. He's kind of fat and doesn't use as much energy on stage as he used to. But he's still looking pretty good and I'll always love him.' It's true that the stringy-haired Le Bon didn't look his best in this period, as he floundered around in oversized, unflatteringly bulky designer clothing. On 20 October, they performed a fifty-minute set to 5,000 fans in Capitol Records' parking lot in Los Angeles and the series of 'intimate' dates ended at the Roseland Ballroom, New York, on 4 November.

When the full *Big Thing* tour hit Europe in November, many shows were cancelled or downsized due to poor ticket sales. Opening at Studio 54 in Barcelona, Spain, on 16 November, the band whirled across the continent, performing in France, Belgium, the Netherlands, Sweden, Norway, Denmark, Germany, Prague in Czechoslovakia, Austria, Hungary and Italy. Such was the strength of feeling against them in the European media, they even tried performing as the Krush Brothers in La Locomotive, Paris. This half-hearted attempt at fooling journalists into listening without prejudice failed, as people soon cottoned on that it was a Duran

Duran show and only the diehard fans turned up. They also tried the idea out with a show at London's Town and Country Club, followed by two unabashed Duran Duran concerts at the NEC, Birmingham and London's Wembley Arena on 23 December. Straight after Christmas, the new year began promisingly for the band when the heavily electronic 'All She Wants is' scaled the heights of number nine in the UK. It was the band's first Top Ten single in their home country since 'Notorious' in autumn 1986. On closer examination, though, the song charted in the post-festivities sales slump when bands with relatively large fan bases are able to leapfrog into artificially high chart positions. Even so, the track also reached a respectable number twenty-two in America. For a moment Duran Duran also recaptured some of their video-age pioneering spirit thanks to director/photographer Dean Chamberlain (the man responsible for the imaginative visuals for the Arcadia track, 'Missing'), who experimented with mannequins wearing masks of the band members and flowing, liquid-like lighting effects to create Duran Duran's best promo since 'A View to a Kill'. Rhodes agrees: 'They did a very good job of painting the masks and after we had finished filming the three heads got delivered to our office. The secretary opened up the boxes and screamed, because it was our three heads inside.'

Duran Duran toured *Big Thing* with the tenacity of a band fighting for survival. They zipped across America from 11 January to 27 February, then set off for dates in South Korea, Japan, Hong Kong, the Philippines and Taiwan. John Taylor recalls, 'On paper, the four-week tour of the Far East looked all right. But it was gruelling.' Duran Duran needed some new lifeblood and after two years hanging around in the wings, Warren Cuccurullo threw his considerable energy into the Duran Duran dates, exploring some interesting tangents with the more experimental *Big Thing* sound on stage and then hosting his own 'Privacy' parties when everyone returned to the hotel. Cuccurullo's nightly ritual involved unpacking his own 'nightclub from out of my suitcase' and then decorating his room with strobe lights, a 'CD player with the laser plugged in so the music goes with the laser', psychedelic posters and incense. Once it was all set up, he'd invite back 'as many girls as possible'. As the tour rolled on, these 'Privacy' parties grew increasingly outrageous, until in the end Cuccurullo hosted them naked except for a feather boa. 'As the host I was always nude, but it was down to everyone else what they did,' he says in 2005. 'I remember one guy dropped in and he looked at all the naked girls in the room and he said I was the sickest motherfucker he'd ever come across. I just have to feed my pleasure centres twenty-four hours a day. I am a sick man, I love pleasure all the time.' Kylie Minogue inadvertently walked in on a 'Privacy' party at the *Top of the Pops* studios; even this didn't faze this American exhibitionist, who had posed naked for *Playgirl* magazine when he was a member of Missing Persons. What's more, he now had a new physique to show off after disciplining himself to a rigorous health and body-building regime: 'I built a new body on top of the old one. Anything I want to change, I do. Sex was my drug; I didn't do anything else. I didn't take drugs at that point. I wasn't drinking or smoking. I was on a macrobiotic diet, stayed out of the sun. I did everything I could to avoid disease. I'd rather eat a head of broccoli raw than cook it.' Cuccurullo's driving, prodigious energy for sex – he claims he's slept with 700–800 girls and eight men, 'although I didn't give it or get it in the bum and three were transsexual' – and body-building didn't take any of his focus away from music. As Nick Rhodes observed, 'Warren plays his guitar more than anyone I've ever seen in my entire life. I mean he plays all day, every day.' He was a generous, charming character who loved to entertain his friends in an extravagant fashion, and a compulsive guitar player with a burning ambition to 'take Duran Duran beyond where they were'. By the end of the *Big Thing* tour, Duran Duran decided to make him a permanent band member. Nick Rhodes also joined Cuccurullo as an admittedly less extreme convert to vegetarianism after tucking into a steak in a gothic-styled Prague restaurant, decorated with candelabra and white tablecloths. The pallid, courteous musician watched with horror as blood splattered over the face and blouse of his dining companion, who was one of Duran Duran's backing singers. She screamed and Rhodes felt a wave of nausea as he observed 'the meat wobbling on the plate, like someone's arm'.

Although *Big Thing* had sold half a million in America, the media were becoming increasingly indifferent towards the band. John Taylor complained to the *Houston Chronicle*: 'I do get frustrated that *Rolling Stone* refused to review our show even though we've played fifty shows in this country and that AOR programmers like our record but won't play it because we're Duran Duran. We're fighting perceptions constantly.' The *Miami Herald* joined the 8,000 fans at the 16,000-capacity Miami Arena, noting enthusiastically that 'the young, half-capacity crowd screamed for each new song and watched in awe as two dancers, backlit and silhouetted behind a giant screen, stripped off their '60s mini-dresses and performed an erotic dance'. At the Coliseum, the band drew 5,000 out of the maximum 15,000, but Rhodes caught the eye of journalists with his 'tomato-red suit and gaunt, cadaverous visage'. The *Arizona Republic* also pointed out that the 12,000 arena was half full, but they too enjoyed the show: 'The group's current album, *Big Thing*, is laced with the influence of Britain's latest musical fad, Acid House. With its strong dance rhythms and neo-psychedelic instrumentation, it is a style with great impact and spontaneity on stage. Duran is the first major act to show its potential to Valley audiences.'

Unable to fill some of the larger arenas, Duran Duran dreamed up the idea of a three-week journey across America, performing in old theatres and old 'show palaces'. The *Electric Theatre* tour included a concert in New York's sumptuous Art Deco theatre, Radio City Music Hall, and ended with a late-April trip to New Orleans. 'Quite frankly, at this stage of our career, we're not sure of our market value,' remarked the band's only remaining Taylor, who took the opportunity to indulge an old rock'n'roll fantasy by wearing some silver leather pants for the shows – just like the ones Iggy Pop wore on the cover of 1972's *Raw Power* album. In America the tour was intended to promote 'Do You Believe in Shame?', the third single from *Big Thing*. When it flopped at number seventy-two in the States and struggled to make the Top Thirty in the UK, Simon Le Bon was absolutely gutted. 'That was one of the worst times for me personally,' he said in 1997. 'Do You Believe in Shame?" was such a lovely song and it just fizzled away.' Its failure also killed off plans to release a reworked version of 'Drug' by dance producer Marshall Jefferson as their next single. The *Big Thing* campaign ended quietly in the UK, where they toured under the radar in April. In fact, the only noteworthy gig was the opening night of the new London Arena in Docklands, where Nick Rhodes dressed in a priest's outfit someone had bought him from the Vatican. He claims it was the suit's one and only outing.

The summer of 1989 therefore brought some fresh changes, with the experimental, open-natured Warren Cuccurullo becoming a full-time member of the band, along with drummer Sterling Campbell. The Brooklyn-born thirty-two-year-old also settled in London after buying the house in Battersea off Simon and Yasmin Le Bon. 'I love living in London,' he enthused. 'I've always loved London. It was the first city I ever came to when I was with Frank Zappa. My first trip away from America was London, England, and I just loved it. I went crazy when I first came here. I was buying, like, women's full-length tiger coats, and I was painting my toenails and wearing open-toed 1950s women's shoes. And I bought these huge glass earrings, and I had my hair slicked, like all greased and punky. I walked out wearing everything I bought in Kensington Market.' Newly restored to a five-piece, Duran Duran decided to write material by 'jamming' together in Stanbridge rehearsal hall near Gatwick. They set up their gear as if it were a stage and attempted to replicate the kind of writing approach that the 'Fab Five' version of Duran Duran had operated with back in the days of the Rum Runner. With the benefit of hindsight, Cuccurullo feels it was doomed to failure. 'It was done in such a disjointed way and I was really disappointed. We were all in a barn, just jamming. That stuff might work for a retro blues band, but it doesn't work when you're trying to make innovative modern pop music.' Nick Rhodes also 'hated it' and, unlike the others, couldn't face staying overnight at the residential studio, choosing instead to be driven back and forth from his house in London every day. In fact he was an uncharacteristically distracted figure as his marriage to Julie Anne was starting to fall apart. Friends had been concerned for a long time that the couple had married too young and Rhodes's long absences while on tour with Duran Duran had put a lot of strain on the relationship. By the time they were thrown back together again, they were virtual strangers, leading separate lives. For the sake of their daughter Tatjana, Nick and Julie Anne Rhodes continued to live together in south Kensington, but privately the pair acknowledged that they were unlikely to be reconciled.

John Taylor was also in an anxious, self-pitying state after breaking up with Renee Simonsen. They'd bought a house in Paris together during the recording of *Big Thing*, but according to the former *Vogue* cover girl, 'Things weren't going great. John's career was going very badly, he was very hard up and the tour wasn't going well, so he was very intent on making everything better and didn't have any time for me. When it did come to an end, it was the biggest disappointment of my life, but we were going in different directions. He wanted to be a pop star and to be recognized and I don't think that's such a big deal. He always complained that I wasn't interested enough in his business and I just wasn't.' Although the split had been on the cards for quite some time, it wasn't until the Danish model returned from a soul-searching, four-month reality check in a kibbutz in Israel that she decided she'd had enough. Simonsen moved back to her home country and the dejected Taylor returned to his Knightsbridge apartment (he'd flogged his flats in New York and Paris) for the duration of the new album's recording. On the rebound, the twenty-nine-year-old bassist started dating former 'wild child' actress (she appeared in *The Rachel Papers* alongside Ione Skye in 1989) and *The Word* TV presenter Amanda de Cadenet, who was twelve years younger. The daughter of the French racing driver Alain de Cadenet, she'd come to the attention of the British media as a rebellious fourteen-year-old at the exclusive all-girls school, Benenden. She met John Taylor when they both went to see a play that Nick Rhodes's wife, Julie Anne, was appearing in. According to Duran's emotionally intense bassist, 'Everything became a living hell for me. I'd split up with Renee and I went running into the arms of Amanda.' 'Amanda and John was not a good combination,' reflected Le Bon years later.

Armed with a dozen or so songs, a battle-weary Duran Duran entered Olympic Studio in Barnes in late 1989 to record the new album, *Liberty* (surely an ironic title given their state of mind at the time), with producer Chris Kimsey and engineer Chris Potter. John Taylor was initially more enthusiastic about the material than some of the others, but his interest in the record began to wane as the sessions dragged on and on: '*Liberty* was a bitch to make. It seemed the worst place you could be in the world was in Duran Duran. I wasn't strong enough to leave, so all I could do by that point was hang on by the skin of my teeth. I certainly wasn't driven to play and practise the way any professional should be doing. I smoked a lot of hash oil; that's all I can really remember about making that album.' Taylor later confessed that he should have worked harder on the project because he felt that he had the key to unlock the songs, but made no effort to do so at the time. Simon Le Bon also experienced the first blank writing period of his career, as he was unable to come up with words for the tracks that were being laid down. He was still disillusioned by the blank reception that had greeted the 'Do You Believe in Shame?' single and the way the *Big Thing* campaign had just petered out due to lack of interest. He'd also become self-conscious about what he should write about, as the band struggled to write political songs like U2 or Peter Gabriel. Given the situation, Le Bon was understandably far more interested in spending time with Yasmin and their new baby girl, Amber Rose Tamara, who was born on 25 August 1989.

In spite of the lunar-dry lack of creativity and lack of financial security – Taylor admitted to being 'practically broke' and Rhodes's debts to Coutts bank were spiralling into gob-smacking seven-figure sums – Duran Duran hung on to their wildly flamboyant, glamorous past by continuing to live beyond their means. During the making of *Liberty*, they had their own in-house chef and a big wine list would appear every day. According to the album's programmer, John Jones, 'I seem to remember at one point someone mentioned that our collective wine bill was over £30,000.' At least there was a useful cash injection in November 1989, when EMI released their first Duran Duran 'best of' compilation, *Decade*. The album shot to number five in the UK – their biggest success since 1984's *Arena*, although that was overshadowed by the album's poor showing in America, where it only limped to sixty-seven. The Frankenstein's monster-like, composite dance single 'Burning the Ground', which Rhodes had constructed out of samples of former Duran glories, fared much worse and stalled at number thirty-one in the UK. It failed to register at all on the US Billboard Top Hundred. Misery was stacked up lasagne-like, when in December 1989 John Taylor was caught drink-driving and banned for twelve months and Nick Rhodes was informed that his friend, Keith Haring, was dying of AIDS (he passed away in February 1990). Some of the 1980s' most colourful, innovative artists had gone (including Andy Warhol and Jean Michel Basquiat, who'd died from an overdose in August 1988), and even the naturally buoyant, optimistic keyboard player feared that the new decade signalled Duran Duran's imminent obsolescence: 'We're as good an example as anybody of what the early 1980s were: excessive, bright and full of hope. And not realizing that you were going to get the bill at the end of the decade. Everybody has been spend, spend, spend and putting it on Duran Duran's tab. We were broke at the end of the 1980s, just like everyone else. And what disturbed me greatly was that at midnight on New Year's Eve 1989, people thought that the door was going to close on the vault and shut people like me behind it.'

Nick Rhodes: *'Plastic is a very dangerous thing. I was, after all, born to shop.'*

Simon Le Bon: *'Duran kind of fell down the back of the sofa and we need to get back on the mantelpiece.'*

John Taylor: *'Bringing Warren in and just giving full rein to his talents is really what* The Wedding Album *was about. Rather than trying to control it, just acknowledging what Warren had to offer is what made that album work.'*

Madeleine Farley: *'I had a pair of couture fangs surreptitiously made for Nick – the dentist and I were in cahoots. Nick would always wear them in bed and I'd have on my six-inch Manolos.'*

Nick Rhodes: *'I think it's important to keep a perspective at all times. In our industry you see such extremes. I saw a guy last night with the longest cigar I've ever seen. And I'm thinking, "My God, he must have a very long limo!"'*

John Taylor: *'When Kurt Cobain died [in April 1994] he made me feel like I was a real sell-out. I wasn't really living my life, I wasn't really doing what I wanted to be doing and it kind of kicked my ass.'*

No one in Duran Duran had very high expectations for 'Violence of Summer (Love's Taking Over)', the first single to be lifted from the *Liberty* album. Released on 23 July 1990 this paper-thin, self-consciously 'poppy' track debuted at number twenty in the UK but failed to reach the Top Sixty in the States. 'It wasn't right; I didn't really like it as a single,' droned an uncharacteristically negative Nick Rhodes in 2005. Le Bon agrees: 'It just doesn't have a proper chorus. Great verse though. Just not paying enough attention, we lost our concentration.' Duran Duran looked as if they'd entered the twilight of their career as they lip-synched 'Violence of Summer (Love's Taking Over)' on *Top of the Pops* and the middle-of-the-road TV chat show, *Wogan*.

Liberty came out in August, charting high at number eight in the UK, but spiralling out of the Top Seventy-five within a few weeks. Over in the States it peaked at forty-six but again swiftly disappeared as Duran Duran no longer enjoyed radio support and even MTV snubbed them. To add insult to injury, the video-age pioneers, who had played such a colourful role in the development of the station in the early 1980s, weren't able to blag any free guest tickets for the 1990 MTV Awards. As dance music, grunge and hip hop crossed over, Duran Duran were regarded as a stigmatized relic from another era completely. American magazine *Trouser Press* was typical in its indifference: '*Liberty* is a senseless collision of tuneless guitar raunch, Motown-inflected soul-pop and numbing dance grooves. The album is idiotic, with lyrics that set new standards for pretensions gone out of bounds.' In the UK, Andrew Martin in *Q* magazine ignored most of the material but did point out three standout moments – 'Liberty', 'Serious' and 'My Antarctica' – commenting, 'The suspicion remains that when they want to write a good tune, Duran can do it. Why they don't bother more often is a mystery.'

Liberty is Duran Duran's weakest album, apart from the three songs highlighted by *Q* magazine: the sweetly produced title-track; 'My Antarctica', which is a pulsing, ethereal synthesizer pop song featuring a fine vocal performance from Le Bon; and the airily upbeat, shimmering 'Serious'. Although it sounds like a lost Hall and Oates classic, 'Serious' didn't break into the UK Top Forty when it was released as a single in November 1990. The rest of *Liberty* is dispiritingly forgettable, especially the lifeless funk-rock of 'Hothead', 'All Along the Water' and 'Can You Deal with It'. The gnarly 'Read My Lips' (US President George Bush's catchphrase at the time) does at least possess a sense of purpose in its eyeballing, declamatory chorus, although the song's rock'n'roll machismo is a bit like seeing your mum with tattoos. 'First Impression' has a scarred potency until you realize that it's a transparent rip-off of The The's 1986 hit, 'Infected', while the wordplays of 'Venice Drowning' have the same toe-curling effect as David Bowie's 'Glass Spider' monologue on his creative nadir, 1987's *Never Let Me Down*.

Wisely the band decided that they should crack on with another album rather than tour *Liberty*, so they set off instead on short promo trips to Australia, New Zealand and Florence. However, only four months after the album's release, Capitol scrapped plans to shoot videos for proposed singles, 'First Impression' (for the USA) and 'Liberty' (UK and Europe). Clearly it was time for some serious soul-searching. Le Bon recalls: 'I don't think any of us were prepared for the duration of the low. You feel that people have got a bit sick of you and we got sick of it as well. There were times when everyone in the band felt like giving up. There were also times when we felt like we hit a low point, only to find a lower point than that later.'

The first thing that happened after *Liberty* sank without trace was that Duran Duran's drummer Sterling Campbell quietly drifted away from the set-up, resurfacing on the cover of *Rolling Stone* magazine as a member of the rock band Soul Asylum. Now the question was, did the remaining quartet have the passion and will to carry on? John Taylor possessed the haunted look of a man on the edge of a nervous breakdown, Nick Rhodes was in the middle of a distressing marital break-up with a young child to protect, and Simon Le Bon was dreaming of escape. He told *Hello!* magazine, 'I'd like to be living by the sea, where it's windy. I like the wind, I like sailing, to me it means freedom.' This left Cuccurullo, the musical obsessive with the Schwarzenegger-meets-Iggy Pop physique, to take control: 'I was the hungriest, I wanted success, I wanted to go beyond where I had gone. The band had a heart transplant. I'm not saying the others weren't motivated, but I didn't have any family to distract me. All I had was my music and I am quite an extreme boy.' Cuccurullo had transformed the living room of his Battersea semi-detached into a studio and invited Nick Rhodes around to consider the idea of recording the whole of the next album there. The keyboard player approved of the notion and later quipped that the décor was an improvement on commercial studios, as 'there wasn't a piece of glass in between us and some horrible plastic plants in there'. A world away from the French villa where they'd started recording *Seven and the Ragged Tiger* nearly ten years earlier, Duran Duran's new album began to take shape on headphones so as not to disturb Cuccurullo's south London neighbours. They were prolific, generating an album's worth of material between January and April 1991, with Le Bon enthusing that they'd finally got themselves into 'a rhythm of working and an attitude we have been aiming for since 1985'. Capitol EMI agreed to an advance for the new album, but this time they policed the deal more closely than their previous arrangements. John Taylor comments: 'It was the first record we made that was tightly A&R'd. On the couple of albums leading up to that one, we'd blown so much cash and not had successes that the label said, "You know what? This time we're only giving you *this* much money and then you're going to come back and play us what you've written, and if we like it, we'll give you some more. And this is going to be good for you." We went away and then came back with "Ordinary World" and they were like, "OK, great, we've got ourselves a hit." It was the first time we'd had that interaction with a label.'

Duran Duran have recorded some great pop songs but the hauntingly beautiful 'Ordinary World' is their timeless moment, written as the four-piece jammed around an acoustic guitar line that Warren Cuccurullo had slowed down and started to play in a different way. 'All I can say is I think that the song goddess looked upon us kindly that day,' grinned Rhodes in 1993. 'It came from air, from space. You know, we were just playing and it came out and somehow all these bits that make up the song came together in one instant. Songwriting is the most powerful artform to me. It's my favourite part of being in a band.' They debuted an early version of the track in April 1991 at the Jerusalem for Reconciliation Concert, in London's Royal Albert Hall, which raised money for the children of the Middle East. Duran Duran also played John Lennon's 'Gimme Some Truth' and 'Do You Believe in Shame?', with the latter closely related to the subject matter of their new composition. Not only does 'Ordinary World' feature a great vocal performance from Simon Le Bon, it's also the finest lyric of his career, written quickly in the first rush of inspiration. It's a very personal song which expresses a universal sentiment, a combination that is a kind of Holy Grail in pop music. On one level Le Bon is still grieving for his 'best friend' David Miles, who died of an overdose in 1987, a life-changing moment which he says haunts him to this day – 'Where is my friend when I need you most? Gone away.' But he attempts to find his way back to some kind of normality as he sings, 'I won't cry for yesterday, there's an ordinary world somehow I have to find.' Given that the track was written in a little house in Battersea as opposed to the Côte d'Azur, Le Bon is also describing his own changed circumstances, especially at the point where he declares, 'Where is the life that I recognize? Gone away.' As Nick Rhodes disclosed to Chris Heath in 1998: 'I think Simon just felt our world was a malaise of complete chaos. "Ordinary World" was written from a heartfelt point of view.' But Le Bon opens the whole song up with the verse: 'Papers in the roadside tell of suffering and greed ... Here beside the news of holy war and holy need, ours is just a little sorrow.' Written at the time of the Gulf War in Iraq, the song captures the sense of shock and insecurity experienced by most people who watched the horrific televised images of war and poverty. As Nick Rhodes articulated in the early 1990s, instinctively 'we all want to get back to something simple and peaceful'. John Taylor agrees: 'I think of the ordinary world as being the one you had as a kid. You know, because when you're a kid, it's like the big philosophical questions are: "Is it going to snow this Christmas and am I going to get what I want for my birthday?" ' Bizarrely, Le Bon has claimed that some band members objected to the word 'ordinary' being used in a Duran Duran song: 'I really had to fight for that!' he revealed.

By July 1991, a fired-up Duran Duran had composed the brooding 'Love Voodoo', 'Sin of the City' (featuring a John Taylor lyric about a fire in New York's Happyland Club which killed eighty-nine people), 'Too Much Information', 'UMF' and the exquisite 'Ordinary World', which went through some subtle changes before they settled on a final version. 'There were little things, like adding the electric guitar at the end,' explains Cuccurullo. 'Simon also added this higher harmony on the last chorus which really helps the song to soar.' Although Duran Duran remained considerate, headphone-wearing creators, sometimes noisy groups of fans upset the neighbours by gathering outside the guitarist's house – not a usual sight in a quiet residential street in Battersea. 'I'm glad to see them and I am glad they support us,' said the open-shirted health freak in 1994. 'But to see the same faces every day just standing there, I just think it's inconsiderate. We have had the police come down here a few times.' The guitarist now admits that he found the female fans a distraction in other ways too. 'I was a low-life. I craved variety in sex. I just wanted to get my dick out. If there were girls standing outside my house, the first thing I'd do was invite them inside, take my pants off and get them to touch my dick. It was like a sport, a drug.'

The sexually compulsive New Yorker continued to work on his own music (in the 1990s he released several solo albums, including *Machine Language* and *Thanks 2 Frank*) as the rest of Duran Duran took some time out in summer 1991. John Taylor and the voluptuous, self-assured Amanda de Cadenet set off for the Caribbean only to discover on their return that the fun-loving TV presenter was going to be a teenage mum. Nick Rhodes had also settled into a new relationship after meeting Madeleine Farley, 'a madcap English beauty' with 'beautiful pussycat eyes and sleek bones'. Although Nick and Julie Anne Rhodes didn't publicly announce that their marriage was over until January 1992, they had been estranged for some time. After releasing a statement to the media, Julie Anne told *Hello!* magazine: 'We were very young and the pressure of Nick's work was a lot for us to cope with. I felt quite restricted in my marriage because we always moved in an entourage of people. Whenever we travelled it would always be for Nick's work and never for ourselves. It wasn't an unhappy marriage but I was unfulfilled ... I realized I was losing my sense of self – all I could talk about at dinner parties was what my husband or my child were doing.' As for vacating the couple's beautiful Art Deco home in south Kensington, she described it as 'stark and cold and that made it a very hard place to live in. It looked great if you were having a party but there was no warm, comfortable furniture to lounge around in.'

Meanwhile Nick Rhodes set about restyling former convent schoolgirl Madeleine Farley, who was still only twenty-three-years old in 1991. 'He used to go to Harvey Nichols and buy all my clothes,' divulges Madeleine. 'He taught me how to wear makeup, how to dress. He's the closest link between gay men and straight women. He was the woman in our relationship.' Described by Rhodes as 'very cultured and educated with this fantastic insanity that English girls can have', the skinny blonde with legs that her friend Elizabeth Hurley is jealous of insists, 'I wanted to be moulded. When I met Nick I'd never worn makeup and I had jeans on. I was a complete scruff and he totally transformed me. I had makeup applied and started wearing six-inch stilettos everywhere I went.' The couple spent days watching movies together, with Madeleine receiving 'an amazing education' as Rhodes guided this fellow Gemini through his favourite directors, film by film. 'He did the same thing with my music education. He went through Velvet Underground, David Bowie, giving me a running commentary the whole time!' She adds, 'Nick and I were soul-mates and we did a lot of writing together. He's an insomniac, he's got a unique mind and it never stops. He doesn't exercise, he doesn't sunbathe, he's not physical at all but he needs intellectual stimulation. He loves talking, he absolutely thrives on it. He's a very loving, warm enthusiast when you get to know him.'

Although the pair met when Rhodes was 'at the lowest point in his entire life', Madeleine didn't detect 'a hint of self doubt. He doesn't have an insecure molecule in his body. His marriage was on the rocks and he owed the bank millions, but he kept going. He's relentless. I remember when I first met him, Coutts had just written him a letter saying, "Dear Nick, you're two and a half million pounds in debt, do you think you might be able to give us some of it back? Your humble servant." It was such a sweet letter that we kept it.'

As the summer of 1991 dissolved into autumn, on 25 September Yasmin and Simon Le Bon had their second child, Saffron Sahara: 'Marriage is fantastic, it saved me as a person,' declared Le Bon. 'They say Jesus saves, well, Yasmin and marriage saved me. Having children is the most exciting thing. You discover things inside you that you never ever imagined. You find a whole new part of your head opens up.' In the same month Andy and Tracey Taylor also celebrated the arrival of their daughter, Bethany. Although hurt by the commercial failure of his debut solo album, *Thunder*, in 1987 ('I had loads of money but a failure is still a failure') the indefatigable rock'n'roller had remained a prolific writer, producer and guitarist. He'd worked with the Scottish band Love and Money, Belinda Carlisle, Gun and in 1988 co-wrote several tracks and added his axe-wielding 'crunch, wallop' style to Rod Stewart's *Out of Order* album. Like Robert Palmer's 1985 *Riptide*, the project was a mini-Power Station reunion as Tony Thompson and Bernard Edwards also worked on the record. In 1989 Taylor bought Trident studios in London, where he recorded his second solo LP, the covers project, *Dangerous*. By now he was being managed by Duran

Duran's former agent Rob Hallett, who recalls, 'We were taking a lot of drugs at the time and thought we were running the world. I seem to remember we spent an absolute fortune at Trident on completely unnecessary things like a games room and a steam room. Andy has no compunction at all; if he wants something he gets it. Of course, the money ran out and it all blew up spectacularly.'

In 1990 the failed entrepreneur (Marcello Anciano also remembers Taylor 'blowing an absolute fortune on a club near Manchester by splashing out on this massive lighting rig only to discover that it hadn't been OKd by the council') returned to what he does best by producing British rock band Thunder on their *Backstreet Symphony* LP. A year later he co-produced Mark Shaw's debut solo album, *Almost*. The pair met by chance when the former Then Jerico vocalist was looking for somewhere to record his album and had wandered into the guitarist's studio at Trident to have a look around. The Geordie was there – dressed as ever in shades and a long, black Jean Paul Gaultier coat – and they immediately struck up a friendship. 'The reason we get on so well is that Andy's the only guy who uses as much hairspray as I do,' laughs Shaw. 'Andy had this huge flat in Wandsworth and I ended up living in the same building. It's called the Royal Victoria Patriotic Building, it's like an old Gothic monstrosity.' Originally built as an asylum for the education of children orphaned by the Crimean War, its foundation stone was laid by Queen Victoria in 1857. Disciplinary measures included the use of solitary confinement and in 1862 one of the girls, Charlotte Jane Bennett, was accidentally burned to death while locked up in a bathroom. Many residents – Shaw included – are convinced that Charlotte's ghost still walks the corridors of the building. Taylor, who also had a home in the Bahamas, took over one of the largest apartments in 1986 and hired Alan Bayne (one of the people involved in the *Sing Blue Silver* stage design) to create a new interior within the vaulted ceilings, exposed beams, baronial towers and Gothic windows. 'The designer did an amazing job,' enthuses Mark Shaw. 'You walked into this forty-foot room and it looked like the prow of ship, complete with portholes. Andy also had hundreds of guitars all over the walls, a steam room and a jacuzzi in one of the turrets of the building, where we'd sit for hours looking right across London. It was a twenty-four-hour party place.

Andy had major problems with the marching powder and so did I. The big joke was, "Oh my God, Andy Taylor and Mark Shaw are working together, all you need to do is bring a straw." There is a self-destructive side to Andy because he has a lot of guilt and doubt inside him. He feels he's been really lucky and perhaps he doesn't deserve to be that lucky.'

Although the singer rates Taylor as 'the best rhythm guitarist in the world', when he delivered his solo album to EMI they weren't convinced by the final product. 'They just said, "It's a bit rock, isn't it?" It didn't do much when it came out.'

Meanwhile, in autumn 1991 John Taylor phoned up the ex-Duran Duran guitarist out of the blue to ask him if he was interested in reforming the original Power Station line-up. It was the first time they'd spoken since the confrontational rocker had walked out on the band. Over dinner they decided to put the past behind them and contacted Bernard Edwards, Tony Thompson and Robert Palmer, who were also enthusiastic about working on a new album. However, John Taylor got cold feet about the project when he suspected that EMI viewed it purely as a vehicle for rejuvenating Robert Palmer's career. Although the project was once again put on the back burner, the pair did stay in touch, which was the first step towards an eventual reunion.

Meanwhile, John Taylor had other things on his mind at the end of 1991, as the thirty-one-year-old bassist married Amanda de Cadenet (still only nineteen) in Chelsea Register Office, London. It was a relatively modest affair and the press coverage was restricted to an exclusive interview in *Hello!* magazine. Taylor later confessed to *Playgirl* magazine, 'Amanda was very pregnant by that point. I wasn't altogether convinced of the necessity of the act, but she was. One sees so much pain in marriage. It doesn't seem to have that magical spell. I don't know whether it ever did, you know?' John Taylor and Amanda de Cadenet became proud parents on 31 March 1992 with the birth of their daughter Atlanta Noo at Wellington Hospital in London. Three months after Atlanta's arrival, the new family moved to Lookout Mountain in Laurel Canyon, Los Angeles, to escape the British press and further de Cadenet's acting career. According to the aspiring thespian: 'In England every time I got my hair cut it was a big deal. And when I was pregnant, I got so much shit. Headlines like, "Amanda De Flabbanet", really horrible stuff.' Taylor built a studio for himself and began writing music, which his friend Allison Anders used as part of the score for her film *Mi Vida Loca*. Inspired by fatherhood, he also successfully quit drugs and alcohol – at least for the time being – telling one journalist that 'drinking was taking me to a place where I would regret so I knew it was a good place to stop'. The bassist was joined in Los Angeles by Nick Rhodes and Simon Le Bon as Duran Duran signed a renewed deal with Capitol. The trio also shopped around for management after an 'amicable' split with Peter Rudge. They selected an LA firm, Left Bank (other clients included Meatloaf and Debbie Harry), who were 'shocked' at the 'unbelievable apathy' that existed within Capitol towards the band and argued that the new album shouldn't be released until these issues were resolved. A collective decision was made to delay the project until 1993, especially as Nick Rhodes had become increasingly immersed in a complicated and protracted divorce settlement that would occupy him, on and off, for the next five years. 'It was a marathon and it did become very painful,' says Madeleine Farley. 'In fact it was physically painful because Nick had this travel case wherever he went, which he called the "divorce case". It contained all of the really important legal documents to do with the break-up of his marriage and weighed a ton. It nearly broke his back every time he lifted it.'

Now that the new record wouldn't be coming out for a few months, Simon Le Bon was able to indulge in another dangerous hobby: racing motorbikes. Once again he faced opposition from Rhodes, who regarded them as 'ghastly, horrible things. I think chess is as dangerous as I get.' Madeleine Farley laughs, 'Nick and Simon are exactly like brothers. I mean, they openly admit that they irritate the hell out of each other but I don't think either of them is afraid to say it – it's just one of those things that's common knowledge. There are things that Simon does that Nick just doesn't understand and yet they're so loyal and close and there's nothing they wouldn't do for each other.' In May 1992, Rhodes was horrified when the accident-prone Le Bon sustained a bruised and swollen testicle after crashing his Yamaha 400cc machine on a track in Dyfed, Wales. 'I went over the handlebars,' he explained, 'and my balls swelled up like a grapefruit and split.'

Duran Duran did use some of this available time for recording, as they toyed with the idea of creating their own covers album.

After completing a grand, echoey version of Velvet Underground's 'Femme Fatale' – apparently at the suggestion of Cuccurullo's friend, Frank Zappa – they decided to include it on their new album. The smoky, alluring ballad 'Come Undone' was another late addition, although because John Taylor was living in Los Angeles at that time, he played no part in the track. 'I had this fucking killer riff going to a drum-beat,' recalls Warren Cuccurullo. 'Me and Nick were saying, "This would be great for Gavin Rossdale," whom we were thinking of using on our own project outside of Duran Duran. At the time I just knew him as this singer around London who always had a wacky poodle with him. I thought his voice was a lot like Pearl Jam. Of course, not long after that he had a massive hit as the front man in Bush. Anyway, that song was going to be for him and then Simon came in, and he was like, "Man, this is amazing." This was Simon at his best. I had a rough vocal line for it but he sang a different bit for the chorus – the "Who do you need? Who do you love?" part. I was screaming. It was fantastic. That's the thing with Simon, when he's excited about something he can come up with these amazing ideas.'

As 1992 drew to a close, Capitol leaked 'Ordinary World' to a couple of US radio stations three months before the intended release date and DJs received hundreds of calls about it in the first day. The label rush-released the track and within weeks 'Ordinary World' had became the band's biggest hit in years, scaling the American charts to reach number three in January 1993. Although they were disappointed with the number six placing in the UK, the song topped the charts in Japan, the Philippines, Taiwan, Singapore, Malaysia, Hong Kong, Venezuela, Mexico, Brazil, South Africa, New Zealand and Australia. Duran Duran had become a major act again with a song that effectively shed their 'teen-band' stigma like an old skin. When Cuccurullo chatted to Sting on *Top of the Pops*, the ex-Police man confessed to the passionate, multi-faceted guitarist that he didn't want to perform his own hit 'If I Ever Lose My Faith In You' after Duran Duran because 'Ordinary World' was 'so beautiful'. This wasn't trashy art or escapist dispos-abilia and it hadn't been sold with an image or a video. In fact it was a few weeks before director Nick Egan filmed an accompanying promo in Huntington Gardens, Pasadena, California, creating some wistful, dreamlike, ambient decoration for the song – all hazy sunshine and a model in a white dress.

Although there's no title on the artwork, the new Duran Duran CD became known as *The Wedding Album* because the cover art incorporates wedding photos of the band members' parents – an ironic gesture suggested by Nick Rhodes, who was going through a painful and protracted divorce at the time. Released in February 1993, it peaked at number seven in America and was still in the Top Twenty five months later. The album also got as far as number four in the UK and was awarded further platinum discs in South America and across the Far East, generating total global sales of around 5 million. Stuart Maconie at *Q* magazine was critical of Le Bon's voice but described *The Wedding Album* as 'polished and listenable in its marshalling of sleek, modernist grooves and occasionally, as in the excellent cinematic single "Ordinary World" or the luxuriant "Breath After Breath", quite brazenly exciting. Only a hideously misjudged stadium rock version of the Velvet Underground's "Femme Fatale" reawakens old suspicions.' The *Independent* summed it up as 'an album of maturity and confidence'.

The Wedding Album is an eclectic, ambitious project with some career-best material alongside a few tracks that suffer from their enduring infatuation with sub-INXS rock-funk. The likes of 'None of the Above', 'To Whom It May Concern' and 'Shelter' are skilfully polished constructs, but it's as if the band had been tied up while over-earnest, world-weary doppel-gängers took their place. 'Drowning Man' features a charmless, half-rapped mid-Atlantic vocal, while on the throwaway 'Shotgun' Warren Cuccurullo plays around with ideas that are as gratuitous as the explosions on *Thunderbirds*, only nowhere near as much fun. In spite of Le Bon's dumbed-down lyric, the crunchy, dissonant, Princey funk of 'UMF' is much better and the seven-minute, epic closer 'Sin of the City' has an intensity that is lacking in the album's weaker songs. Although marred by a fragmented, random running order that appears to have been programmed by a bored, channel-changing thirteen-year-old, some of Duran Duran's finest moments are also on display, especially the million-selling single 'Ordinary World' and 'Come Undone', which combines the elegant romanticism of David Bowie's 'Wild is the Wind' with a moody, Cure-like riff. This darkly sensual ballad became the album's second single in March

1993, reaching number thirteen in the UK and seven in America, where it generated more airplay than 'Ordinary World'. *The Wedding Album* also features a rare foray into world music on the uplifting 'Breath After Breath', a collaboration with Brazilian artist Milton Nascimento. 'Love Voodoo' is a dusky, moody grower and their version of Velvet Underground's 'Femme Fatale' is an intriguingly atmospheric treatment, relocating the song from the icy, street hassle of New York into LA's glimmering Californian sunshine. As for the album's opener, 'Too Much Information', it's classic Duran Duran – shiny, energetic, rowdy, plastic and full of great hooks. Lyrically, it's a paradoxical swipe at the over-hyped, pop-trash culture that the band are part of, containing the line, 'Destroyed by MTV/I hate to bite the hand that feeds/There's too much information.' 'We're living in a decadent society,' said John Taylor, sounding like a man who was now digging Lego out of the soles of his feet rather than attending Felliniesque orgies. 'There's too much television, too much media. I don't know whether we're in our last throes but it's like the rise and fall of the Roman Empire. It's not owning up – that's for sure.' Rhodes targeted the televised coverage of the Gulf War as inspiration for the song, which he argued was an 'immoral' trivialization of a world event into something more like 'sports coverage or *Top Gun*'.

Although the songs are built around programmed, machine-made beats, *The Wedding Album* is a richly produced collection, with John Taylor's subterranean, savant bass-lines adding a warm, organic feel to the songs. Nick Rhodes's keyboards play a lesser role but his electric piano layers the underrated 'Femme Fatale' with a cinematic, melancholy glow. Aside from the odd self-indulgence, the album's star performer is Warren Cuccurullo, who blitzes 'Too Much Information' with dense, Fripp-like guitars and eastern Zeppelinisms; 'Breath After Breath' features joyful, acoustic-led instrumentation inspired by his frequent visits to Brazil, where his girlfriend and her son were living at the time; his sky-scraping solo and pretty acoustics are an essential part of the soulful 'Ordinary World', and the chiming, atmospheric playing on 'Love Voodoo' is almost as darkly evocative as the James Bond-meets-post-punk guitar line on 'Come Undone'. Although Cuccurullo's stutter-funk workouts and imaginative texturing flow through the rest of the album, it's not enough to rescue the lesser tracks.

The increasingly confident guitarist also stamped his musical authority over Duran Duran by reworking the band's back catalogue. This process began at the end of 1992 when the charged-up body-builder had been given only ten days to rearrange material for an unplugged-style annual acoustic festival held by LA radio station K-ROQ. Inspired by the results, Duran Duran went on to play stripped-back concerts in Toronto and New York in February, which consolidated their newfound maturity after the lilting, wistful beauty of 'Ordinary World'. In addition to a cinematic, string-ornamented version of 'The Chauffeur', they also started throwing in bizarre cover versions such as the Doors' 'Crystal Ship' and 'Success' by Iggy Pop as off-the-wall surprises rather than obvious crowd-pleasers. All this was a long way from the accelerated, car-chase pop of their early days, but the new set illustrated Duran Duran's developing gift for character-acted, lived-in melancholia. Featuring a nine-piece new line-up enhanced by former Soul II Soul singer Lamya and a string section in black dresses, their *Dilate Your Mind* tour opened at the Paradiso in Amsterdam, before travelling to Germany, Spain and Le Cigale in Paris. It reached the UK on 19 March, where Duran Duran staged their hamburger-to-foie gras reinvention at a swanky homecoming concert in Birmingham's Symphony Hall. They also played matinee and evening shows at London's Dominion Theatre, and Naomi Campbell and U2's Adam Clayton were among the audience who witnessed their National Stadium date in Dublin on 22 March. The UK leg of this acoustically restyled tour ended at Barrowlands in Glasgow and was followed by a trip to Dubai in the United Arab Emirates. As an illustration of the international reach of *The Wedding Album*, their next port of call was South Africa, where they arrived to discover a country in turmoil following the assassination of black Communist Party leader Chris Hanni. Although constantly flanked by armed guards, the band went ahead with the scheduled nine dates in South Africa and also attended the première of the Malcolm X biopic, *X*, in Johannesburg. There was more drama in Argentina, where Duran Duran played four shows in late April 1993. According to Madeleine Farley, who joined Nick Rhodes for the whole tour, the band went missing after chartering a jet from a friend of Simon Le Bon's in Buenos Aires. When she didn't hear back from them that night, she feared the worse: 'I was convinced that they'd crashed and that they were all dead, until Nick came strolling in casually the next morning. It turns out that the plane did have a problem and they'd had to make an emergency landing in the middle of nowhere. I think the worst part for Nick was sleeping in this out-of-the-way place with no phone, completely cut off. He kept his clothes on because he didn't want to touch the sheets and all the time he was thinking of me sleeping in this beautiful hotel in Buenos Aires.'

The concert in Argentina's capital turned out to be one of the tour's highlights as Duran Duran played to a rowdy, intense 50,000-strong audience, who added to the drama of the show by illuminating the night sky with firecrackers and flares. The band filmed the concert for a 'Breath After Breath' promo (included in their 1993 video documentary, *Extraordinary World*), which also included some footage shot at the stunning Iguacu Falls on the border of Argentina and Brazil. Surrounded by semi-tropical forest and the high-rising mist of the turbulent water, this wonder-of-the-world famously provided the dramatic backdrop to the opening scene of the 1986 movie *The Mission*, starring Robert De Niro and Jeremy Irons. Following the full-on excitement of Argentina, 20,000 fans saw Duran Duran in Paraguay, another 6,000 attended a show in Uruguay and the tour ended on a grand scale at the outdoor stadium, Velodromo, Santiago, Chile on 9 May 1993. Despite the inspiring mix of Latin culture and breathtaking natural panoramas, Warren Cuccurullo admits: 'I travelled around the world with Duran Duran, but I hardly saw any of it. All I wanted to do was find the hottest babes and take them back to my room. I didn't see much past my own four walls.' 'He's such an extremist,' laughs Madeleine Farley as she recalls his psychedelic, strangely romantic seduction zone. 'He'd decorate his room so it was absolutely the same wherever he was in the world. Warren was only interested in playing guitar, girls and his body-building. I remember on that tour he showed me how he shaved – he'd start on his cheek and then he'd work all the way down his body!'

After celebrating the end of the tour in Chile, Duran Duran flew to California where they joined Madonna and others at the Arsenio Hall Fourth Anniversary Show in the Hollywood Bowl. Two days later the band signed records at LA's Tower Records, where they also performed an hour-long show with their three-piece string section, which was broadcast by satellite to Hard

Rock Cafes in London, Sydney, Tokyo, Berlin and Beverly Hills. The *LA Times* noted, 'This nine-strong version of Duran played with more passion here than veteran viewers might remember seeing in larger, more electric settings.' Much of the next two months were spent rehearsing for the American tour, which opened on 14 July 1993 in the Sundome, Tampa, Florida (they also played four dates in Mexico as a stadium-sized 'warm-up'). For these US shows they erected a lavish stage set that had visual echoes of David Bowie's *Diamond Dogs* cityscape from the mid-1970s, but modernized with projected visuals and the swaggering, apocalyptic camp of U2's *Zoo TV* tour. Later described by Nick Rhodes as 'a cross between Flash Gordon and Kafka', the staging featured a slum tenement block, a rocket-sized lipstick tube and a giant eye, which looked over the audience and had images and films beamed into it. For 'A View to a Kill', the thirty-year-old film fanatic volunteered to make 'a very campy B-movie' starring Madeleine Farley's friend, Elizabeth Hurley. According to Rhodes, 'She has that film noir type of look that we wanted and so we had a lot of fun shooting this very kitsch thing with lingerie and fake blood in the Chateau Marmont in Los Angeles.' In addition to an eyeball with a slinky, silhouetted actress writhing at its centre, there were also numerous video screens, a red telephone box, a wall-smashing globe and a TV set, which a choreographed Le Bon demolished during the show. Rhodes says: 'It was all my fault. I saw an opera in London and for weeks after I was thinking how magical it was, so I contacted the set designer. We had a lot of fun with it but we soon realized that we'd bitten off more than we could chew.' The designer Stefano Lazaridis was used to working on fixed sets that would be erected in the English National Opera and then taken down at the end of the run. As a result, he'd built this surreal, nightmarish vision out of huge, heavy wooden pieces that were extremely difficult to break down at the end of the concert, costing the band a fortune in union fees as the hours ticked on. Not only that, but it required six trucks to transport from show to show and was actually too big for some of the venues. This included the cavernous Hollywood Bowl, because Lazaridis's surreal metropolis didn't fit underneath the shell-like overhang, so the band were forced to relocate into the nearby LA Forum. 'The whole thing had been constructed and we'd rehearsed with it and then we were advised, "If you just leave this right now, you'll be much better off than if you take it," ' recalls Cuccurullo. 'Of course we thought that was crazy after all the expense of building it in the first place. But then I went to see Frank Zappa around that time and when I told him about it he said, "Do you know how much six trucks will cost in gas?" And then he told me, "Don't go spending all your money on scenery." He was right.'

Duran Duran's 1993 tour of America was a showy, glitzy thirty-date affair with the athletic, eccentric Terence Trent D'Arby as support. They had the air of conquering heroes and the reviewers seemed to fall under their spell, with the *LA Times* raving about a 'revitalized' Le Bon, 'full of barely contained energy'. When Duran Duran arrived in New York to play the Jones Beach Amphitheatre in Long Island on 24 July, Michael Bracewell from *The Times* was waiting to talk to them. By now, a pincer-cheeked John Taylor was dyeing his hair red and Nick Rhodes had switched back to peroxide blond after a brief flirtation with purple, much to the relief of his girlfriend Madeleine, who says, 'It was like waking up with Mrs Slocombe every morning.' Bracewell's first impression of the charismatic, fashion-loving keyboard player summed up the lavish atmosphere around the band, which was like a Broadway production of a rock'n'roll tour: 'The air-conditioned, fragrant calm of the lobby of the Royalton Hotel in New York was suddenly disturbed by a caravan of minders, promoters, publicists, assistants, record company officials, children and glamorous women, all of whom appeared to have descended in the same lift. At the centre of the throng, dressed in a scarlet satin jacket and Vivienne Westwood bondage trousers and sporting platinum-blond hair, was Nick Rhodes. It was a moment designed to be bathed in flashlight and consequently, it was. As the procession approached the double doors and prepared to slide into limousines, Rhodes paused, bringing the whole platoon to a sudden halt. The doors were opened by black-clad bellboys with cheekbones like wing mirrors and a few pre-emptive teenage screams shot in from the oven of the pavement. "This," said Rhodes, surveying the scene before him, "is going to be rather like an episode of *The Simpsons* ..." ' Not to be outdone, Simon Le Bon was spotted in a pink satin suit and John Taylor went 'Vivienne Westwood crazy', varying his look from a three-piece velvet suit that he had in three shades – red, brown and royal blue – to a modernized New Romantic style, complete with ruffles. As for Warren Cuccurullo, he paraded around New York in a black fishnet top, high-heeled boots and gold lamé jeans. When Michael Bracewell later observed Duran Duran signing autographs at a Manhattan record store, he confessed, 'The stars look frail and glamorous. You cannot help but be impressed.'

Yet despite the hype and myth-making (as a result of the come-back, the band were also immortalized in Tinseltown with their own star on the Hollywood Walk of Fame) Duran Duran's next single 'Too Much Information' not only failed to break into the Top Thirty in the UK, it only got as far as forty-five in America. Did fans prefer their pretty ballads to the swaggering, slightly tongue-in-cheek spirit of the new single? Capitol certainly felt so and were already lining up 'Femme Fatale' as the next single, complete with an androgynously styled video shot by photographer Ellen Von Unwerth. However, the idea was scrapped because 'Too Much Information' had lost so much momentum on radio that it effec-tively killed off the campaign. If the US radio programmers weren't keen on trash-rock or plastique-soul it presented Duran Duran with a commercial problem. In fact they weren't alone in 1993, as U2's *Zooropa* had failed to replicate the multi-million sales of the more 'authentic'-sounding guitar rock of their 1987 album, *The Joshua Tree*. By the time of 1997's *Pop*, even the world's biggest band seemed to have alienated large sections of their audience in an extravaganza of disco beats and a giant, hydraulic lemon.

But while U2's glittery, leering 'showbiz' creation was an experi-ment, Duran Duran are in essence a cocky, romantic, fashion-obsessed band. They are MTV pioneers. They are CNN rockers. Although the likes of 'Ordinary World' and 'Come Undone' proved they were capable of writing beautiful songs, it didn't mean that they could seamlessly mutate into a ballad act for the rest of the 1990s – not without ripping out the heart of the band. With the benefit of hindsight it's clear that by early September 1993, Duran Duran's rediscovered Midas touch was slowly fading from their fingertips. Bad luck played a part in this as, after performing in Germany, Switzerland and Turkey, the high-spirited, glammed-up rockers had suddenly to halt their show in Rotterdam, Holland when Simon Le Bon's voice gave in after one and a half songs. The disconsolate singer was diagnosed with swollen vocal cords, forcing the postponement of the remaining three weeks of their European tour. Duran Duran tried again a month later with another sequence of American shows, but after five dates Le Bon lost his voice again. This time he had 'lacerated' his vocal cords and the band had no choice but to cancel a further month of gigs. Duran Duran didn't perform again until 17 November, when they adapted their acoustic set for an MTV Unplugged Special at the Sony Music Studios, New York City. Two days later they resumed their American tour – minus the opera-inspired set and string section – but the flamboyant, celebratory mood was tinged with sadness when Warren Cuccurullo received the news that his mentor Frank Zappa had died of prostate cancer.

In January 1994 Duran Duran set off for yet more American dates, followed by the rescheduled shows in the UK, which included a night at the NEC where they were supported by Andy Wickett's new band World Service. Also in attendance that night was the band's ex-guitarist Andy Taylor, who once again was having discussions with Duran Duran's restless, changeable bass player about re-forming The Power Station: 'It was a bit strange. I went down to see John and make my peace with everybody. I was at a point where I was ready to say, "I've got to see what they're up to." I sort of stood at the side and I was OK until they put the lights on and this sea of people caught on to who I was. It was like, boom! All of a sudden I was running for the dressing room. It was quite scary.'

At Wembley Arena, Duran Duran were joined by Grandmaster Flash and the Furious Five for a version of the anti-drug anthem 'White Lines' and Amanda de Cadenet presented a live broadcast from the after-show party for an edition of *The Word*. *The Guardian*'s Caroline Sullivan was also at the concert: 'Their renewed success gave John Taylor the temerity to appear onstage wearing a kilt. Not to be outdone, Simon Le Bon turned up in a pair of blue, Vivienne Westwood bondage trousers, an eighteen-inch strap tethering one knee to the other. One imagines that they were not designed with the hearty Le Bon in mind. Yet his enthusiasm, the group's matured style and the sound of old hits made this a memorable show.' After Simon Le Bon joined Paula Yates for one of her infamous 'in-bed' TV interviews for *The Big Breakfast*, Duran

Duran left the UK for concerts in Europe, Israel, Turkey. The tour ended in the Far East, where they played in Hong Kong, Singapore, Bangkok in Thailand, Malaysia and Indonesia.

This was an emotionally raw period for the addiction-battling John Taylor who had been understandably reluctant to go on the road so early in his rehabilitation, confessing, 'I hadn't got a choice as I didn't have any money in my bank account.' He later owned up that he 'started drinking again' during the later stages of the globe-trotting marathon. Paradoxically Madeleine Farley recalls that 'it was only later on that I saw a lovely side to John. To be honest, I didn't really get to know him until then. John was always on the phone to his sobriety sponsor and was very hard to talk to. I think he was going through a really tough time. It's funny, although they've known each other for years and years, I didn't see him and Nick interact that much. I think Nick found John's problems hard to understand and I don't think he felt comfortable with the whole concept of giving yourself over to something like the twelve-step programme.' She adds, 'Simon was quite lonely at times too. He missed Yasmin and the kids. She loves to party and have a good time, but she's a family girl. She's Super-Mum, very loyal and dedicated to her kids. Whenever you see her, there are always lots of children around.'

Meanwhile, inspired by the likes of Bryan Ferry's *These Foolish Things* and David Bowie's *Pin-Ups*, Duran Duran's rough-edged version of 'White Lines' was one of the tracks the band had laid down as part of their own covers album. Although the first completed track, 'Femme Fatale', had, of course, ended up on *The Wedding Album*, they had continued the project via intermittent recording sessions in Paris, London, The Power Station in New York and at Prince's Paisley Park studios in Minneapolis. The ever-eager, get-up-and-go Cuccurullo was keen to release this material as quickly as possible. 'The idea behind the *Thank You* album was to do it on tour,' he explains. 'We intended to record it fast, keep it raw, get it out quick. That's what me and John wanted to do, but then Simon wanted to do more recording after the tour and they went to France in the summer. Time started going past and it ended up being presented as a follow-up to *The Wedding Album*, which it was never intended to be.' Ken Scott, the Bowie producer and former Missing Persons manager, was initially drafted in as an engineer on the *Thank You* sessions. 'I'd fly out to wherever they were playing,' he recalls. 'My understanding was that they wanted to keep something out there in the market, so we were piecing it together while they were on tour. The rough mixes sounded nothing like Duran Duran. They were much more rock'n'roll and I thought they were fantastic. The version of "White Lines" was amazing and really kicked butt! Then someone must have started voicing concerns at the label or management and I got the impression that after that some band members also changed their minds. They went to France and spent ages mixing the record and as a result I think some of the songs, including "White Lines", lost a lot of their energy.'

However, Duran Duran's engineer/programmer at the time, John Jones, insists there was still a sense of urgency when he received a call from Nick Rhodes, who wanted to set up a temporary studio in a villa on the Cap d'Antibes in the south of France. 'Nick said, "We need to finish the covers record right away." He thought that we should work in the south of France as he was planning on spending the summer there.' The band's self-appointed decision-maker and his girlfriend Madeleine Farley arrived in the French summer heat to complete the album with Jones and Simon Le Bon, although Yasmin stayed in London with their children. 'It was a difficult time for Simon in some ways,' explains the friendly, open-natured Madeleine. 'Yasmin had the children and she had to make sure they were doing their ballet or yoga, all that sort of thing. But he's like a big kid really and he'd find stuff to do. He had this habit of coming around to our villa, taking all his clothes off and then climbing a tree. Simon also jumped out of a window on our first floor. He just liked to do mad things and it was like he was made of rubber – he landed on gravel but he wasn't hurt.' During this spell in the south of France, Le Bon hooked up with INXS singer Michael Hutchence, who was a fun-loving, kindred spirit with his own villa close by. Their combustive relationship was a 'disaster waiting to happen', according to one friend, 'but Michael was so sweet, so talented and so funny that you understood why they were best buddies'. Duran Duran's outwardly composed keyboard player later confessed, 'Trying to pry Simon away from Michael Hutchence and get him in the studio was something of a feat.' Le Bon subsequently enthused, 'Michael and I had a great time. I hadn't had so much fun with anyone in ages.' 'This is typical of the two of them,' chuckles Madeleine. 'They were driving on this road, winding through a beautiful forest and on a whim Simon decided to go off-road. Of course he drove straight into a tree. Amazingly they weren't hurt – Simon just said that he wanted to make sure the front bumper worked.' Bono from U2 was also living in the south of France at the time and soon started partying with the other two larger-than-life front men. Jokingly calling themselves 'The Lead Singer Club', they sat by Rhodes's swimming pool, experiencing a renewed sense of freedom and bonhomie as they talked, drank and listened to music. Bono later described this period in his life as 'a couple of years of pure joy, just listening to music and people came from far and wide to stay. I grew a beard, put on a few pounds and drank a lot of whiskey, and it was the most extraordinary life, just one of those stupid times when you fall in love with music and everything.' 'We had a lot of fun with U2,' recalls Rhodes's former convent school girlfriend. 'We'd all go into town and they had these wonderful, mad Irish friends with them. People were lovely and drank a lot. There weren't any security bouncers with us; it was all very real. I remember one night we went out for dinner – there was Bono, Michael Hutchence, The Edge – and everyone decided to write and draw pictures on the tablecloth. Whoever's got that, it's probably worth a fortune!' In the end, Le Bon and Rhodes spent ten weeks in Cap d'Antibes with the singer rarely in work mode. This was followed by three months of mixing in Los Angeles, which took them through to the autumn. All hope of releasing *Thank You* in 1994 faded when Capitol suggested more work was required on their version of Bob Dylan's 'Lay Lady Lay'. Not only that, but Simon and Yasmin had their third child, Tallulah Pine, on 10 September, so the album was rescheduled for 1995. These constant delays meant that the prolific musical zealot Cuccurullo forged ahead with some of his own solo shows (the guitarist's band included Nick Beggs from Kajagoogoo) and over in Los Angeles, a troubled John Taylor restarted his recovery from drug and alcohol addiction. In 2005 he confessed to *The Sun*: 'I'd got to the point where I was pretty miserable. I didn't like anybody and I was afraid of my own shadow. I didn't like the person I'd become and it was all about survival. It's very depressing when drugs don't work like they used to. Anyway, I needed to be "born again", for want of a better expression.' The grim-faced musician was also trying to save his marriage, which was being contorted by the stresses of parenthood, addiction, ambition and the twelve-year age difference. After meeting up again with Andy Taylor, he decided to keep himself occupied by re-forming The Power Station after all – the original Robert Palmer-fronted line-up. However, the sessions never came to life. 'It was a pretty miserable experience,' said John Taylor years later. 'I got halfway into it and we started hitting walls and I couldn't hack it. I think I realized I couldn't tour it and I just didn't like what we were doing all that much.' Although he backed out of The Power Station just days before they were due to sign with Polydor Records in America, John Taylor had the personal support of the other band members. Andy Taylor told *Goldmine* magazine: 'John was in rehab and he'd started going through a divorce and all that, the complete mess. His wife was giving him a hard time and he wasn't dealing with it very well at all. It doesn't matter a hoot about the band, you've got your baby there, you've got to take care of things. When he said, "I can't go on", he didn't go into a full explanation, but I knew why. He's a dear, sweet guy and no one should end up like that. I know it was a difficult thing for him to do, to phone up and say he couldn't continue, but it was the right thing for him to do. If a guy quits a band and you lose a million-dollar record deal, he usually gets sued until he starts bleeding – everybody sues, the band, the management – but that never even entered anybody's head. You don't kick someone when they're down.'

As the relationship started to break down, Amanda de Cadenet made Kurt Cobain's equally traumatized, emotionally volatile widow Courtney Love her confidante. After the friends were spotted together at the 1995 Oscars in matching dresses, the Hole singer (who a year later performed 'Hungry Like the Wolf' as part of her band's MTV Unplugged set) interviewed Amanda for the *Hollywood Reporter* in August of that year. They gossiped about Keanu Reeves (whom Amanda was later linked to) and when Courtney mentioned the 'horrible rumours' about her friend's marriage, Amanda de Cadenet could only reply, 'You know how my marriage is – you hear about it on a daily basis from me when I phone you.' Within weeks she and John Taylor had separated for good with de Cadenet confessing that she had married 'too young'.

In the immediate aftermath John Taylor focused on completing a 'therapeutic' solo album co-written with his LA mate, the former Sex Pistol, Steve Jones. Entitled *Feelings are Good (and Other Lies)* the album came out through Taylor's own label B5 and via his *Trust the Process* website, packaged in a cardboard gatefold with a picture of a crying girl on the cover. As for ill-fated Power Station, they were hit by further tragedy when John Taylor's hero, Bernard Edwards (who had rerecorded all of the bass-lines on the new album), died of pneumonia on 18 April 1996. According to the band's singer, Robert Palmer: 'The guy dropped dead from an acute pneumonia attack that wound up his whole respiratory system. He died in his sleep. What a weird ass thing to happen.' In 1997 The Power Station eventually released a new album, *Living in Fear*, and toured it in mid-sized venues such as the Fillmore, San Francisco and the House of Blues in Hollywood. Sadly two more band members have since died: Robert Palmer himself had a fatal heart attack aged fifty-four in September 2003 and Tony Thompson passed away two months later on 15 November after suffering from renal cell cancer.

Meanwhile, Duran Duran attempted to pick up momentum again in spring 1995 as they prepared for the release of two singles from the now completed *Thank You* album: 'White Lines' was scheduled for America and a cover of Lou Reed's 'Perfect Day' (taken from his 1972 album *Transformer*) had been allocated for the UK market. Given the traumas that John Taylor was going through at the time (he fuelled rumours of a split with Duran Duran when he didn't show up for a festival in San Remo at the start of the campaign), 'White Lines' was a raw expression of his own relationship with cocaine. Le Bon comments, 'I last did coke in 1986 but for John it was like the sign of the devil. We'd lived through it and seen the shit and we felt we were the right people to record the song. Coke has always been a problem for me because it drips corrosive mucus on your vocal cords. Most people can only do it for about two years. It makes you feel like shit.' Although Ken Scott argues that the final version lost some of its edge, Grandmaster Flash himself not only guested on Duran Duran's power-dressed, exuberant rock-rap crossover, he also described the band as 'the funkiest bunch of cats since the Average White Band'. *Rolling Stone* were also upbeat in their assessment: 'It's fun hearing Duran Duran gee-whizzing its way through "White Lines" along with Grandmaster Flash and the Furious Five. Although it's not a terribly inventive interpretation, mixing straight-off-the-record imitation with laughably overblown special effects (the snort and the giggle at the beginning of the track), it's hard to argue with the spirit of the performance.' However, 'White Lines' flopped on US radio, partly because in 1995 there was still a very clear division between stations that played rock music and those that stuck to rigid, hip hop-only playlists. 'It was a disaster because US alternative radio didn't want to play a song which had a black rapper on it,' claims Cuccurullo. 'So an edit was done without the rap but the trouble is that once you get a negative reaction to something it's pretty much over.'

While 'White Lines' was being chopped up and re-presented in America, their UK single 'Perfect Day' (featuring a cover of Neil Young's 'Needle and the Damage Done' and a more keyboardy version of 'Femme Fatale as bonus tracks) lurched to number twenty-eight and then dropped out of the charts. Simon Le Bon's voice has always suited ballads and on this song he transforms Lou Reed's glacial intellect into a warm, dreamy, fuzzy account of a lovely moment in time. 'That was something Nick and I had talked about for years,' explained Le Bon. 'When I was recording it I kept getting this image in my head of Lou Reed on the cover of the *Transformer* album and I couldn't help doing an imitation of Lou's vocal style, because I'd sat around and stared at that album cover from the ages of fourteen to seventeen. So I had to invent a new picture in my head and a new story. I imagined I was singing it to my daughter Amber and suddenly the song became mine. It's such a beautiful song, it doesn't have to be about heroin.' The cantankerous Lou Reed was uncharacteristically effusive after hearing Duran Duran's shined-up version of 'Perfect Day'. 'It's the best cover ever completed of one of my songs,' he gushed. 'He sings it better, they recorded it the way I meant it, so thank you Duran.'

After the failure of both singles on either side of the Atlantic, *Thank You* arrived without much of a fanfare. For one week, a mobilized fan base took it to number twelve in the UK and nineteen in America, but after that sales collapsed and the album stuttered to around half a million units shifted worldwide – a huge drop after the multi-platinum success of *The Wedding Album*. In America, the *Miami Herald* summed up the project as 'so laughably lame it should win a Grammy as Best Comedy recording'. The *Observer* in London named and shamed Duran Duran's version of Public Enemy's '911 is a Joke' as the 'Worst Cover Version of All Time', describing it as 'shockingly misconceived in both theory and execution'. *Q* magazine's Ian Cranna awarded *Thank You* two out of five, although he did enjoy their self-plagiarizing, reworked cover of their own track, 'The Chauffeur', which the band had now retitled 'Drive By'. The best review on either side of the Atlantic ran in *Rolling Stone*: 'As tempting as it may be to snicker at their shamelessness, think about the daring that goes with it. How many other bands would have the guts to try to update Sly and the Family Stone's "I Wanna Take You Higher", much less work in an allusion to Queen's "Another One Bites the Dust"? ... Admittedly, some of the ideas at play here are stunningly wrongheaded, but it takes a certain demented genius to recognize Iggy Pop's "Success" as the Gary Glitter tune it was meant to be or to redo "911 is a Joke" so it sounds more like Beck than like Public Enemy. Had the band indulged in more such remakes, *Thank You* would have been even more welcome.' Le Bon himself declared, 'We've always been cocky bastards and with this record we've got our balls back. The mere fact that we did those songs is quite an act of irreverence. I don't really give a fuck about what anybody else thinks. You don't have to pass a test to be allowed to do a Led Zeppelin or a Lou Reed song. All you've got to do is love the music.' Although *Thank You*'s original, fast-moving, bang-it-out ethos was lost in the final product, it is a perversely enjoyable collection. 'White Lines' (which reached number seventeen in the UK when it was released as the album's second single) and 'Perfect Day' are the strongest tracks, but the glossy electro-dub of Elvis Costello's 'Watching the Detectives' is a sugary treat (featuring Roger Taylor on drums, who briefly joined them for a one-off session in Paris) and their version of 'I Wanna Take You Higher' has plenty of health-food-assisted muscle provided by Cuccurullo. Duran Duran also suit the grandeur of Led Zeppelin's 'Thank You', especially as it flows seamlessly into the ultra-pretentious 'Drive By', which is a seductive, string-arranged mix of David Bowie's 'Future Legend' (the opening monologue on *Diamond Dogs*), a Los Angeles traffic report and 'The Chauffeur'. Bob Dylan has described their version of 'Lay Lady Lay' as 'the best yet' and it's an attractive, stadium-rock rendering of the 1960s ballad. However, the album's disasters are rooted in Simon Le Bon's vocals, which are completely unsuited to some of the tracks, especially 'Ball of Confusion', later dismissed by the singer himself as 'so bad it spoils the album for me'. Public Enemy's Flavour Flav said he was 'honoured that Duran Duran' had covered their '911 is a Joke' but the megaphone-assisted, gratingly nasal delivery ruins the promising slacker-blues backing. Regrettably, Le Bon also sucks all the life out of the glammed-up 'Success' (featuring ex Missing Persons drummer Terry Bozzio) by delivering a strangely muted performance and his Jim Morrison impression on the mercifully short 'Crystal Ship' is pure karaoke.

CHAPTER ELEVEN

Simon Le Bon: *'Painkillers are awful if you've broken a leg but they can be quite good fun in other cases. Same as sleeping pills: if you have to use them to fall asleep, they're a right pain in the arse, but otherwise they can be brilliant.'*

Nick Rhodes: *'I had fun wearing black about my eyes to get that Marlene Dietrich look. Then putting a dab of Vaseline on it and letting it run.'*

Andy Warhol: *'I always like to work on leftovers, doing the leftover things. Things that were discarded, that everybody knew were no good. I always thought that had a great potential to be funny. It was like recycling work. I always thought there was a lot of humour in leftovers.'*

Simon Le Bon: *'There used to be times when I wouldn't go home for months and months.'*

Simon Le Bon: *'I can never remember orgasms. They have this effect of wiping my memory clean. That's the beauty of living right in the present. That for me is the ultimate. I couldn't describe an orgasm right now.'*

In the summer of 1995 John Taylor needed to find a way of venting his frustration and anger after the twin catastrophes of a failed marriage and the commercially disastrous *Thank You* album. The faux-Californian found his safety valve when he formed the Neurotic Boy Outsiders with the cleaned up and sober Steve Jones, along with Duff McKagan and Matt Sorum from Guns N' Roses. They made their debut as a one-off pub-rock band on 28 June 1995, performing at a charity gig in LA's infamous Viper Room on Sunset Boulevard. Owned by the actor Johnny Depp, the dark corners and black vinyl booths of the club had immediately drawn a crowd of celebrities and sleazy hangers-on when it was launched in 1993.

However, its reputation for rock'n'roll excess went out of control when River Phoenix collapsed and died of a drug overdose after a Halloween party during its first year of opening. Eighteen months later, the Neurotic Boy Outsiders revitalized the club's rock'n'roll spirit when they thrashed through a twenty-five-minute set of Iggy Pop covers ('I Wanna be Your Dog', 'No Fun'), punk songs ('Pretty Vacant' by the Sex Pistols) and Duran Duran's 'Planet Earth'. Enlivened by this new camaraderie, Taylor enthused, 'We're a think-tank for male menopause, a bunch of old slags and a bunch of sweethearts.' In fact, they enjoyed themselves so much that they regrouped again at the Viper Room on 11 September, where they were joined on stage for a version of Iggy's 'No Fun' by Guns N' Roses' distinctive-looking guitarist, Slash. A hyped-up Taylor later told *Metal Hammer* that he was inspired by the band's direct contact with their audience: 'We just went, "Out of the fucking way!" It was very reassuring that I could get it on, with the audience, face to face.' Duran Duran's most instinctive, emotionally up-front band member felt frustrated by the external machinery around his day job, arguing that the Neurotic Boy Outsiders 'didn't need smoke and lights and a promotions staff to generate excitement'. After agreeing to a two-month, Monday-night residency at the venue, they invited a disparate bunch of musicians on stage with them, including the bequiffed rock'n'roller Brian Setzer from the Stray Cats, lip-snarling Englishman abroad Billy Idol and Simon Le Bon.

By the autumn, the Neurotic Boy Outsiders had started gigging around America, performing in clubs such as New York's Irving Plaza, New York and Mama Kin in Boston, where they were watched by crowds that included actor Dan Aykroyd, Aerosmith's Stephen Tyler, Joe Perry and Tom Hamilton, plus former Led Zeppelin legends Jimmy Page and Robert Plant. Although they'd been formed in a spur-of-the-moment manner, events took a surreal twist in early 1996 when Matt Sorum's neighbour Madonna decided to sign them to her label, the Warners-financed Maverick. Recordings for the Neurotic Outsiders album (they shortened their name after inking the contract) took place at the Plant studios, Sausalito, near the home of the project's producer, the Talking Heads keyboard player Jerry Harrison. In September 1996 they toured across the States again, this time in support of their twelve-track self-titled debut, which included John Taylor's composition

'Feelings are Good' and was described by *Q* as 'nowhere near as bad as it promised on paper'. In addition to the US gigs, this grizzled collective of tanned muscle (most of the band members had taken up mountain biking, including John Taylor) and fading tattoos played gigs in France and Germany, as well as the UK, before breaking up at the end of the year.

Initially invigorated by the early Neurotic Boy Outsiders gigs, the reborn punk rocker participated in a two-week Duran Duran recording session in August 1995 with Warren Cuccurullo and drummer Steve Alexander. At that time the positive-thinking guitarist felt that John Taylor was 'in great form, enthusiastic and full of ideas' and the trio demoed fourteen songs, including a track called 'Butt Naked' which featured the bassist on vocals. In fact it wasn't Taylor's input that was lacking at this stage – of greater concern was an increasingly absent Simon Le Bon. In 1995 Nick Rhodes indicated there was a problem when he told the *Independent* that the worst thing about making records 'is trying to get the singer to write some words. You finish the music and think, "I wonder if he's got any words coming to his head today?" Maybe we could put some through his postbox, or paint something on his window.' What even he didn't realize was that Duran Duran would have to wait until October 1996 before Le Bon added some of his own lyrics and vocals to the band's ageing backing tracks.

The singer had a lot of things on his mind that weren't being acknowledged by the other band members. Simon Le Bon missed the LA-based John Taylor, and realized that despite the bassist's writing trip, Duran Duran had once again lost their collective spirit. As a result the balance of power increasingly tilted towards the conceptual approach of Nick Rhodes and the virtuoso skills of Warren Cuccurullo. Not only that, but he found it hard to accept that Duran Duran's glory days were over for a second time and his moods alternated between brooding over why it had all gone wrong to losing himself in a non-stop round of ego-massaging, celebrity-filled parties. Although he savoured the moment when he performed 'Ordinary World' with Luciano Pavarotti for the Children of Bosnia/War Child Series on 12 September 1995, Le Bon settled into a mixture of family-based home life and socialising that was broken only by sporadic, forced attempts at creativity. As he didn't communicate what was on his mind, these were usually in response to pressure from an irritated, clock-watching Nick Rhodes. The lowest points came when Le Bon's ideas ended up on the cutting-room floor – either torn up by himself or rejected by his Duran colleagues. 'One of the issues that hurt Simon was that Warren was not at all nice about his lyrics,' recalls Dave Ambrose. Cuccurullo concedes that 'sometimes when Simon came up with things, Nick and I would step in and say, "We can't really put this out. The third word can't be 'nostril', you know." Lyrics are very important.' However, the guitarist insists, 'Everyone loved him in the room when we had those discussions. There was no malice in it at all.'

Nick Rhodes found this absenteeism hard to understand because he felt intellectually stimulated and creatively inspired by his work with Warren Cuccurullo. In fact as Duran Duran fell into a prolonged slumber, the insomniac ideas man and the musical obsessive formed a complete unit, often working through the night in the guitarist's Privacy studio. After a few months they'd generated three albums' worth of bizarre, electronic-based material, described by the Brooklyn-born musical maestro as 'very Art of Noise, very unconventional, very hooky'. Calling themselves TV Mania, they improvised around tapes of dialogue and weird sound effects that Rhodes had sampled off the television (apparently the Fashion TV cable channel was a particular favourite source of inspiration). The aural scavengers then began to link these completely random samples into a storyline. 'The TV was feeding us lyrical content,' laughs Cuccurullo. 'We started discovering common stories and sub-plots and before we knew it we had ourselves a Broadway show!' *Bored with Prozac and the Internet* was described by Duran's keyboard player in 1998 as 'a strange observation on modern life and how simple families deal with the technology enforced upon then. You could call it a cyber-soap or,' he added with a flourish, 'a social-junk-culture-triptych-opera.' For the staging of *Bored with Prozac and the Internet*, the ever-ambitious Rhodes wanted to rig up a whole auditorium and turn the theatre into a giant TV set, with the onstage family being filmed at all times. According to this self-proclaimed cultural connoisseur, 'It largely predicted the idea of reality TV, but at the time no one really understood it and we realized that it was also going to be terribly expensive to stage. So in the end we had to give up on the idea, although we're still hoping to release the music one day.'

Inspired by the themes of this side project, Rhodes also started writing lyrics for new Duran Duran songs. For the moment, the ego-deflated, creatively bankrupt Le Bon went along with this, accepting that the band was bigger than one individual. 'Nick stepped in and wrote some of the words because Simon just couldn't do it,' explains Cuccurullo. 'I really respected Nick for doing that, but yes, I could see a problem was starting to develop. We all knew it.' Le Bon experienced a further shock when he arrived at the studio one afternoon to discover that the role-playing, platinum-haired Gemini had added his own spoken-word part to the title-track of the new album, *Medazzaland*. 'You know that was going to be an instrumental,' explained Rhodes in 1997. 'Then one day I was sitting there with Warren when Simon hadn't arrived yet, and I thought, "This would sound so cool if it had a voiceover on it," and I just started writing these words out about paranoia and fear of trusting people. I used the analogy of the operating theatre and slowly sinking into a world where you have no control over anything and you don't know what the hell is going to happen to you, or whether you'll ever come out of it. And if you do, you won't even know what's happened. Once it was completed, Simon came in and heard it and at first he wasn't sure about it at all – it was like, "Oh my God, Nick's on a track now!" '

Meanwhile, John Taylor's time away from Duran Duran had given him the freedom to think about the future and weigh up his options. During his tour with the Neurotic Outsiders in autumn 1996, he sounded increasingly world-weary and distant whenever he was questioned about the band he had formed back in 1978. 'I think that Duran has to do something unusual or something different to stand out,' he told a Canadian radio DJ in October of that year. 'We're not always on the same page. We have a lot of disagreements about the way we want to do things, and I don't know. Sometimes I just get sick and bored to death with even talking about it. It dominated my life for twenty years and I know all the jokes, all the punchlines, all the stories. I don't want to tour. I don't want to do the same old shit. We have to find ways of doing things differently to make it interesting.' When he was asked by *The Groove* magazine if Le Bon's creative problems spelled the end of Duran Duran, Taylor shrugged, 'Well, if it is, then it is. Life goes on.' He then argued that the band will carry on for ever but, 'whether I'll be playing with them, I don't know. I think we've done a lot of stuff that we shouldn't have done. Just crappy TV shows, crappy radio fucking festivals.' Taylor argued that Duran Duran had ended up prostituting themselves: 'It's lost all integrity. And I don't know. I mean, I'm so bored with it.'

Given such open-wounded public declarations and the fact that he was still trying to come to terms with the break-up of his family, it was no surprise when John Taylor officially announced that he was leaving Duran Duran on 18 January 1997. He revealed that as a last throw of the dice, he'd suggested a reunion tour featuring all the members of the 'classic line-up' and Warren Cuccurullo. However, when this idea was rejected by Andy Taylor, he couldn't see a way forward: 'At times it didn't feel like Duran Duran any more. I think Nick and I were in denial, perhaps Simon wasn't.' Le Bon still sounded emotional about John Taylor's decision when he stated in 1998: 'I kind of guessed John would leave but I really miss him. I wish he hadn't got himself into the personal mess he got himself into.' However, the alabaster-skinned keyboard player kept his composure on the surface at least: 'We were sad to see him go but at the same time we've never been afraid of change. I don't think his heart was in it any more, really, and I've never been one to stop progress. It's like one of those rockets that takes off and then you lose the one bit and then the next bit and then you move on. John leaving has became part of the evolution of the band. To be honest, he wasn't around much after 1992, so we kind of got used to him not being there.'

After rejecting the idea of changing the band's name on the basis that Simon Le Bon's voice is the thing that makes them sound like Duran Duran, the three remaining members pulled together in a way that they hadn't done for years. According to Rhodes, 'We had a heart-to-heart about what we had between us, what was really good out of what we'd created over the previous couple of years and how we were going to move forward. I suppose it was a cata-lyst.' Le Bon adds, 'When John left we listened back to what we'd done and to be really, really honest with ourselves, it just wasn't good enough. It's as simple as that.' Compared to the previous two years, their new burst of creativity – six songs in four months – was something of a revelation, especially as it was all sounding like the kind of cybernetic dream pop Rhodes had been fantasizing about for years.

The first taster for the new album came out in March 1997 when 'Out of My Mind' appeared on the soundtrack to the disastrous box-office flop *The Saint*. Featuring Talvin Singh on 'tabla and santoor', this moody, rhythmic ballad has a strikingly melodramatic chorus (there was also a fantastic mix by Paul Oakenfold) and a more left-field, atmospheric sound. Lyrically there are echoes of 'Do You Believe in Shame?' and 'Ordinary World' as Le Bon sings: 'Got to get you out of my mind but I can't escape from the feeling/as I try to leave the memory behind what's left to believe in?' The accompanying video was filmed in Prague by Dean Karr (responsible for Marilyn Manson's perverse 'Sweet Dreams' promo) and features Le Bon as a bizarre, decaying man, achieved after more than five hours of makeup. Combined with the song, it repositioned Duran Duran as a more alternative act after the maturity of 'Ordinary World' and their self-consciously cocky liaisons with other people's songs on *Thank You*. Two months later 'Out of My Mind' came out as a single in the UK, peaking at number twenty-one and then dropping out of the Top Forty the following week. In fact it was in and out so fast that no one but Duran's fan base even heard it.

The campy, spacey synthesizer-led 'Electric Barbarella' was their next US single, climbing to number fifty-two on 16 September 1997. It wasn't just the sound of Duran Duran attempting to escape cultural mummification by reclaiming their early history as an electronic pop band, it was illuminated by a tongue-in-cheek sense of fun that had been missing from much of their own late 1980s and early 1990s material. They also set about pioneering musical downloads by making available an internet-only mix, which was a nice futuristic detail that tied in well with the robotic, sci-fi spirit of the song. 'Electric Barbarella' features a light-hearted lyric courtesy of the gadget-loving Nick Rhodes about a man who has a relationship with a female robot, described by the protagonist as 'princess of my dreams, emotionless and cold as ice'. In contrast to one of the sources of inspiration, Roxy Music's darkly humorous, twisted story of a blow-up dolly in 'Every Dream-home a Heartache', 'Electric Barbarella' is a light-hearted tale of a doe-eyed loner who seems perfectly satisfied with his 'deviation'. Essentially, it's a male fantasy of 'perfect skin', like staring at pictures in a fashion magazine, and Rhodes doesn't pass comment. He is, after all, something of a visual fetishist himself, who possesses a collection of *Vogue* magazines dating back to 1912, all stacked up in piles on the ground floor of his home. In fact the odd thing about this plastic, Pop Art lyric is that it's actually full of ideas that are very personal to Nick Rhodes. Not only are there cultural references to Kraftwerk (who presented the idea of models as beautiful robots in their number-one single 'The Model'), his creative guru Andy Warhol and the film that inspired the name Duran Duran, but the song's presentation of an idealized image is a character-defining, Rhodesian fixation. His old friend, the fashion designer Anthony Price, informed *Tatler* in 2002 that 'Nick has an obsession with photographic image. He's like Bryan Ferry. They both know more about what is going on in *Vogue* than what's happening in the music business. And it's no coincidence that all his girlfriends are very photogenic.' The art dilettante with a fascination for Hollywood screen goddesses and the cool, iconic Factory starlet Edie Sedgwick took up portrait photography in the 1990s because 'I like to make somebody look better than they think they look. I think it's exciting committing someone to celluloid.' He's also pontificated with the air of a brilliant brain surgeon that he's continually on ocular alert: 'I think about furniture, light fittings, door handles, magazines, window displays, cars, fruit. I sometimes sit and muse to myself, God, the person who designed fruit must have been cool, but the person in the vegetable department wasn't quite so together. I mean, potatoes and carrots are real drab but when you look at pineapples, wow!' According to Simon Le Bon, 'Nick feels it's his business to choose my socks and underwear!'

'Electric Barbarella' is also an updated twist on the inspiration behind the long-lost Duran Duran track 'Hold Me Pose Me', as it's essentially about a doll-like character that can be prettified, controlled and admired. One girl who was recently photographed by Rhodes for a style magazine revealed, 'Nick likes girls to be doll-like. He enjoys choosing clothes for them and making them pretty. There is an element of control in that.' Anthony Price agrees: 'There's no one quite like Nick. His idea of heaven is being in a top restaurant surrounded by ten supermodels, discussing makeup. He's a girl with male genitals.' As for his girlfriend at the time, Madeleine Farley, she confesses with a laugh: 'Nick wanted someone to mould, that is true. He kind of wanted to clone himself and I loved it.' 'Electric Barbarella' is an absurd, throwaway, plastic track that expresses a lot about the writer's tastes, influences and personality – from its Kraftwerkian, jerky electro riffage to the love of different design elements ('ultra-chrome, latex and steel') and a fascination with photogenic women, all delivered with a self-effacing, camp sense of humour.

Meanwhile, the band ran into a controversy when some viewers didn't get the 'irony' of the video to 'Electric Barbarella', filmed by one of Rhodes's favourite fashion photographers, Ellen Von Unwerth. The promo features a life-size Barbie dressed in a plastic sheet who is taken home by Duran Duran and given various household chores before she rebels and electrocutes them. Although it's directed by a woman and is clearly a kitsch wind-up, the video was banned in Canada. 'There were meetings in church halls,' deadpanned Rhodes in his nasal, slow-mo drone. 'She's young, she's beautiful, she's nearly naked and she's hoovering,' laughed Le Bon. 'We're taking the piss out of ourselves and out of men's idea of women, out of cyber-sex and technology.' Cuccurullo was incredulous, arguing, 'My motivation was to do everything with her on video that I wouldn't do if she was really in my home. I certainly wouldn't waste time having her vacuum, and I wouldn't be sharing her with two other guys.'

The new album, *Medazzaland*, was released by Capitol in America on 14 October 1997 and charted at number fifty-eight. Although it also broke into the Canadian Top Twenty, in the rest of the world the project was delayed until the new year. Duran Duran accepted that it was going to be an uphill struggle after the failure of *Thank You* but the reviews were OK, with *Rolling Stone* awarding the album three out of five: '*Medazzaland* sets jazzish noodling, adult-contemporary sincerity, Queen-camp crunch and sad, "Dust in the Wind" acoustic tapestries to new-fangled mechanical clanks. It finds its dizziest hooks in the updated Eurodisco of "Electric Barbarella", a runway-model-seduction number titled after the 1968 movie that inspired Duran's name. That very name, you might notice, has always embodied an assembly-line sense of repetition in and of itself.'

The bizarre album title was inspired by a dental drug called Medazzalin which Simon Le Bon had been given intravenously one day. 'He sort of floated into the studio six feet above the floor, and we said, "What on earth did you take now?" recalled Nick Rhodes.

'He kind of explained it and said, "It's the strangest thing … in dentistry you need to be awake so that you can respond to commands to keep your mouth open and move your jaw and things. So they give you this stuff and you go into this state where you are awake and you respond, but don't really know what's going on. Afterwards, you don't know what happened at all. It's like losing three hours of your life." That's when we said to him, "Yeah, you're still in Medazzaland." ' Opening with the heavily electronic title-track, *Medazzaland* is conceptually a Nick Rhodes album through and through. The panstick-wearing thirty-five-year-old fashionista explained that he wanted to make a record that 'has that controlled hysteria and that organized chaos of the late 1990s – it's little bits of space-junk glued together with really beautiful classical things'. He described the album's key themes as 'technology, kitsch things, insanity and obsession … Everything has become quite mystical to me, particularly with the whole renewed interest in space – everything from *The X-Files* to the Mir station to the flood of alien movies out there these days.' From that starting point – which was closely related to the ideas he was exploring with Cuccurullo in TV Mania – Rhodes then joined the dots back to the band's early albums, claiming, 'I wanted *Medazzaland* to capture the 1990s in the way *Rio* expressed the 1980s.' That's why there's a vandalized *Rio* painting on the back sleeve, with Duran's visual ideas man working closely with the artwork designer Andrew Day, a young protégé he'd recently discovered at art college. 'That's our Dorian Gray – that's what's happening to it upstairs in the loft,' laughed Rhodes. This back catalogue association also tied in seamlessly with *Medazzaland*'s retro-futuristic electronic sound, which reminded people of Duran Duran's history at a time when they had no Taylors left from the classic line-up. In addition, the machine-based style of the album plugged them into America's growing interest in 'electronica' in 1997, with the media hyping up new dance acts such as the Prodigy, the Chemical Brothers, Leftfield and Underworld. He declared, with the words of a great orator, though his intonation remained sleepy, 'Now I am the longest-serving original member, I see my role as the standard bearer, keeping the band exciting and relevant, and moving ahead without jumping on the bandwaggon. The day we make records that aren't as exciting as those we've done previously, we should stop making records.' Rhodes's boxed-up, multi-layered, prettily packaged vision was executed with vivid panache and an impressive eye for detail, but it soon fell apart as 'electronica' failed to become the Next Big Thing and Duran Duran's fan base not only openly mourned the loss of the last Taylor but were turned cold by the album's artificial styling.

Medazzaland is the most experimental album of Duran Duran's career, swarming with special effects, sci-fi atmospheres, weird guitar sonics and treated vocals. Rhodes patently enjoyed himself as he went back to his old analogue texturing and even rebought a Wasp, but the synthesizers are only one element of this off-beat, mildly hallucinogenic album which has layer upon layer of abstract sounds. They also used a lot of studio trickery, such as on the track 'Undergoing Treatment', which has a different, 'schizoid' vocal effect on every line. All this gizmo-fashioned intricacy is so culturally in a different place to the mind-set of LA-based Neurotic Boy Outsider John Taylor, it's not surprising he left the band when he did (he plays bass on three of the tracks, 'Medazzaland', 'Big Bang Generation' and 'So Long Suicide'). As for Le Bon, he found it hard to find a way into the album's edgy, dysfunctional noise (credited on the sleeve as 'production by TV Mania') which at times was not to his taste: 'The sound was very toppy after John Taylor left. My wife was like, "Where's the fucking bass, Simon?" ' However, behind this synthetic veil, the album has a very human side to it and contains the band's best collection of songs since *Rio*. From the epic thriller 'Midnight Sun' (featuring a Le Bon lyric about a relationship that has been through difficult times) to the Iggy Pop-style futurism of 'Be My Icon' ('Butt Naked' rewritten by Rhodes into a creepy stalker song), it's still a pop album rather than the over-complicated, self-indulgent project that threatened to be its likely mutation. 'Big Bang Generation' sounds like a hit single as designed by NASA; the Eastern-sounding 'Buried in the Sand' is rich with exotic machinery, violin samples and a farewell lyric for John Taylor written by a quietly emotional Rhodes; 'Silva Halo' initially appears to have been transmitted at the wrong speed on an alien frequency, but emerges as a tender love song penned by the keyboard player for his girlfriend Madeleine Farley; 'So Long Suicide' offers an abstract twist on Nirvana's quiet–loud dynamics in a song about Kurt Cobain and, in the midst of all this technology, they also include the rousing 'Who Do You Think You are' and Simon Le

Bon's 'Michael, You've Got a Lot to Answer for' – a touchingly straightforward song inspired by his friend Michael Hutchence. According to Le Bon, '*Medazzaland* is a place of lost dreams and that's what I tried to do with "Michael, You've Got a Lot to Answer for". It has that guitar motif at the end which is like a Tibetan temple bell. It's supposed to wipe out the rest of the song from your memory, like a forgotten dream.' Unfortunately the album also faded away almost as if it had never happened, with Rhodes confessing two years later, 'It was pretty much a commercial disaster but I stand by it, absolutely. There are a few songs on there that are as good as anything we've ever done.'

Although Rhodes camped it up on 12 October by wearing 'giant bug-eye sunglasses, a flamingo-pink dress shirt and a tinfoil-silver jacket' for a show in the Tower Records parking lot in Los Angeles (it was all part of a combined launch with a Duran Duran tribute album containing bizarre ska-punk versions of their classic hits), it was a show of confidence at a new low point. Following the poor performance of *Medazzaland*, the band received an ominous phone call from Capitol EMI, who told them their relationship was 'at a crossroads'. By the time Duran Duran appeared at an Andy Warhol benefit show at New York's Whitney Museum on 6 November, they no longer had a record deal. 'We'd been given a huge advance for *Thank You* and it hadn't done well,' says Cuccurullo. 'After that, they just thought we'd peaked.' When the official announcement was made two months later, Le Bon insisted that it was a mutual decision: 'I think they wanted us to lie down, be quiet and be a "catalogue" band, and for them not to put any backing into it. They weren't taking it as we wanted it to be taken.' Duran Duran were handed back the rights to *Medazzaland* (although it remains unreleased in the UK and Europe) and the backstage 'bloodletting' continued when the band parted company with their management company, Left Bank.

In some ways it was the perfect time for Duran Duran to get back on the road as at least it gave them a more direct sense of contact with a fan base that they now needed more than ever. Their *Ultra Chrome Latex and Steel Tour* opened in Boston on 13 November, featuring Steve Alexander on drums and a new bassist, Wes Wehmiller, who was a friend of Cuccurullo's. As the band walked on to music created by TV Mania, they performed in front of relatively small audiences (at least compared to the arena venues they'd played in the wake of 'Ordinary World') with the biggest concert scheduled at the Wiltern in Los Angeles, which held around 5,000. The tour featured a brave, forward-looking set list that included eight new songs alongside the hits such as 'A View to a Kill' and 'Hungry Like the Wolf', plus a rare airing of the 1983 B-side, 'Secret Oktober'. The *Houston Chronicle* enthused about the band's 'edgy' treatment of the old album track, 'Friends of Mine', and 'the breakneck, rousingly emphatic "Careless Memories" ', adding that the best new songs were 'Out of My Mind' and the 'dynamic anthem' 'Who Do You Think You are'. However, the dates seemed to be cursed from the start, with the band forced to deal with illness (Rhodes was hospitalized with flu, forcing the cancellation of several shows) and two deaths (sadly, Warren Cuccurullo's father passed away from prostate cancer and Michael Hutchence was found dead from asphyxiation in the Ritz Carlton hotel in Sydney, Australia). Le Bon cried on stage in Cleveland as he performed 'Save a Prayer' on the day of the news and 'Michael, You've Got a Lot to Answer for' was dropped from the set: 'I still don't know if I will ever be able to sing that song again in public. Michael was tremendous fun, a gentle man, but he had this way of getting you into trouble. I'd go out with him and he had this way of making the maddest things happen. It never occurred to me that he would take his own life. I suppose the thing that really hurts is that you believe you know someone so well, you believe they will turn to you if they need help. But people have these secret lives, these inner lives that aren't visible even to their nearest and dearest.' After all these painful revelations, the mania and glitter of Duran Duran's show in Los Angeles provided a welcome distraction. On 9 December the guest list included Bruce Willis and Steve Buscemi, while according to the visiting *Vox* magazine, the after-show party 'was pure LA decadence. It seems you have to be a movie star, a six-foot blonde model or a transvestite to gain entry.' As if to prove that even at their most debilitated, life in Duran Duran is rarely boring, Le Bon was asked by a Madonnaesque she-male whether he'd like her to 'pee in his mouth'. As the party fluttered on in the background, Le Bon concluded, 'Everyone agreed it was a great tour, but these things, these bolts out of the blue, they can flatten you if you let them.'

After the artificial experimentation of *Medazzaland*, Duran

Duran enthusiastically agreed to a back-to-basics approach for their next record: classic songs recorded on old analogue gear but with a contemporary, slightly surreal twist. 'We wanted to go in a more organic direction,' explains Cuccurullo. 'I suggested we try Ken Scott again, who'd produced the early Bowie stuff. I wanted to get a lot of vintage amps and started preparing.' Ken Scott, who had last worked with them on the *Thank You* album, immediately detected that there was a problem. 'Simon would always enter the studio with a swagger because there would be girls there, but I could see he was feeling dejected. He was trying to put on a brave face.' Although they'd agreed to self-finance the album and wanted to find a new record deal as soon as possible, Le Bon's absenteeism reached a chronic state in 1998 and the first half of 1999. 'I remember two months before I arrived to work on the record I'd been given tapes and was told that Simon was adding lyrics to the music,' says Scott. 'Of course, when I got there, still no lyrics.' Cuccurullo adds, 'If your heart isn't in it one hundred per cent then it shows. Simon came in; we set a schedule. First week, Simon would be there for three days; second week he would be in one day and by the third he wouldn't be there at all. Meanwhile, you've hired a producer or an engineer, so work has to be done whether he's around or not. That was the pattern. At times he wasn't involved in the music at all and we really missed his input.'

Dave Ambrose believes that the changing musical relationships, with Rhodes and Cuccurullo now in charge, had left Le Bon feeling more isolated than ever before. 'That was a very difficult period for Simon,' he asserts. 'Nick and Warren were very together and that left Simon out in the cold. Simon has to be buoyed up by his own ego – for God's sake, to get up on stage and do what he does, you've got to be brave to do it, and I sensed he was starting to feel very down. It was fairly disturbing to see him.' According to Yasmin Le Bon, 'John leaving had changed the whole dynamic. Simon began to find it depressing and wasn't enjoying it any more. I wouldn't have had the staying power or the loyalty to go on, but he did.' In turn, Rhodes had grown increasingly impatient with the singer: 'Simon kept up a punishing social schedule. I was at the studio until ten at night and he would be at the opening of a toilet seat.' He then tempered his comment by adding, 'He's still prone to going off on benders, which is frustrating when we've got work to do, but it's difficult for him, chiefly because he is Simon Le Bon. Simon loves people, he loves to socialize. It's what he does.' Such was the level of communication breakdown between the band members that Ken Scott remembers on one occasion 'everyone turned up at the studio expecting Simon to finish the lead vocal and we waited for hours. Then finally someone called to say that he'd flown out to Naomi Campbell's birthday party in Ibiza, but not a word from Simon.' Oddly enough on one of his nights out, Le Bon ran into Roger Taylor and his wife Giovanna who was being employed as a body-painter for the première of the glam-rock movie, *Velvet Goldmine*. In a further twist of fate, one of the models was ex-Then Jerico singer Mark Shaw, who encountered Le Bon in one of his aloof moods: 'I was there with the whole Ziggy thing going on and I said, "All right, Simon" and he just blanked me totally. I said, "It's Mark from Then Jerico." And he went, "I know who you are." So I put my arm around him later and got body-paint all over his jacket. Because that's the difference: some people are nice, other people are just wankers, aren't they?'

As 1998 drifted on, the more time the increasingly remote singer spent away from the studio, the less input he had into the direction and flow of the music. Songs were simply completed without him, such as 'Hallucinating Elvis', which was an idea originally sparked by Le Bon: 'I had this suit, this gold suit made for the video that we did for "Perfect Day". This suit was made of upholstery plastic and it had a mind of its own. I could actually stand it in the corner. When I put it on, I never felt like it was doing what I wanted it to do. It always felt like it was doing what it wanted to do. And I kind of got into that mentality, and people would say, "What's happening to you? Hey, Charlie, have you got a hangover or something?" And I would say, "I'm hallucinating Elvis," with this suit on. It became a sort of catchphrase, really. There's even a photo I did with Ellen Von Unwerth where I look like Elvis. And I thought that would be a good idea for a song. Then I left the studio for about a week and disappeared somewhere. When I came back they'd pinched the title and worked this track up without me.'

Rhodes now feels that it might have been better to postpone the album for a while and allowed the rock'n'roll truant some time to get his head together: 'Simon was too distracted, he was more interested in his personal life at the time.' In fact on top of mourning the death of Michael Hutchence and having no record deal or management, Simon Le Bon was having to fight press allegations about problems in his marriage, not helped in 1998 when the tabloids started printing stories linking him to other women. Le Bon told *Q* magazine, 'Unless you're married to a very suspicious partner, going out and having a drink with a friend – a female friend – is not a problem. Being seen at a club with someone isn't a problem. Being seen leaving their house at dawn, however, would be a problem. Fortunately, I've never been in that situation.' 'Simon was going through a lot of emotional turmoil,' says Cuccurullo. 'That was the inspiration for the song "Someone Else Not Me", which does have his lyrics on it.' Featuring lines such as 'I guess you've know it for a while but I mean trouble', 'the hardest thing is to let go but it's not defeat' and 'I know you're meant to give yourself to someone else not me', it's not surprising that the front man was given a grilling by the newspapers when the song was finally released (a long time after it was written) in 2000. He told the *Daily Telegraph*: 'It was about a real experience but not a divorcing matter. It's not really a break-up song. I think of it more as a self-realization song. Some guys just think they are going to love every woman in the world or be loved by every woman in the world. And sometimes there's a realization that maybe she's the one.' The couple worked through their problems, and six years later Le Bon reiterated his conviction that he and Yasmin 'have something I've never found with anyone else. My priorities are very simple. The family comes first.' In the late 1990s the Le Bons moved in to a house with a big garden in Putney, which Yasmin explained was 'perfect for our little girls'.

Although he'd blacked out creatively, the singer did regroup with the remainder of Duran Duran to promote a new compilation, *Greatest*, which came out at the end of 1998, achieving platinum sales in the UK and going on to sell over a million in America. 'Electric Barbarella' was added to the album and released as a single in the UK, but it failed to break into the Top Ten despite a ten-date tour backed up by appearances on *The National Lottery*, *The Big Breakfast* and *Never Mind the Buzzcocks*. In March 1999 Capitol/EMI raided the vault again by releasing an album of 12" mixes, *Strange Behaviour*, and Le Bon appeared briefly in a spoof

New Romantic TV show, *Hunting Venus*, starring Neil Morrissey and Martin Clunes from *Men Behaving Badly*. When the *Independent* encountered Le Bon around this time, they observed a 'frowning, sulky and slightly truculent presence with a constant air of pissed-off disappointment'. His friends were also starting to worry about a self-destructive side of Le Bon's personality that had emerged as he lost the ability to write. After having corrective eye surgery for short-sightedness in April 1999, the singer drove around London on his motorbike at dangerous speeds. Although his Formula 1- and sports-car-loving wife has always understood Le Bon's fascination for death-defying machines, she was becoming concerned that he'd reached the crossover point between life-affirming risk-taking and bloody-minded recklessness. 'We were all starting to really worry about him,' says Dave Ambrose. 'I thought to myself, "For him to drive that fast, something is obviously disturbing him." It was a very tricky time for him.' Cuccurullo adds, 'I said to him one day, "How could you get on your motorcycle and drive to my place in the rain?" It was absolutely pouring down, really dangerous to drive in and this wasn't long after a guy we knew had been killed on a bike.'

Meanwhile, throughout the second half of 1999, Duran Duran started talking seriously to record labels about a new deal as the self-financed *Pop Trash* (featuring lyrics almost exclusively written by Rhodes) was now almost ready. 'No one really wanted it,' argues Ambrose. 'I had a label through Sanctuary and I wanted the album because I knew they were strong enough people to evolve out of this period. But my label wasn't big enough for them.' '*Pop Trash* was the beginning of it being hard to get a deal,' admits Cuccurullo. Eventually, in June 1999, Duran Duran flew to Los Angeles to negotiate a new contract with the Disney music label, Hollywood Records. On the paperwork lawyers stipulated the sales territory as 'the universe'. Rhodes sent it back saying, 'excludes Pluto'. A Hollywood executive responded: 'We refuse to exclude Pluto. That territory is of the utmost importance to us.' However, in spite of this early bonhomie it was downhill from there as the company 'requested' changes be made to the album. As a result, strings were added to the record and because Hollywood didn't like most of Ken Scott's mixes, they handed the project over to an American, Chris Lord-Alge. The English producer-engineer was understandably upset: 'It was the same thing as *Thank You* all over again. *Pop Trash* had this really organic approach, which was radically different for Duran Duran. It was very rock'n'roll I suppose, a mix of the 1960s, 1970s, 1980s and 1990s. And they lost that. I don't know what went on. Nick seemed happy with the original mixes. Then I got a call that they wanted to do these strings for the album. It was a question of acceptance. I went along with it.' Cuccurullo describes the changes as 'unfortunate. They got in this guy who was very hot at the time. Before you knew it we had a very different album to the one we'd recorded with Ken Scott.' As for Rhodes, he is uncharacteristically brusque: 'We weren't trying to make an album that was an exact copy of something made in the 1970s.'

In August 1999, Duran Duran tried out some of the new material live during a month-long journey across America, dubbed the *Let It Flow* tour. Opening with three nights at the House of Blues in Chicago and climaxing at the Universal Amphitheatre on 3 September, the band previewed four new songs: 'Lava Lamp', 'Pop Trash Movie', 'Hallucinating Elvis' and 'Someone Else Not Me'. Warren Cuccurullo confesses that by the time of the appropriately titled *Let It Flow* shows, he'd been experimenting with 'liquid ecstasy', otherwise known as GHB, for several years. Taken as a powder that you mix with your drinks – absolutely not alcohol – it is notoriously difficult to control the dosage and many users collapse and black out. 'GHB was a drug that I'd been introduced to via body-building as it's supposed to help with the release of growth hormones,' he explains. 'I'd mix it up and take a little before I'd go to bed, as it puts you into a very deep, recuperative sleep. Then I started mixing it a little earlier and eventually I realized I liked the side-effects. But it's a very tricky drug. You don't know what grade it is; I couldn't get a consistent dose. So I started cooking up my own and that's when I really started taking it. I guess I took it for about four and a half years in total before I decided I'd had enough.'

In December the band returned to the UK to play the ironically titled *Overnight Sensation Show* at London's Earl's Court on 8 December, where they were watched by the *Guardian*: 'Le Bon is taking the markedly ungentle Mick Jagger route into that good night, high-kicking in tight trousers, scrambling atop amps to strike attitudes of defiance against age, his fall from fashion and the erosion of his band.' Duran Duran spent New Year's Eve 1999 in Atlanta, USA, where they performed at the home of a very wealthy American woman called Stephanie. She spent at least half a million pounds on the party, which included Dom Perignon fountains, ice sculptures and two acts – Joe Cocker and Duran Duran – performing in an enormous tent. 'It's the most I've ever made in fifty minutes,' laughs Cuccurullo.

Five months later Duran Duran released the confessional, Beatlesesque ballad 'Someone Else Not Me' as a single. Although it's a pretty song with an honest lyric and a very pure-sounding vocal, it disappeared off American radio play lists after only two weeks. The *Pop Trash* album arrived in mid-June, when it scrambled to number 135 in America and fifty-three in the UK. The *Independent* argued, 'As they flit like gadflies from style to style, the overwhelming impression is of a band that has sadly lost its moorings', although the *Mail on Sunday* was more positive, asserting that it's 'quite a good, if uncommercial return to their art-school roots'. Just as with *Medazzaland*, the new album was another TV Mania production, with Cuccurullo playing the gifted foil to Rhodes's very particular vision. 'To me *Pop Trash* is all the stuff we're surrounded by,' he announced in 2000. 'It's soundbites from television, it's things on the internet, it's displays in shop windows and new gadgets that we buy and packaging.' The keyboard player's professed love of Vegas tack is displayed on the back cover artwork, which features a pink telephone, a toy robot, leopard-skin prints, a fake white poodle and his own gleaming silver trousers. The front image is a photograph of a customized rhinestone car that once belonged to Liberace. The pop culture aficionado also composed the lyrics to the Vegas kitsch of 'Hallucinating Elvis' and the Warhol-inspired 'Pop Trash Movie', a track originally written by TV Mania and recorded by Blondie, although their version has yet to be released. Other songs are more personal, such as 'Starting to Remember', with a lyric dreamed up by Rhodes to accompany a piece of music written by Cuccurullo after his father died. The thirty-eight-year-old keyboard player also opened up about his own life on 'The Sun Doesn't Shine Forever', a break-up song inspired by Madeleine Farley, who had lived with him for several years in Chelsea. 'He didn't tell me about the track at the time,' recalls Madeleine. 'We were soul-mates, we had a fantastic relationship. He was very, very encouraging but Nick's personality is so big, there comes a point where, even though he encouraged me to be creative and try ideas, it was too difficult. I'd start a project and he would come and help me and then suddenly it became his. It sounds corny but I just needed to go off and do my own thing and I couldn't do it around him.' Madeleine has since established herself as a film-maker and photographer, re-creating famous movie scenes by using Q-tips (including a life-size Marilyn cotton bud at the doorway of her London and LA exhibition) and even collaborating with designer Jimmy Choo on shoes with a perspex heel and a Q-tip inside. In 2004 she completed *Trollywood*, a movie about the home-less in Los Angeles which has been shown at the Sundance film festival and was nominated for the best British documentary at the British Independent Film Awards. 'Nick helped me with the sound-track,' she laughs, 'so there's lots of Velvet Underground, Goldfrapp and "Drive By", the very beautiful version of "The Chauffeur" from the *Thank You* album.' Back in 2000 Rhodes took solace for a while in a relationship with socialite Tara Palmer-Tomkinson and he was also briefly linked with 'It Girl' Lady Victoria Hervey. On the *Pop Trash* song 'Lady Xanax', he describes a lonely, paranoid girl who 'can't be alone when the darkness falls/got to make it to the party', but insists that it wasn't written about Tara: 'It's actually inspired by two people I've met. One man and one woman. And I'm not going to tell you who it is.'

Musically *Pop Trash* is a mixture of elegant, melancholy ballads ('Starting to Remember', 'Someone Else Not Me', 'Lady Xanax' and 'The Sun Doesn't Shine Forever') and heavier tracks, such as Simon Le Bon's finest moment 'Playing Like Uranium' which sounds like Duran Duran being produced by Garbage. 'Mars Meets Venus' is an unlikely collision of Devo and Oasis, while 'The Last Day on Earth' is heavier still, a techno-rock hybrid with echoes of both Smashing Pumpkins at their most epic (Le Bon had joined the band for a version of 'Nightboat' at a London gig in 1998) and the James Bond theme, 'Live and Let Die'. It was later released as a single in Japan and in 2001 the Universal Theme Park in Osaka used it to welcome visitors during their grand opening. The string-led 'Pop Trash Movie' is the centrepiece of the album and largely succeeds in pulling it all together. However, although Cuccurullo's playing is melodic and inventive throughout, the faux-psychedelic 'Lava Lamp' still fails to convince and 'Hallucinating Elvis' is a throwaway, humorous oddity. The tone of *Pop Trash* is also very strange and almost impossible to define – is it organic or machine-made? Art or bubblegum? A naturally pretty face or cleverly applied makeup? Either way, in spite of Le Bon's lack of involvement, the album is a fascinating mixture of ideas with a very serious commercial flaw – *Pop Trash* sounds like a lot of things (Velvet Underground, ELO, Lennon, Jobriath, James Bond), but very rarely like Duran Duran.

CHAPTER TWELVE

John Taylor: *'Act like a rock star, live like a monk, that's my philosophy these days.'*

Nick Rhodes: *'I've got everything in storage. Very early on in my career David Bowie told me he kept everything that he had worn and, being a fan as a child, I obviously wowed at the whole idea of all those outfits, so I've kept all my own ever since.'*

Andy Taylor: *'Simon is a pop writer and a pop singer. He's not a rock singer, he's not a chanteur, he's a very good pop singer and a great pop writer. He's a pure pop person.'*

Nick Rhodes: *'All these invitations are making me socially confused. I class the importance of invites in order of how thick they are and how much gold they have around their edges.'*

Simon Le Bon: *'We've got families and making money makes you feel like a man.'*

By the time Duran Duran started the thirty-three-date American leg of the *Pop Trash* tour at the end of July 2000, they'd already resolved to leave Hollywood Records, although it wasn't officially announced for a few months. 'Hollywood really dropped the ball on *Pop Trash*,' says Cuccurullo, who now owns the album along with Rhodes and Le Bon. 'They didn't have a clue about how they wanted to market us, which singles to release, nothing. From what I've heard, they really wanted the Duran reunion. At the very least they wanted John back in the band.' According to an increasingly frustrated Le Bon, 'It was a complete disaster. I was thinking, "How do I get out of this?" I missed John terribly. The reason we never got a permanent bass player was quite simply because the seat was still left there for him. I didn't think he'd come back, not then anyway. I'd have had him back in a shot, but Nick and Warren maybe felt a bit different about it.'

Performing a set that included the 'Planet Earth' B-side, 'Late Bar', Duran Duran travelled around America for a month, ending with six successive shows in late August at the House of Blues, west Hollywood, California. While they were there, John Taylor invited Rhodes and Le Bon over to his house for lunch. According to Rhodes, 'We were seeing an old friend and having a very pleasant lunch and then Simon started talking about how he'd been unhappy for some time and wanted to move on. The background to this is that as far as Simon was concerned his relationship with Warren had come to an end. I think he'd decided that much earlier than he actually told me, in fact. It wasn't anything personal but Simon wasn't happy and didn't want to make another Duran Duran album with Warren. He wasn't sure what he wanted to do. There wasn't a big plot behind Warren's back to put the five back together again.'

After yet another commercial failure with *Pop Trash*, Le Bon was probably right in his assessment that the band didn't have a future if they carried on as they were: 'We realized that Duran Duran without a single Taylor was pretty tricky and not something people would readily accept, no matter how good the album might have been. It was a marketing nightmare. So, for a number of reasons, it all got very serious. I felt that the plug had been pulled out and the water was draining away. And that's a very depressing feeling. I love Nick, I really love him, but it's a very intense relationship when it's just the two of you. Morale in the band was at an all-time low. Eventually I thought, "I just need to stop this thing altogether," and I said to Nick, "You know what, mate? I'm not going to do it any more, it's not fun." It was at that time that I got a message on my answer phone from John. He said, "I've got a great new place in the Hollywood Hills, why don't you come over and sit by the pool?" We went up there and spent the afternoon with him. I told him everything that was going on in my life and my heart, and he said, "Look, this is perfect – let's get the original band back together!" '

Since leaving Duran Duran, Taylor had briefly rejoined the Neurotic Boy Outsiders, who played a few gigs again at a newly designed Viper Room in early 1999, with guests Ian Astbury and Billy Duffy from the Cult. The forty-one-year-old also toured with his own band Terroristen, compiled some of his solo material on releases such as *Metafour* and *Retreat into Art*, and tried his hand at acting in a few movies – as a faded rock star in *Sugar Town* and then in the role of Keith Rockhard in *Flintstones 2: Viva Rock Vegas*. On 16 March 1999, the Americanized heart-throb put down his Los Angeles roots even deeper when he married the co-founder of the Juicy couture T-shirt label (as worn by the likes of J-Lo, Madonna and Kate Beckinsale) and mother of two Gela Nash, in a private ceremony at the Chapel by the Bay in Las Vegas. Sadly, his mother Jean wasn't around to see him marry again as she died in 1998. He composed a song, 'The Only One', for her and wrote in his journal, 'I had perfect closure with her. I was there when the spirit left her and she had a long, strong, happy life.' Through all these highs and lows, John Taylor has shown tremendous determination and at times real courage in remaining sober.

As Rhodes and Le Bon returned to the *Pop Trash* tour, John Taylor started ringing around the other band members almost immediately. 'John called me out of the blue,' related Roger Taylor in 2004. 'He asked if I fancied getting the band back together soon. I was really shocked as I really thought it was in the past and there had been a lot of water under the bridge. To be honest, I was a bit sceptical at first and said, "A bit late, isn't it?" ' But after twenty-four hours the quiet-living drummer called back and agreed to the idea. Once it was confirmed that Roger was on board, the third Taylor, Andy, also signed up. 'I wouldn't have done it if Roger hadn't said, "Yes",' he explained. 'But I think we all came to the same realization that you're never going to do anything as spectacular as Duran Duran again.' The roving guitarist and his family had spent the last few years in Ibiza, the north of England and Beckbury Hall, where he'd worked on a new Then Jerico record, *Orgasmaphobia*. 'We recorded the album in Andy's lovely, haunted fifteenth-century rectory,' says Mark Shaw. 'I was at Beckbury Hall in this beautiful four-poster room and I heard this sound, like a bunch of men with spurs running up the stairs, but it's like six in the morning. They're going, "crunch, crunch, crunch" and then there's this sound of furniture moving above me. I later found out that I was the only person there that night but there are priest holes in the house and they used to move the furniture and hide from the soldiers. When

I told Andy this he turned to Tracey and said, "See, I told you the place was still fucking haunted." They had the place exorcized twice!' In addition to dealing with ghostly apparitions and having more kids (the couple now have four – Andrew, Georgina, Elizabeth and Isabella) Andy Taylor toured with Luke Morley from Thunder in the early 1990s, set up 'a music-industry-destroying' internet project with the photographer Denis O'Regan and recorded a lot of material which has remained unreleased: 'Dave Ambrose told me, "Don't worry, Andy, these are your 'wilderness' years. Every artist has them!" '

In late 2000, the 'Fab Five' met up in London and discussed the idea of playing together live and recording a new album. Andy Taylor says, 'When we sat down and decided how to do this, Nick said, "We've got to do an album." And I said, "Thank God you've said that, because we don't have a future if we don't actually do something new." ' After that the full complement of Taylors reunited in a studio in Wales to jam and rehearse together, blowing away the cobwebs after sixteen years apart. The bassist was as intense as ever, psyching himself up by having the letters DD tattooed on to his right bicep. As for Rhodes and Le Bon, they continued to work with Cuccurullo, who was still in the dark about the proposed reunion. Duran Duran's schedule included an appearance on BBC1's *Children in Need* on 17 November, during which they played two songs, 'Girls on Film' and 'Hallucinating Elvis'. The band also toured the UK, climaxing with two dates at Wembley Arena, where they were watched by the *Guardian*'s Elisabeth Mahoney: 'Le Bon tries to do a rock'n'roll leap from a very low-level amp, he trips and goes flying. In another rock-star gesture – mike-stand twirling – he knocks the whole thing over. In between he cavorts, dances badly, punches the air, stoops to pick up some red roses and a pair of black undies, thrown by an adoring crowd. In the corner, twiddling with synthy knobs, is Nick Rhodes, still sporting David Sylvian's old haircut and lashings of scary Goth makeup. They make an odd couple, especially during "Hallucinating Elvis", one of the more painful parts of the evening. With a backdrop of virtual-reality projections in which the King comes among us, Le Bon adds a silver shirt and Brains glasses to his ensemble, presumably wanting to look like an Elvis impersonator. He doesn't; he looks like Les Gray, erstwhile lead singer with Mud, while Rhodes has something of Andy Warhol about him in certain lights. It is like being stuck in a really giddy episode of *Stars in Their Eyes*. Except that this tour clearly has a much smaller budget. It's the cheapness of the proceedings that really pulls you up, marks the time that has been passed between the days of that video for "Rio" and now. The screen on which they show art videos and the cyber-Elvis is a big crinkled sheet; they have no backing singers, only perky female voices on tape. As a big finale, they kick a few balloons into the audience in a forlorn, under-whelming gesture. They get kicked back.' According to Ben Clancy from the *NME*, 'They do play a few more hits, but not enough to please this child of the 1980s. Still, ask any member of the crowd and they'd tell you it was fantastic. Being a Duranie is a case of selfless love.' The trio's last show of 2000 was a New Year's Eve party concert at Pleasure Island, 'Downtown' Disney, Orlando. 'You're doomed when you end up playing things like that,' concedes Cuccurullo. 'It's probably my least favourite place in the world.'

In January and February 2001 Duran Duran travelled to the Ukraine, Moscow, St Petersburg and Estonia for more dates. This was followed by *The Up Close and Personal* tour across America through March, which ended with a one-off concert in the Dominican Republic. 'We'd just done our last interview and the tour was over,' says the hairless, shaved-from-top-to-toe Cuccurullo. '*Pop Trash* hadn't performed, Hollywood had dropped us and we didn't have a publishing deal. I said, "We're at a crucial time right now and I don't know what we're going to do." I had no ideas, I certainly didn't want to finance another record and shop it around. We all went back home and the next thing I heard was when a letter arrived by special delivery at my house sacking me from the band. I read it and I was absolutely shocked because no one had said anything to me, I didn't have a fucking clue. I called Simon straight away and he said, "Sorry, Warren, it's got to be like this" because they were getting the original band together. I said, "We have to work out a deal for me." The initial feeling was one of loss. I'd dedicated everything to Duran Duran and then it was gone. And I was shocked that they didn't tell me to my face. I had a meeting later with their business manager and he said, "Warren, I'm talking to you here and I have to say your partners were absolutely petrified of your reaction – they didn't want to be in the same room when they told you, they're terrified of you." That shows how little they know me, I would never get aggressive in a situation like that. There were things that had to be sorted out in a professional manner, so, that's what I did.' With the benefit of hindsight Nick Rhodes was not entirely convinced that it was the right way round to do it. He understood that Simon wanted to put all his thoughts down in a letter first, but he could see how that must have looked to Warren: 'After that Simon and Warren did speak at great length about everything. But it wasn't as if Warren had done anything particularly wrong. Simon just felt that it had run its time and he would have started the ball rolling in any case, whether the rest of Duran Duran got together or not.'

Cuccurullo sold his Battersea house, moved back to America and hooked up with Nick Rhodes and Simon Le Bon for three final Japanese shows in June 2001. Although Rhodes insists that Cuccurullo wanted to play them, the guitarist now exclaims: 'They were the worst shows ever! Not fun. Japan has never been so depressing, overcast and gloomy every day ... ughhh!' It was also the last Duran Duran show for the bassist Wes Wehmiller, who had filled in for John Taylor for the last four years (tragically, he died of cancer, aged thirty-three, on 30 January 2005). Following this sombre experience in Japan, Warren Cuccurullo flew to Los Angeles to play some Missing Persons reunion gigs and also had a meeting with the man behind the porn-mag *Hustler*, Larry Flynt. Cuccurullo was there to shop his 'Rock Cock' concept. 'I wanted to make a toy, a mould so if people wanted my dick, they could get it,' laughs the gym-trained womanizer. 'Meeting Larry Flynt was really something. He'd just gotten over pneumonia and he had fluid in his lungs so it was hard to hear what he was saying. So I kneeled down next to his wheel-chair and he whispered into my ear, "Even John Holmes didn't get his own sex toy." He suggested that he'd only be interested in a whole range of rock star dildos and I was trying to explain to him that there was no way that was ever going to happen!' During the *Pop Trash* period, the Brooklyn body-builder had also posed naked in a gay Brazilian porn magazine. 'They asked my girlfriend in Brazil, "Can we get him to do it?" he says. 'It was an interview and a nude shoot. Good money. I didn't know they wanted me to be hard until an hour or two in the shoot. By the time I moved back to LA there were lots of gay sites charging money for people to download my pictures.'

Cuccurullo figured that if other people were making money out of the images, he might as well do some of his own porn and sell it directly from his website. Visitors to his Privacy website were able to download clips of Cuccurullo having sex and conducting interviews in his shower. 'There was a lack of love in my life. When I came back to LA, I'd gone through the biggest upheaval of my life. Also this was around the time of 9/11 and so it felt like a double whammy because the whole world had changed too. I was hanging out with these two girls all the time, it was a loose three-way relationship and the whole thing only lasted about eight months. I did it out of fun and ignorance. There are no mistakes. It was like entertainment and I knew there were people out there who would be interested. Once you've posed erect in a magazine, and other people are downloading your pictures, you might as well go all the way.' His life spectacularly combusted when he spent eight days in hospital suffering from an illness and mental exhaustion, but he has overcome it through a characteristically intense spiritual revelation, meeting a new girlfriend who has recently become his fiancée, and he also successfully launched an Italian restaurant, Via Veneto (he had apparently considered the name Gen-Italia) in Santa Monica, California. 'Here I am, I have a restaurant in LA and no one from the band has been to see it,' he says with obvious regret. 'Not once. If I was travelling the world and Nick had opened up a restaurant somewhere I would have dropped in to see him. I have spoken to Nick on the phone because I needed him to write a couple of lyrics for me, but I haven't seen him properly since we performed together in Japan. They've all been in Los Angeles a few times – they had a listening party at the Chateau Marmont for the new album. But no one called. I thought, "Jesus, is the album that fucking bad!" It would have been great if they had come by, met my girlfriend, hung out one last time. That would have been beautiful. I've had Dustin Hoffman, Spielberg and Quincy Jones in my restaurant but not Duran Duran.' He was also snubbed by his former bandmates when they played their 2003 show in Los Angeles. 'I was supposed to go and see them play in LA. I rang

Simon and said, "Hey, I'm planning to come to the show and maybe I could come along to Vegas with you." He said, "We'll take care of you, man, come to Vegas." Then their manager rang me up and said, "Warren, we'd really rather you didn't come to the show. It's not so good if you were photographed with the band." That was practically the final straw for me, I mean these guys were like my brothers, we'd laughed and loved and created together for years and years. I'd always put Duran Duran first in my life and then to be treated as no longer a friend ...'

While Cuccurullo rebuilt his life in Los Angeles, back in 2001 the 'classic' Duran Duran line-up rented a house near San Tropez and shipped over all their equipment and an engineer. Working together every day until midnight and financing the sessions themselves, according to Rhodes it was like 'treading on eggshells. It was so fragile. We had a few incidents where people were thinking: "Is it really worth it? Do I really want to give up my life to these four people? Again?" But when you spend as much time together as we do, you get to know everybody's dynamic. Who's tired and grumpy that day. Who's suffering from anxiety because they've been on the phone to home. You just have to try to be patient.' 'Fortunately nobody turned up with a sitar or a bunch of John Coltrane albums,' quipped John Taylor. 'We know that as individuals none of us is a genius like Prince. Together, though, we can still be a vital force.' Duran Duran subsequently claimed that during their first session together they immediately worked up an idea for a new song. 'Nick pressed a button on his keyboard and this sequence started happening,' recalled Le Bon in 2003. 'Within minutes Andy was playing this riff. I heard a melody line in that, Roger was playing the drums and John had a bass in there and within twenty minutes we had a song happening. It was fantastic.' Three songs written in this initial twelve-day San Tropez session made it on to their comeback album, *Astronaut*: 'Bedroom Toys', 'Taste the Summer' and 'Nice'.

As Duran Duran continued to record new material in Barnes, London and at Nile Rodgers's home in Connecticut (he was their initial choice of producer although only one untouched song remains from the session – 'Point of No Return'), they had to consider who was going to manage them. The first people they approached were Paul and Michael Berrow, with the globally successful 'seven' reuniting for the first time in fifteen years at a restaurant in Covent Garden, London. 'There was talk of managing them again,' confirms Paul Berrow. 'We met and we chatted and it did get heated. Some people seemed to have a very different view of events. We had to say, "Hang on a second, you fired us, we didn't walk away!" It came to nothing.' Rhodes adds, 'The formula of the original team had worked. No one argued with that. But once we were all there together we realized it was a complete impossibility. It was ridiculous, we couldn't agree on anything.' The Berrow brothers are currently working on producing a series of 'epic, fantasy adventure' films , own the 'musicians' community' website bandname.com and have two new bands in development (including the Coldplayesque Meeky Rosie). Due to Paul Berrow's interest in hydrogen-fuel technology, he has also invested in a new car being designed by Philippe Starck. Interestingly, he claims there are plans to race *Drum* again in 2005 and that Simon Le Bon has expressed an interest in joining the crew.

As for Duran Duran, they worked for a while with former IRS label founder Miles Copeland (and older brother of Stewart Copeland from the Police), who started shopping around for a new deal, but according to Rhodes, 'seeking out a record label proved to be a lot harder than we imagined. Every time we sidled up to someone, the chief executives would get fired or the company would be cannibalized by a bigger company.' After a few months they changed management again, settling on Wendy Laister (who is Nick Rhodes's cousin) and Magus Entertainment as their joint representatives.

While news of the reunion was enough to send Duran Duran's *Greatest* back into the UK Top Thirty, there was less hype about Stephen Duffy and Nick Rhodes working together again for the first time in over twenty years. Rhodes had bumped into Duran Duran's original singer at a Vivienne Westwood show in 1999 and the pair discussed the idea of this more 'culty' reunion. Rhodes says, 'We started chatting and at one point I said, "You know that album we made in late 1978, do you think we should finish it?" It still took us another year or so before Stephen eventually came around with a cassette. The ideas, the embryos were all there.' Calling themselves The Devils, the duo worked 'intensely' for a few weeks at AIR Studios in London, re-creating songs that Duran Duran had performed back in 1979. 'I had to try to remember what voice I used in those days,' reveals the Lilac Time and solo singer, who remains one of the UK's most underrated artists. 'It was somewhere between Iggy and Howard Devoto,' he laughs. Released on their own Tape Modern label in July 2002, *Dark Circles* has echoes of Brian Eno's 1970s solo albums and his pioneering work with David Bowie, *Remain in Light*-era Talking Heads, Ultravox! and Roxy Music. *The Sunday Times* described the album as 'outstanding – Duffy's sense of melody is sublime and Rhodes's often overlooked talent for understatement helps to create subtly shifting musical backdrops'. According to *Q*, 'Duffy's melodies ooze period pop charm, leaving "Come Alive" and "World Exclusive" sounding like hits. The album also manages to be soulful and moving. Excellent.' *Time Out* assessed the work as 'beautiful songs and Nick Rhodes conjures drones and shrieks and shudders that would impress the Aphex Twin. *Dark Circles* is a window on a more innocent, less homogenous world. You'll feel better for looking through it.' The release of The Devils also seemed nicely timed with the emergence of 'Electroclash', a much hyped smash-and-grab of early 1980s synthesizer pop and Studio 54 glamour. Tiga and Felix Da Housecat, two leading lights of this short-lived scene, remixed some Devils tracks for the dance floor but despite the rave reviews and a swanky gig/party at the Knightsbridge designer shop Harvey Nichols (there was also a press photo call with Duffy and Rhodes performing in one of the store's famous window displays), The Devils quietly faded away.

Meanwhile, a pretty, long-legged New Yorker, Meredith Ostrom, was spotted dancing the night away at the Devils' Harvey Nichols launch. It was the first time she'd seen her partner Rhodes play live since the pair had met while hailing the same taxi in August 2001. The strangers discovered they were both going to a Mario Testino book launch at the Sanderson hotel. 'Nick's friend suggested we share the cab,' revealed the young actress/model to *Tatler* magazine. 'I thought that very rude but we found out that we were going to the same event. His haircut made me laugh. I had no clue who he was. When we stepped out the cab and all these flash-bulbs went off, I felt like I was in a Woody Allen movie.' Raised on New York's Upper East Side, Meredith's father is an engineer and her mother worked as a successful interior designer with clients such as the late Richard Nixon and the music mogul Russell

Simmons. 'Nick's so intelligent, I really respect him,' says Meredith. 'I love the way his mind works. He invests carefully, he chooses the people he surrounds himself with. I feel lucky to know him because he gives such good advice. Before meeting him I'd have assumed all rock stars take drugs. He's a very steady guy – more like an invest-ment banker.' When asked by *Tatler* in 2002, 'Is he controlling?', the twenty-three-year-old responded, 'How much time do you have?' She also revealed Rhodes's love of 'dingy little bookstores' and the meat substitute, Quorn: 'He loves it, so I cook Quorn burgers, Quorn sausages – I even make him turkey-flavoured Quorn sandwiches to take to the studio.' In 2004, the couple made it to number twenty-eight on *Tatler*'s list of the '100 Most Invited', highlighting the year's 'key social players'. However, his previous girlfriend Madeleine Farley believes that more often than not Rhodes would prefer to stay at home with his diamante-collar-wearing cat, a pile of lists ('he suffers from list-ism – he makes lists and then compiles them into master lists and sub-lists') and a bottle of red wine. 'He's definitely not a party animal. He doesn't work the room, he usually attaches himself to one person whom he likes to talk to. The reason he goes out is that Nick likes to gain informa-tion and contacts. He's interested in meeting someone who he can start a project with or who can help him in some way. Nick also has this remarkable ability to have a superior attitude no matter who else is in the room, but he does it in such a way that it isn't conde-scending or arrogant. Whereas Simon has a huge social life with lots of friends, very few people are allowed to get close to Nick. He only opens up emotionally to a very few people.'

While Rhodes was promoting The Devils he'd mentioned to journalists that he'd started work on another project, co-producing the Dandy Warhols' next album, *Welcome to the Monkey House*. The band's singer Courtney Taylor later explained, 'We wanted some-thing that reflected that we're now people who are immersed in a world of international, big-city sexuality. Just coked out of your head, horny … You stumble out of this club into the morning light of New York City in some filthy meat-packing district club with these pseudo-supermodels and they're smart and they're fucking beautiful and scary and you just want to get naked and be with someone, and you realize that the Eurotrash shit that you've been listening to has something – a certain dark, cosmopolitan desperation – to it. "Another One Bites the Dust" had that. And so did Duran Duran.' The Dandy Warhols also roped in Simon Le Bon on backing vocals for the track 'Plan A' and Nile Rodgers (who was still working with Duran at the time) appears on 'I am a Scientist'. Once Courtney Taylor had met Nick Rhodes, he seemed to be utterly charmed by the composed, designer-loving thirty-nine-year-old. 'Nick is so smart and clever: just the perfect elegant English guy. He just sits on the floor in his expensive Italian suits and beautiful shoes, and goes, "No, darling, that's dreadful ... Now this one, perhaps ... [makes keyboard sound]." We'd get drunk at night and go to these fantastic private clubs in London.' The Duran Duran influences are easy to spot on *Welcome to the Monkey House*, which came out on 19 May 2003. Featuring the hit 'We Used to be Friends', the Dandy Warhols created a cool, witty pastiche of arty, New Wave pop, but critical acclaim failed to sell it to the fan base, many of whom found the changed emphasis from guitars to keyboards, bass and drums a little disturbing. A year or so later, various eyeliner-wearing young-men-in-black, such as the Las Vegas indie-fops The Killers (whose *Hot Fuss* album has gone platinum on both sides of the Atlantic) and New York's The Bravery, started breaking through with their own Duran Duran mutations. In fact The Killers' singer Brandon Flowers has described their hit 'Somebody Told Me' as ' "Rio" with chest hair'. As ever, timing in music is everything and by summer 2005 more Duran Duran-styled acts such as VHS or Beta and Clear Static were also starting to emerge.

Back in May 2003, as the Dandy Warhols hit the charts with their new album, Duran Duran also relaunched themselves by appearing in their first fashion spread in eighteen years with various models in *Vogue*. The Armani-styled band still looked the part, with John Taylor (described by one magazine as resembling 'a well-funded art school professor in his skinny black suit, thin black glasses and grown-out bleach blond mop') revealing a typically glamorous approach to jogging: 'In the last few weeks I've run around Central Park in New York and Hyde Park in London, along the Seine in Paris and across Sydney Harbour Bridge.' Even the restaurant-loving, napkin-scribbling Nick Rhodes confessed that he'd invested in a running machine, although he always walked and usually had his mobile phone glued to his ear.

On 12 May, EMI released the Duran Duran *Singles Box 81–85*, a thirteen-CD set of their early singles with reproductions of their early artwork (*Singles Box 2: 1986–1995* came out in November). A few days later the band announced a twenty-fifth-anniversary show at the massive 12,000-capacity Budokan in Tokyo, Japan, which sold out in less than half an hour. The band were reportedly 'gob-smacked' by this news, which suddenly added a lustre to the reunion that had been sorely lacking while they toiled away in a studio in south-west London. As the cool US magazine *Blender* ran a six-page article on the history of the band, Duran Duran flew to Italy for an exclusive Juicy Couture launch in Florence – the first time 'the five' had actually been photographed together in public. By the time they arrived in Tokyo on 2 July 2003, they'd completely sold out shows in Osaka, Fukuoka, Nagoya and both nights at the Budokan. There were also manic scenes on 14 July, when they returned to the Roxy in Hollywood for a US club date which was watched by Brad Pitt (who later does a karaoke performance of 'The Wild Boys' for his then wife and Duran fan, Jennifer Aniston), Gwen Stefani, Nicolas Cage and Beck, whose dad went to Duran Duran's first ever Roxy show, back in 1981. According to the *NME*, 'tonight, this is Duran Duran the way God intended, the Fab Five. It doesn't matter that Roger's as grizzled as a North Sea fisherman, that Andy's even less cute than he was during his unfortunate hair-extensions phase, or that jowly, sweaty Simon resembles a wet bulldog. No, all that matters is they're playing all their Old Romantic classics ('Girls on Film', 'Hungry Like the Wolf') and that bassist John Taylor is, at age forty-three, still hotter than Rio asphalt. JT reminds everyone that Duran Duran were once the coolest band on Planet Earth – and that tonight they still are.' Britney Spears turned up at the band's next sold-out show on 16 July, which was held in the 8,500-capacity Pacific Amphitheatre in California, and their 19 July show at the Joint, Hard Rock Hotel, Las Vegas took only six minutes to sell out. Yet the best was still to come as Duran Duran received two Lifetime Achievement Awards – the first from MTV on 27 August and then on 2 October, they were honoured by *Q* magazine in the UK. 'It's great to get recognition,' said Roger Taylor of this newfound credibility. 'We didn't get much recognition first time around as people were just dazzled by the videos and the hysteria. But people are now thinking, "Actually this is a great band." They can see beyond the glitz.'

In the autumn Duran Duran appeared at K-ROQ's Inland Invasion Festival in front of 65,000 people on a bill that also included the Cure, Interpol and Soft Cell. On 13 October 2003 EMI released the *Greatest* DVD featuring all their era-defining videos and the next day Duran Duran performed their first UK reunion show at the Forum in London, where there were reportedly 20,000 applications for tickets, which sold out in four minutes. Steve Sutherland, who had been the only voice of support in the music press at the start of their career, was there to review it for the *NME*: 'Duran Duran were the original Strokes. They had their Julian in Simon Le Bon – a cherubic singer prone to the podge. They had their Fab in John Taylor, the chiselled hunk who still elicits most of the screams. They had their own Nick in Nick Rhodes – snooty, pretentious and sometimes a twat. They had their Albert in Andy Taylor – a bit of rough washed up from another band entirely. And they had their Nikolai in Roger Taylor, the dull one who left in the 1980s and went a bit Frank Bruno. We shed a communal tear to lost youth during "Save a Prayer" and made strange robotic gestures to "Wild Boys" – which sounds like an epileptic outbreak in a woodwork class. In other words, fucking excellent fun.' Simon Price from the *Independent on Sunday* was also impressed: 'Opening song, "Friends of Mine", an obscure early album track but always a fan favourite, provokes a reaction which utterly refutes my long-held belief that Duran are a band you could like, but never love. If pop won't give us a new Duran, we'll stick with the old one. Some people call it a one-night stand but we can call it paradise.' The *Independent*'s Steve Jelbert wrote, 'There's more glamour on this stage than all the Roger Moore Bond movies put together. Duran Duran are certainly daft these days and they surely know it. Why else would they crack into "We are Family" during "Notorious"? "The Wild Boys" is played, rightly, for laughs, while "Rio" is pure panto. Best of all is the bubblegum punk of "Careless Memories". It was all great fun, especially when the crowd sang along loud enough to drown out Le Bon's voice (recently compared to "a drunkard attempting Chinese opera"). Duran Duran remain a glorious anomaly.' The year ended with a seventeen-date sold-out tour of America and a rare 'support slot' for Robbie Williams (Duran Duran claim they'd originally been told it was a 'double bill') on a stadium tour of New Zealand and Australia.

When 50,000 tickets for the Sydney concert were sold an hour after going on sale, a second date was added.

Duran Duran were relieved to be back at the top of the bill at the start of 2004, performing 'The Wild Boys' to millions during the pre-game commentary of Superbowl XXXVII on 1 February. Two weeks later Justin Timberlake presented them with an Outstanding Contribution Award at the Brits, where they played a selection of their hits including 'Ordinary World' and 'The Wild Boys'. Afterwards the band hosted a party at the Adam Street private members club, attended by Justin Timberlake (he discovered he lives within walking distance of John Taylor), Liz Hurley and Scarlett Johansson, who danced with Nick Rhodes. Moet & Chandon champagne and melon martinis fuelled the celebratory atmosphere as Duran Duran's campaign continued to build momentum. John Taylor says, 'The awards ultimately suited our agenda. They rebuilt the brand and put the name back in lights. After the Brit Awards ceremony we realized we couldn't have released the album any earlier. We thought, "Phew, there is a God." Everything's happening in order.'

After the success of the Brits, the *Greatest* album shot into the UK Top Ten and Duran Duran started rehearsals for the twenty-fifth-anniversary reunion shows in the UK, consisting of sixteen arena shows. Opening in the Odyssey Arena in Belfast on 7 April and including five nights at Wembley Arena which were recorded for a live DVD, the band performed a selection of their hits and a few new songs ('What Happens Tomorrow', 'Sunrise' and an unre-leased track, 'Beautiful Colours') in front of 250,000 people, grossing over £7.2 million in ticket sales. They also got to cherry-pick some cool support acts, including Nick Rhodes's personal favourites Goldfrapp and the New York disco band, Scissor Sisters. The *Observer*'s Akin Okjumu flew out to see the opening night: 'Thoughtfully, Duran put strong hooks at the start of many of their hits, useful for indicating when it's time to come back from the bar. The rattle of drums signalling "Wild Boys", the flashbulbs popping on "Girls on Film" and the vocal trill "Ta Na Na Na" that heralds "The Reflex" put everyone on alert that it's time for another singa-long before singer Simon Le Bon opens his mouth. Each time you imagine Duran have run out of hits, they strike up another. "New Moon on Monday" is plastic pop heaven, "Notorious" starts with a terrace chant then becomes a Chic-inspired funk workout, and I rush back from the toilet to catch the a cappella start of "Is There Something I Should Know?" Le Bon isn't cool ... But every over-the-top move is greeted with delight. When he comes to the side of the stage and does a wiggle, I worry that he is going to be knocked off his feet by a barrage of underwear.' Dave Simpson from the *Guardian* attended their show at Nottingham Arena: 'Unusually for a comeback band, they sound better than they did in their heyday. Drummer Roger Taylor maintains a thud-bang beat for 120 minutes and diminutive guitarist Andy Taylor plays with restraint and danger, perhaps aided by dressing like an LA hitman. The set list reflects the unrecognised breadth of their canon, dipping into the eerie side with 1981's sinister "The Chauffeur" and the instrumental "Tiger, Tiger", never played live before. Perhaps most impressively, Le Bon brings a new maturity to songs that were once just about escapism. "Save a Prayer"'s line about a one-night stand being "paradise" now sounds more sad than boastful, while "Ordinary World" (which Le Bon reveals helped him over the death of a friend) has an emotional wallop not generally associated with a man in tight trousers. The forty-somethings manage to sing "Wild Boys" without sounding ridiculous and, as a refurbished "Rio" kicks in, the message is that the Wild Boys are definitely back.' The *Independent*'s Kevin Harley was a rare voice of dissent, arguing that, 'while the likes of "Notorious" and "The Wild Boys" are forgivably silly, their oafish, bawling charmlessness is another thing altogether.'

In the wake of the hugely successful tour, Duran Duran finally signed a new record deal with Epic Records, described by John Taylor 'as the kind of deal people can lose their jobs over'. The band lined up two producers for the project – Don Gilmore (his credits include David Bowie and Linkin Park) and Dallas Austin, a self-confessed 'Duran Duran nut' who has recently worked with Gwen Stefani on her album *Love. Angel. Music. Baby*. According to Nick Rhodes, 'Dallas said, "I want to stack up the harmonies. I want that uplifting sound that you always had in those big Duran Duran choruses." '

Three years since they'd got back together, Duran Duran's make-or-break new single, '(Reach Up for the) Sunrise' arrived in October 2004, debuting at number five in the UK, bizarrely the same week that the Stephen Duffy-penned Robbie Williams single 'Radio' topped the charts. It also gave them their first chart entry in America since 'Electric Barbarella' in 1997, although it didn't get any higher than ninety-five. They had better luck in Europe, especially in Italy, where the song broke into the Top Five. '(Reach Up for the) Sunrise' is part rehab mantra, part football terrace anthem, full of air-punching optimism as Duran Duran grasped what they sensed could be their last chance after a decade of relative obscurity. Although it's a return to the feel-good energy of their early hits, the singalong chorus does save the day after a rather forgettable verse. 'I was disappointed when I heard the track, "Sunrise",' affirms Cuccurullo. 'I heard it in a mall in Baltimore while visiting my mother and I'm like, "Oh, no, this sounds a bit like Duran Duran and the verse is horrible fake soul." Then I heard the chorus. I thought to myself, "Man, there's just a little bit too much helium in Simon's voice." They're trying to make him sound younger, I guess. I called Nick a few days later and said, "I heard that song, it's dreadful but tell Simon I can still remember that chorus." ' Andy Taylor summed up the song's aesthetic: 'I always thought it would be weird if Duran Duran came back but didn't have a great song the whole world could sing. That's one of the things that drives us – melodic songs that people can relate to has always been our thing. I was a Beatles fan as a kid – that song sensibility where you have to get a perfect four minutes out of things. In this fucking dark gloomy world, we're a sunny day. Music is escapism. It's entertainment.'

Duran Duran performed the track on *Top of the Pops* and then flew off around the world to do a radio promo tour of America, Australia, Japan, Hong Kong, Spain, France, Germany, Sweden and Italy. They appeared on Jonathan Ross's Friday-night TV chat show, followed by another trip to the States, where they signed records at Virgin Megastores in Times Square, New York and Sunset Strip, Hollywood. Their frenetic, gruelling schedule (especially for five men in their forties!) also included appearances on huge-rating TV programmes, *Good Morning America* and *The Late Late Show*.

Duran Duran's new album, *Astronaut*, came out on 11 October 2004 with sumptuous artwork designed by John Warwicker, who had actually first worked with the band back in 1980 when he came up with cover artwork for their planned but subsequently scrapped indie release of 'Planet Earth'. As explanation for the CD's title,

Rhodes dreamily claimed that 'there's something very romantic about astronauts' and perhaps it was also inspired by the fact that Duran Duran's music had recently been heard in space. In 2001 the crew of the US shuttle *Atlantis* woke to the sound of 'Hold Back the Rain' from the *Rio* album – NASA's Mission Control were playing it as an effort to ward off bad weather and it seemed to work as the spacecraft landed safely later that day at Cape Canaveral. In 2004 Duran Duran were also celebrating as the new album shot to number three in the UK and sold 54,000 copies to debut at seventeen in America. The album went to number one in Italy, Top Ten in Canada and a very respectable twenty-nine in Japan, where the CD included the bonus track 'Virus'. So far so good, but *Astronaut* dropped out of the Top Twenty in the next two weeks and the media's response was generally one of disappointment in the UK. *Mojo* felt the album was 'over-cooked' and *Q* magazine preferred the ballads: 'The moody "One of Those Days" shows introspection now suits them best. When they strain for sexy modernity – the clunky techno-pop of "Astronaut", the pull-your-ears-off horror of "Bedroom Toys" – it's as appealing as Mr Burns writhing round in satin sheets.' *Uncut* concluded, 'it's sleek, groomed and genetically engineered to within an inch of sonic perfection but there's very little that's memorable' and the *NME*'s Rob Fitzpatrick gave the album five out of ten: 'No one in the world sounds like Duran Duran. This is good in the sense that as soon as Simon Le Bon sings, "Groovin' now to X-Ray Spex/Something tells me you're the alien sex" across Andy Taylor's funk-rock guitar flurry in "Astronaut" – a song quite clearly about hammering rock-star-quality pharms – you can practically smell the wildly expensive video. The same goes for "Bedroom Toys" – hey, splashy rubber sex with strangers rules! – which is the sort of copper-bottomed dub-funk the impossibly mental Grace Jones used to scowl over about a thousand years ago ... "Still Breathing" is a genuinely great song.' Over in the States, the band were greeted like an old friend, with *Rolling Stone* enthusing, '*Astronaut* revitalizes Duran's early synth-pop magic. The lush, moody tones of "Point of No Return" and uplifting charm of "Finest Hour" recall the seductive sounds of *Rio* and remind us that Duran Duran always had a knack for radiant melodies.' Meanwhile, *Billboard* praised the band for 'sounding more vibrant and exciting than it has in eons'.

Opening with '(Reach Up for the) Sunrise', the album occasionally reads like a self-help book written by an emotionally revitalized Le Bon who can't quite believe his luck. Unfortunately when he's not trading in darkness-into-light imagery, he's making one-dimensional statements about the state of the world in the wake of the 9/11 tragedy. The album's second single, 'What Happens Tomorrow', is one of the worse offenders but its sky-scraping, panoramic sentiment and soft rock balladry were enough to take it to number eleven in the UK and one off the top slot in Italy. Fortunately, once you can get past Le Bon's autistic sloganeering, *Astronaut* is a fantastic, cinematic-sounding album, full of textures that are genuinely uplifting, warm, space-age and playfully escapist. Nick Rhodes's bubbling electronics flow through everything, as if he'd invited Air, Jean-Michel Jarre and William Orbit to join him on Duran's machines. Two of the Dallas Austin-produced tracks, the driving, synthesizer-based 'Want You More!' and the ecstasy-munching sci-fi pop of the title-song, are early highlights in the running order. The Le Bon rap song 'Bedroom Toys' is refreshingly throwaway, 'Nice' is a very pretty, dreamlike dance track and 'Taste the Summer' does what it says on the tin. Meanwhile, the backs-to-the wall grit of 'Finest Hour' is surrounded by a pupil-dilating rush of Goldfrapp-styled strings and analogue electronics. This is the elegant start of a five-song section (also including 'Chains', 'One of Those Days', 'Point of No Return' and 'Still Breathing') that is the most beautiful twenty-five minutes of Duran Duran's career. These tracks in particular reveal a band fluently in command of their material, with Andy Taylor playing in a wider variety of styles than ever before (an eclecticism that Duran Duran have become used to after the input of Cuccurullo) but always retaining an emotional, atmospheric edge, especially on the Ennio Morricone-style 'Still Breathing'. In contrast to their heavily programmed 1990s albums, the natural dynamics of the returning rhythm section open up the sound and a freshly inspired Simon Le Bon has never sounded better – from the Suede-like romanticism of 'One of Those Days' to the layered harmonies of 'Point of No Return' and his wistful soul-baring on 'Still Breathing'.

Duran spent the last two months of 2004 promoting the record, but were hit by an unexpected disaster on 23 November when it was announced that Andy Taylor was 'suffering from exhaustion' and that his doctors had told him to rest for a 'few weeks'. A stand-in guitarist took his place until January 2005 when he rejoined the band for a one-off gig at Hammersmith Palais in London, which was later broadcast by Radio 2. There were more problems during that show as by the end of the set Roger Taylor was in some discomfort and X-rays revealed that he'd broken the fifth metatarsal bone in his foot, forcing the cancellation of Duran Duran's January-scheduled arena tour of Japan. The drummer also announced his 'trial separation' from his wife Giovanna after twenty years of marriage. He moved out of the family home in south-west London but the couple, who have three kids, James, Elliott and Ellea, stressed that it would not necessarily be permanent and that no one else was involved on either side. Despite these troubles Roger Taylor was still part of the line-up on the North American *Astronaut* tour, which also featured backing singer Anna Ross and the band's old friend, saxophonist player Andy Hamilton.

Opening in Puerto Rico on 8 February and closing two months later at New York's Madison Square Garden on 13 April, the tour was a forty-four-date, smoothly executed road trip, apart from Andy Taylor pulling out of some dates to be with his father, who died after a long fight against cancer on 22 March. Dom Brown was drafted in as replacement guitarist until 24 March when Andy Taylor rejoined the tour, which was starting to regularly appear in *Billboard* magazine's Top Ten grossing concerts of the week. One of their biggest successes was their sold-out (13,909) show in Los Angeles on 6 April where they generated a total revenue of $794,755. Cate Blanchett and Juliet Lewis were among the stars in attendance that night and Duran Duran spent the next day hobnobbing with more Tinseltown actors at Oscar parties hosted by *Esquire* and *Vanity Fair*. The US concerts also went down a storm with the critics, including *Times Dispatch* writer Melissa Ruggieri, who gave the best visual description of the show in her review of the band's Fairfax concert: 'The strobe lights snapped, and fans nearly broke eardrums with their screams. It could have been 1984 for Duran Duran as the fivesome stood at the lip of the stage in the blinking darkness. But twenty years have passed since the band's last foray, and finally, these gracefully ageing men are swimming in long-deserved respect. John Taylor, the lanky bassist with a jaw line that could shred thick glass, remains the favourite judging by the shrieks. But his nimble fingering during "Notorious", which slyly dipped into Sister Sledge's "We are Family", and his dense anchoring of "Planet Earth" proved his often-unsung prowess. Coupled with the drumming of Roger Taylor, Duran's quiet rhythm machine, John funked up even the still-pedestrian "A View to a Kill". It wasn't until midway through the concert that keyboardist Nick Rhodes, in all his pouty stoicism, garnered much attention. Standing behind his mission-control set up under a circle of white lights, the platinum-haired Rhodes tiptoed into the instrumental "Tiger, Tiger" before neatly segueing into longtime fan fave "The Chauffeur". That one also brought out the drama school background in singer Simon Le Bon. Clad in a black tux jacket and driver's cap, Le Bon emerged from the shadows to croon the moody song and play the recorder. But most impressive about Le Bon is that he sings better now than he did twenty years ago (one listen to *Arena* should confirm that). He also looks the healthiest, somewhat like a less thuggish Russell Crowe or, perhaps, the father of *The OC*'s Benjamin McKenzie. Most of the time, guitarist Andy Taylor, cigarette dangling from his mouth and black shades never revealing his eyes, provided that grittier edge, even if it meant overpowering Le Bon's vocals, as happened during a muddled "Astronaut". But the occasional speed bump was easily forgiven by the time the band ripped into its slamming version of Grandmaster Flash's "White Lines" and the seductive funk of "Girls on Film".' The *New York Times* cast an eye over their Madison Square Garden show, commenting that 'while video screens showed the band as cartoon heroes between glimpses of women in lingerie, Duran Duran was just a five-man band (plus a female backup singer and, very occasionally, a saxophonist) socking away at the songs like troupers, getting sweaty and just about as silly as the songs deserved. You don't have to be a teenager to scream like one.' The *New York Post* was also buoyant in its assessment of the show: 'In concert, you'd expect oldies like "Hungry Like the Wolf" to satisfy fans but at the Garden, there was equal strength in such new tunes as "(Reach Up for the) Sunrise" and "What Happens Tomorrow". Both of those songs have a bright, optimistic appeal and make an air-tight case that Duran Duran have re-established themselves with contemporary relevance.' By the end of the tour, Duran Duran had played to 400,000 fans and US sales of the *Astronaut* album had reached

250,000 – a decent comeback, but not an all-conquering, multi-platinum success. In fact the album that has returned to the US charts in the wake of the tour is *Greatest*, which re-charted at number 146 after selling 7,900 in a week. One suspects that the band are disappointed that *Astronaut* hasn't sold more at this stage and that what happens in 2005 will dictate whether there's another new Duran Duran album or not. At the time of writing this, the band were set to play a one-off homecoming show at Birmingham City's St Andrews football stadium (supported by The Bravery and Daniel Bedingfield) plus an extensive European tour in support of the third single from the album which Nick Rhodes expected to be 'Nice'. When asked about Duran Duran's future, he insisted from a hotel in Las Vegas that they are enthusiastic about getting back into the studio together again, but added, 'I never know what's going to happen next. We could all stay together or someone could leave tomorrow. I just don't know … We're all very much live-in-the-moment people.'

ACKNOWLEDGEMENTS

Notorious includes a substantial amount of exclusive material, including several hours of unpublished transcripts with the band, plus my own two-hour interview recorded in Nick Rhodes's back garden three years ago. Several people spoke to me 'off the record' and over thirty agreed to talk openly about Duran Duran, some over the course of several meetings and phone calls. Thanks to – Warren Cuccurullo, Stephen Duffy, Andy Wickett, Paul Berrow, Michael Berrow, Amanda Berrow, David Twist, Dave Ambrose, Rob Hallett, Gary Numan, John Foxx, Brandon Flowers, Billy Currie, Paul Humphreys, Ken Scott, Nick Beggs, Marcello Anciano, Bob Lamb, Mike Caddick, Martyn Ware, Richard Barbieri, Madeleine Farley, Hazel O'Connor, Mark Shaw, Patti Bell, Tim Dry, Sean Crawford, Alan Bayne, Angus Margerison, Colin Thurston, Denis O'Regan and Eric Fellner.

Special thanks to: Isobel & Lil, Zak, my mum and her husband Alan, Brian Malins for the jazz lullabies, Sal & Al, Alice & Emily, Danni, Sav, John & Paul, Gary & Gemma & the gang, John Foxx, Jane & Matt, Ian Abraham, Rich & Tina, Kevin Cook, John Aizlewood, Fiona, Webbo, Rico, Ian & Virginia, Don, Ian Macdonald, Sarah Watson and my editor, Sarah Hayes.

Finally, thanks to Duran Duran (Simon, Nick, John, Andy, Roger, Warren).

Books

Buckley, David: *The Thrill of It All: The Story of Bryan Ferry & Roxy Music* (Andre Deutsch, 2004)

Buckley, David: *Strange Fascination: David Bowie the Definitive Story* (Virgin, 1999)

Easlea, Daryl: *Everybody Dance: Chic and the Politics of Disco* (Helter Skelter, 2004)

Frisa, Maria Luisa & Stefano Tonchi: *Excess: Fashion and the Underground in the '80s* (Charta, 2004)

Garfield, Simon: *Expensive Habits: The Dark Side of the Music Industry* (Faber & Faber, 1986)

George, Boy & Spencer Bright: *Take It Like a Man: The Autobiography of Boy George* (Sidgwick & Jackson, 1995)

i-D Magazine: *A Decade of Ideas – The Encyclopaedia of the '80s* (Penguin Books, 1990)

Napier-Bell, Simon: *Black Vinyl White Powder* (Ebury Press, 2002)

Power, Martin: *David Sylvian: The Last Romantic* (Omnibus Press, 1998)

Rimmer, David: *New Romantics: The Look* (Omnibus Press, 2003)

Rimmer, David: *Like Punk Never Happened* (Faber & Faber, 1985)

Savage, Jon: *Time Travel* (Chatto & Windus, 1996)

Savage Jon: *England's Dreaming: Sex Pistols and Punk Rock* (Faber & Faber, 1991)

Strange, Steve: *Blitzed! The Autobiography of Steve Strange* (Orion, 2002)

Warhol, Andy: *The Philosophy of Andy Warhol: From A to B and Back Again* (Harcourt Brace Jovanovich, 1975)

Thanks also to Stephen Duffy for the excerpts from his unpublished memoir *Memory & Desire*

Video/DVD

Duran Duran: *Sing Blue Silver* DVD, 1984

Duran Duran: *Arena & the Making of Arena* DVD, 1984

Duran Duran: *Extraordinary World* VHS, 1994

Duran Duran: *Greatest* DVD, 2003

TV

VH1: *Ru Paul Show*, 1997; VH1: *Behind the Music*, 1999; VH1: *Storytellers*, 2000; VH1: Interview with Nick Rhodes, 2000; MuchMoreMusic: *The Story of Duran Duran*, 2004; BBC 3: *Liquid Assets: Duran Duran's Millions*, 2005

Articles

Where possible I have credited the writer and publication but some of the articles researched on the internet did not have complete credits, plus many news stories do not name the journalist. My heartfelt apologies to anyone I missed out. Thanks to Mark Blake at *Q* for the access to all the back issues of *Q*, *Smash Hits* and *Sounds*. I'm also grateful to certain key journalists who have written about Duran over the years: Peter Martin, Steve Sutherland, Chris Heath, Michael Odell, Betty Page and Gordon Barr.

All Anon: 'Duran Duran Interview', *The Face*, 1980; 'Simon Le Bon Personal File', *Smash Hits*, 1981; 'Duran Duran Interview', *The Face*, 1981; 'Review of Duran Duran Debut Album', *Trouser Press*, 1981; 'Duran Duran Interview', *Teenbag*, 1982; 'Hungry Like the Wolf for Stardom', *People Weekly*, 1983; 'Roger Taylor Interview', *16 Magazine*, 1983; 'Interview with Andy Taylor', *Smash Hits*, 1983; 'Julie Ann Backs Her Man', *People Weekly*, 1984; 'Nick Rhodes Interview', *Teen Magazine*, 1984; 'Review of *Arena*', *Rolling Stone*, 1984; 'Pop's Dynamic', *Teen Magazine*, 1984; 'What the Papers Say', *Smash Hits*, 1984; 'Duran Duran Interview', *The Face*, 1985; '20 Questions – Nick Rhodes', *Smash Hits Yearbook*, 1985; 'Nick Rhodes Interview', *Smash Hits*, 1985; 'Review of Arcadia' – *Rolling Stone*, 1985; 'Rock Idol Le Bon Escapes Death', *The San Diego Union-Tribune*, 1985; 'A View to a Spill', *People Weekly*, 1985; 'Singer's Yacht Capsizes', *Chicago Tribune*, 1985; 'Simon Le Bon Tests Matrimonial Waters', *People Weekly*, 1986; 'Andy Taylor vs Duran Duran', *Smash Hits*, 1986; 'Review of *Notorious*', *Rolling Stone*, 1986; 'A Day in the Life of Simon Le Bon', *Smash Hits Yearbook*, 1987; 'Simon Le Bon Interview', *News of the World*, 1987; 'Duran Star Banned from Driving', *Associated Press*, 1989; 'John Taylor Interview', *The Music Paper*, 1990; 'Review of *Liberty*', *Trouser Press*, 1990; 'Fast Popstar', *CosmoDutch*, 1991; 'Nick Rhodes Interview', *Song Talk*, 1993; 'Warren Cuccurullo Interview', *Hot Press*, 1993; 'New Album Is Lame', *Miami Herald*, 1995; 'Review of Neurotic Outsiders', *Q* Magazine, 1996; 'Simon Le Bon Interview', *Ego Trip Magazine*, 1997; 'Duran Duran Interview', *Recording Magazine*, 1997; 'Simon Le Bon Interview', *Nuvo Sound*, 1997; 'Save a Prayer for Duran', *Lexicon* Magazine, 1997; 'Simon Le Bon Interview', *Sunday Pink*, 1997; 'Duran Duran Interview', *Mix Magazine*, 1997; 'Duran Duran Interview', *Smug Magazine*, 1997; 'Le Bon Viveurs', *Vox*, 1997; 'Duran Duran Interview', *AOL*, 1997; 'Duran Duran Interview', *Dallas Morning News*, 1997; 'Duran Back on Track with *Medazzaland*', *Billboard*, 1997; 'Calling Planet Earth', *The Independent*, 1998; 'Nick Rhodes Interview', *Ceefax*, 1998; 'Nick Rhodes Interview', *Wolverhampton Express & Star*, 1999; 'Duran Duran Interview', *Attitude*, 1999; 'Nick Rhodes Interview', *Yourmanchester.com*, 2000; 'Duran Duran Interview', *Sunspot*, 2000; 'Warren Cuccurullo Interview', *G Mag*, 2000; 'Review of Pop Trash', *The Independent*, 2000; 'Original Duran Duran Lineup to Reunite', *Jam! Music*, 2001; 'Nick Rhodes Interview', *Sleazenation*, 2002; 'Worst Cover Versions',

The Observer, 2004; 'Memories of Nick', *Birmingham Post & Mail*, 2004; 'John Taylor Interview', *Max*, 2004; 'Superbowl Isn't a Hit with Duran Duran Girl', *Daily Telegraph*, 2004; 'Review of *Astronaut*', *Billboard*, 2004; 'Revealed: The Girl Behind the Curtain', *Daily Telegraph*, 2004; 'Simon Le Bon Gives Up 'Vodka And Dirty Women', *Ananova.com*, 2004; 'Back to Business', *Melodicrock.com*, 2004; 'Duran Duran Interview', *Music OHM*, 2004; 'Old Boys on Film *The Age*, Australia, 2004; 'John Taylor Interview', *Peavey*, 2004; 'John's Just a Toy Boy', *Sunday Mercury*, 2004; 'Union Of The Drummer Is No Longer on the Rise', *Divorcemagazine.com*, 2005

Adams, Cameron: 'Back on Planet Earth', *The Cairns Post*, 2004; Adrianson, Doug: 'Duran Duran Gets Visual', *Herald*, 1989; Adrianson, Doug: 'Duran Duran Tries Harder Rock', *Herald*, 1989; Alexander, Hilary: 'The Old Rockers Who Never Go Out of Fashion', *Daily Telegraph*, 2004; Allen, Joseph: 'Duran Duran Interview', *Jam TV*, 1997; Amabile, Michele: 'John Taylor Interview', *Home News Tribune*, 1998; Amerson, Cookie: 'The Wild Boys Branch Out', *Teen Magazine*, 1985; Aquilante, Dan: 'Fans Get a Double Dose', *New York Post*, 1997; Aquilante, Dan: 'Duran Duran Live Review', *New York Post*, 2005; Arnold, Gina: 'Can Pretty Pop Stars Survive Their Good Looks?', *Again Again*, 1997; Ashworth, Andrea: 'Once More with Feeling', *The Observer*, 2005; Baber, Brendan: 'Liquid Listening', *Interview Magazine*, 1997; Barry, Rebecca: 'Duran Duran Interview', *Entertainment News*, 2004; Beckley, Fred: 'Duran Duran a Hit', *Philadelphia Inquirer*, 1997; Birch, Ian: 'Kajagoogoo', *Smash Hits*, 1983; Barr, Gordon: 'Andy Taylor Interview Parts I & II', Evening Chronicle, 2004; Bell, Max: 'I Wouldn't Fancy Being Pregnant', *No. 1 Magazine*, 1986; Benson, John: 'Duran Duran Not Giving Up on *Astronaut*', *Billboard*, 2005; Birch, Ian: 'The Big League', *Smash Hits*, 1981; Birch, Ian: 'Le Bon Viveur', *Smash Hits*, 1982 ; Birch, Ian: 'Best Group', *Smash Hits*, 1982; Birch, Ian: 'On a Wing and a Prayer', *Smash Hits*, 1982; Birch, Ian: 'The New Romantics: The Truth Behind the Makeup', *Smash Hits*, 1983; Black, Johnny: 'History of Duran Duran', *Tiger Beat*, 1986; Blagg, Christopher: 'Band Puts on Killers Impression of Duran Duran', *The Herald*, 2004; Bonner, Michael: 'Review of *Astronaut*', *Uncut*, 2004; Bougeral, Elizabeth: 'Duran Duran Interview', *Mike Magazine*, 1997; Bracewell, Michael: 'Kiss of Life for the Old Romantics', *The Times*, 1993; Bracewell, Michael: 'The Human League Interview', *GQ*, 2000; Bradley, Lloyd: 'Review of *Big Thing*', *Q Magazine*, 1988; Braunagel, Don: 'Duran Delights Frenetic Fans', *The San Diego Union-Tribune*, 1984; Bream, John: 'Idols No More', *Star Tribune*, 1989; Brown, Mark: 'Duran Duran interview', *Rocky Mountain News*, 2004; Brownstein, Bill: 'Duran Fighting Back', *Montreal Gazette*, 1987; Buckingham, Robert: 'Interview with Yasmin Le Bon', *Vogue*, 2000; Buckley, David: 'Review of *Astronaut*', *Mojo*, 2004; Burton, Ronnie: 'Fans No Longer Save a Prayer for Duran's Success', *The Campus Press*, 1995; Campbell, Mary: 'Duran Getting Older Fans', *The Ottawa Citizen*, 1987; Cantacuzino, Marina, 'Julie Anne Rhodes Interview', *Hello!*, 1992; Cantacuzino, Marina: 'Julie Anne Rhodes Interview, *Hello!*, 1994; Caramanica, Jon, *Anon*, 2004; Carl, Charmian: 'Duran Duran Interview', *Playgirl*, 1995; Cashmere, Paul: 'Duran Duran Interview', *Ondercover Online*, 2003; Catlin, Roger: 'It's a Good Phase II', *The Hartford Courant*, 1993; Chamberlain, Vassi: 'Renaissance Man Nick Rhodes', *Tatler*, 2004; Chamberlain, Vassi: 'Who's a Pretty Boy Then?', *Tatler*, 2003; Chiose, Simon: *The Globe and Mail Toronto*, 1997; Clancy, Ben: 'Duran Duran Live', *NME*, 2000; Cohen, Howard: '80s Redux', *Miami Herald*, 1993; Cohen, Scott: 'All Dressed Up & Everywhere to Go', *Spin*, 1987; Collingbourne, Huw: 'Going Their Own Way', *Kicks Magazine*, 1982; Colon, Suzan: 'Different Drummer', *Star Hits*, 1985; Consindine, J.D.: 'Duran Duran Discovering Success', *The Baltimore Sun*, 1993; Consindine, J.D.: 'Duran Duran Interview', *The Globe & Mail*, 2004;

Consindine, J.D.: 'Review of *Thank You*', *Rolling Stone*, 1995; Cooper, Carol: 'Review of *Medazzaland*', *Newsday*, 1997; Cooper, Carol: 'Duran Duran 90s Style', *Long Island Newsday*, 1997; Cooper, Tim: 'Nick Rhodes Interview', *Evening Standard*, 2003; Cranna, Ian: 'Review of Thank You', *Q Magazine*, 1995; Crisafulli, Chuck: 'Warren Cuccurullo Interview', *Guitar Player*, 1993; Cromelin, Richard: 'Duran Duran: Oh No!', *Los Angeles Times*, 1993; Dallas, Karl: 'Gary Numan Live Review', *Melody Maker*, 1981 ; Davis, Johnny: 'Famous and Dandy', *NME*, 2003; Dee, Johnny: 'Review of *The Singles 1986-1995*', *Q* Magazine, 2003; De Graaf, Kasper: 'Duran Duran Interview', *Smash Hits*, 1981; De Lisle, Tim: 'One for the Dedicated Durannies', *The Mail on Sunday*, 2004; Dellar, Fred: 'Review of *Rio*', *Smash Hits*, 1982; Dickie, Mary: 'Durable Duran Launched *Astronaut*', *Toronto Sun*, 2004; Dickie, Mary: 'Duran Duran Shoot for the Sky', *Toronto Sun*, 2004; Doenchuck, Bob: 'Nick Rhodes Interview', *Keyboard*, 1984; Doenchuck, Bob: 'Idylls in Arcadia', *Keyboard*, 1986; Domostroy, Patrick: 'The Music of Duran Duran', *Youthquake Magazine*, 2004; Drew, Dr: 'Nick Rhodes Interview', *DrDrew.com*, 2001; Duffy, Thom: 'Duran on Track from '93 Comeback', *Billboard*, 1993; Duerden, Nick: 'The Ridiculous Life of Simon Le Bon', *Q* Magazine, 1998; Duncan, Alistair: 'On the Grid', *The Evening Standard*, 2004; Eddy, Chuck: 'Review of *Medazzaland*', *Rolling Stone*, 1997; Edwards, Mark: 'A Reputation For Endurance', *The Times*, 1995; Ellen, Mark: 'Review of "Careless Memories"', *Smash Hits*, 1981; Evans, Simon: 'Nick Rhodes Interview', *Birmingham Post*, 1998; Faris, Mark: 'Power Station No Lightweight', *Beacon Journal*, 1985; Faris, Mark: 'New Duran Duran Is Better Better', *Beacon Journal*, 1989; Ferman, Dave: 'Attitude for Gratitude', *The San Diego Union-Tribune*, 1995; Fischer, Blair R: '*Pop Trash* to Be Released on Hollywood', *Rolling Stone*, 1999; Fitzpatrick, Rob: 'The Artists Formerly Known as Swoon', *Word*, 2004; Fitzpatrick, Rob: 'Review of *Astronaut*', *NME*, 2004; Flans, Robin: 'Roger Taylor Interview', *Modern Drummer*, 1985; Flick, Larry: 'Duran Duran Gives Thanks to Fans', *Billboard*, 1995 ; Fricke, David: 'Review of the Power Station', *Rolling Stone*, 1985; Fulton, Rick: 'A Bon Voyage', *The Daily Record*, 2004; Gladstone, Jim: 'Duran with Pursuit of Happiness', *The Inquirer*, 1989; Glass, Cyndi: 'Warren Cuccurullo Interview', *Youth Quake Magazine*, 2003; Glick, Beverley: 'The Rebirth of the Savvy Band', *Sunday Express*, 2003; Goddard, Kay: 'Ronnie Taylor Interview', *No. 1 Magazine*, 1983; Goddard, Peter: 'Duran Feel Energised', *The Toronto Star*, 1986; Graff, Gary: 'Duran Comes Around Again', *Free Press*, 1989; Graham, Polly: 'Duran Duran Interview', *Daily Mirror*, 1998; Grant, Kieran: 'Durable Duran Duran', *Toronto Sun*, 1995; Green, Jo-Anne: 'Mission Accomplished', *Goldmine*, 1998; Green, Jo-Anne: 'Duran Duran Interview', *Interface*, 1998; Green, Michelle: 'The Five Faces of Duran Duran', *People Weekly*, 1985; Griffin, John: 'The Power Station Generates a Buzz', *Montreal Gazette*, 1985; Grigoriadis, Vanessa: 'Still Pretty', *Rolling Stone*, 2005; Hanna, Lynn: 'The Ultimate Warrior', *NME*, 1980; Hanley, Lynsey: 'Review of Astronaut', *Daily Telegraph*, 2004; Harley, Kevin: 'Duran Duran Live', *The Independent*, 2004; Harrington, Richard: 'Beatlemania for the Video Generation', *The Washington Post*, 1984; Harris, John: 'Phone Home', *Mojo*, 2003; Hauptfuhrer, Fred: 'Wedding Bells Toll for Nick Rhodes', *People Weekly*, 1984; Hay, Carla: 'Duran Turns Avant Garde', *Billboard*, 2000; Heath, Chris: 'Mr & Mrs Le Bon', *Smash Hits*, 1985; Heath, Chris & Tom Hibbert: 'Around the World in 150 Days', *Smash Hits*, 1986; Heath, Chris: 'Are Duran Down the Dumper?', *Smash Hits*, 1987; Heath, Chris: 'Duran Duran Interview', *Deluxe*, 1998; Hedges, Dan: 'Duran Duran Minus Two', *Newsday*, 1986; Henke, Jim: 'Middle Class Heroes', *Rolling Stone*, 1984; Hepworth, Dave: 'Review of "Planet Earth"', *Smash Hits*, 1981; Hibbert, Tom: 'Review of Arcadia', *Smash Hits*, 1985; Hibbert, Tom: 'Review of *Big Thing*', *Q* Magazine, 1988; Hillier, Bev: 'Review of *Duran Duran*', *Smash Hits*, 1981; Hughley, Marty:

'Duran Duran Returns', *Portland Oregonian*, 1993; Hughley, Marty: 'Age Is Kind to Duran Duran', *Portland Oregonian*, 1993; Iannacci, Elio: 'Duran Duran's Pop Romeo', *Icon*, 1998; Irwin, Colin: 'A View to Another Kill', *Planet Sound*, 1998; Jaeger, Barbara: 'Making Do with Less', *The Record New Jersey*, 1987; Jaeger, Barbara: 'Looking for a Little Respect', *The Record New Jersey*, 1989; Jaeger, Lauren: 'Duran Set To Tour', *Amusement Business*, 1997; Jardine, Cassandra: 'Simon Le Bon Interview', *Daily Telegraph*, 1998; Jelbert, Steve: 'Duran Duran Live', *The Independent*, 2003; John, Richard: 'Mini Tour Hits Canada', *Jam! Showbiz*, 1997; John, Richard: 'Duran Duran Are Back in the Loop', *Jam! Showbiz*, 1997; Johnson, Heather: 'Recording Notes', *Mix Magazine*, 2004; Kerins, Suzanne: 'Rocky Rhodes to Fame', *Sunday Mirror*, 2004; Kim, Jae-Ha: 'Duran Still Attracts Notoriety', *Chicago Sun-Times*, 1987; Kim, Jae-Ha: 'Duran Returns with More Maturity', *Chicago Sun-Times*, 1989; Kopf, Biba: 'Puppie Love', *NME*, 1985; Kolson, Anne: 'Duran on the Road Again', *The San Diego Union-Tribune*, 1987; Kolson, Anne: 'Glamor, Clamor', *Inquirer*, 1987; Kutner, Julia: 'Simon Le Bon on Family, Music & the Brits', 2004; Leston, Kimberley: 'Review of *The Power Station*', *Smash Hits*, 1985; Linfield, Carole: 'The Adventures of Tin Tin', *Sounds*, 1982; Logan, Brian: 'Christmas Crooning', *The Guardian*, 1999; Love, Courtney: 'Amanda de Cadenet Interview', *Hollywood Reporter*, 1995; Lui, John: 'Duran Returns from Dry Spell', *The Singapore Straits Times*, 1994; Lyster, Simon: 'Nick Rhodes Interview', *The Birmingham Post*, 2000; Maconie, Stuart: 'Review of *The Wedding Album*', *Q* Magazine, 1993; Martin, Peter: 'My Own Way', *Smash Hits*, 1986; MacDonald, Vici: 'Review Of *Election Day*', *Smash Hits*, 1986; MacDonald, Vici: 'Duran Duran Live', *Smash Hits*, 1987; Mahoney, Elisabeth: 'Duran Duran Live', *The Guardian*, 2000; Manes, Billy: 'Nick Rhodes Interview', *Orlando Weekly*, 1999; Manning, Toby: 'I Want to Be a Machine', *Q Special*, 2005; Martin, Andrew: 'Review of *Liberty*', *Q* Magazine, 1990; Martin, Peter: 'Review of *Seven & the Ragged Tiger*', *Smash Hits*, 1983; Martin, Peter: 'The Greatest Live Video Ever Seen', *Smash Hits*, 1984; Martin, Peter: 'A Day to Remember', *Smash Hits*, 1984; Martin, Peter: 'War!', *Smash Hits*, 1984; Martin, Peter: 'Band Aid', *Smash Hits*, 1984; Martin, Peter: 'Welcome to the Power Station,' *Smash Hits*, 1985; Martin, Peter: 'The Future of Duran Duran', *Smash Hits*, 1985; Martin, Peter: 'Interview with John Taylor & Bob Geldof', *Smash Hits*, 1985; Martin, Peter: 'What Are Duran Duran Up To?', *Smash Hits*, 1985; Matre, Lynn Van: 'Arcadia Interview', *Chicago Tribune*, 1985; McDonald, Patrick: 'Romancing Again', *The Advertiser*, 2004; McCullough, Dave: 'Review of *Duran Duran*', *Sounds*, 1981; McCullough, Dave: 'The Thoughts of Sylvian', *Sounds*, 1981; McCullough, Dave: 'Manifestation of the Insect God', *Sounds*, 1981; McCullough, Dave: 'Review of *Rio*', *Sounds*, 1982; McCullough, Dave: 'Review of *Seven & the Ragged Tiger*', *Sounds*, 1983; Means, Andrew: 'Missing Pieces', *The Arizona Republic*, 1987; Means, Andrew: 'Duran Duran Live', *The Arizona Republic*, 1987; Means, Andrew: 'Duran Duran Acts Its Age', *The Arizona Republic*, 1989; Moon, Tom: 'Duran Enjoys Its New Found Respect', *Inquirer*, 1989; Morley, Paul: 'A Salmon Screams', *NME*, 1982; Morse, Steve: 'Duran Defies Detractors', *Boston Globe*, 1984; More, Steve: 'The Merchants of Fantasy', *Boston Globe*, 1984; McIver, Joel: 'Duran Duran Interview', *Record Collector*, 2004; McIver, Joel: 'Pioneers – Nick Rhodes', *Future Music*, 2005; McNiece, Andrew J.: 'Andy Taylor Interview', *Melodic Rock Classics*, 2003; McOmber, J. Martin: 'Those Weren't the Days', *Los Angeles Times*, 1992; Mehle, Michael: 'Nick Rhodes Interview', *Rocky Mountain*, 1999; Merritt, Stephanie: 'Review of *Astronaut*', *The Observer*, 2005; Mundy, Chris: 'Simon Le Bon Interview', *Rolling Stone*, 1995; Nash, Jesse: 'Duran Does Stint as House Band', *Billboard*, 1993; Neil, Beth: 'Fans Are Still Wild on Duran', *Newcastle Evening Chronicle*, 2004; Newman, Melinda: 'Duran Duran Makes Grand Re-entrance', *Billboard*, 1993; Noah, Sherna: 'Duran Duran Hope for Top 10 Glory a Decade On', *PA News*, 2004 ; Novak, Ralph: 'Review of *Notorious*', *People Weekly*, 1986; O'Connell, John: 'Duran Duran Interview', *Time Out*, 2004; Odell, Michael: 'In Their Own Words', *The Observer*, 2003; Okjumu, Akin: 'What Became of the Wild Boys?', *The Observer*, 2004; Orr, Andrea: 'Old Rockers Refuse to Fade Away', *Reuters*, 1997; Overall, Rick: 'Duran Duran Return', *Ottawa Sun*, 1997; Page, Betty: 'Enter the New Romantics', *Sounds*, 1980; Page, Betty: 'Go Vest Young Man', *Sounds*, 1981; Page, Betty: 'Non Rock Non Pose', *Sounds*, 1981; Page, Betty: 'Review of "Girls On Film"', *Sounds*, 1981; Page, Betty: 'Duranosaurus Rocks', *Sounds*, 1981; Page, Betty: 'The Art of Parties', *Sounds*, 1981; Page, Betty: 'From Brags to Riches', *Sounds*, 1982; Parker, Lindsey: 'The Long and Winding Rhodes', *Launch*, 1997; Parker, Lindsey: 'Duran Duran Tribute Concert', *Launch*, 1997; Parker, Lyndsey: 'Duran Duran Live', *NME*, 2003; Parney, Lisa Leigh: 'John Taylor Interview', *The Christian Science Monitor*, 1997; Paul, George: 'Duran's Not So Ordinary Show', *The Orange County Register*, 1993; Pendlebury, Richard: 'The Duran Star and the Ex-Wife', *Daily Mail*, 1997; Phalen, Tom: 'Second Time Around', *Seattle Times*, 1993; Picardie, Justine: 'A Few of Our Favourite Things', *The Independent*, 1995; Pratt, Sarah: 'Review of *Astronaut*', *Rolling Stone*, 2004; Price, Karen: 'Return of the Wild Boys', *The Western Mail*, 2004; Price, Simon: 'Duran Duran Live', *The Independent*, 2003; Puterbaugh, Parke: 'Duran Duran Meets Chic', *Rolling Stone*, 1985; Randall, Mac: 'Review of *Medazzaland*', *Musician Magazine*, 1997; Raub, Kevin: 'Duran Duran Interview', *Rolling Stone*, 1997; Raub, Kevin, 'Hungry Like John Taylor', *Rolling Stone*, 1997; Rayman, Graham: 'Duran Rides Three Hits Back to the Top', *San Francisco Chronicle*, 1993; Reece, Doug & Larry Flick: 'Electronica: The Beat Goes On', *Billboard*, 1997; Rimmer, Dave: 'Review of "My Own Way"', *Smash Hits*, 1981; Rimmer, Dave: 'Human Nature', *Smash Hits*, 1981; Rimmer, Dave: 'Review of "Hungry Like the Wolf"', *Smash Hits*, 1982; Rimmer, David & David Keeps: 'Five Go Solo!', *Smash Hits*, 1984; Rimmer, David: 'Life in the Land Down Under', *Smash Hits*, 1987; Robinson, Lisa: 'Back on the Charts', *New York Times*, 1988; Roberts, Gordon: 'Duran Duran Talking Trash', *Lexicon*, 2000; Rogers, Forrest: 'Duran Duran Is Back', *Atlanta Journal*, 1989; Rumbold, Judy: 'The Old Romantics', *The Guardian*, 2003; Sakamoto, John: 'Simon Le Bon Interview', *Toronto Sun*, 1993; Sakamoto, John: 'New World for Durans', *Toronto Sun*, 1993; Sakamoto, John: 'Duran Fly out of Medazzaland', *Jam! Showbiz*, 1997; Sandall, Robert: 'Duran Duran: The Old Romantics', *The Independent*, 2004; Segal, Victoria: 'Review of *Astronaut*', *Q* Magazine, 2004; Sinclair, David: 'A View to a Second Killing', *The Sunday Times*, 1998; Shaar Murray, Charles: 'Glam Rock', *NME;* Sheffield, Rob: 'Review of *Pop Trash*', *Rolling Stone*, 2000; Simon, Jane: 'Review of Arcadia', *Sounds*, 1985; Simmons, Sylvie: 'World Domination by 1984', *Sounds*, 1982; Simpson, Dave: 'Duran Duran Live', *The Guardian*, 2004; Simpson, Richard: 'The Brits', *The Evening Standard* (London), 2004; Smith, Russell: 'Power Station Super Group', *Dallas Morning News*, 1985; Smith, Russell: 'Power Station Gets Plugged Back In', *Dallas Morning News*, 1985; Sommer, Allison Kaplan: 'Pop Group Arrives', *The Jerusalem Post*, 1994; Sommer, Allison Kaplan: 'Better Late than Never', *The Jerusalem Post*, 1994; Stand, Mike: 'In New York New York with Duran Duran', *Smash Hits*, 1981; Stark, John: 'Chatter: Nick Rhodes', *People Weekly*, 1985; Stevenson, Jane: 'Monster Album Gives Duran Freedom', *The Ottawa Citizen*, 1995; Stevenson, Jane: 'Duran Duran Can't Get No Respect', *The Toronto Sun*, 1997; Stevenson, Jane: 'Vintage 80s Pop Fivesome Has Aged Very Well', *The Toronto Sun*, 2003; Sullivan, Caroline: 'Duran Duran Live', *The Guardian*, 1994; Sullivan, Jim: 'Duran Duran the Comeback Kids', *The Boston Globe*, 1993; Sullivan, Jim: 'Riding High in the Saddle', *The Boston Globe*, 1993; Sumrall, Harry: 'Music Takes Center Stage', *Mercury News*, 1987; Sutherland, Steve: 'So This Is Romance', *Melody Maker*, 1981; Sutherland, Steve: 'Review of

Rio', *Melody Maker*, 1982; Sutherland, Steve: 'Prayers and Promises', *Melody Maker*, 1982; Sutherland, Steve: 'Fantasy Island', *Melody Maker*, 1983; Sutherland, Steve: 'Duran Duran in New York New York', 1984; Sutherland, Steve: 'Live Review', *NME*, 2003; Takiff, Jonathan: 'John Taylor Interview', *Daily News*, 1985; Takiff, Jonathan: 'Big Time Comeback', *Daily News*, 1989; Teotico, Rochelle: 'Duran Duran Interview', *Firstcut*, 1997; Tennant, Neil: 'Duran Duran Live', *Smash Hits*, 1981; Tennant, Neil: 'That Was the Week that Was', *Smash Hits*, 1983; Tennant, Neil: 'A Public Figure', *Smash Hits*, 1984; Thomas, Karen: 'Le Bon Throat Injury', *USA Today*, 1993; Triplett, Gene: 'Similar to Beatlemania', *The Daily Oklahoman*, 1984; Van Der Veene, Valac: 'Polaroid Gentleman', *Sounds*, 1980; Van Der Veene, Valac: 'Review of "Planet Earth"', *Sounds*, 1981; Varela, Neneta: 'Interview with Renee Simonsen', *Hello!*, 1990; Vaziri, Aidin: 'Nick Rhodes Interview', *Allstar News*, 1999; Vineyard, Jennifer: 'John Taylor Interview', *Orange County Edition*, 1998; Vivinetto, Gina: 'And Did He Mention that Renee Is Lovely, Bubbly', *St Petersburg Times*, 2000; Wallace, Carol: 'A Week Simon Won't Forget', *People Weekly*, 1985; Walters, Barry: 'Simon Le Bon Interview', *San Francisco Examiner*, 1995; Watson, Ian: 'Duran Duran: Old Romantics's *The Evening Standard*, 2004; Weatherford, Mike: 'Power Station Interview', *Las Vegas Review Journal*, 1997; Welles, Robin: 'Quintet Now a Trio', *Copley News Service*, 1987; Werner, Ben: 'Duran Duran Baffled Too', *The Orange County CA*, 1997; Westbrook, Bruce: 'Not Booming but Back', *Houston Chronicle*, 1989; Westbrook, Bruce: 'Duran Back with Album', *Houston Chronicle*, 1993; Westbrook, Bruce: 'Duran Sound Survives', *Houston Chronicle*, 1997; Wictor, Thomas: 'Learning to Survive', *Bass Player Magazine*, 1994; Wigney, James: 'Bedroom Toys a Hit for Wild Boys', *Sunday Mail* (SA), 2004; Wilkinson, Roy: 'Review of *Notorious*', *Sounds*, 1986; Williams, Zoe: 'Still Playing Rio with Brio', *London Evening Standard*, 1998; Wilmot, Howard: 'Open Rhodes', *Boyz*, 1998; Willman, Chris: 'Up Close to Duran Duran', *Los Angeles Times*, 1988; Wilman, Chris: 'Duran Duran Turns up the Techno-Heat at Tower', *Los Angeles Times*, 1993; Wilson, Joanna: 'Nick Rhodes Interview', *BBC2 Teletext*, 1998; Worley, Gail: 'Scandalous! The Duran Duran Interview', *Ink 19 Magazine*, 1997; Yakir, Dan: 'A View to a Success', *Chicago Sunday Times*, 1986.

Internet Sources

There are so many great websites on Duran Duran, it would take another book to list them all. But the following have been a fantastic source of information over the last few months and I recommend that anyone interested in the band should pay them a visit. Thanks to:

www.duranduran.com

www.trusttheprocess.com

www.andytaylor.com

www.cuccurullo.tv

www.lizardkingduran.com

www.durandurantimeline.com

www.duranduran.co.uk

www.templeofsaintnick.com

www.stephenduffy.com

This is a very basic, easily accessible guide to the new albums Duran Duran have released over the last twenty-five years – refer to the original track listings. Details of compilations, singles, DVDs, videos, side projects (including the Power Station and Arcadia) and solo releases are all discussed within the main text of the book.

ALBUMS

1981 *Duran Duran*
Girls on Film/Planet Earth/Anyone out There/To ohe Shore/Careless Memories/Nightboat/Sound of Thunder/Friends of Mine/Tel Aviv

1982 *Rio*
Rio/My Own Way/Lonely in Your Nightmare/Hungry Like the Wolf/Hold Back yhe Rain/New Religion/Last Chance on ohe Stairway/Save a Prayer/The Chauffeur

1983 *Seven and the Ragged Tiger*
The Reflex/New Moon on Monday/ (I'm Looking for) Cracks in the Pavement/I Take the Dice/Of Crime and Passion/Union of the Snake/Shadows On Your Side/Tiger Tiger/The Seventh Stranger

1984 *Arena* (Live Album)
Is There Something I Should Know?/Hungry Like the Wolf/New Religion/Save a Prayer/The Wild Boys/The Seventh Stranger/The Chauffeur/Union of the Snake/Planet Earth/Careless Memories

1986 *Notorious*
Notorious/American Science/Skin Trade/A Matter of Feeling/Hold Me/Vertigo (Do the Demolition)/So Misled/Meet El Presidente/Winter Marches On/Proposition

1988 *Big Thing*
Big Thing/I Don't Want Your Love/All She Wants Is/Too Late Marlene/Drug (It's Just a State of Mind)/Do You Believe In Shame?/Palomino/Interlude One/Land/Flute Interlude/The Edge of America/Lake Shore Driving

1990 *Liberty*
Violence of Summer (Love's Taking Over)/Liberty/Hothead/Serious/All Along the Water/My Antarctica/First Impression/Read My Lips/Can You Deal With It?/Venice Drowning/Downtown

1993 *The Wedding Album*
Too Much Information/Ordinary World/Love Voodoo/Drowning
Man/Shotgun/Come Undone/Breath after Breath/UMF/Femme Fatale/None
of the Above/Shelter/To Whom It May Concern/Sin of the City

1995 *Thank You*
White Lines/I Wanna Take You Higher/Perfect Day/Watching the
Detectives/Lay Lady Lay/911 Is a Joke/Success/Crystal Ship/Ball of
Confusion/Thank You/Drive By/I Wanna Take You Higher Again

1997 *Medazzaland*
Medazzaland/Big Bang Generation/Electric Barbarella/Out of My
Mind/Who Do You Think You Are?/Silva Halo/Be My Icon/Buried in the
Sand/Michael You've Got a Lot to Answer For/Midnight Sun/So Long
Suicide/Undergoing Treatment

2000 *Pop Trash*
Someone Else Not Me/Lava Lamp/Playing with Uranium/Hallucinating
Elvis/Starting to Remember/Pop Trash Movie/Fragment/Mars Meets
Venus/Lady Xanax/The Sun Doesn't Shine Forever/Kiss Goodbye/Last Day
on Earth

2004 *Astronaut*
(Reach up for the) Sunrise/Want You More!/What Happens
Tomorrow/Astronaut/Bedroom Toys/Nice/Taste of Summer/Finest
Hour/Chains/One of Those Days/Point of No Return/Still Breathing

Additional Songs as B-Sides

Duran Duran have often included album tracks and remixes as B-sides but
the following are exclusive to the release.

Late Bar (Planet Earth) – 1981
Khanada (Careless Memories) – 1981
Fame (Careless Memories) – 1981
Faster than Light (Girls On Film) – 1981
Faith in Colour (Is There Something I Should Know?) – 1983
Secret Oktober (Union of the Snake) – 1983
Make Me Smile (The Reflex) – 1984
We Need You (Skin Trade) – 1987
I Believe All/ I Need to Know (All She Wants Is) – 1989
God (London) (Do You Believe in Shame?) – 1989
This Is How a Road Gets Made (Do You Believe in Shame?) – 1989
Throb (Violence of Summer (Love's Taking Over) – 1990
Yo Bad Azizi (Serious) – 1990
The Needle and the Damage Done (Perfect Day) – 1995
Sinner or Saint (Out of My Mind) – 1997
Know It All ((Reach Up For The) Sunrise) – 2005
Silent Icy River (What Happens Tomorrow) – 2005